Innocence and Victimhood

Critical Human Rights

Series Editors
Steve J. Stern ❦ Scott Straus

Books in the series Critical Human Rights emphasize research that opens new ways to think about and understand human rights. The series values in particular empirically grounded and intellectually open research that eschews simplified accounts of human rights events and processes.

Grounded in fifteen years of ethnographic research, this study of postwar Bosnia-Herzegovina examines efforts to rebuild society after an ethnically charged conflict that was notorious for targeting women. In working to promote peace following mass atrocity, human rights initiatives by and for Bosnian women paradoxically reinforced elements of traditional gender hierarchies and notions of ethnic difference through affirmative images of morally superior, peace-loving women. In a study that connects the local, the national, and the international, Elissa Helms shows how such ideas can become embedded in strategic and political relations with local nationalisms as well as donors and other partners at home and abroad. Her findings thus reveal the potential risks of peacebuilding efforts that reinscribe stereotypes.

Innocence and Victimhood

Gender, Nation, and Women's Activism in Postwar Bosnia-Herzegovina

Elissa Helms

The University of Wisconsin Press

Publication of this volume has been made possible, in part, through support from the Andrew W. Mellon Foundation and from Central European University.

The University of Wisconsin Press
1930 Monroe Street, 3rd Floor
Madison, Wisconsin 53711-2059
uwpress.wisc.edu

3 Henrietta Street
London WC2E 8LU, England
eurospanbookstore.com

Library of Congress Cataloging-in-Publication Data

Helms, Elissa.
    Innocence and victimhood : gender, nation, and women's activism in postwar Bosnia-Herzegovina / Elissa Helms.
        pages   cm — (Critical human rights)
    Includes bibliographical references and index.
    ISBN 978-0-299-29554-7 (pbk. : alk. paper) — ISBN 978-0-299-29553-0 (e-book)
    1. Women—Bosnia and Hercegovina 2. Women political activists—Bosnia and Hercegovina. 3. Women human rights workers—Bosnia and Hercegovina. 4. War victims—Bosnia and Hercegovina. 5. Bosnia and Hercegovina—Social conditions. 6. Bosnia and Hercegovina—History—1992– I. Title. II. Series: Critical human rights.
HN639.A8H45   2013
323.14974—dc23
2013011468

Cover image: Still from Maja Bajević's 2001 performance "Washing Up." The artist together with refugee women Zlatija Efendić and Fazila Efendić spent five days in a women's *hamam* (bathhouse) in Istanbul washing and hanging up pieces of cloth upon which they had embroidered quotations from socialist Yugoslav leader Josip Broz Tito that have taken on ironic meanings since the Bosnian war. They washed the cloths repeatedly until the material disintegrated.

TO THE VICTIMS AND SURVIVORS OF THE BOSNIAN WAR

AND TO TIBOR AND EDGAR

Contents

Illustrations

Acknowledgments

A question from the audience when I recently presented my work on rape survivor activists was discouraging. Why would I question the victimhood of these women, I was asked. I had been careful, as I have in this book, to stress the difference but also compatibility between my sympathy for survivors and condemnation of war atrocities on one hand and academic and feminist critique on the other. In my years of involvement with Bosnia and Herzegovina (BiH) I have wondered if I am not perhaps *too* drawn to its Muslim traditions and to the worldview of those who consider themselves Bosniacs and Bosnians. The last thing I wish to do is to downplay the extent and severity of war-related suffering among this population when I have witnessed its effects all too intensely. At the same time, as I have tried to make clear in this book, I find it crucial to interrogate the assumptions behind the politics of victimhood just as rigorously as that of violent nationalisms and war atrocities. Doing so does not take away from the gravity of crimes or the suffering of its victims. It is precisely the logic of competing victimhoods—in relation to BiH but also in many other contexts—that leads many to jump to this conclusion rather than engage in reasoned debate. This book is in part an attempt to consider the consequences of such intellectual and political avoidance. It is my sincere hope that the survivors, advocates, activists, and others I got to know in the course of this research understand these intentions and still feel that I have rendered their words fairly and in the context of their everyday realities, even when I come to critical conclusions.

This book has been many years in the making and so my list of people to thank is inevitably long. In the first place are the many people in BiH who welcomed me to their offices, homes, and gatherings. I thank Duška Andrić-Ružičić and the rest of the Infoteka activists—Meliha, Belma, Rada, Sabina, Jaca, Arijana, Nasiha—who gave me a base, put up with my questions, and shared their archive, activities, and thoughts with me, as well as countless pots of coffee and nights in the disco. Marijana Senjak, Edita Ostojić, Sabiha Haskić-Husić, and the rest of Medica's therapists were also very helpful and generous with their time and insights, as were many other familiar faces in the organization from the kindergarten to the kitchen to the administrative staff. Šida Jašarspašić was incredibly welcoming, introducing me around, having me tag along on activist and social errands, field trips, and hikes. Other NGO women in Zenica and beyond deserve thanks—from those who took me in and fed me to others who talked to me on many occasions, to those I only saw for one interview or chatted with at a conference. For especially illuminating conversations, shared events, and hospitality I thank Emsuda Mujagić, Zejneba Saraljić (*rahmetlija*), Safija Imamović, Nada Ler, Hasija Branković, Enisa Salćinović, Jadranka Milićević, Selma Hadžihalilović, Nuna Zvizdić, Rada Sesar, Lana Jajčević, Nada Golubović, Natalija Perić, the women of the SULKS sewing workshop, and many more who appear in this text in one way or another.

Both my research and social life would have been much less interesting without the friendship and hospitality of many more people: Sefke, Ada, Mersiha, Aras, and Asifa and others in Zenica; the Grahovac family in Prijedor; Sabina, Nana, and Rasema in Žepče; and the former refugees I have known since the war years, some now back in their homes—the Švrakas in Rizvanovići and the Linić, Hidić, and Redžić families in Bosanski Petrovac—not to mention others around BiH or scattered across the world who were responsible for my getting hooked by this country and who have taught me more about Bosnia and life than I can describe.

I also appreciate the time that many "internationals" and "locals" working for intervention agencies and donor organizations took out of their busy schedules to meet with me, and to activists from Zagreb and Belgrade, particularly Đurđa Knežević and Lepa Mlađenović, who also made time for me. Wenona Giles welcomed me to the Budapest Women in Conflict Zones workshop in 1999, which was a fascinating activist-academic encounter. Gabi Mischkowski and Monika Hauser offered their reflections and feedback on parts of this book when it was in the final stages. Further reflecting the fluidity of local/global distinctions and the difficulty of dividing these acknowledgments into logical sections, I thank Jennifer Erickson, Holly Peele, Paul Stubbs, Michael Szporluk, Peter Lippman, Jill Benderly, Cynthia Cockburn, and Gabi Mischowski for sharing their insights and experiences as fellow foreigners pursuing overlapping activist/research/policy projects in BiH at different times. I especially thank Jen for her insights and for being a wonderful *cimerka*; I hope she doesn't blame me too much for having become an anthropologist herself. Milena Marić-Vogel has my gratitude for her help as my go-to language guru for difficult translations from BCS, as well as her general critical reflections on life and culture in BiH. And I owe huge thanks to Armin Alagić and Marina Bowder, Naia and Sara, for years of friendship, stories, and a second home in Sarajevo.

The first phases of the research for this book were made possible by a Foreign Language and Area Studies Fellowship and grants from the International Research and Exchanges Board (IREX), the Institute for the Study of World Politics, the Council for European Studies, and the University of Pittsburgh's Stanley Postrednik Nationality Room. During my research in 1999 and 2000, I was graciously hosted by the Institut za Istoriju in Sarajevo where Sonja Dujmović, Seka Brkljača, Senija Milišić, Vera Kac, and Husnija Kamberović were helpful colleagues and warm friends with a constant supply of coffee. Dino Abazović, Asim Mujkić, and Nerzuk Ćurak at the Faculty of Political Sciences have also been gracious and insightful colleagues. I thank them for organizing our Young Scholars conference in 2005 from which I learned a lot. I treasure the conversations I had in the early 2000s with Nirman Moranjak-Bamburać and the chance to take part in the international feminist "Balkans" conference she organized in 2004. Her death was a blow to all who knew her but also to feminism and gender studies in BiH. The MA program she founded at the Center for Interdisciplinary Postgraduate Studies (CIPS) lives on and I was grateful for the opportunity to lecture and to learn from the faculty and students there. Zilka Spahić-Šiljak must also be thanked for our inspiring conversations and her help in locating materials. Dragan Golubović at the Media Center archive, himself a mental archive, was wonderfully efficient in locating what I was after in the wartime press. I am further thankful for friendship and intellectual exchange with Jasmina Husanović and Damir Arsenijević of the University of Tuzla, Danijela Majstorović of the University in Banja Luka, as well as the amazing group Jasmina and Damir gathered for the ReSET seminar on Cultures of Memory and Emancipatory Politics in the former Yugoslavia. I especially thank Nebojša Jovanović and Šejla Šehabović for offering many insightful perspectives and details.

Certain people will recognize the kernel of a doctoral dissertation in this book. For inspiring me then and helping me develop the ideas that remained in the text, I thank Nicole Constable, Joe Alter, Kathy Blee, Janine Wedel, and other teachers and mentors, especially my always supportive advisor Robert Hayden. Bob took me on as a novice in anthropology coming out of some intense years in refugee camps speaking a strange mix of provincial Bosnian dialects and challenged me to strengthen my arguments even when we disagreed. The late Denison Rusinow has my great appreciation for being a constant source of instructive and humanizing observations of the history of Eastern Europe and especially of what was Yugoslavia as he had lived it firsthand. And

Milica Bakić-Hayden taught me much more than just the grammar of Bosnian/Serbian/Croatian. The University of Pittsburgh offered a great community of scholars working on the Balkans and Central/Eastern Europe. I am especially grateful to Rada Drezgić, Nevena Dimova, Neringa Klumbyte, and Ed Snajder for their continued friendship and collegiality, and to my other anthro friends who influenced this research and grad student life in different ways, especially Abby Margolis, Patrick Wilson, Elizabeth Blum, and Greg Smith.

In the wider academic world, I have enjoyed the critical feedback, inspiration, and friendship of a wonderful circle of anthropologists and other researchers of what was Yugoslavia who continue to challenge and inform my work while also making conferences and Bosnia visits more fun. Xavier Bougarel, Jessica Greenberg, Andrew Gilbert, Stef Jansen, Larisa Kurtović, Damir Arsenijević, Michaela Schäuble, Edin Hajdarpašić, Azra Hromadžić, Marko Živković, Isabelle Delpla, Cornelia Sorabji, Paul Stubbs, Christian Nielsen, Jasna Dragović-Soso, Dubravka Žarkov, and Pam Ballinger have all influenced this book in some way. I was especially inspired by our 2007 and 2008 workshops in the anthropology of hope and postsocialism in the former Yugoslavia, for which I cannot thank Stef, Jessica, Drew, and all the participants enough. I am also grateful to Paula Pickering, Robert Donia, Lara Nettelfield, Sarah Wagner, Erika Haskell, Dan Hammer, and Peter Locke, as well as Drew, Xavier, Paul, and Edin again, who all shared valuable contacts, insights, and commiserations from their own research experiences while we overlapped in BiH. Thanks go also to Ana Croegeart, Renata Jambrešić-Kirin, Sanja Potkonjak, Nicole Lindstrom, Kristen Ghodsee, Eric Gordy, Sasha Miličević, Chip Gagnon, Keith Brown, Ana Dević, Julie Mostov, Tone Bringa, Frances Pine, Gerald Creed, and countless others for various forms of feedback, advice, help, and inspiration.

My colleagues at the Central European University and particularly the Gender Studies Department have supported me in carving out time for the research and writing of this book. Jasmina Lukić, Hadley Renkin, Anna Loutfi, and Allaine Cerwonka offered valuable feedback that is reflected in this text. I have also learned a lot from our wonderful students and their research. A CEU faculty research grant supported the second phase of my research in 2005–7.

When CEU granted me a sabbatical year, Susan Gal and the Anthropology Department at the University of Chicago welcomed me as a visiting scholar. There I am grateful to Victor Friedman and Meredith Clason at the Center for East European and Russian/Eurasian Studies for providing me with office space and other support. I also thank Drew Gilbert, Andrea Muehlebach, Larisa Jašarević, and participants in the Anthropology of Europe workshop for their friendship and helpful feedback. I especially thank Sue for her comments on the theoretical and methodological framings of the book.

For advice on how to navigate the world of publishers, my gratitude goes to Kristen Ghodsee, Sarah Green, Dubravka Žarkov, Erin Jenne, Tijana Krstić, Éva Fodor, and others. In the end the process was amazingly quick and efficient, thanks to the enthusiasm and responsiveness of Gwen Walker at the University of Wisconsin Press and series editors Steve Stern and Scott Straus. I also thank manuscript reviewers Pamela Ballinger and Wendy Bracewell for their thoroughness, appreciation, and productive suggestions. I have tried to incorporate the feedback I have received while working on this project but inevitably and regretfully could not do justice to every suggestion.

Behind this have always stood my parents Robert and Sharon Helms and sister Julie Favin and her family. They have put up with my Bosnia references and talk about some elusive book for years now, also tolerating my disappearances to write during our visits. They have helped with practical details during research trips and in general living abroad; most importantly, I thank my dad for heroically excavating my boxes of pre-digital photos stored in his basement in search of printable images for publication.

Finally, in addition to offering perspective on various aspects of Yugoslavia (past and former), Tibor Mesman sustained me with his delicious soups and gave me the space to write by taking on more than his fair share of domestic duties and child-care. Edgar came along only in the final phases of this book. He did not exactly help me finish more quickly but he made sure that breaks were filled with the kind of silliness only a (now) three-year-old can conjure up. Both he and his father are probably even happier than I am that this book is finally going to press.

❧

Earlier versions of material in chapters 4, 5, and 6 appeared in the following publications and are reprinted here with permission of the publishers: "Women as Agents of Ethnic Reconciliation? Women's NGOs and International Intervention in Post-War Bosnia-Herzegovina," *Women's Studies International Forum* 26 (1): 15–33; "'Politics Is a Whore': Women, Morality, and Victimhood in Post-War Bosnia-Herzegovina," in *The New Bosnian Mosaic*, edited by Xavier Bougarel, Elissa Helms, and Ger Duijzings, 235–53 (Aldershot, UK: Ashgate, 2007), copyright © 2007; "The Gender of Coffee: Women and Reconciliation Initiatives in Post-War Bosnia and Herzegovina," *Focaal* 57 (Summer 2010): 17–32; "Justice et genre: Mobiliser les survivantes de guerre bosniaques," in *Peines de guerre: La justice internationale et l'ex-Yougoslavie*, edited by Isabelle Delpla and Magali Bessone, 249–65 (Paris: Editions de l'EHESS, 2010), translation by Magali Bessone.

Language and Pronunciation Guide

The language in Bosnia-Herzegovina is called variously Bosnian, Croatian, or Serbian (but also BCS, our language, local language[s], and other expressions). They are all variants of the south Slavic language (formerly) known as Serbo-Croatian. Spelling is phonetic; each sound has its own corresponding letter in both the Cyrillic and Latin alphabets, both used in BiH, with Cyrillic associated mostly with Serb variants. The following uses the Latin alphabet, as found in this book, and only those letters that differ significantly from English.

a   a as in *father*

c   ts as in *cats*

č   ch as in *church*

ć   ch as in *Chile* but softer

dž   j as in *John*

đ   a softer j, nearing a 'ty' sound

e   e as in *let*

g   hard g as in *go*

h   h as in *loch*, from the throat

i   long e as in *he*

j   y as in *yes*

lj   lli as in *million*

nj   ny as in *Sonya*

o   o as in *no*

r   rolled with one flip of the tongue

š   sh as in *she*

u   u as in *rule*

z   z as in *zebra*

ž   zh, as the s in *measure*

Abbreviations

AFŽ	Antifašistički Front Žena (Front of Antifascist Women)
BiH	Bosna i Hercegovina (Bosnia and Herzegovina)
BWI	Bosnian Women's Initiative
CEDAW	Convention on the Elimination of All Forms of Discrimination against Women
CEE	Central and Eastern Europe
CRPC	Commission on Real Property Claims
CRS	Catholic Relief Services
Dayton	General Framework Agreement for Peace in Bosnia and Herzegovina (signed at Dayton, November 1995)
DP	Displaced person
EU	European Union
Federation	Federation of Bosnia and Herzegovina (entity of BiH dominated by Croats and Bosniacs)
HDZ	Hrvatska Demokratska Zajednica (Croatian Democratic Union)
ICTY	International Criminal Tribunal for the former Yugoslavia
IDP	Internally displaced person

IPTF	International Police Task Force
IZ	Islamska Zajednica (Islamic Community) (official religious authority)
KM	Konvertabilna marka (Convertible Mark) (BiH's currency)
MP	Member of Parliament
NATO	North Atlantic Treaty Organization
NGO	Non-governmental organization
OHCHR	Office of the High Commissioner for Human Rights (UN)
OHR	Office of the High Representative
OSCE	Organization for Security and Cooperation in Europe
RS	Republika Srpska (Serb Republic) (entity of BiH dominated by Serbs)
RVI	Ratni vojni invalidi (Wounded war veterans)
SDA	Stranka Demokratska Akcija (Party of Democratic Action)
SDP	Socijaldemokratska Partija (Social Democratic Party)
STAR	Strategies Training and Advocacy for Reconciliation
SULKS	Savez Udruženja Logoraša Kantona Sarajevo (Association of Concentration Camp Torture Survivors of the Canton Sarajevo)
SzBiH	Stranka za Bosnu i Hercegovinu (Party for Bosnia and Herzegovina)
UN	United Nations
UNFPA	United Nations Population Fund
UNHCR	UN High Commissioner for Refugees
ŽŽR	Udruženje Žena Žrtve Rata (Association of Women Victims of War)

Innocence and Victimhood

Introduction

Grbavica

On February 18, 2006, nearly fourteen years after the beginning of the Bosnian war, a film by a young Sarajevan woman director won a Golden Bear award at the Berlin International Film Festival. Jasmila Žbanić's *Grbavica* was billed as a movie about the infamous mass rapes committed mainly by Serb forces against Bosnian Muslim (Bosniac) women as a weapon of what has become known as ethnic cleansing during the 1992–95 war. The story was indeed about one such woman who had borne a child after being raped by Serb soldiers, but it was more about the difficulties of the postwar period and coping with the effects of trauma than about the war or violence themselves. But the war and its victims, the largest number of whom had been Bosniacs like Žbanić and the protagonist of her film, formed a strong subtext to the poignancy of the story. Žbanić had underscored this in her acceptance speech in Berlin by calling for the arrest of Radovan Karadžić and Ratko Mladić, respectively the political and military leaders of the Bosnian Serb forces charged with committing mass rapes, ethnic cleansing, and, at Srebrenica, genocide.[1] Muslim women rape victims, along with the women survivors of Srebrenica, had become a major symbol of the suffering of the Bosniac people and the cause of a multiethnic Bosnia and Herzegovina (hereafter Bosnia or BiH). Both mass rape and the sex-selective killings of ethnic cleansing were made to stand for the brutality of the enemy, the drama of Bosnia's plight, and the suffering of the Bosniac nation. The film thus immediately took its place in the familiar narrative of national innocence and victimhood.

Rape survivors, however, had mostly been left to fend for themselves and to continue their suffering in silence. Only foreign-funded non-governmental organizations (NGOs), most of them run by and for local women, had offered the women victims any concrete aid or psychological support. Publicity of the rapes and other images of helpless refugee women had in fact been a major impetus for the many international aid projects launched on behalf of women after the end of the Bosnian war. (The existence of male survivors of sexualized violence was hardly acknowledged.) As Žbanić publicly stated, no Bosnian government had offered the survivors anything but rhetoric. This reflected a general ambivalence toward female rape victims as well as toward female refugees,[2] despite their importance as symbols. Soon after the award for *Grbavica*, state benefits were extended to some sexual violence survivors, the culmination of a prolonged campaign by local women's activists, but the new law was far from perfect. The publicity around *Grbavica* and a later controversy involving Hollywood actress Angelina Jolie, however, brought questions of gendered war victimhood back into public debates and exposed hidden tensions in Bosnian women's activists' relationship to ethno-nationalism(s), politics, and the state.

This book is about the awkward and ambivalent relationship between victimhood and nation that is made apparent through the logics of gender. Through an ethnographic study of women's activism, I show how initiatives by and for Bosnian women in the aftermath of ethnicized war perpetuated and complicated the association of women with victimhood, armed conflict, and ethno-national affiliation. Bosnian women activists[3] actively sought to portray themselves as victims, but only of a certain sort and for certain audiences. Most, in fact, tried to distance themselves from association with the most prevalent images of Bosnian women, the rural refugee and the rape victim, even while claiming the moral status of victims of male-led violence and nationalism. Claims to victimhood are a double-edged sword, precisely due to their gendered connotations: the point of such claims is not victimhood itself but its association with innocence, distance from responsibility, and thus moral purity, which in turn affords a basis for claims to legitimacy in the field of the social. Women's activism in Bosniac-dominated BiH brings these dynamics to light, raising questions about the gendering of nationalism, representations of gender and culture, and feminist engagements in areas of conflict and corrupt politics in democratizing states. Ultimately, I argue that the ways in which these dilemmas have been approached in BiH point to the need for sustained critique of the gendered logics that enable both nationalist war violence and the politics of victimhood in and after ethno-nationalist conflicts.

Furthermore, the dilemmas and paradoxes these women faced are revealing not only for what they say about gendered processes. In the words of Susan Gal and Gail Kligman, "attending to gender is analytically productive, leading not only to an understanding of relations between men and women, but to a deeper analysis of how social and institutional transformations occur" (2000, 3). The focus on gender sheds light on areas of contestation, unease, and blurriness that may not be fundamentally or only about gender but are often made sense of and naturalized through representations of gender and gender difference. Such areas appear in Bosnia around contestations over what is political and what is not, delineations of the private from the public, and gendered notions of the place of sexuality, religion, ethnic identity, or social activism within these ever-shifting spheres. Ultimately, these distinctions emerge from judgments about moral and immoral behavior in a time of major fluctuation in values, institutions, possibilities, and hierarchies of privilege.

Gender, Nation, Victimhood

From time to time, in the face of the intense public presence of wartime topics in the Bosniac-dominated areas of BiH, some of my educated, consciously anti-nationalist (and arguably jaded) acquaintances exasperatedly complained that it was as if some of their leaders were *happy* that so many Bosniacs had died in the war. During my research, I certainly came across accounts that focused in macabre detail on the cruelty of the war violence, the brutality of its logic, and the ongoing suffering of the victims, together with an unmistakable identification of those victims as "ours" in the ethno-national sense. A victim apparently had to be seen to be continuing to suffer, too, as if the violence would lose its gravity otherwise. As perpetrators no doubt knew, continued suffering was an integral part of the violence. This sense was sustained by the attention paid in the Bosniac-dominated areas of BiH to commemorations of genocide in Srebrenica, to other war crimes, and the language of genocide applied not only to Srebrenica but to the whole war. Victimhood was foundational to claims to collective innocence and moral righteousness, but primarily on ethno-national terms, as has been common throughout this region (see Ballinger 2003; Jalušič 2007; Nielsen 2013) and elsewhere (e.g., in the Great Lakes region of Africa: Burnet 2012b; Malkki 1995; Turner 2010). Ethno-national victimhood was crucial, even fundamental, to postwar politics, the distribution of state benefits and NGO aid, and social hierarchies both within the community of the "self" nation and in efforts to restore a multiethnic BiH. This meant that other sorts of collective claims to social and political legitimacy were most readily channeled through categories of ethnic victimhood, even when their advocates explicitly tried to transcend such frameworks.

These constraints posed particular challenges for women's activists interested in challenging entrenched gender hierarchies and ethno-national thinking. How to call attention to the gender dimensions of war violence or postwar inequalities without reproducing images of passive female victimhood and support for patriarchal notions of the protection of women? How to honor the undeniable suffering of war victims and condemn brutal violence without fetishizing victimhood? How to point to the intensely gendered nature of war suffering without fetishizing sexualized violence and rape? How to name the victims without reinforcing essentialist gender tropes or ethno-national logics? Would the principled activism of a handful of anti-nationalist feminists push the public's capacity for change too far to be politically effective?

The representation of victimhood has been an ongoing concern in feminist debates, especially in the past twenty years. In fact, it was during the Bosnian war in the early 1990s that several prominent critiques of "victim feminism" were published in the United States (see, e.g., Schneider 1993; Siegel 1997; Sorisio 1997). The critics, for the most part young, educated white women from what was being called feminism's third wave, assailed the earlier generation's second wave claims that women are everywhere victims of patriarchal ideologies, violence, sexualization, and rape. Largely ignoring what had by then already been a sustained critique by women positioned as Third World, lesbian, and women of color (e.g., Ahmed 1982; Collins 1991; hooks 1984; Mohanty 1988) of the idea that women were everywhere oppressed in the same way—that gender should be the only important axis of difference for feminists—their critique of victimhood did not extend into analyses of women in places coded as non-Western. Outside of middle-class, white society, violence and social restrictions against women continued to be represented as dictated by culture and tradition (Kapur 2002; see also Mohanty 1988; Narayan 1997). The counterpart to the woman-victim for the critics of so-called victim feminism was the educated, employed Western woman who had control of her life as an autonomous individual. Such a scenario was apparently unimaginable in non-Western societies where life was organized around community, ethnicity, religion, and tradition.

This is how Bosniac women were represented when news of the war violence was publicized. The dominant Western (Euro-American) feminist response to reports of mass rapes in Bosnia was to reinforce the image of women as victims—or at least *those* women as victims. These were rapes committed on the basis of what was being described as ancient ethnic hatred. They were happening in the semi-exotic Balkans to a community of Muslims. Victimhood was thus easily culture-ized in a way that fit into Orientalist assumptions about gender oppression. In this way, ethnicity and religion were also essentialized and, through the construction of nations as extended (patriarchal) kinship groups (McClintock 1993; A. Smith 1988), the large numbers of Bosnian Muslim women who had been raped, widowed, and expelled from their homes were easily understood as symbols of the innocence and victimhood of the Bosniac nation as a whole.

Moreover, much like extreme iterations of victim feminism, the focus on victimhood was apparently irresistible; as with some nationalist narratives, some feminist analyses of post-Yugoslav nationalisms and the Bosnian war seem to revel in the brutality of the violence and the ways in which gendered nationalism was taken to its logical conclusion. In some cases, as I discuss in chapter 2, it was the feminist analysts themselves who took the violence to its logical conclusions, even in the absence of evidence that things had actually gone so far (and as if the atrocities were not bad enough). There seems to be a seductive quality to the realization of just how deep oppressive ideologies run, how vulnerable the powerless are when society breaks down, and how devastating the consequences of violence can be long after it has been committed. For feminists, these realities prove, against all those who claim that women in the modern world have been emancipated, or even that it is men who are now the victims, that there remains a need for feminist activism and campaigns for women's rights. For NGO activists, it is a necessary basis from which to claim legitimacy, the basis of institutional and financial support to keep these organizations running. The local community must be shown that women are disadvantaged and vulnerable to violence; feminist donors must be convinced that local conditions foster women's oppression and vulnerability, including in BiH the continued need to fund NGOs that work on ethnic reconciliation. Narratives of victimhood must apparently be total, with no hint of complicity, responsibility, or even agency, for such ambiguity may lead to suspicions of guilt or inauthenticity on the part of the victim.

Affirmative Essentialisms

A key facet of gendered representations after the Bosnian war, and what lent themselves so readily to claims to various forms of collective victimhood, were what Richard G. Fox (1996) has termed "affirmative essentialisms." Fox used this phrase in countering Partha Chatterjee's (1989) assessment of the gender discourses of late-colonial Indian nationalism, which had assigned women the valued but ultimately subordinated domestic roles of keepers of tradition, spirituality, and national essence. Women were said to be naturally suited to nurturing roles and to embody the purity of the nation. Fox argued that, in the long run, these essentialist representations mobilized women, providing them with legitimacy and opportunities to be active in the public, male sphere. Once engaged, Fox asserted, women's actions actually "superceded the original gender stereotypes" (1996, 48). While some eventual change can no doubt be traced, we should be skeptical of Fox's optimistic assessment of a set of gendered associations that ultimately, as Chatterjee argued, reinforced patriarchal hierarchies that restricted women's access to power. I adopt Fox's term in relation to the positive cast on women's roles and the *intentions* behind the use of such representations as they envisioned a scenario similar to what Fox describes. Ultimately, however, much as Chatterjee argued for colonial India, I argue that in postwar BiH affirmative essentialisms placed limits on the range of acceptable and possible spheres of engagement for women by failing to fundamentally challenge conservative gender norms and stereotypes.

To be sure, BiH was a case like many others in which unambiguous narratives of group entitlement were far more politically effective than nuanced argumentation. Indeed, the widespread common sense association of women with motherhood and nurturing meant that such representations were easily accepted and reproduced by both foreign and local actors, whether operating in donor and intervention agency circles, local NGOs, or the wider community. Gayatri Chakravorty Spivak famously pointed to the use of "strategic essentialisms" by subaltern groups, including women, as a conscious means of glossing over, at least temporarily, potentially disruptive differences within such groups even as the very notion of identity was rejected (1993). For some Bosnian women's activists with more nuanced and critical views, among them many of those who self-identified as feminists, this concept might be applied. Indeed, as I show in chapter 4, there were activists who explicitly acknowledged strategic elements of their avoidance of certain topics in order to facilitate cross-ethnic cooperation, affect government policies and laws, or garner funding. Very few of these women rejected the very notion of identity, however. The identity category of woman was meaningful to them, a fundamental part of their own sense of self, rather than a knowing construction of political strategizing, as Linda Alcoff (2000) has suggested is contained in the postmodern critique of identity and the notion of strategic essentialisms itself. Essentialist representations appeared as common sense and natural, even when used in strategic ways.

The power of such representations lay in their moral weight, which is why I find the affirmative designation important. Men were called upon with much fanfare in times of war to make sacrifices for the nation, but women were called upon and expected every day to make sacrifices for their families. Perhaps the most evocative of the affirmative characteristics claimed by and for women were therefore those attached to motherhood. As the most important role assigned to women as members of ethno-national collectivities in a variety of contexts (Anthias and Yuval-Davis 1989; Peterson 1999) including the states of former Yugoslavia (Bracewell 1996; Mostov 1995; Žarkov 2007), motherhood has been both a reason given to restrict women's activities and a powerful argument justifying women's engagement beyond the home. Groups of mothers such as the Mothers of the Plaza de Mayo in Argentina (Bejarano 2002; Taylor 1997) and the Mothers' Fronts in Sri Lanka (de Alwis 1998; Samuel 2003) have in many ways succeeded in publicly shaming the state precisely because their engagement in the public, political sphere was as mothers and widows in performances (Taylor 1994, 1997) of grief and mourning. Public, activist identities were based on their positioning outside the male realm of politics, on their relationships with male kin as mothers, and on their responsibility for domestic roles. In Bosnia, women survivors of Srebrenica have played a similar role.

In some places, this form of women's protest may be the only way possible for women to successfully achieve their goals (Samuel 2003), especially under conditions of extreme state repression (Taylor 1997). But conservative political and social climates can also favor such representations. In another postsocialist context, Armine Ishkanian found that women NGO activists in Armenia stressed an image of "moral motherhood" engaged on behalf of the nation to legitimate their activism in the eyes of local elites, even as they utilized "modern" discourses of women's rights and gender equality with their Western donors (Ishkanian 2000, 2003). Similarly, given the climate in BiH, in which politics was perceived as immoral, and moral status was derived from categories of wartime victimhood, Bosnian women activists achieved more immediate respect and standing—even avoiding outright dismissal—by mobilizing such essentialist representations. In this sense, the alignment with motherhood and other affirmative characteristics was certainly strategic. The focus in most cases was not, however, on a wider movement for women's rights as Spivak discussed, but a more immediate calculation frequently combined with what I understood as sincere conviction about women's and men's essential characteristics. I therefore refer to the often strategic use of affirmative essentialisms in the ways in which women were represented and represented themselves in relation to the male realms of nationalism, the political, and war.

In BiH, affirmative essentialisms lay at the crux of contestations over women's roles, especially in the NGO sector, which was new and located at a muddled border between what was public (typically gendered male) and what belonged to the (female gendered) realm of the private or domestic. The war and collapse of Yugoslav socialism had in many ways reinforced masculine roles (e.g., through the celebration of military heroes) and conservative gender regimes (especially through nationalist and religious revival), but these spheres had also been delegitimated in many ways: the brutality of the war, especially atrocities committed by enemy forces, had brought only suffering to the population despite its gratefulness to "its own" (ethnic, male) defenders; while many were happy to be rid of the strictures on religious and ethnic identity affirmation, the economic realities of market capitalism in the context of ruined infrastructure, an ineffective state, and the political corruption of a nominally democratic system run by clientelistic nationalist cabals had hit the population hard and many were bitter (see, for example, Jansen 2006). Postwar BiH society was thus particularly conflicted in terms of what behavior was morally respectable and what should be condemned and changed for the good of all (as Maček [2009] shows was even more the case during the war itself). Similar to (and intersecting with) the mobilization of simplified us-versus-them dichotomies of ethno-national character, neatly dividing naturalized gender representations into essentialized dichotomies of men's and women's spheres was one way to smooth out these uncertainties, offering people a way to make sense of situations in which the standards of morally correct behavior had been thrown into flux.

Claiming Distance

These circumstances created an opening for women and their advocates to argue for the legitimacy of women as public actors on the basis of their higher moral standing. They had not been involved in the decisions that had led to recent disasters and thus could hold their heads high and try to "clean up the mess" that men had made. In other words, women—as a group— were victims, innocent and morally uncompromised. Which (male) forces had victimized them was another question and one about which women's activists did not always agree. In fact, there was enough contextual fluctuation in the moral assessment of men's and women's roles, as well as of nationalism, politics, and wartime roles, that representatives of almost any position regarding gender, ethno-religious identifications, political configurations, or the war could in some way embrace affirmative notions like those attributing peacemaking roles to women. As no one wanted to be associated with nationalism, political corruption, war profiteering, or offensive war aims, the essentializing rhetoric celebrating women's innocence, victimhood, and peaceful nurturing nature found its place in a variety of political orientations, from conservative religious nationalists, to mainstream patriots with a vague sense that women's rights were a desirable part of the modern, democratic package, to anti-nationalists and feminists.

To be sure, many activists we will meet in this book did not explicitly use the term victim. It is not the victim *label* that interests me per se, but claims to moral standing, or goodness, that are implied through pronouncements of collective disempowerment, non-implicated-ness in the processes that create oppression and violence, the plausible denial of responsibility that lies at the root of certain claims to collective victimhood. The claim to victimhood is ultimately not about the wretched position of actual victims but about moral purity. And so moral purity must be absolute; innocence cannot be compromised. Moreover, none of these kinds of victimhood claims assumes a perpetual state of suffering and victimhood *for the collective*: while the victims are often required to remain as such, the group aspires to a brighter future. These associations made victim images focused both on women and on ethnic collectivities particularly difficult to dismantle, and not only at the local level. Internationally, there have been many activists, journalists, scholars, and others with intense investment in the victimhood narratives of a particular ethnic group in BiH, of women, or of particular ethnically defined women.

Differences in the terminology used by activists reflected wider uses of the victim label. In popular discourses, victims were mainly those who suffered in the war, although there was also an older notion of female victimhood within the patriarchal family, now relegated in the urban Bosnian sensibility to the rural and the past (see Helms 2008). Many women's activists in BiH deliberately referred to women who had been expelled from their homes or raped during the war, as well as women experiencing domestic violence, as *survivors*, in keeping with feminist positions elsewhere. Although relatively few in number compared to more conventional women's groups, there was a growing circle of self-described feminists who actively eschewed the victim label out of principle and who also fundamentally opposed the organizing logic of ethno-national collectivities that had come to dominate Bosnian society. Yet even these activists could be seen making use of collective representations that distanced them from morally compromised activities such as politics, nationalism, and war. Sometimes the (implied) victim was women, sometimes it was Bosniacs or BiH as a multiethnic state; much of the time it was all of these together. But like the dangers to progressive gender politics posed by positioning women as victims, representations of ethno-national victimhood also carried risks for various actors who wielded them. The conditions under which victimhood or, more to the point, moral purity could be claimed or even denied were thus varied and diverse.

Given the sensitivity and the stakes of this topic, and indeed because of the widespread sense that to examine the workings of power and moral claims among victims is to call into question the very facts of their victimization, I must stress from the start that the atrocities of the war and the suffering experienced by survivors are decidedly real, and devastating. Ethno-nationalist ideologies and the violence that sought legitimacy from them have created rigid, territorially based social hierarchies that have profoundly affected people's lives, both during the war and after. It is irrefutably clear that Bosniacs made up the large majority of those killed, expelled, and abused during the war; women make up most of the survivors of this violence.[4] Atrocities deserve to be condemned and punished in the strongest possible terms. Serious, too, are the material and symbolic exclusions of women in everyday life and the effects of traditionalist gender ideologies in all parts of BiH, effects that are felt more intensely by differently positioned women as well as men in ways that can truly be understood as discrimination, oppression, or victimization. By critically examining how people make sense of such inequalities and real effects, I by no means intend to suggest that the injustices they have suffered are not real or should not be taken seriously. Quite the opposite: because these issues are so important—even matters of life and death—I feel deeply that they must be better understood, that analysis should not be based on stereotypes and unexamined assumptions, and that advocates and activists would better serve their causes through representations that avoid reproducing oppressive hierarchies like sexism and nationalism. Ultimately, I am concerned with the political (mis)use of such suffering, which rarely has in mind the well-being of the less powerful.[5]

Studying Bosnia

This book offers an ethnographic account of Bosnian women's NGO activism in the years after the end of the war. This was not only a period of recovery from war and confrontations with nationalism(s) and the strong presence of international intervention. BiH was also struggling to adjust to new market logics after the dismantling of Yugoslavia's unique brand of socialism. At the same time the country was also feeling the effects of wider, global trends, among them the consolidation of social service provision and advocacy for social and political change into NGOs and civil society. Transnational networks of activists, government agencies, and United Nations (UN) bodies channeled their visions of victimized Bosnian womanhood into support for newly formed local women's NGOs with varied agendas: from alleviating the pain of trauma, to housing issues and income generation for newly destitute and homeless populations where women dominated, to various initiatives aimed at gender equality.

I examine the constructions and consequences of dominant discourses among and about those who were the very objects of such representation—women in the Bosniac-dominated areas of BiH—offering more nuanced ways in which to understand the terrain of gender activism and the lives of women in BiH since the dissolution of Yugoslavia.[6] Crucially, my point is not to merely suggest an alternative truth or to recover a more authentic subject but to uncover the implications of particular framings and the ways in which they are mobilized, challenged, or negated as activists pursue various agendas. In short, like Donna Murdock (2003), I find it less important to determine whether NGO activists are "doing good" according to some preset standards of what successful activism should look like than to situate activists' narrated experiences, choices, and motivations within the social and political context in which they operate (see also Sharma 2008). I thus ask how the discursive framing of Bosnian women as victims has shaped actual practices and strategies of representation given the multidirectional traffic—the circulation (Gal 2003)—of traveling theories, images, resources, and people. How were academic, activist, and media discourses of female victimhood mobilized, challenged, or ignored by those who were the objects of such depictions? And how did women in BiH attempt to shape the ways in which those dominant representations were received?

Research Choices

The fieldwork on which this study is based was conducted over fifteen years after the end of the Bosnian war, starting with doctoral dissertation research in the summer of 1997 and two years in 1999–2000 when I was based in the central Bosnian town of Zenica. In subsequent years, I made multiple research trips ranging from a few days to several months. Chapter 6 especially reflects the most recent research, undertaken during summers and teaching breaks from 2005–8, but supplemented by media analysis and a few more short visits until fall 2012. My perspective has also been shaped by experiences and relationships I established while working for local NGOs, first in refugee camps for Bosnians in Croatia (1993–94) and later with children and youth in the Herzegovinian city of Mostar (summer 1996). Data come from written sources, formal and informal interviews, everyday interactions with women activists, and attendance at NGO conferences and other gatherings. All research was conducted in the Bosnian language aside from interviews and interaction in English with foreign donor representatives and officials. Translations from the Bosnian language are mine unless otherwise noted.

When I began my research, the war had been over for less than two years. As I was intrigued by the wartime debates among feminists over gender, ethno-nationalism, and wartime violence, I set out to investigate how women's NGOs navigated the relationship between gender and nationalism and in what ways they were moving on after the war. I began in Sarajevo, which was important as the capital of Bosnia-Herzegovina, the political and cultural center of the Bosniac-dominated territories, and also a focal point for most foreign intervention agencies and NGO donors. I was to return to Sarajevo at various points throughout my research, but in those first phases, I wanted to focus my study outside the capital, somewhere that was not so flooded with foreigners, to get a better sense of the embeddedness of NGO activism into everyday life.

I chose Zenica mostly because it was home to Medica Zenica, one of the strongest, oldest, and best-known women's NGOs, which also described itself as feminist and anti-nationalist. In Zenica were also several other women's organizations with various approaches to issues of gender, nationalism, identity, and social change, including Bosanka, which (at first) focused on the affirmation of Bosniac identity. Following the activities and networks of these varied groups took me to places throughout BiH, to Serbia, Croatia, even nearby Hungary, and into contact with many other women's NGO activists, donors, representatives of international organizations, and ordinary Bosnians. I got to know activists from Medica and Bosanka especially well, but I also spent time with the members of several other NGOs from Zenica and other places as they participated in joint activities and meetings with Medica or Bosanka women. While most of these organizations were connected in some way, they represented different clusters of donor organizations and activist networks, which in turn affected the ways in which they articulated their concerns and how they represented themselves.

Zenica was also interesting for its politics. An ethnically mixed town before the war, the already large percentage of Muslims had increased to over 80 percent with the influx of Muslim refugees from other parts of Bosnia and the flight of many Serbs and Croats. Zenica retained its reputation as a center of Islamic fundamentalism and Bosniac nationalism, gained during the war when divisions of foreign jihadists fighting on the side of the Bosnian Army had been headquartered there and maintained by the fact that the main Bosniac party, the Party of Democratic Action (Stranka Demokratske Akcije, SDA), whose leaders had backed the creation of explicitly Islamist units in the military, held firm political control. But it was also a workers' town, having been built up around an enormous steel mill, where socialist industrialization had benefitted many in the recently urbanized population. In this atmosphere, I hoped to find a variety of gendered expressions of Bosniac and Muslim identity and perhaps opposition to its dominant forms. Of course, as is often the case, none of this played out in such stark terms—there were ethnically tinged tensions and doubts about feminism at Medica, Bosanka leaders abandoned their concern with Bosniac identity, and in the spring of my second year of major fieldwork (2000) the SDA lost its hold on the municipal and cantonal assemblies to the ideologically multiethnic Social Democratic Party (Socijal-demokratska Partija, SDP).

Research from Day to Day

Zenica is BiH's third largest city, a good hour's drive northwest from Sarajevo in the days before the four-lane highway (see fig. 1). It was less than picturesque with its concrete high-rises and the sprawling, rusting mess of pipes, chimneys, and machinery of the severely crippled steel mill that had employed nearly 23,000 workers in its heyday. Like similar postindustrial towns in the postsocialist world, it suffered from its loss of both jobs and sense of modernizing purpose (see Ghodsee 2009), but the war had made this change even more abrupt while adding to it the traumas of deprivation, ethnic polarization, and demographic shifts. In contrast to Sarajevo or Mostar, Zenica was more sagging with age than damaged by the war; it had very little Ottoman, Austrian, or other pre–World War II architecture. But it was also bisected by the wide Bosna River and surrounded by Bosnia's characteristic green mountains dotted with orange-roofed houses and white flowering fruit trees. With a population of less than 90,000,[7] Zenica was big enough that I could move through it anonymously, yet I also found that nearly everyone I met was connected to each other in some way and I frequently encountered acquaintances on the street.

I lived in the upstairs apartment of a house on the edge of a neighborhood of high-rises, at the base of one of the hills that delimited the town, near Medica and a ten-minute walk from the center. I shared the flat with a Medica team member, a young American woman whose experiences offered another perspective on Medica's work. We saw our landlady, an elementary school teacher, and her family frequently over thick Bosnian (Turkish-style) coffee or as they worked in their substantial garden behind the house. Friendly quarrels between our newly religious landlady, her "communist" husband, and her patriotic Muslim brother mirrored general divides in Bosniac-majority areas. Such dynamics were also palpable as I kept up a regular schedule of visits with other acquaintances and friends in the town as well as in other parts of the country.

In Zenica, Medica was the starting point of my research, especially the information and advocacy wing, Infoteka. I stopped by the office nearly every day, especially at afternoon coffee time, where discussion topics ranged from local political developments to the media to personal family issues to the latest fashions or TV shows. I participated in discussions and activities and helped out where I could with translating, editing, and report writing for Infoteka. I also visited Bosanka's leaders regularly, and attended activities of several other Zenica women's organizations. Over time, I conducted multiple interviews with key activists from all groups.

Figure 1　Political map of Bosnia-Herzegovina. (*The World Factbook*)

In following the activities especially of Medica and Bosanka, I was drawn away from questions of ethno-national identity and into several overlapping Bosnia-wide networks of women's activists working on issues of political participation, gender equality, legal reform, and domestic violence prevention. When, through these networks, I got to know the members of several refugee women's NGOs based in other parts of BiH, and later (from 2005) with the campaign for official recognition of rape survivors, ethnic identities and nationalism naturally did play a more central role, though not always exclusively or in expected ways.

Participating in the activities of these networks meant attending countless meetings, round tables, trainings, and conferences organized by international officials or other NGOs (usually with funding from a Western donor) in all

Figure 2 Downtown Zenica. Apartment blocks and teenage boys outside the Bosanka department store, July 2005. (photo by author)

parts of Bosnia as well as nearby countries. These were typically all-day affairs held in the conference rooms of once modern but now fading socialist-era hotels accompanied by heavy lunches and frequent coffee breaks. Participants were often divided into working groups where they went through an activity or held discussions before the whole group reconvened to decide on a tangible list of conclusions (*zaključci*), whether consensus had been reached or not. Some of the gatherings seemed more useful to the women's cause than others; activists complained about the constant travel just to see the same women and say the same things over and over again. Others praised the meetings for their networking (*netvorking* or *umreživanje*) utility. For my purposes, these gatherings allowed me to compare the "Western-looking" activists who operated in Western donor-funded circles with those who rarely left Zenica for their organizational activities or who had no contact with Western donors (but sometimes with "Eastern" ones). Their rhetoric and ideological stances were markedly different, reflecting different strategies of representation for different circles and audiences (cf. Phillips 2008).

Thus, as much as a large part of this study reflects my experience in the community of Zenica as a place, it is more a multi-sited study of the cultural

Figure 3 A meeting of women's activists. Federal Parliament hall, Sarajevo, April 2007. (photo by author)

unit of the Bosnian women's NGO scene in both its multilevel connectedness as well as its rootedness in particular places. Spending time in Sarajevo and many of the smaller communities where activists lived and worked but also moving with them from place to place offered insights into the doing of activism as well as the issues that motivated them. This movement was especially important when it came to refugee women's NGOs, as I was able to travel with them to their former (or again current) homes to appreciate the challenges they faced. Getting to know this multi-sited network was further a useful base from which I was later able to study the engagement of some of the same women's NGOs with the issue of women rape survivors.

And so travel itself was part of my research. I rode buses, trams, and taxis to get to NGO offices, meetings, and workshops. I bought a used car (an old Volkswagen Golf II, the car of what seemed like half of Bosnia) in which I gave rides to Medica or Bosanka members and women activists, politicians, journalists and so on from other towns who joined us at various gatherings. Riding through the winding, narrow highways of the mountainous terrain, we discussed all kinds of issues facing women in postwar BiH. They waxed nostalgic about the prosperous days of Yugoslavia, exchanged gossip about other activists and prominent figures, shared their satisfaction and frustration about the meetings we attended, and patiently explained to me why opening the car windows to create a draft (*propuh*), even against the stifling summer heat, could be deadly.

The CIA in Wonderland

In the Bosnian language, my first name is rendered phonetically as Alisa, a common "modern" first name among Bosniacs and also the Bosnian/Croatian/Serbian translation of Alice. So I was often addressed as *Alisa u zemlji čuda*—Alice in Wonderland. I was indeed in a land of wonders, I was told. Anything can happen here; this is the Balkans. Here was a reflection of dominant Balkanist representations, as Sarah Green, who was told much the same thing in northern Greece, argues (2005). At the same time, it was one of several common "litanies and laments" (Ries 1997, 83–125) on the ruptures of the normal—what was being experienced as a particular sort of chaos of life since the disintegration of socialist Yugoslavia (see Greenberg 2011; Jansen 2006, 2007; Živković 2011). As Alice, I was hardly expected to be able to make sense of all of this when it was not even clear to Bosnians themselves.

Bosnians of all walks of life had become accustomed to foreigners in their midst—making pronouncements in the media, driving around in SUVs, busily attending meetings, inspecting projects, and asking them questions—few of whom spoke the local language or had much prior knowledge about the society and its history (see Coles 2007).[8] In some cases, therefore, NGO women saw me as part of the international community, that is, a potential donor, and I sometimes heard statements that, to me, resembled what people thought donors might want to hear. Sometimes this meant requests to use my assumed connections to find a job for a relative or fund an NGO project (cf. Kuehnast 2000); others lost interest when I insisted I was *not* a donor. I had occasional encounters with those who pounced on what they were sure were my Western prejudices against Muslims or intentions to portray them as primitive and patriarchal, especially since I was interested in gender relations (see Helms 2008). Some even intimated I might be a spy, wondering aloud, maybe only half-jokingly, what else the CIA might want to know (cf. Green 2005; Silverman 2000; Zanca 2000). To drive the point home, for my birthday the young women at Medica once gave me earrings that said "FBI" ("CIA" hadn't been among the choices). Several leaders of the war survivor associations I met in 2005–7 were especially reluctant to talk, as they were, in one leader's words, "up to here with journalists" and other researchers to whom they had told their stories without seeing any visible benefits to them.

Fortunately, those with whom I developed more sustained relationships grew accustomed to me as a researcher and fellow traveler in the circles of women's meetings. My status as an American was never completely forgotten, but this positionality was illuminating as it sometimes prompted people to reflect on their activities to me and to compare the situation in BiH with their views of the United States and "the West." Early on, the director of Infoteka pointed out, echoing warnings about the pitfalls of feminist solidarity through research (e.g., Abu-Lughod 1990; Stacey 1988; Visweswaran 1994), that my access to and participation in spontaneous exchanges alongside more official presentations was an advantage but also carried with it a deep responsibility. I have remained deeply conscious of this responsibility in my efforts to honor my friendships and respect for the people I write about even as I critically analyze the implications of some of their choices and stances.

This book is populated by real people whose own words I have endeavored to convey as much as possible, while at the same time affording them a measure of anonymity given the sensitive political climate and competition among activists in postwar BiH. The quotations I give, when not otherwise indicated, come from recorded interviews and meetings as well as less formal conversations detailed in field notes. The bulk of these examples come from the period of my initial research, 1997 and 1999–2000, with the exception of material presented in chapter 6, or where otherwise designated. Though I do not disguise the names of organizations and places, following anthropological convention, I use pseudonyms, here designated by first names only, for most of those with whom I interacted. Where I give both first and last names, these are the real names of people who requested to be identified or who were publicly visible, although the latter distinction is somewhat arbitrary given the public nature of activism itself. While far from a perfect solution, my aim is to grant credit to the organizations for their work and to offer ethnographic details for other researchers while also protecting individuals. In many cases, while I am fully aware that thorough disguise is difficult, I retain pseudonyms because I find that they create a degree of distance that draws attention more to analytical points than to individual personalities. In a few instances, I have intentionally omitted names and places in order to avoid identifying people and groups whose statements, or my analysis of them, might be interpreted negatively in the sensitive political climate of BiH, despite their having been conveyed to me in good faith.

I sometimes specify people's ethno-national background as it is relevant to the context. I do this as a regrettable shorthand for categories that are portrayed as clear-cut, but are inevitably experienced with much more subtlety and fluidity than such labels imply. Ethnicity in BiH is presumed through well-recognized cues such as religious affiliation (a reference to religious rituals, mosque/church attendance, or pendants with religious symbols); use of ethnically marked language; ties to geographical location, especially in reference to wartime movements (e.g., whether a person was expelled from or had stayed in an area known to have been ethnically cleansed); political affiliations; and above all names. These cues are not always accurate, however, and names can obscure as much as they reveal, most obviously in the case of people with mixed ethnic parentage or whose spouses came from a different ethnic background. Some names are ethnically ambiguous, often purposefully chosen by "mixed" or "communist" parents who believed in Yugoslav "brotherhood and unity." Readers familiar with names in BiH will therefore notice ethno-religious associations, or ambiguity, conveyed in the pseudonyms I use, as they would with informants' real names. I do this to retain a sense of the socially significant information conveyed by names, even as the practices and stances of individuals often complicated or undermined dominant usages.

Outline of Chapters

I begin in chapter 1 by mapping the landscape in which Bosnian women's activists operate, from the terms and effects of international intervention, to pressures from local nationalist movements, to the multiple transformations and changed moral codes that informed social and political life in postwar BiH. I then discuss the dominant frameworks through which gender in Bosnia has been analyzed by scholars, activists, and policy makers, and which structured the possibilities for and obstacles to activism. These include Orientalist and Balkanist representations, as well as older notions of honor and shame, while frameworks of postsocialism have been conspicuously absent.

In order to understand the tensions produced among local, regional, and foreign women's activists and feminists as well as the stakes of public representations of victimhood, it is also necessary to examine the gendered violence of the war, the regional ethno-nationalisms that fueled it, and the feminist debates of the period over how to interpret war rapes in Bosnia. This is my task in chapter 2. As background, I briefly review the socialist period from the perspective of women and gender equality. I then explain the gendered patterns of the war violence and show how the events and disagreements around interpretations of the war brought out contested linkages between gender, nation, and victimhood that have provided an often unexamined tension for women's activists in the region, especially when it comes to forging solidarities across ethnicized boundaries. This includes a critical examination of gender in discourses of genocide in the Bosnian war and of statements that the loss of husbands and sons or the experience of rape was especially difficult for Muslim women or that women were the biggest victims of the war. I further show how Bosniac nationalism shares much of the logic of gender and nation with the notoriously patriarchal nationalisms in Serbia and Croatia, just as it shares with these, and perhaps all nationalisms, a need to portray the nation as the ultimate victim. I therefore argue for an understanding of the war violence and nationalist politics that takes gender and ethno-nationalism as mutually constructive, rather than separate explanatory lenses.

In the third chapter, I map the social, ideological, and economic terrain in which postwar international intervention took place, and introduce the reader to the main activists and women's organizations featured in this study. I discuss the approaches of foreign intervention agencies and donors toward women's NGOs and gender issues, emphasizing the models they put forth and the goals they encouraged local NGOs to pursue. Further, I trace the strong continuities with, and ruptures from, socialist forms of women's organizing, and contrast them to new models of civil society advocacy promoted by donors and foreign intervention agencies. The interweaving of these competing models produced new and stronger notions about women's roles vis-à-vis nationalism, politics, and war, notions that fed back into representations of female victimhood and agency.

The remaining chapters of the book explore activists' strategies of representation in relation to three gendered categories that define the discursive arena of postwar Bosnia: ethno-nationalism, the political, and war victimhood. In all three areas, I critically examine affirmative essentialist assertions that women have opposed, and are the primary victims of, nationalism and violence, along with the unspoken corollary of female innocence and moral purity.

Chapter 4 interrogates women activists' relationship to nationalism, a concept that implicated notions of ethnicity and religion as well as stances toward a multiethnic Bosnian society, the return of refugees to their original homes, interethnic reconciliation, and ultimately narratives of collective war victimhood. Donor approaches and local NGO strategies in many cases converged to *strengthen* both ethnic and gender divisions, and to foreclose certain avenues of activism even while many of these actors advocated ethnic togetherness and/or gender equality. On one end of a spectrum of approaches, I show how some activists reproduced a moral hierarchy of ethnic difference through profoundly conservative narratives of gender difference. I thus show how representations of women as peacemakers can carry with them assumptions about incompatible ethnic collectivities in ways ill-suited to reconciliation initiatives. On the other end, self-described feminists managed to rise above ethnic divisions, engaging in effective cross-ethnic cooperation that was enabled by what one activist called "strategic avoidance" of "ethnic" issues in favor of notions of women's solidarity—affirmative essentialisms of a different kind. Finally, I tease out some of the thornier questions raised by the specific relationship between feminism and national narratives of victimhood detectable in activists' responses to assertions about wartime rape and to the 1999 North Atlantic Treaty Organization (NATO) bombing of Serbia.

Chapter 5 turns to the political, a concept associated with gendered constructions of public and private; with issues of activism, feminism, and public visibility; and with the relationship to male-dominated arenas held responsible for war violence, corruption, economic woes, and crime. Here I analyze the rhetoric of foreign agencies, donors, women's activists, and groups of female Srebrenica survivors, as well as women in formal party politics, showing how they constructed women as innocent bystanders to male-led violence and corruption. Women were essentialized as mothers, actors uninterested in "dirty" politics but compelled to get involved out of concern for the future of their children. They were thus charged with leading reconciliation efforts, paradoxically a highly political endeavor. I argue that this discrepancy was resolved through a temporal construction in which women distanced themselves from the politics of the past and present, aligning themselves with an idealized politics of hope for the future.

The representational strategies presented thus far made use of various forms of female victim identities, yet in different ways activists avoided direct association with the iconic figures of female victimhood from the war: the rural refugee and especially the rape victim. Chapter 6 focuses on the figure of the woman wartime rape victim. I argue that public identities were much more difficult to sustain for rape survivors than for refugee women such as the survivors of Srebrenica, despite the stigma attached to both categories. Drawing on more recent research, I trace the successful 2006 campaign by Medica Zenica and a broad coalition of women's NGOs to achieve official recognition in the Federation of BiH of rape survivors as civilian war victims, a status which made them eligible for a small state pension. This process and the subsequent dispute sparked by the making of a film by Angelina Jolie brought out the lingering stigma against rape victims and the tensions created as women's organizations and state institutions struggled between the political value of such victimhood for the nation, the concrete needs of actual survivors, and the politics of authenticity over who had the moral right to speak on behalf of women victims. I argue that women's activism in BiH and all of former Yugoslavia has so far avoided an open discussion of their stances on wartime rape and thus a full articulation of a gender critique that might challenge the dominance of ethno-national victim narratives.

In the conclusion, I reflect on the dynamics of gendered victimhood in contexts of war and nationalism and argue for the importance of masculinity in understanding the implications of gendered nationalism for both women and men. Through this lens, some of the limits of gender rhetoric for ethno-nationalisms become apparent. I further note the limits of claims to collective victimhood for gender politics and feminism. This leads me to reflect on the potential traps of gender-sensitive mechanisms of transitional justice after conflict. Through insights drawn from the experiences of other societies with more victim-centered approaches, I suggest that the increased attention to war violence against women, including by well-meaning human rights and feminist activists, carries more potential drawbacks for victims and for local women's activism than are readily apparent. I end by considering some recent feminist scholarship that attempts to locate pockets of hope in the potential for feminist public and artistic expression in BiH to create an emancipatory politics. While I recognize these attempts as valuable contributions to such a politics in themselves, following the material presented in this book, I caution that there are many more obstacles than usually acknowledged to these messages coming across, given the dominance of gendered narratives of collective guilt and innocence rigidly constructed in ethno-national terms.

1

Victims and Peacemakers

Contextualizing Representations

Kad čujem "žene žrtve" odmah mi zlo dođe.
(When I hear "women victims" I immediately feel sick.)

Jasna Zejčević, president of Vive žene

Representations of Bosnian Women

Mention women and Bosnia and your first association is likely to be one of two iconic images: distraught women in headscarves and traditional Muslim dress fleeing ethnic cleansing, their ragged children and few belongings in tow; or the shamed and silenced young Muslim victim of rape and forced pregnancy, doubly victimized by her attackers and then by her own patriarchal community. These were the images that flooded the world media during the war and that have been instrumentalized in various political discourses of the region ever since.

Bosnian women activists were well aware of this representation. If they had not noticed it on CNN (see Mertus 1994), it became obvious in their interactions with visiting foreign journalists, aid workers, activists, or donors. When I interviewed her in 2005, Jasna Zejčević, president of the Tuzla women's NGO Vive žene, summed up the sentiment of many urban Bosnian women I had met over the years: "Whenever I meet foreigners, there's always the question, 'Were you in the war?' Of course I was here. And then they look at you and—they do everything but poke me to see if I'm real! Because a Bosnian woman is uneducated, wearing *dimije* [colorful baggy trousers], a victim, from a village. So when they see someone who speaks English, who knows something, who can talk intelligently, they're surprised." Even though she had been working for a decade with women survivors of the Srebrenica massacre, with survivors of wartime rape, and more recently with women and children fleeing domestic violence, Zejčević was fed up with these images, as this chapter's epigraph indicates. This sentiment had been behind their choice of name for the NGO: as she emphasized, "Vive žene" meant "Women *live!*" Anger over dominant media images also affected the way in which another women's NGO, Bosanka in Zenica, was founded, as we will see in chapter 3. Many other women's activists told of similar encounters with foreigners' assumptions and were equally as incensed, even as they also reproduced dominant images in various ways.

Importantly, Zejčević added that she blamed local media as much as foreign outlets for the perpetuation of the image of oppressed rural women: "All they show are poor Bosnian women with nothing but suffering in this patriarchal world of the village." There were local prejudices and stereotypes but also real social cleavages that had fed into how international media coverage had been presented by locals and that continued to shape the landscape in which women's NGOs operated after the war. At the same time, I suggest, there were also reasons why different actors might emphasize such images or allow them to be perpetuated. At the crux of such motivations were often questions of victimhood and innocence, which in turn underpinned various kinds of moral claims.

The Bosnian war became notorious for campaigns of ethnic cleansing and mass rapes, the victims of which were overwhelmingly Muslims. As socialist Yugoslavia disintegrated and parts were consumed by war, newly powerful nationalisms, through patriarchal logics of ethno-national superiority and territorial control, were positioning women as passive symbols and powerless targets. The nation was cast as a woman in need of protection from "our" men, while the rape of "their" women signaled the defeat of "their" men, as they had not been men enough to protect "their" women. In Bosniac and Bosnian nationalist discourses, the rapes have been invoked as a symbol of the innocence and victimhood of the Bosniac nation/Bosnian state, and as evidence of the barbarity of the Serbs (and to a lesser extent, Croats).

Women were thus placed in the role of passive victims, active only in their capacity to reproduce and nurture new members of the nation. Fierce debates that flared during the war among feminists over how to represent the rapes in Bosnia (and neighboring Croatia)—as crimes of gender or of (ethno-) nation—further highlighted the fraught relationship between gender and ethno-national categories.

These newly powerful discourses and the horrific ways in which they came to life in the war became the grist for renewed feminist interest in gender, nationalism, and ethnic conflict in the 1990s. This attention from academics, activists, psychologists, and legal specialists brought forth valuable insights into the workings of ethnic violence, nationalisms, and the wars in what had become the former Yugoslavia. It also led to solidarity campaigns, humanitarian actions, and a successful effort to have sexualized violence recognized as a crime of war. To counter nationalist and mainstream accounts, feminist analysis has striven to highlight the *active* roles of women in the successor states of Yugoslavia in aiding victims, rejecting violence, and working for peace. Donor agencies and international organizations working to build a unified, multi-ethnic state have also portrayed Bosnian women mostly in (re)active roles, as noble peacemakers working for ethnic reconciliation, cleaning up the mess made by violent and greedy men. As I argue in this book, however, these interventions have paradoxically reinforced the image of female victimhood—for women in general but specifically in the case of Bosniac women—and foreclosed other avenues of academic inquiry, activist engagement, and policy approaches. There is no denying that Bosniac women were the most numerous among those who survived ethnic cleansing and rape, but through a variety of dominant representations they have become the only victims, and, more worryingly, *only victims.*

These representations have been constructed largely without the voices of Bosnian women themselves, or in ways that downplay their agency, leaving intact an Orientalized image of silenced, shamed, and powerless victims of patriarchal, Muslim culture. This pattern shares much with accounts of women in other Muslim or Balkan societies, as well as other contexts of violence and rupture. But existing literature has surprisingly little to say about how such representations have resonated among the women depicted, in this case Bosnian women themselves.

This book thus offers an alternative to images of the passive, Muslim female victim, focusing on women's active roles. But it is far from a celebration of women's resistance to patriarchy, nationalism, and war. Instead I show how the context of conflict and social upheaval posed different dilemmas for women and men, how women made a variety of choices, and how they positioned themselves very differently in the face of such forces, some trying to challenge, others trying to escape, and still others reinforcing the nationalisms, violence, and other patriarchal political currents that have held sway in BiH since the disintegration of Yugoslavia. To understand these choices, it is necessary to map the terrain in which Bosnian women activists have operated since the recent war. As relatively marginal but not insignificant actors in the local political arena, women's organizations have had to navigate the discursive, material, political, and moral fields defined by more powerful forces.

Postwar, Postsocialist Bosnia-Herzegovina

State(s) and International Intervention

The Bosnian war ended in late 1995 with the Dayton Peace Agreement (properly, the General Framework Agreement for Peace in Bosnia and Herzegovina), brokered by American diplomats and the nationalist leaders of the warring parties. Though the issues that had sparked the war remained far from settled, the cease-fire paved the way for reconstruction efforts to begin. Dayton had shored up the Bosnian state, yet it had also established two internal entities, each ethnically[1] defined and controlled: the Serb Republika Srpska (RS) and the Bosniac and Croat dominated Federation of Bosnia-Herzegovina. The Federation, created in 1994 with the Washington Agreement that halted fighting between Bosniac and Croat forces, was further arranged into ten ethnically controlled (and populated) cantons. Within the two mixed cantons, in turn, ethnically controlled municipalities took on primary significance. Governance was thus highly fragmented and ethnicized, creating territories now largely segregated by ethno-national identification. Refugees and internally displaced persons (IDPs), most having fled to "their own" ethnic territories, were given the right to return to their homes where they would become ethnic minorities,[2] while ethnic others who stayed in areas that came to be controlled by the forces of a different group also became minorities without moving anywhere. Bosniac-controlled areas of the Federation retained the greatest amount of ethnic heterogeneity, which increased slightly in both entities when the return process got under way starting in 1998.

To oversee and ensure its implementation, Dayton established a quasi-protectorate role for the (Western-dominated) institutions led by the Office of the High Representative (OHR) and including a variety of private, governmental, intergovernmental, European Union (EU), and UN agencies as well as peacekeeping forces led by NATO and later by the EU.[3] While peacekeepers, humanitarian aid organizations, journalists, and diplomats had been operating in Bosnia during the war, the peace agreement ushered in much bigger swarms of development and aid workers, international administrators, advisors, consultants, trauma experts, mine-clearing specialists, doctors, youth workers, specialists in nonviolent conflict resolution, feminists, human rights activists, and many others. Bosnia was incorporated as another project site in the networks of humanitarian crisis response, democracy aid to postsocialist countries (i.e., Central and Eastern Europe [CEE]), as well as development agencies whose traditional targets had been Third World countries. Though these foreigners mainly came from Western Europe and North America, a number of Islamic organizations from Arab and other predominantly Muslim countries also took up projects in the Bosniac areas of Bosnia (as they later did in other parts of Southeast Europe with indigenous Muslim populations; see Ghodsee 2009). These diverse actors had many different goals and visions but the most powerful (Western) ones shared a general commitment to building a viable, democratic Bosnian state with a market economy that would eventually join the EU (see, for example, Bose 2002; Pugh 2005). They were thus often referred to en bloc as the international community, or "internationals" (Coles 2007); Bosnians often called them simply "foreigners" (*stranci*).[4]

The most prominent obstacle for the OHR and other international institutions in building a functioning, multiethnic state was the power of nationalist parties. In the immediate postwar years, they were especially concerned with Serb and Croat parties that opposed placing the territories they controlled under the authority of state institutions as they vied for increased autonomy and sometimes outright opposed the state itself. Bosniac nationalists' goals generally overlapped with support for a multiethnic state, such that Bosniac leaders were not as often perceived as obstructing Dayton, although they grew increasingly critical of the existence of the RS. All those in power were pressured by international institutions and foreign governments to engage in interethnic cooperation and reconciliation, including allowing the return of "minority" DPs (displaced persons), secular politics, respect for human rights, and sustaining non-ethnic definitions of citizenship. At the same time, the very structures of governance established by Dayton were based on a fundamentally "communitarian" (Bougarel 1996) logic of ethno-national representation and citizenship defined through ethnicity (Bieber 2004; Mujkić 2007b).

Moral Worlds and Social Categories in a Time of Flux

Nationalism and recovery from war were not the only challenges facing Bosnian society, nor the only ones being addressed by international institutions. Things like the collapse of the economy, destruction of factories, and the imposition of new borders were obviously attributable to the war. But the disappearance of the social safety net, accessible health care, housing rights, and various perks like cheap seaside vacations had more to do with the transition from socialism to neoliberal market capitalism. Likewise, the political system and the ways in which the population related to it had shifted, at least on paper, from communist one-party self-management to pluralistic democracy. Bosnian society was at the same time caught up in various global and regional processes, from shifts in humanitarian aid and intervention approaches, to the worldwide boom in NGOs, to the growth of the Internet, and later, to increased concern over Islamic terrorism, to name just a few. Everyday worries revolved around intertwined effects of all these changes, which had produced times of profound precariousness (Jansen 2007; Jašarević 2007) but, for some, also unprecedented opportunity (cf. Nordstrom 2004).

In these times of uncertainty and flux, social categories were also undergoing change. The war had brought about what Veena Das and Arthur Kleinman have called "the distortion of local moral worlds" (2000, 1), the recovery from which entails a negotiation of public space for the expression of individual experiences and ultimately a "transformation to a different moral state" (ibid., 23) and attempts to remold a working political society (ibid., 4; see also Bougarel et al. 2007b). We see this in BiH in the intense struggle to reestablish a moral order in the face of widespread feelings that morality had broken down, that those who least deserved it—war profiteers, politicians who stirred up hatreds, men who avoided fighting on the front lines—were living well at the expense of the suffering masses.

Ivana Maček (2009) vividly captures these dilemmas among wartime residents of Sarajevo as they tried to cope with the destruction of the social world around them. The postwar period continued the processes she describes, with categories of wartime victimhood and behavior adding to preexisting notions of worthiness and morality. Thus, social categories created or given new significance in the war—victims and perpetrators, veterans, deserters, fallen soldiers and martyrs, civilian victims, former camp detainees, rape victims, war profiteers, those who stayed or left the country or went to the "other side," those who helped their neighbors and those who betrayed them, and so on— were frequent referents in postwar claims to legitimacy and entitlement. At the same time, though often not coded as such, moral claims also invoked categories that had existed before the war, both positive and negative: distinctions between cultured and uncultured (*kulturno/nekulturno*), rural (primitive) versus urban (modern), humanitarian work versus politics, politicians versus ordinary citizens, mothers versus whores, and the like (Bougarel et al. 2007b). All of these categories and moral referents were highly gendered and subject to contestation, though not always as malleable as some of the activists I studied hoped.

Moreover, especially among the urban educated classes, to which most of the activists I worked with belonged, there was a stubborn adherence to identities as modern Europeans that had been cultivated under socialism, especially in reference to the modernizing socialist project (see Maček 2009; Jansen 2009). Sarajevo had hosted the 1984 Winter Olympics, Yugoslavia had been a leader in the Non-Aligned Movement, and its citizens had enjoyed the freedom to travel that went with Yugoslavia's neutrality between the Soviet bloc and the NATO members of Western Europe. Bosnians were thus incredulous that they could be so quickly cut off from the world and portrayed as uncivilized "Balkan tribes." As is not surprising in such a time of rapid change, the whole society seemed to be preoccupied with its place in the world and the judgment of outsiders, especially what was perceived as the powerful and prosperous but not wholly perfect West. Thus, even as they stressed their modern and European identities, some women activists were also wary of embracing neoliberal Western models. Although most of these activists were dependent on Western aid for the survival of their organizations, and in many cases also their personal livelihoods, these models, with their emphases on democracy, civil society, even feminism and gender, seemed at times to clash with the women's senses of self. While this contested emphasis on NGOs and civil society offered women new opportunities and spaces for a redefinition of gender roles and women's public/political activism, they were also constrained in various ways by dominant notions of morality, gender order, and identity. It was this range of meaning and discursive opportunities and barriers that shaped the ways in which representations of women and gender relations resonated and circulated.

The Politics of Gendered Dead Bodies

Regardless of their connection to these multiple transformations, most every social, political, or economic issue was narrated through idioms of ethnicity and nation, reflecting the success of nationalist discourses and the violence that solidified and *produced* new notions of ethnic difference that had been much more diffused and complicated before the late 1980s and the breakup of socialist Yugoslavia (see Bringa 1995; Gagnon 2004; Woodward 2000). The violence, in turn, became the main referent for all manner of claims to legitimacy, from the level of everyday life through the world stage, in which the morally superior position was always that of victim, particularly when one's enemy could be cast as especially barbaric and evil.

In their attention to narrative as a crucial element of nationalist expression, Rada Iveković and Julie Mostov note: "The ethno-national story is a closed narrative. It is a story in which the contents of the identity in question are given through the official version of a unique and absolute truth/event. All of the multiple possibilities of the event (which could have happened) are discarded and reduced to one sole interpretation, which fixes the official interpretation of the event into a 'unique truth'" (2002, 19). Such stories come to be mutually exclusive, even or especially when they narrate the same events. In postwar BiH, these ethno-national narratives were not restricted to events of the war, as significant a place as the war tended to inhabit. They were competing and often clashing world views that emerged out of different social, geographical, and political positionings. And while they had a profound effect on everyday lives and practices, as well as governing structures and policy, it is important to see them as narratives because it is the stories they told about the origins and character of the nation, its actions and suffering, and its eternal desires that incited emotional responses, demanded loyalty, and underlay claims to both individual and collective morality and legitimacy.

Nationalisms everywhere strive for their nations to be recognized as collective victims, perhaps defenders but never aggressors. Throughout the former Yugoslavia, national politics have been infused with what Katherine Verdery has aptly termed "dead body politics" (1999) through commemoration and glorification of victims of past wars and oppressive regimes to project ethnonational designations onto the past and thus to legitimize the political claims of the present. Dead bodies, but also, as we shall see, the ongoing and visible suffering of certain surviving tortured bodies, become the moral argument for the purity of collective character and aims, for the innocence and thus goodness of the nation (Ballinger 2003; Schäuble, forthcoming). Particularly powerful has been what Marko Živković, writing about Serbian nationalism, calls "the wish to be a Jew," or the aspiration to be collectively equated with the ultimate victims and the most devastating genocide of the Holocaust (2000).[5] This ultimate victim status is not desirable for its association with passivity and vulnerability, rather for its implications of innocence, the absolution of responsibility, and ultimately moral purity. No ambiguity is allowed: members of one's own nation can only be victims, enemy groups only perpetrators, and those victimized by conflicts can only be identified in ethno-national terms.

Such rigid parameters also open up spaces for contestation that threaten to negate whole episodes of atrocities in the name of defending nationalist causes. For one of the problems with the hyperbolic rhetoric of what Samantha Power (1999) calls "Holocaustizing" is the impossibility of living up to the role of helpless victim and the pattern of Nazi killings; if a group can be seen as "implicated victims" it is therefore not completely innocent (54, quoting Helen Fein). Indeed, as Pamela Ballinger notes, "this exclusivity constructs the other side's victims as compromised or guilty (hence meriting their fates and not genuine victims)" (2003, 135). Ballinger's work on the politics of memory after the violence and population movements of Italians and Slavs in Istria and the region of Trieste during World War II shows how political and military affiliations were later read in ethnic terms, shifting the stakes of the politics of exile decades after the end of that war. Accordingly, Yugoslav officials described victims murdered and thrown, sometimes alive, by partisans into crevasses and pits of the karstic mountains as fascists implicated in the Italian and German regimes, while an Italian judge ruled in the 1975 trial of those accused of responsibility for war crimes in a Trieste concentration/death camp that the camp's victims had included both innocent and "noninnocent victims," the latter designated as antifascist partisans and Communists (ibid.). Implicatedness here blurred the line between political and ethnic affiliations, allowing later narratives to construct the conflict in ethnic terms. Implicated-ness could also come from questions about the civilian status of victims, with soldiers, even if disarmed, seen as legitimate targets.

In a further implication of this logic, Vlasta Jalušič has argued that the nationalisms of the former Yugoslavia (but certainly also elsewhere) are built not only on various distortions and selective remembering of the past but also on what she terms "organized innocence," which allows for, even justifies, further victimization of "others" (2007; see also Turner 2010). Indeed, in the 1980s, excavations of mass graves from World War II and renewed accusations of past genocides (Denich 1994; Hayden 1994; Nielsen 2013) played a decisive role in fueling the nationalist outrage that turned into secession movements and war violence, including ethnic cleansing and, many argue, genocide again.[6] And some saw worrying signs that Bosniac narratives were starting to make similar claims, moving from arguments about war atrocities and genocide to claims of collective righteousness and superiority over ethnic others (see P. Miller 2006). I return to this phenomenon and its gendered components in the conclusion. Here, the connection between innocence and victimhood are important to consider for the ways in which they structured the possibilities and obstacles for gendered citizenship and women's activism.

Gendered Nationalism

Women and associations with the feminine serve as perfect symbols of this victim-innocence, especially in situations of armed conflict. They, along with the children and elderly in their care, epitomize the civilian, widely rejected as a legitimate target of war violence, whether directly or as "collateral damage," despite the fact that modern wars tend to produce higher civilian than military casualties. Innocence thus stems from essentialist presumptions about sex roles: women are assumed to be unconnected to political or military spheres while men are targeted as potential (political or military) threats (Carpenter 2003, 2006; Jones 2000). Whether war or the threat of war is real or symbolic, territories, nations, or states are often feminized, rendering attacks on them illegitimate and barbaric. We need only recall how phrases like "the rape of Kuwait" or "the rape of Nanking" simultaneously admonished the world, cast as male, for its failure to protect those (feminized) places and acted as a call to arms to avenge the victims or to prevent further outrages. They are framed as outrages to be understood through the normative lens of patriarchal heterosexuality and the gendered laws of war and statehood: men act as defenders of the nation's territory and honor while women symbolize and embody the passive (feminized) nation, whose body/land and honor must be defended by men (see, for example, Massad 1995; Mosse 1985; Peterson 1999; Verdery 1994).

Though it is still largely marginalized in mainstream accounts, there is now a substantial literature showing not only that nationalisms are gendered but that notions of gender and sexuality are in fact *constitutive* of discourses about ethnic groups, nations, and states.[7] Fears of enemy rape are part of larger concerns over the reproduction and ethnic purity of the self group. Nationalist discourses and policies have thus commonly encouraged "ethnically correct" (along with class exclusive) births and attempted to limit interethnic sexual contact and marriage (see, for example, Das 1995; Heng and Devan 1992; C. Smith 1996). Broadening this line of reasoning, nationalists have also linked (re)traditionalized gender role expectations to national loyalty, as when women are exhorted to remain in the domestic sphere to bear and nurture a new generation for the nation, while men are expected to lead and defend the nation in the public roles of politicians and soldiers (e.g., Chatterjee 1989; McClintock 1993).

In patterns familiar from this literature, nationalist projects in the former Yugoslavia targeted not only ethnic selves and others in gendered ways but also different men and women within these groups. Beginning in the late 1980s, nationalists especially in Serbia and Croatia began putting forth traditionalist, essentialized constructions of women as reproducers, nurturers, and objects of protection, while the male roles they promoted became ever more militarized and aggressive. As I outline below, the available scholarship on these processes says next to nothing about strains of nationalism in Bosnia itself, especially among the Bosniacs, most likely, I suggest, because there is no will to cast a critical eye on the group that suffered the worst violence of the recent wars—the victims and therefore the good guys. Yet, given the gendered logic of claiming victimhood, the constellation of shared gendered meanings across the former Yugoslavia, and what we know of other nation-building projects, it should not come as a surprise that conservative, patriarchal notions of gender and sexuality have figured prominently in Bosniac and Bosnian nationalisms as well. Further, the logic of gendered nationalism can be a double-edged sword: rape and sexualized violence carry with them the risk of stigma and the stain of humiliation for both the victim and her (or his) erstwhile protector. The Bosnian case lays bare the gendered logics by which national and individual victimhood are negotiated, and the ambiguous moral terrain thus created for women and men victims, for advocates of social change and gender equality, and for supporters of the Bosniac or Bosnian national causes.

Muslim, Bosniac, Bosnian

It is important to distinguish between Bosniac and Bosnian. Bosnian, as adjective (*bosanski*) or proper noun (*Bosanac*, fem. *Bosanka*), refers sometimes to the geographic area within BiH (as opposed to Herzegovina) and is frequently (also) short for Bosnian-Herzegovinian. Bosnian thus denotes anyone from BiH regardless of ethnic or religious background.[8] Depending on the context, it can connote affiliation to a multiethnic polity, support for the existence of the state, non- or anti-nationalist orientation, as well as loyalty to the state as protector of the Bosniac nation. Bosniac (*Bošnjak*, fem. *Bošnjakinja*) has, since 1993, replaced Muslim (*Musliman*, fem. *Muslimanka*) as the official national name for Slavic-speaking Muslims, though Muslim continues to be used in everyday speech.[9] It is understood as an ethnic rather than a necessarily religious label, even as religion is the primary marker of difference among what have come to be understood as ethno-national groups in BiH (see Bringa 1995; Sorabji 1995). Just as Catholics living in BiH had become Croats and the Orthodox had become Serbs,[10] the (re)introduction of "Bosniac" was a move toward a more ethnic-sounding name (firmly tied to a specific territory), rather than "just" a religious one, even as religion remained a key component of all nationalisms in the former Yugoslavia.

In the leading Bosniac party, the SDA, secular nationalists lost out to the group of more religiously oriented pan-Islamists around the late Alija Izetbegović (Bougarel 1997). The SDA and its allies in the religious hierarchy have dominated the Bosniac leadership since the breakup of Yugoslavia and have promoted a strong role for Islam while officially also supporting the multiethnic state and "life together" (*suživot*) with Serbs and Croats.[11] The place of Islam in politics and in definitions of Bosniac identity has been contested, more subtly by the less religious in Bosniac nationalist parties and more openly by opponents of nationalism who support secular, non-ethnically based political structures (see Maček 2009). There is no more vivid illustration of these contestations than recent debates (as this text goes to press) over how Bosniacs should declare themselves in the population census now scheduled for October 2013.

Religious revival and the debates over national identity have had significant gendered effects. On one hand, the new prominence and legitimacy of religious discourses has meant the promotion of "traditional" patriarchal gender roles, a focus on women's sexual purity and their role as the bearer and nurturer of new generations of Bosniacs. As an anti-communist ideology, religious nationalism has sought to denounce and reverse many of the benefits women enjoyed under socialism, though with limited success. On the other hand, especially in urban areas, the fundamentally secular and modern, "European"-oriented population has resisted much of this re-traditionalization (Helms 2008; see also Jansen and Helms 2009), although, as local feminists have argued, socialism had done little in the first place to erase the gendered division of labor and patriarchal norms, especially in the family. Still, feelings of loyalty to BiH in the face of threats, violence, and political obstruction by Serb and Croat nationalists ran strong in Bosniac-dominated areas, making it difficult to point out, much less challenge, the gender imbalances in experiences and narratives of the war and victimhood. The considerable overlap between Bosniac nationalism and support for a multiethnic state meant that these positions were often indistinguishable, even for individuals themselves, though what sort of relationship this implied to Islam or religion in general, to ethnic others, or to gender relations varied widely.

In these dramatically unsettled times, as they attempted to redefine their senses of self in the face of abrupt changes in (what was remembered as) comfortable patterns of life, people in BiH were particularly preoccupied with their place in the world. The recent wars were not the first occasion for Bosnians to come under outside scrutiny and intervention,[12] yet the constant presence in their midst of war correspondents, aid agencies, and later a whole range of foreign intervention officials, donor representatives, not to mention activists and researchers, created an atmosphere of being intensely watched. This outside gaze was often resented but so was the panicked feeling, beginning five years or so after the end of the war, that attention was slowly shifting to new global crisis zones, leaving a still fractured BiH to gradually fend for itself.

Knowledge Production: Bosnia, Balkans, Islam, and Gender

The outside gaze is also produced by various depictions of gender relations and the roles of women in Bosnia. The dominant modes of representation and analysis that have circulated—in the sense elaborated by Susan Gal (2003)—in academic, journalistic, and activist discourses have strongly influenced the ways in which donors and international organizations have understood problems in BiH, as well as how Bosnian women activists have felt they were viewed. Common to all of these accounts is the near exclusive lens of nationalism and war. In tracing this production of knowledge, it is important to stress that this is not a question (only or always) of outsiders getting it wrong; as much as these representations incorporate outside stereotypes, they also reflect the success of *local* nationalists in setting the terms of discourse, even for those bent on opposing them. Media representations, activist and policy assessments, along with academic analyses have variously upheld, complicated, and challenged nationalist perspectives, but their arguments have remained to a large extent within the parameters of ethnic conflict.

It is also important to stress that I am characterizing a constantly changing discursive field in which I am also a participant, especially when it comes to feminist analyses. I therefore do not aim to account for all examples of knowledge production, but to characterize the major and most prominent trends, especially those that have been frequently read and cited by academics, policy makers, or Bosnian activists themselves.

The most visible mode of representation was the international media. Journalists quickly took to explaining the breakup of Yugoslavia and the accompanying wars in the idiom of Serb nationalists, who insisted that Bosnia's peoples could not live together. Media bemoaned the violence as an inevitable eruption of "ancient ethnic hatreds," as exemplified in Robert Kaplan's notorious *Balkan Ghosts* (1993). This thesis is said to have convinced key political figures, notably President Clinton, that no outside intervention could make a difference in the conflict. Such narratives were bolstered by descriptions of the violence as primitive, barbaric, and premodern,[13] with the brutal logic of mass rapes and ethnic cleansing fitting readily into this picture. Despite attention to the victimization of civilian men, coverage of the violence also reproduced widely shared gendered ideas about war, in which armed males victimize "womenandchildren" (Enloe 1990b), notions that may reflect the logic of many attacks, but that mask a much more complicated gendering of roles, actions, and intentions. Images of Muslim women victims, and especially rural women in headscarves and traditional dress, became iconic figures (Helms 2012; Mertus 1994; Penezić 1995; O. Simić 2012; Stetz 2000), and, together with the way they were explained, triggered associations with a deeply rooted set of assumptions about Balkan and Muslim societies in ways that foreclosed other avenues of inquiry.

Gatekeeping Concepts

Ethno-nationalism and ethnic war have thus acted as what Arjun Appadurai termed a "gatekeeping concept" in the discipline of anthropology

(1986). Appadurai was concerned with the way in which certain forms of social organization come to "limit anthropological theorizing about the place in question" and further to "define the quintessential and dominant questions of interest in the region" (357). As he noted, certain regions were automatically associated with certain topics and theorizing about them, and conversely, topics with regions: gift exchange was studied in Polynesia, segmentary states in Africa, hierarchy in India, and the honor-and-shame complex in the so-called Mediterranean culture area.

This bit of largely defunct, but apparently returning, categorization is interesting to revisit, given that (at least part of) Yugoslavia was included in the "Mediterranean culture area," and that honor and shame were seen as key to explaining gender dynamics in the region as a whole.[14] In anthropology, the idea of the Mediterranean as a region of cultural unity was roundly criticized in the 1980s, not least because the notion of region-wide common traits such as honor and shame failed to hold up in the face of local variation; ultimately it was seen as an imperialist construct of northern Europeans (e.g., Herzfeld 1980; De Pina-Cabral 1989).[15] However, Western analyses of gender regimes in the former Yugoslavia never did excise the essence of the honor and shame complex from their explanatory frameworks, neither during the socialist period nor especially in analyzing gender-based violence in the 1990s wars.

A major effect of the ethno-national lens has been the reification of ethnic blocks as actors in political and military conflict, as in statements about what Serbs want, Croats think, or Bosniacs reject. Rogers Brubaker (2002) has succinctly outlined the problems with social analysis that assumes "groupness," or a sense of group cohesion and homogeneity, with every invocation or marker of ethnic identity—an ethnic "coding bias" that many analysts, especially those assessing postwar BiH, have incorporated into their analytical frameworks instead of treating the invocation of ethnicity as a social process of constituting a sense of group cohesion and of ethnic conflict. Nationalist discourses together with the violence itself succeeded in framing the wars as ethnic leading to the reification of ethno-national groups,[16] a framing that was inscribed in the Dayton Peace Agreement and therefore powerfully structured the terms of debates and realities to follow. Even those writing against nationalist exclusivity and the brutal logic of the violence it spawned have not gotten away from this ethnic bias in their often romanticized efforts to recover histories of ethnic tolerance or present spaces of ethnic cooperation and rejection of nationalism. This phenomenon is analogous to, and in ex-Yugoslavia feeds into, the tendency of feminists and women's activists to find peacebuilding behind every stated goal of reconciliation or opposition to war.

An ethnographic perspective reveals a much more complicated picture, as my colleagues and I have argued elsewhere (Bougarel et al. 2007b). To summarize the argument, the logic of the war violence undeniably ensured that ethnic categories would become much more rigid and tied to religion than during the socialist period. They have thus remained a major category of social organization, political mobilization, and conflict, as well as identification on the individual level. At the same time, interethnic cooperation and rejection of nationalist logics were not completely wiped out, and ethnic categories have remained fluid, contested, and relative in terms of other social categories. Furthermore, the salient categories of a given situation are not only those forged during the war but are frequently (also) social concepts carried over from before the war, albeit in new forms. Categorizations such as those by class, education, rural/urban origin, age, war experiences and actions, and gender can alternately exacerbate, undermine, or obviate ethnic divisions in ways that belie simple "ethnic" explanations.

A second, related gatekeeping effect has been the failure to take postwar Bosnia (along with other parts of former Yugoslavia) seriously as a post*socialist* as well as simultaneously a postwar place, or, for that matter, one caught up in a number of other global and regional processes (Jansen 2006; see also Gilbert et al. 2008). This tendency is part of the ethnic bias, in that, when socialism is discussed, it is only in terms of ethnic relations and politics (a topic that often focuses even more attention on World War II and earlier than on the socialist period). This can be said of academic as well as policy analyses and certainly also of policy discourses in Bosnia. A prime example is the refugee return process, as Stef Jansen has vividly shown (2007). International institutions stressed the rights of refugees enshrined in Dayton to return to their former homes, couching their arguments in a moral discourse of undoing the injustices of ethnic cleansing (Ito 2001; Dahlman and Ó Tuathail 2005). It was seldom made explicit that this was at the same time a process of property transformation from socialist forms of ownership into private hands.

To be sure, these discourses and analyses, whether produced by academics, policy analysts, or members of international institutions in Bosnia, both reflect and help to create the framing put forward in Bosnian political life and everyday discourses. Andrew Gilbert (2006) argues that in postwar BiH the socialist period has been "bracketed" as a significant set of referents or causal paradigms. Forms, ideologies, and effects of the socialist system still abound as they do in other former state-socialist countries, but they are not often talked about as such except in simplistic caricature. International actors are thus able to gesture toward "communist" habits, and nationalists can invoke dark scenarios of religious repression under the Yugoslav regime, without allowing the socialist period itself to become a subject of serious discussion. Academic analyses, however, need not ignore these continuities and effects, even as they are often taken for granted by our informants as some of the few elements of normality that were not disturbed by the totalizing event of the war (Maček 2009). Moreover, as I found among women's NGO networks, there are certain pockets of discussion and action where engagement with the socialist system and its ideologies are primary while ethnic divisions and nationalism take a back seat.

Symbolic Geographies and the Ambiguous Balkans

Accounts of the Bosnian war and its aftermath, as well as everyday framings of political discourses in BiH, draw on histories of culturally essentialist symbolic geographies, those often stereotypical invocations of cultural traits as explanations or indices of the characteristics of a certain place, region, or civilization. As is particularly evident when it comes to Islam and Muslim societies, the underlying messages of such "culture talk" are ultimately political (Mamdani 2002).

Southeast Europe has figured differently in the Western imagination, through what Maria Todorova (1997) terms "Balkanism," a pattern of Western representations that construct the Balkans as a less-than-civilized, backward zone of not quite belonging to (Western) European culture. Whether the taint is attributed to Orthodox Christianity, Islam, or Ottoman domination, the region has been portrayed as hopelessly mired in tradition and violence, but also with an exotic tinge of the "real Orient," which was just beyond its boundaries. While this mode of representation resembles the workings of Edward Said's Orientalism (Said 1978), it differs in that the Balkans were not constructed, as was the Orient, as an alien "other," but as an incomplete "self." Furthermore, while Orientalism is tied to (histories of) direct Western colonization, Balkanism is built on much more diffuse and indirect relationships of domination and subordination vis-à-vis the West (Bakić-Hayden and Hayden 1992; Fleming 2000). Nevertheless, several scholars have argued that the *language* of Orientalism can be detected in discourses on the Balkans (Bakić-Hayden and Hayden 1992),[17] especially when the subject is Islam or Muslim society (Helms 2008; Žarkov 1995). Often, it is far from clear which of these "isms" is at work, owing, I suggest, to the profound ambiguity attributed to this region (Green 2005; Todorova 1997) and the blurring of categories resulting from the unmooring of Orientalist rhetoric from the specific geographies and colonial histories outlined by Said (Fleming 2000, 1224).

Thus the Balkans are neither fully West nor fully East, giving rise to their own brand of metaphors invoking crossroads, bridges, fragmentation, and mixing.[18] As Sarah Green insightfully points out (2005), the Balkans even disappear altogether during periods when the region, or parts of it, is not behaving in a "Balkan" way, that is, engaging in violence leading to fragmentation into smaller parts. At the same time, the consternation produced by the Balkans' apparent failure to conform to neat modernist categorizations—neither one thing nor the other, but at the same time too much of both—is an indication not of chaos but that there is too much connection, too many relationships (see also Irvine and Gal 2000). Green goes further, arguing that not only are realities on the ground seen as chaotic but the oppositional categories suggested by hegemonic discourses, such as East/West, Balkan/European, are themselves not fixed or stable but a "wavering form" (2005, 132–33).

It is this ambiguity and liminality that opens the space for multiple contestations of such East/West (Balkans/Europe) frameworks by those doing the labeling as well as by those being labeled. In what was Yugoslavia, this has taken the form of what Milica Bakić-Hayden (1995) calls "nesting orientalisms," through which members of one nation attempt to portray themselves as superior/Western/European while casting their southern and eastern neighbors as part of the inferior, Oriental East. Such positionings, however, are not always so unequivocal about the merits of East and West, even in many instances seeking to combine elements of both. Nor do they always reject the East or construct the West as superior, as for example in discourses about the morally bankrupt, decadent West.[19] In another form common among activists and urban intellectuals, the local society, especially the rural, is denigrated as Balkan, while speakers align themselves and their agendas with an enlightened, cosmopolitan, "good" West devoid of the sorts of problems they associate with their Balkan surroundings (cf. Böröcz 2006). With Green, we again see "the appearance and disappearance of things" (2005, 158), the shifting and fragmenting of categorization and of their meanings and valences.

These shifting constructions—Green's "Balkan fractal"—conform to a more general pattern of social distinctions, what sociolinguists have called fractal recursions, in that oppositional pairs such as West/East, European/Oriental, male/female, public/private can recur within one half of a broader oppositional pair, making for endless possibilities of repositioning within categories of superiority and inferiority like those associated with East and West.[20] Despite this shifting of boundaries and meanings, however, the notion of Western versus Eastern (or Southern, as in the Third World) civilizations or cultural-political blocs are remarkably stable, forming the basis for hegemonic constructions of the role of culture itself.

Gendered Balkanism, Gendered Orientalism

The history of Western depictions of the Muslim world, from the era that defined Said's Orientalism to the present, provides ample evidence of the power of gendered and sexualized images to amplify these representations, from older evocations of erotic allure or backwardness, to current warnings about the political dangers lurking in Muslim societies. Balkanism, too, has been gendered, but in its own way. As I have elaborated elsewhere (Helms 2008), images of violent, backward, but fun- and drink-loving male peasants have been joined and even replaced by representations of women as the victims of male brutality through ethnic cleansing and war rapes, and more recently through domestic violence and human trafficking.

As with nationalisms, Balkanist and Orientalist discourses in and about Bosnia are frequently constituted through representations of women and gender regimes. Among Bosnians, and especially in Bosniac-dominated areas of BiH, many were preoccupied with the role of Islam and the degree to which Bosnian Islam is tolerant of ethnic differences, respectful of women, not supportive of terrorism—in short, "European" (see Cerić 2006; Karić 2002). "Emancipated" Muslim women, that is, educated, secular members of the work force, became the marker of this Europeanness and distance from what were depicted as more primitive Muslims further to the east or in the villages. The evidence for this was frequently said to be the scores of fashionable, sexy young women to be seen on the streets of BiH's cities. Thus, peasant-ness or rurality was also a repository of negative, "Balkan" attributes, as a further fractal copy of the dichotomy. Generalizing comparisons were frequently made with the West, only occasionally differentiated by country, in terms of policies, services, or attitudes related to women to be found there, in contrast to the situation in BiH, whether described as traditional/patriarchal, Balkan, not-Western, or simply in a state of chaos.

While Balkan generally remained a derogatory label, it also sometimes served as a means by which people embraced a purportedly more primitive identity as a sort of resistance to relentless Western scrutiny, as I found in the case of Bosnian men jokingly performing the role of the violent, patriarchal Balkan peasant (Helms 2006, 2008). It was this sort of play with stereotypes of East/West, Balkan/European in which the activists I worked with continuously engaged in their interactions with local officials, representatives of foreign donor agencies, visiting activists and researchers, and members of their own organizations and social networks.

As already mentioned, there were times when "the Balkans" seemed to disappear, as during the period of socialist Yugoslavia. Yugoslavia was even then in an in-between position, both part of the Communist East but not in the Soviet bloc, a leading member of the Non-Aligned Movement of Third World countries, and with its own brand of self-managing socialism. The English-language literature on women in Yugoslavia was mainly concerned with women's roles in paid work and politics, as fighters in World War II—the famous *Partizanke*—as well as more "traditional" subjects like folklore, ritual, kinship, and the family. Within the country itself, second-wave feminists tackled the discrepancies between official socialist ideology and the real lives of women who still did the bulk of domestic chores and care-giving work (see Lórand, forthcoming). Within the focus on modernization, however, ran a distinct echo of Mediterraneanist anthropology: persistence of norms and values from village culture was situated within notions of honor and shame, said to restrict women's activities outside the home despite the official ideology of equality.

The central problems addressed by academics changed abruptly with the dissolution of Yugoslavia and the onset of war. Suddenly the place was again Balkan, rife with ancient ethnic hatreds, heavy reliance on patriarchal traditions and religious prescripts, and soaked in histories of violence and Ottoman taint. However, a focus on gender reveals some continuities even in the wartime and postwar literature. When it came to the Bosnian Muslims, and BiH itself as symbolized through Muslim victims, there remained an overlap between Orientalist assumptions about gender relations in Muslim societies and those connected to "Mediterranean honor and shame" (if not readily iconic of the Balkans, then associated with the many Muslim societies falling within the confines of the Mediterranean).[21] From the longstanding Balkanist assumptions about violent, primitive men, the appearance during the recent war of female victim images, as victims of those men's violence, was a logical extension. The figures of bereaved widows in traditional rural Muslim dress or shamed rape victims therefore did not require much explanation. Their mention or images merely served as confirmation of the barbarism still rife in the primitive Balkans and the patriarchal strictures of a Muslim society that would surely reject its "dishonored" women and girls or read the loss of sons and husbands as the ultimate devastation for a woman (Žarkov 1995, 2007). These depictions only strengthened narratives of female victimhood.

Feminist Framings

The gatekeeping functions of ethno-nationalism and war, along with the stereotypes of symbolic geographies, have been especially evident in wartime and postwar analyses of gender in the former Yugoslavia. Nearly all analyses of gender dynamics since the breakup of Yugoslavia have been put forth by feminists—whether activists, academics, policy analysts, or some combination of these.[22] Most often, they wrote out of a desire to expose and denounce nationalist violence and to call attention to the suffering of women (even if these were sometimes limited to only certain women and certain nationalisms). These works have maintained a focus on women, taking on topics such as nationalist discourses about women's roles; wartime sexualized violence; women as refugees, rape survivors, and other victims; women and national/religious identities; or women's organized opposition to ethnonationalism and war. Invariably and unsurprisingly in these circumstances, questions asked have to do with ethno-nationalist conflict, even when the goal is to challenge such logic. Without doubt this has been a very productive avenue of research and analysis, leading to a well-grounded understanding particularly of war violence against women and the courageous initiatives that women have undertaken to alleviate suffering and oppose war and militarism. Paradoxically, however, this focus has meant that the quintessential questions about gender in the former Yugoslavia continue to be framed though ethnonationalism, thus limiting both theorizing and empirical research on the region. Even more problematic have been analyses focusing on women in BiH that tend to rest on unexamined assumptions based on ready-made stereotypes about the Balkans and Muslims.

In fact, as I argue in chapter 2, while at first glance there seems to be a great deal written about gender in Bosnia, the opposite is in fact true: very little is based on actual empirical research *in* BiH itself. Furthermore, most analyses and accounts are concerned only with women; men as gendered beings, either as victims or perpetrators, or masculinity have failed to attract much serious interest (Helms 2006). Even in terms of women, the focus on victimhood has meant that Bosnian women are exemplified by Muslim women, leaving women of Croat, Serb, or any other background invisible—as victims but even simply as inhabitants of Bosnia. Gender scholarship on BiH has thus obscured roles and experiences of women and men that did not fall into the gendered victim/victimizer pattern.

These are broad tendencies concentrated in the 1990s, which have dissipated only somewhat with time and as the successor states of Yugoslavia experience increasingly divergent realities. In one sense, the violence led to some very productive studies: Croatia, Serbia, and Bosnia were included in some illuminating comparative projects on women in conflict zones around the world.[23] These have usefully placed the former Yugoslavia within a global political economy of peacekeeping and humanitarian missions, and provided evidence that the gendered patterns of violence, resistance, and recovery were not unique to the Balkans.

As a postsocialist place, however, the post-Yugoslav countries were often overlooked, left out of collections on gender and postsocialism in Central and Eastern Europe, or included only as illustrations of nationalist resurgence and its negative impact on women.[24] This categorization is all the more striking given that very similar trends of re-traditionalization and gendered nationalism also appeared, and were analyzed early on, in other postsocialist countries (e.g., De Soto 1994; Gal 1994; Verdery 1994). For the Yugoslav successor states, there appears to be a continuum—the less a country is associated with war, the more likely it is for analyses to tackle typically postsocialist topics relating to gender: citizenship, abortion rights, democratization, political behaviors, employment, welfare, property ownership, consumption, advertising and film, and so on. The treatment of Slovenia is illuminating in this regard: although Slovenian feminists wrote about gender and conservative nationalist trends, and although the country did feel some of the impact of war, it was largely successful in distancing itself from the taint of ethnic violence and nationalism in the mode I am concerned with here. Slovenia was thus increasingly analyzed from perspectives other than that of ethno-nationalism or war, most notably the lens of postsocialist transformation.

It is thus not that issues of postsocialism were completely ignored in ex-Yugoslavia, but that analyses tended to be driven by questions relating to nationalism and war while processes that are usually examined in the postsocialist literature were either ignored or addressed under the nationalism and war rubric.[25] This approach served to mark the former Yugoslavia as different (or Slovenia as not-so-different from the European norm), thereby reinforcing the notion of a Balkans mired in primitive, patriarchal, ethnic hatreds. It further tells us little about the peculiarities of gender under the unique system of Yugoslav socialism or the ways in which continuities from that system have shaped postwar processes. To be sure, it is often impossible to disarticulate postsocialist issues from those connected to nationalism and war, a dynamic that naturally complicates comparison with other socialist countries, as does the uniqueness of Yugoslav socialism. However, local variation has always posed challenges to theorizing about (post)socialism; some of the most productive insights have come precisely through attention to such differences. Inclusion of formerly Yugoslav countries should therefore offer new insights into the study of postsocialism rather than standing only as an exception.

A further obstacle to analyzing BiH from a postsocialist perspective is that local discourses have also privileged ethno-national and postwar recovery framings, a reflection of Gilbert's (2006) bracketing of socialism in Bosnian public discourse. This was noticeable in the arena of women's activism, too, but closer attention revealed that the issues women were most concerned with were as much postsocialist as postwar, and that they often adopted a rhetoric of transition to signal not only postsocialist processes but the complicated package of multiple transformations they were living through. "I'm a woman in transition," they were fond of joking, even when referring to the challenges of their personal lives.

In sum, the frameworks through which gender in Bosnia or the Balkans has typically been understood are overlapping and mutually reinforcing. Older paradigms like Orientalism or Mediterraneanism seem to creep back, or never went away in the first place. Newer developments like the mass rapes in Bosnia were in some ways made to fit into these frameworks, as with culturalizing logics like Orientalism, but in other ways nearly completely sidelined existing approaches, as with the abrupt change in feminist analysis from critiques of political or economic structures under Yugoslav socialism to intense focus on nationalism and war. It is obvious that scholarship needs time to broaden and deepen after such dramatic events and multiple ruptures. But in the case of BiH, as I explore further in the next chapter, the accounts of the 1990s solidified impressions of gender relations without having delved much into the particulars. Instead, ready-made notions about the oppression of women in Muslim societies and of male violence against women victims were even further reinforced, given new life through the gripping tragedy that was the Bosnian war.

Wartime

Gender, Nationalism, and Sexualized Violence

The gatekeeping effects I have described are of course based in the realities of war and ethno-nationalism as major factors in the profound transformations that Bosnian society has undergone in recent years. There is thus no escaping these topics in any discussion of present-day Bosnia, but they must be approached critically. War violence against women, especially mass rapes, drew donors and sympathetic activists to the country, informing foreign intervention policies toward women as well as the ways in which women figured as poignant symbols of victimhood in national(ist) narratives. It was the war that created the two most visible images of female victimhood: the refugee and the rape victim, both iconically Muslim. And it was nationalism-fueled war occurring at a particular moment after the end of the Cold War (Harrington 2010, 2011) that mobilized a transnational network of feminists to call attention to and take steps to mitigate their gendered implications.

Reactions to these processes included major contributions to the feminist critique of nationalism, ethnic violence, and international legal standards, as well as successful efforts to recognize and prosecute rape as a war crime. In various localities in BiH, women's NGOs were formed and began tackling different aspects of social and political issues affecting women (and men). Responses to the war also created bitter rifts among women's activists, exposing in practice what academic analyses had pointed out as a troubled relationship between nationalism and feminism, nation and gender (e.g., G. Kaplan 1997; Moghadam 1994).[1] These histories are closely tied to those of gender practices

Figure 4
Mannequins in
Baščaršija. Old town
Sarajevo, July 2007.
(photo by author)

and women's activism in what would become the former Yugoslavia. Feminists from these circles made it plain that the war violence could not be understood outside of a critique of how gender and sexuality figured in Serbian and Croatian nationalisms. I argue, however, that these dynamics must also take critical account of nationalism(s) put forth in the name of those who made up the largest number of war victims: Bosniacs but also other Bosnians who supported a multiethnic BiH state. This chapter outlines the background of nationalism and war as a foundation for understanding many of the identity categories and concrete issues around which women's activists organized during and after the war. To begin the story, but also as an entry to understanding the simultaneous postsocialist transformations that have affected postwar BiH, we must go back to the aftermath of another war.

Socialist Yugoslavia

The socialist state of Yugoslavia that emerged out of World War II made gender equality official policy, a daunting task in a country of widely varying gender ideologies and levels of economic development. The country was overwhelmingly rural, the economy based on agriculture and pastoralism. But women, many of them teenage girls from the countryside,[2] had played a significant role as *Partizanke* (partisan fighters) with several later rising to top positions within the Communist Party. Through the party-affiliated AFŽ (Antifašistički front žena, or Antifascist Front of Women), these women took an active role in teaching literacy among the uneducated female population and advocating for the socialist cause.

Women were to be emancipated from the patriarchal system through the uplifting of the working class as Yugoslavia underwent rapid industrialization and urbanization. From the outset, women were granted equal legal status, the right to vote and run for political office, the right to own and inherit property, equal rights in marriage and divorce, generous maternity and child-care benefits, and equal access to education and employment (Morokvasić 1986; Ramet 1999; Woodward 1985). Because of historical regional differences in legal codes, the new laws represented more drastic changes for women in some areas than in others (Woodward 1985). Religiously based family law codes (such as *šari'a* law governing Muslims) were abolished so that marriage and divorce were placed under civic authorities and applied equally to all citizens regardless of sex, region, or religion (Jancar-Webster 1990; Ramet 1999). The wearing of the *zar* and *feredža*, garments worn by Muslim women to conceal their faces and bodies, was outlawed in 1950, "to remove the age-old mark of subordination and cultural backwardness of Muslim women," and to allow them to equally participate, along with other women and men, in the building of the country (Radić 1995, 216; see also Achkoska 2004; Milišić 1999). Women AFŽ activists, especially the Muslims among them, led the campaign. Abortion was legalized in 1952 and liberalized in a series of subsequent laws that eventually guaranteed all citizens the right to decide on family size (Morokvasić 1986; Ramet 1999). Indeed, abortion became a widespread method of family planning (see Drezgić 2000, 2004, 2010).

As women gained education and began to be employed in wage labor outside the home, their dependence on husbands and families decreased (see Olsen 1990). Marriage patterns were duly altered, as women began to be evaluated for their potential as wage-earners as well as for their household and reproductive labor. Urbanization and industrialization also affected women's possibilities (Denich 1976), though, as Susan Woodward has pointed out (1985), these varied widely according to economic status. Young women whose parents lived in university towns and cities had more support for completing higher education and thus got better jobs. These women tended to marry men of similar educational backgrounds, to initiate divorce in the case of problems, and to hyphenate their maiden names with their husbands' surnames as a display of independence. In this way, Woodward argued, "class differences among women [were] rapidly replacing the cultural [i.e., ethnic and religious] divisions that [had] formerly separated women of one region from another" (1985, 255). Class and overlapping distinctions between rural and urban continued to be the most significant differences among women in terms of beliefs and practices related to gender and sexuality even after the ethnic polarization of the war.

Among rural families, however, the changes brought by socialism meant that women were more likely to be isolated in their villages as men commuted to factories and towns to work (Bringa 1995; Woodward 1985). It was also common for villagers, especially Muslims, to flout the law that now mandated eight years of schooling. Many families even opted to pay rather than send girls to school, especially beyond the fourth grade when girls would have to travel outside their villages. Further education was seen as unnecessary for leading lives as housewives and mothers, but more important was the strong fear of compromising a girl's sexual reputation or risking her dating and marrying a non-Muslim (Haskić 2000). As an elderly Bosniac man I know (who had educated his own daughters) explained of the early socialist period in his small town, "A female going to school? Must be a whore! That's how it was" (*Žensko ići u školu? To je kurva! Tako je bilo*). While such attitudes dissipated over time, this points to another aspect of the uneven "emancipation" of women in Yugoslavia (Žarkov 1991) and especially in areas with large rural and Muslim populations. And while education levels among urban Muslim women have been consistently high, even overtaking those of men, the problem of girls not being allowed to continue in school has resurfaced since the end of the Bosnian war among the rural poor of all religious backgrounds.

Ultimately, despite many gains for women—including rates of employment and education that exceeded those in the West—Yugoslav socialism failed to destroy patriarchal ideologies and male privilege. In fact, Žarkov argues that the (deceptive) prosperity of the 1970s contributed more to women's emancipation than did socialist policies of legal equality (1991). As the new generation of Yugoslav neo-feminists pointed out, women had been brought into a male-dominated system as workers and supporters of the socialist system but the roots of their subordination had not changed. Although women had moved into paid employment in large numbers, they remained concentrated in sex-stereotyped jobs of low status and pay (Denich 1977). Despite legal safeguards and generous maternity leaves, pregnant workers could be laid off and many employers were up-front about preferring to hire men (Sklevicky 1989a; Woodward 1985).[3] The biggest indicator of socialism's failure, in the eyes of both Yugoslav and Western feminist critics, was women's continued responsibility for housework and child-care (Benderly 1997a; Jancar 1988; Morokvasić 1986; Woodward 1985). This remained a widespread ideal, to the extent that womanhood was often equated with motherhood, an association that persisted into the postsocialist era. As a result, women had less time or incentive to strive for advancement into jobs with higher salaries or positions of power (Jancar-Webster 1990; Ramet 1999; Woodward 1985).

These contradictions with official socialist ideology led to the development of what has been termed Yugoslav second-wave feminism, which critiqued the system from a Marxist standpoint, but which was also well connected to international feminist networks. This was a new generation of women, the AFŽ having been disbanded in 1953 and the "woman question" declared solved by the party. The second wave arose in the 1970s, coming to wider attention with the international conference "Drug-ca" or "Comrade Woman" held in Belgrade in 1978 (see Bonfiglioli 2008; Lórand, forthcoming). The conference and the subsequent activities of these women were condemned by the authorities as bourgeois frivolities. But they were allowed to exist and in the 1980s they gave rise to the first feminist and lesbian organizations as the Yugoslav system grew more decentralized. On the whole, however, Yugoslav feminism was an elite phenomenon of intellectual women centered in the capital cities of Slovenia, Croatia, and Serbia. BiH was largely untouched by these activities until the war called feminists' attention to the gendered consequences of violent nationalisms.

Nationalisms and Gender in a Disintegrating Yugoslavia

The story of how gender and sexuality were central to nationalist mobilizations and the violent breakup of Yugoslavia is well known in the feminist literature. Nationalisms of the region were profoundly conservative and traditionalist, opposing what was seen as the emancipation of women under socialism and advocating a return to an imagined past of religious piety and clearly defined patriarchal (and heteronormative) gender roles. Beginning in the late 1980s but especially during and just after the wars of the 1990s, feminists in Serbia, Croatia, and Slovenia publicly opposed the growing power of these nationalisms while also organizing to offer aid to women victims of the wars that broke out in Croatia and then BiH. They, along with observers from elsewhere (with varying degrees of knowledge about the region), exposed the ways in which nationalist ideologies advocated (re)entrenched patriarchal gender roles among their own people while demonizing the sexual and gender patterns among ethnic others, now represented as enemies.[4]

Croatian feminist Rada Iveković summed up much of this critique by pointing to how women became both the inside and the outside "other" (1993). While men were constructed as the central actors of the nation, the heroic defenders, virile, powerful, and noble, women were given more symbolic roles as reflections of the nation's purity and honor, as pointed out in the scholarship on gendered nationalism emerging at the time (e.g., Anthias and Yuval-Davis 1989; McClintock 1993). Women's active roles were thus restricted to the reproduction and nurturing of new (loyal) members of the nation: future soldiers and mothers (Bracewell 1996; Drezgić 2000). Based on this important duty, women of the nation were admonished to marry among "their" people, to remain chaste and religiously devout, to give birth to as many children as possible, and to care for the home rather than "meddling" in politics. This logic was intensified in times of ethnicized conflict. It was women and the children in their care who were to be defended by the nation's men, especially from rape, defined as a violation of the national territory as well as pollution of ethnic purity (see Massad 1995). In turn, the way to best humiliate and incapacitate the (male) enemy was to rape "his" women and (much less frequently addressed) sexually abuse him, placing him in feminized roles, thus taking away his manhood. Such abuses are precisely what happened in the Bosnian war.

These developments alarmed feminists, who focused on their consequences for women, but there were wider implications for men and the construction of masculinities, for gender relations and sexual norms in general, and also for the very way in which ethnic differences were being constructed. Dubravka Žarkov analyzed what she terms the media war in Serbia and Croatia that preceded and accompanied the actual ethnic war as played out in Croatia and Bosnia, arguing that gender and sexuality distinctions actually *produced* ethnic difference:

[W]ithout notions of masculinity and femininity and norms of (hetero)-sexuality, ethnicity could have never been produced, and the practices of the two [media and ethnic] wars would have remained unintelligible. We would make little out of the stories of state borders and threatened territories were they not conveyed through familiar gendered and sexualized imagery. What made both the media war and the ethnic war so powerful, so effective in mobilizing people's sentiments, and ultimately so deadly, is the familiarity and the casualness of notions that gave meaning to the bodies of chaste maidens and men in dresses [as in examples she gives from the Serbian and Croatian media]. (Žarkov 2007, 8)

This insight is crucial for understanding the war violence, which, it became apparent, operated not only according to strict us/them religious-ethnic distinctions, but also and at the same time through notions of gender and sexuality. These were assumptions shared not only by the perpetrators of violence and the nationalist ideologies to which they subscribed but also by the target populations and their own ways of expressing collective victimization.

Gendered Patterns of Violence

The war in BiH became notorious for attacks on civilians, from the televised sniper and shelling attacks on city residents by Serb forces besieging Sarajevo to the terrorization and forced expulsion of ethnic others from desired territories that became known as ethnic cleansing, to genocide (on the war in general, see, e.g., Burg and Shoup 1999). Such campaigns were initiated by Serbian and Bosnian Serb paramilitary and regular forces who, in a systematic pattern, terrorized, tortured, and murdered non-Serb, that is, Muslim and Croat, civilians, rounded many of them up into detention camps, expelled them from territories now designated as Serb, and razed mosques, Catholic churches, and the houses of those being expelled. Similar tactics were later used by Croat forces when their alliance with the Muslim-dominated Bosnian Army broke down and they attempted to secure and Croat-ize territories for themselves. Due to its goals of keeping BiH together but also because it was hardest hit in the early years of the war by the international arms embargo on the region, the Bosnian Army did not commit atrocities on the same scale. But it participated in the same game; crimes against "undesirable" civilians and soldiers, including inhumane treatment and torture in detention camps, were also committed by Bosnian forces and against Serbs and Croats. As the war progressed, the Bosnian Army, too, despite its initial formation as a multiethnic force, was increasingly defined as a Muslim/Bosniac army with ethnicized territorial aims (see Hoare 2004). The most widespread attacks on civilians, including ethnic cleansing and prolonged siege warfare, were committed by Serb forces, followed by violations by Croat forces and lastly by the Bosnian Army; the majority of those attacked, abused, and killed were Bosniacs, followed by Serbs and then Croats. Each "side," however, had its own genuine war crimes victims, both civilian and military, as well as perpetrators of atrocities within its own ranks. In other words, seen from the ethnic logic of the violence, while Bosniacs were the most numerous victims and Serbs the biggest perpetrators, they were not the only victims or perpetrators: no group was entirely innocent. Nor was sexualized abuse the only form of gendered wartime suffering.

Victims and territories were targeted not only according to ethno-religious criteria. The violence followed gendered patterns that stemmed directly from the logic of nationalist ideologies that feminists were pointing to, as well as from globally dominant constructions of gender roles in war. Women and children made up a large proportion of the victims, shown in the international press as refugees who flooded into the safer areas of BiH or into neighboring countries. When detention camps and mass rapes were uncovered in late summer 1992, they were widely publicized, launching a successful international feminist campaign for the prosecution of rape as a war crime and crime against humanity. Near the end of the war, in July 1995, came the most devastating atrocity, later ruled to have been genocide, when Serb forces overran the

Figure 5 A mosque destroyed by Serb forces in the war, Kozarac. Photographed May 1999. (photo by author)

Figure 6 War damage to both traditional-style structures and markers of the modern, Bosanski Petrovac. Photographed April 1999. (photo by author)

UN-protected "safe area" of Srebrenica, deporting around 25,000 women, children, and elderly and executing around 8,000 Bosniac men, burying the bodies in mass graves.

In the early phases of the war, when most of these atrocities took place, Serb forces quickly took over large areas of northern and eastern Bosnia, expelling the non-Serb (mostly Muslim but also Croat) population. Forces attacking a town, village, or neighborhood typically killed or detained its non-Serb leadership, the educated, and those who might put up armed resistance. In one small town, for instance, refugees told me how Serb forces had tracked down and killed the best male athletes among the Muslims at the high school so as to eliminate future agile soldiers. In place after place, attackers entered the houses and apartments of ethnic "others," looking for weapons and men and tormenting the residents in the process. This was one of the situations in which women were raped and subject to sexualized abuse, as were men, and both men and women were beaten and humiliated. Attacking forces then drove people out of their houses, separating out those deemed to be fighting-aged men. Sometimes the men fled or were killed on the spot but there were also places where they were simply forced to leave with the rest of the population (after being harassed and robbed of valuables). In many other instances, men were taken to detention camps where they endured inhumane conditions and torture, including sexualized abuse; many were also killed there, often in gruesome ways. Women and girls were detained as well, separately, and, in a widespread pattern, subjected to gendered and sexualized humiliations from having to clean, cook, and serve their captors, or being forced to dance naked for soldiers' entertainment, to gang rapes, prolonged sexual slavery, and forced pregnancy. In places like Foča, Serb commanders also forced young women to pretend they were the men's girlfriends or sold their victims to other men for cash.[5] While many were killed after being raped, significant numbers of women were released once their pregnancies had advanced too far for an abortion or otherwise allowed to survive as living reminders of their having been "dishonored."[6]

The logic of the violence clearly followed from the ways in which gender and sexuality figured in nationalist ideologies. At the same time, the violence also continued to *create* nationalist narratives, both by justifying ethnic territorial separation and by underpinning claims to collective victimhood. Again, I turn to Žarkov's analysis of media discourses in Serbia and Croatia (2007), which traces how raped female bodies, always with an ethnic designation, were constructed as (conquered) ethnic territory and simultaneously expelled from that territory as ethnically other. As such, the function of rape, both discursively and through the actual war violence, was "to establish a particular ethnic geography" (153). Or, in the analysis of Robert Hayden, the rape of women in ethnicized conflicts became a weapon by which cross-ethnic social ties and peaceful coexistence were brutally severed; any further sharing of the same territory, now reinscribed as belonging to one ethnic group only, was made unthinkable (2000; see also Hayden 1996).

The violation of women's bodies thus seemed intended to send a message of defeat from the (male) rapists to the men of the women's ethnic group (Das 1995). It was the men of the other nation who had failed to protect "their" women, symbolically linked to the nation, and whose pride and honor, both masculine and national, had now been diminished. Thus, as Žarkov's analysis shows, in the Croatian press raped Croat women were not talked about, preserving the purity of Croatia/n women and the honor of Croatian men while exposing the evil of the Serbs through crimes against Muslims/Muslim women. Raped Serb women were presented with full empathy in the Serb press, but as proof of the victimization of Serb *men* and the savagery of Muslims (2007, 116–42).

Given this concern for the image of the nation's men, it should therefore not be surprising that males from "undesirable" ethnic groups were also assaulted in sexualized ways. As was made clear in more recent cases like the abuse of prisoners by American military personnel in the Abu Ghraib prison in Iraq or at Guantanamo Bay, a particularly effective way to humiliate males is through sexualized violence that places them in positions understood as feminized or homosexual. The intended, and often well-received, message is that the masculinity of men forced into feminized roles is thereby diminished to a point from which it is difficult to recover.

Within this logic, such acts cannot be spoken about without the risk of compromising the victims' masculinity even further (Žarkov 2001). In the Bosnian war, the most notorious such abuses occurred in Serb-run camps where men were beaten on the genitals and castrated, forced to perform oral sex or penetrated anally, usually with foreign objects.[7] In most cases it appears that sex acts were not performed by the guards themselves (so as not to cast doubt on their own heterosexuality); in fact, the humiliation was intensified by forcing male prisoners to sexually abuse each other, very often in father-son pairs, just as perpetrators also forced men to rape their own daughters or mothers. Dejan Ilić (2009) argues that such forced sexual acts between fathers and sons was a deliberate attempt to break the continuity of the nation as imagined as an endless, and inexplicably female-less, line of male ancestors, as Katherine Verdery (1994) has shown for Romanian national imaginaries. Even absent such motivations, these atrocities were clearly aimed to humiliate the victims as men and as Bosniacs, a message that all involved would have understood well given the shared understanding of the relationship between masculinity and sexual dominance.

There was one more aspect of sexualized violence that caught attention: forced pregnancies as the result of rape. A pattern emerged of non-Serb women held in Serb-run camps being repeatedly raped until they were pregnant and then deliberately detained until it was too late for an abortion, at which point they were released into territory controlled by Bosniacs or Croats as living message boards to the men of their communities. Camp survivors reported that pregnant women were given better conditions and not abused as frequently once they became pregnant, indicating that their abusers' intention was for them to make it back to their families alive and to successfully give birth. Survivors also said they were told by Serb rapists that they were being impregnated with the enemy's seed or that each woman would give birth to a *Četnik* (Serb nationalist fighter) who would one day kill her. Men beaten on the genitals were similarly told they were being prevented from making more Muslims. Attackers thus seemed to adhere to a strictly patrilineal logic by which women were empty vessels of reproduction for male (ethnic) identities.[8]

Nationalist imaginaries took this logic seriously, concerned as they were with future reproduction of the (patrilineal) nation. In public discourses, therefore, the focus shifted from the women to the nation itself, whose purity and possibly future reproductive capacity was damaged by the rapes. In the case of Serbia, as Žarkov shows, the victim was even more specific: it was not just the Serb nation but the Serb man who had been deprived of his pure offspring, while raped Serb women were described as "destroyed," not so much by rape but by the continued trauma of carrying an "alien" child (2007, 116–24). In the Bosniac/Muslim community, discussed further below, the concern of religious officials was that children born of wartime rape be raised both in the Muslim community and specifically *by their mothers* (Omerdić 2002, 430).

There were other more banal ways in which the war affected men and women differently. Even among the urban populations where gender roles were not as sharply delineated as in rural areas, expectations for men and women were suddenly starkly different. Men for the most part joined the military, both out of a sense of masculine duty to their families and their communities and because they were forcibly conscripted. There were some males, derided as *podrumaši* (basement dwellers), who tried to avoid going to the front lines by running from conscription raids and keeping a low profile, hiding in basement bomb shelters with other civilians (see Bašić 2004; Maček 2005; Milićević 2006). I knew young men, too, who spent their time within the army trying to avoid serving on the front lines. There were women who joined the army and many who fought bravely, but they were not conscripted. Nor did they face the same social pressure to fight as did men.[9]

For the most part, women were burdened with daily survival for themselves and their families under harsh conditions, whether it was the shortages, deprivation, and dangers of life in the war zones or the monotony and uncertainty of refugee camps. Sarajevo writer Alma Lazarevska praised the stoic persistence of women as "hewers of wood and carriers of water" during the siege (1995). After the war, Bosnians still joked about how they had made *pita* with nettles or cake out of air.[10] Humorous and bitterly ironic stories abounded, as Ivana Maček also encountered during her fieldwork in wartime Sarajevo (2009). Coffee and sugar, the basis of domestic hospitality, cost enormous amounts on the black market (see Andreas 2008); household appliances could be run only sporadically when the electricity or water would suddenly go on. Women told stories of being awakened at four in the morning by the electricity going on and jumping up to frantically vacuum the apartment and praying that it would last long enough for *pita* to cook in the oven. But such predicaments and deprivations affected all civilians and even soldiers living partly at home. One young woman incredulously recalled being given two raw eggs by a humanitarian organization when she was living in a students' dorm. Without electricity or any way to cook the eggs, she didn't know whether to laugh or cry. An older woman told me how she had clutched a rare piece of chocolate to bring to her small niece, who was too young to have even seen it before to know what it was. By the time she reached the child, the chocolate had melted. Not wanting to waste such a precious treat, she had the girl lick the chocolate out of her palm.

More seriously, it was women's lot to worry about loved ones trapped in zones of ethnic cleansing, and especially males who were detained in camps, fighting on the front lines, or hiding from conscription raids. Women were the ones who more often had to cope on their own with unfamiliar roles when they lost husbands and other male family members to war violence, a position that fell especially hard on less-educated rural women. And the new ethnic divisions and war separations were hard on all marriages but took a particular toll on women in ethnically mixed marriages (Kaufman and Williams 2007, 79–113; Maček 2009, 100–105).

Debates over Rape: Gender versus Nation

Despite these varied forms of gendered war experiences, it was the mass rapes of women by Serb forces that called the world's attention to the

Figure 7 Bosniac returnee women visit men's graves in Kozarac, May 2010. (photo by Peter Lippman)

violence as a gender issue. Speaking out were journalists, human rights advocates, and feminists in Western Europe and North America as well as feminists from the former Yugoslavia. When the first rape survivors began appearing in areas of relative safety, local feminists reacted quickly, setting up aid and counseling organizations and raising awareness and funds to help survivors. They published academic and activist texts of their own but also became (often unacknowledged) local sources about the nature of the rapes (see, e.g., Lindsey 2002). What eventually became a deep divide among feminists in the former Yugoslavia was thus mirrored in the ways in which the rapes were represented elsewhere.

Feminists split over the characterization of the rapes: were these crimes of gender or crimes of nation?[11] Ultimately, they disagreed over how to name the victims and the perpetrators. They all pointed to women as the victims of rape and also agreed on the need to condemn Serbian nationalism[12] and Serb forces that were clearly using rape in a widespread manner against Muslim and Croat women as part of the rapid and violent spring and summer of ethnic cleansing in 1992. But feminists in Serbia were also encountering Serb women who had been raped by Croats or Muslims (see, e.g., Nikolić-Ristanović 2000;

Nizich 1994). For Serbian feminists, the pariah status of Serbia and their own firm anti-nationalism and anti-militarism directed them to focus more on the gender dimensions of the war rapes, one group of radical feminists even at first eliding the ethnic component altogether (Žarkov 2002). This put them uncomfortably close to what I term the global feminist position taken by some US feminists in particular. It pointed to rape as a crime against women in all wars and, as Susan Brownmiller asserted long ago (1975), an extension of women's oppression in patriarchal society even in peacetime.[13] This view was made to fit easily into second-wave arguments that women (as an undifferentiated group) are constant (potential) victims of male violence, a kind of claim to innocence through victimhood that I also identified in some forms among Bosnian activists.

The global feminist approach therefore privileged gender as a social category in a much too simplified way; most egregiously in this case, it largely ignored ethnicity. With the increasing international publicity around wartime rape, therefore, some feminist and women's groups in Zagreb began to object to the focus on gender: yes, women were the victims but it was only happening to *certain* women. Focusing solely on the gender dimension implied an "all sides did it" position that equated victims with perpetrators, they argued. This group, led by the radical feminist group Kareta, came to be known as nationalist or "patriotic" feminists (Benderly 1997b).[14] They insisted that Serb crimes constituted a unique, genocidal strategy against the Croatian and Muslim nations and could not be compared to "incidental" rapes or other attacks committed by Croat or Muslim soldiers. In fact, they argued that these rapes, together with forced pregnancies, by Serbs should be classified as an altogether different, even unprecedented phenomenon of "genocidal rape."[15] Nationalist feminists also held all Serbs responsible, including Serbian feminists as they were "women of the group committing the genocide,"[16] and refused to participate in gatherings where they were invited. In fact, they, along with their most famous advocate, US feminist law professor Catherine MacKinnon, were publicly hostile to Serbian feminists as well as to the opposing camp of Croatian feminists, often referred to as anti-nationalists.[17]

The Croatian anti-nationalist feminists, many of them veterans of Yugoslav feminist networks, were determined not to let nationalist divisions sever their solidarity with Serbian feminists.[18] Despite closed borders and severed phone lines, they made efforts to maintain contact, meeting in Hungary or elsewhere abroad and communicating through foreign friends or through Zamir (For peace), an early e-mail network. What bound them together was their feminist critique of patriarchal norms for women and their opposition to nationalism and militarism. This is what they stressed.

In their theorizing of the war violence, anti-nationalist feminists criticized Serb nationalism and the use of rape as a weapon of ethnic cleansing but analyzed this as an extension of patriarchal nationalist ideologies in which both gender and ethnicity were relevant. It was thus to be expected that Croatian and Muslim soldiers had raped, too, and that Serb women were also among the victims. Taking this stance publicly was precisely the crime of these feminists from the perspective of Croatian nationalism. In a notorious incident in late 1992, an anonymous article in the Croatian weekly *Globus* attacked five Croatian women writers—Slavenka Drakulić, Vesna Kesić, Rada Iveković, Jelena Lovrić, and Dubravka Ugrešić—calling them "witches" for their open criticism of Croatian nationalism (*Globus*, December 11, 1992, 33–34). Drakulić, Kesić, and Iveković had written specifically about the rapes in Croatia and Bosnia as crimes of men against women instead of (only) Serbs against Croats and Muslims. The headline of the *Globus* article said it all: "Croatian Feminists Rape Croatia!"[19] The women were accused of "concealing the Serbian rape of Muslim and Croatian women" (Korać 1994, 505), and the article went on to attack the writers' physical appearance, what was said to be a political choice of (non-Croatian, even Serb!) marriage partners, and their ties to the West, thus challenging their Croatian-ness (Kesić 1994; Korać 1994; Mostov 1995; Tax 1993). The women's home addresses and phone numbers were published and the five were "'witch hunted' throughout the national media for almost a year and a half" afterward (Kesić 1994).[20]

In denunciations of the "witches," much was made of their feminism and how the adoption of this ideology proved their anti-Croatian, pro-communist loyalties; they were "Yugo-nostalgics" who had benefited from the socialist system that had denied Croatia its freedom and true identity as part of Europe (Benderly 1997b; Kesić 1997). (Ironic since the same feminists, in their critiques of socialist realities, had been dismissed by the Communist authorities as following a foreign, bourgeois ideology.) It was thus curious when the nationalist media and authorities in Croatia, which were otherwise quite hostile to feminism, began to embrace "patriotic" groups who stressed the unique evil of Serb crimes, despite their explicit identification as feminists (see Žarkov 2002, 62).

The rhetoric of the nationalist feminists in fact began to mirror that of the nationalist mainstream in Croatia, for example when they denounced two veteran Yugoslav feminists who took anti-nationalist stances as having benefited from the Communist system,[21] or in the way they spoke not only of raped Croat and Muslim women but raped *Croatia and Bosnia*, women's honor equaling the honor of the nation/land. These positions were starkly displayed in March 1993 in reaction to a speaking tour of the United States organized by MADRE, a US group of antiwar feminists, to call attention to the use of mass rape in the wars in Croatia and BiH. The nationalist women's groups from Zagreb strongly objected to the choice of speakers—anti-nationalist feminists from Croatia and Serbia who had been active in the Yugoslav feminist scene—and angrily denounced the whole tour on the grounds that its message obscured wartime rape as a unique Serbian crime against Croatia/n women and Bosnia/n women (see Batinic 2001; Carr 1993; the March 1993 issue of the US feminist magazine *off our backs*; and the group of articles in the *Village Voice*, July 13, 1993).

Nationalists in Croatia were also keen to pick up on the idea that this was "genocidal rape" and should thus be prosecuted more severely. Anti-nationalist feminists argued back that this concept only reinforced the logic by which the rapes were committed and understood in the first place.[22] For how else was one to determine whether rapes were genocidal, that is, aimed at the destruction of an ethnic group or nation, without reinforcing the same relation of women to the nation assumed by the very perpetrators of rape—the equation of women's honor and reproductive capacities with that of the nation? Accepting this categorization meant privileging only those rapes that could be determined to be ethnic, thus downplaying other rapes and sexualized assaults. In this formulation, only Muslim and Croat women come to be seen as victims, much as Doris Buss shows has happened along similar reasoning for Tutsi women after the Rwandan genocide (2009).[23] Insisting on genocidal rape implied that "only certain [ethnic] victims count" (Kesić 1994, 276).

Indeed, this is what made such an approach so attractive to nationalists and what underlay the intensive competition over numbers of the victims.[24] It was not the first time, either, that ethnic categories had been used to define rape, an otherwise underreported and little noticed crime. In the late 1980s, in response to stories that Albanian men were raping Serbian women in the disputed province of Kosovo, Serbian authorities introduced a new category of "ethnic rape" into the criminal code.[25] "Ethnic rape" carried harsher punishments than "non-ethnic" rape and was thus understood as a crime against the ethno-nation rather than an injury to women. As several scholars pointed out, this episode prepared the conceptual groundwork for later uses of rape as a strategy of ethnic war in BiH (Bracewell 2000; Jalušič 2004; Meznarić and Moghadam 1994; Žarkov 2007). When it came to the war in BiH, then, politicians at peace negotiations bickered over whose soldiers had raped more women of their own nations (Skjelsbaek 2004, 25); Croatian nationalists charged that "a raped Croatian woman [*Hrvatica*] is a raped Croatia!" (Kesić 1995); Biljana Plavšić, then vice president of the Serb Republic in Bosnia, reportedly complained that most of the women raped in the war were actually

Serbs that Muslims and Croats were unfairly counting as "their victims" (Knežević 1993, 13). Žarkov (2007) shows how this competition for victimhood shaped representations in the Croatian and Serbian media; I take a closer look at how war rapes figured in Bosniac and Bosnian narratives below.

To avoid the danger of manipulation by patriarchal nationalists, antinationalist feminists therefore stressed the rapes as crimes perpetrated by men against women. This stance carried consequences, too, however. The preoccupation with the rape of women, rather than the wider patterns of gendered and sexualized violence that also affected men, as Žarkov argues, reinforced the identification of "The Rape Victim" with females, and females as therefore vulnerable, violable, "rapable" (2007). There is thus a cruel reality involved in discussing the use of sexualized violence in this war that was imposed by the ethnic and gender categories produced through the violence itself. As Skjelsbaek (2001a) similarly argues, only an approach that takes the interrelation between systems of both gendered and ethnicized meanings can adequately make sense of how men and women were differently victimized in this or any conflict.

Representation and Bosnia

Throughout this discussion, I have said very little about BiH or Bosnians themselves. And this is the effect of the way in which the war rapes were represented: Bosnian women were reduced to a caricatured image of silent victimhood, one that was intensified by Orientalist assumptions about the Muslim, Balkan society in which they were said to live.

The overwhelming majority of discourses about wartime rape in BiH (and Croatia) were produced by those in Croatia, Serbia, and Slovenia and from outside the former Yugoslavia. At best, Bosnian women were interviewed as usually anonymous refugees who talked about the war violence or their relationships to new surroundings—in other words as victims (e.g., Mertus et al. 1997; Nikolić-Ristanović 2000; Stiglmayer 1994; Vranić 1996). To be sure, groups aligned with the nationalist feminist stance included Bosnian Croat and Muslim refugee women's organizations that had decided to organize precisely because of this situation. As Almasa, a Bosniac refugee who had been active at the time with Žena BiH in Zagreb, later explained to me, "We . . . saw other NGOs in Zagreb like Kareta, etc., and we thought, why should they speak for us [Bosnians] when we can do this for ourselves?" (interview, September 2000). But in published accounts the Bosnian groups were only occasionally named—their members did not publish analyses or get quoted in public statements.[26] Instead, Croatian feminists appeared to speak for them, even though some of the Bosnian women rejected the Croatian women's feminist ideas.[27] Those from outside the region, too, tended to look to Serbian and Croatian women to speak about, and often *for*, victims of wartime rape in BiH, not only silencing the voices of Bosnian Muslim women (as members of the group most affected by war rapes) but also obscuring Serb and Croat women (and others) from Bosnia, just as separatist nationalists would have it.[28] Feminist analyses, too, even those that condemned nationalism across the board, in many ways reinforced the nationalist notion of the guilt and innocence of national collectivities by leaving the gendered aspects of Bosnian Muslim/Bosniac nationalism unanalyzed and unacknowledged.[29]

There were good reasons for this. Serbian and Croatian nationalisms were doing much more dramatic and visible damage to women or hopes for gender equality; there was not much interest in scrutinizing the politics of the victims, the "good guys," in an atmosphere in which criticism of political leaders was interpreted as an attack on the nation as a whole. Furthermore, most of these debates occurred while the war was still going on. The Bosnian women working with war rape survivors in BiH itself had little access to world media and scholarly journals, not to mention that they were too consumed with survival and helping other war victims to have the luxury of reflection and writing. The refugee women in Zagreb had existential issues of their own as well. However, not many of them were inclined to analysis and publication.[30] BiH had not had a feminist scene before the war like those that existed in Zagreb and Belgrade.[31] I am not suggesting that Croatian and Serbian feminists were out of line in speaking out; their aid to victims and their critical voices were crucial at a time when many ill-informed observers were making all kinds of well-circulated pronouncements. Feminists in Croatia and Serbia of course shared a former country with Bosnians and many of them had worked with Bosnian war survivors and experienced the effects of living under nationalist regimes. Their critiques of the rape discourse were, furthermore, not primarily about BiH but were an integral part of their critiques of nationalisms in their own communities, although that emphasis often contributed to the static image of Bosnian victims. I am also not suggesting that Bosnian women's voices be seen as more authentic because of this positioning. Nevertheless, the absence of Bosnian women as actors in shaping debates over the Bosnian war had particular consequences for the construction of dominant images.

Most striking was the Orientalizing effect similar to that noticed by feminists from other Muslim or Third World societies in their critiques of Western feminist representations (e.g., Ahmed 1982; Mohanty 1988). The relative absence of women from Bosnia meant that "The Muslim Raped Woman" could remain the archetypal victim, forever the secluded and silent Muslim woman whose only role is as passive victim of male power. Žarkov's work (1995, 1997, 2007) shows how this effect was produced through both the nationalist media in Croatia and Serbia and through feminist representations in those countries and globally. Muslim rape victims appeared as visible but mute, numerous but anonymous, bearing witness to Balkan savagery much like the African refugees pictured in great throngs, never appearing as persons but as signifiers of pure victimhood, which Liisa Malkki (1996) termed "speechless emissaries."

Orientalist descriptions of the society in which the victims lived facilitated the easy association of Muslim women with victimhood. In feminist and nonfeminist texts alike, there have appeared unsubstantiated assertions that coping with rape was especially difficult for Muslim women, and that such women were rejected by their families and communities as damaged goods. It hardly had to be spelled out, although many did, that virginity before marriage was especially prized, that wives were chaste, that marriage and motherhood were the unavoidable norm for women, and that rape was therefore a particularly harsh blow for Muslim women. Žarkov discusses several examples from both journalistic and feminist accounts where it is confidently asserted that the (rural) culture and religion of the Bosnian Muslims meant both more intense trauma caused by rape and that Bosniac women experienced greater shame and stigma and therefore refused to speak about their ordeals (1995, 144–48). Writing from the perspective of international law and war crimes prosecutions, Karen Engle singles out another genre of analysis that has especially relied on such assumptions with scant evidence or knowledge of Bosnian society (2005). Fisher, for example, asserts, "A policy of rape is particularly damaging in the Bosnian Muslim culture," because of the norms of gender and sexuality in "traditional Islamic culture" that consider rape victims unfit to become wives and mothers (1996, 123). Other telling examples can be found in studies by Askin (2003) and Kalosieh (2003), the latter of whom discusses social norms in BiH under a generalized, stereotyped, and misplaced framework of Islamic law.

In the first place, not all rape survivors came from conservative rural communities, nor were they all religious or religious in the same ways. As discussed earlier, while Muslim women were historically more visibly sheltered and constrained, by the time the war broke out, Muslim women as a whole were (are) just as educated and independent (or not) as other women in BiH. Differences in adherence to patriarchal norms varied much more by education level, religious piety, and most importantly rural versus urban background than by ethnicity, patterns that owed much to socialist modernization. As Žarkov also asked, regardless of these realities, why would one—especially a feminist—

assume that rapes would be less traumatic for non-religious or urban women? Or for Serb or Croat or other women who also came from conservative communities in which female chastity, marriage, and motherhood are prized? (2007, 146).

In my research with rape survivor advocates, therapists who worked extensively with survivors, and among survivors themselves, I found no indication that Bosniac women experienced rape any differently from women of other ethnic or religious backgrounds. The few other researchers who have interviewed survivors in BiH have found the same: some Bosniac women have spoken out, others have remained silent; they have experienced a wide range of responses from family and community members, including forms of rejection *and* support (Mischkowski and Mlinarević 2009; Skjelsbaek 2006; see also Hromadžić 2007; Žarkov 2007, 148).

This does not mean there was no stigma against raped women or the children born from the rapes (and even stronger taboos around the sexual abuse of men). It also does not mean that Bosniacs themselves, including women rape survivors, did not reproduce these Orientalized tropes. In fact, at the time of the intense debates on war rapes, one of the only frequently cited texts by a Bosnian woman, a journalist with a Muslim name herself, offered an extremely romanticized and Orientalized view of Muslim women as upholders of family honor in a patriarchal, rural culture, ending with the suggestion that truly honorable Muslim women would rather die than be dishonored through rape (Zalihić-Kaurin 1994). It was precisely this notion that was reproduced in a publication of rape testimonies tellingly titled *I Begged Them to Kill Me*, which I discuss. Complicating matters, I was frequently assured by Bosnians of various social positions, including some women's activists, that rape *had* been especially difficult for Muslim women given the patriarchal rural communities many of them came from. I return to this phenomenon in later chapters.

Representations of forced pregnancies posed a similar problem. Without interrogating actual practices and beliefs among the survivors and members of their communities themselves, many authors concluded the worst about the lives of the women victims and the basis of their social rejection, even murders, for having betrayed the nation by bearing a "child of the enemy." Patrilineal kinship is the rule in BiH among all ethno-religious groups. Children are usually given their father's last name and in many places, patrilocal traditions have survived in the ideal that new families live with or close to patrilineal kin. But this did not mean that women's relatives did not continue to participate as part of the family or that children were not seen as equally sharing their mother's and father's "blood." Nor does it mean that there was a general rejection of modern science in favor of some primitive folk beliefs. And while nationalist leaders favored patrilineal notions by which women and children took on the ethnic and religious identities of the male-defined kinship groups into which they married, the high rates of what was tellingly termed "mixed marriages" in BiH pointed to the widespread acceptance of "mixed" children who retained both or neither of their parents' ethno-religious identities or chose one or the other according to individual circumstances. In fact, children of rape were likely to be raised either as adoptees or orphans who were unaware of their origins or as members of their mothers' ethnic group and believers in her faith rather than to be determined solely by the genetic input of the rapists, social stigma notwithstanding. And of those women who killed or attempted to kill their babies, we cannot assume without evidence that their desperation stemmed necessarily or solely from the notion that these were *Serb* babies, as there were many more traumatic experiences that might have led them to reject their children.[32]

While there was certainly evidence that rape did prevent many victims from having future children, whether for medical or psychological reasons or because they also lacked husbands with which to reproduce in a socially acceptable way, this was not necessarily or always the outcome (see Jansen and Helms 2009). Bosnians appear to have responded in much the same way as the Hindu, Sikh, and Muslim survivors of the violent partition of India that anthropologist Veena Das describes (1995) employing Bourdieu's notion of "practical kinship." After this episode of "communal" violence among people who adhered to similarly patrilineal kinship norms, families and communities were far from comfortable with accepting what they did see as dishonored women and children of the enemy, or with the situation that a daughter who had been abducted and raped (but in some cases saved) by a man from another group had stayed with him to raise her children. But they made accommodations and maintained strategic silences in their rendering of family histories, allowing themselves to save face and move on with their lives. As in India, victims and members of their communities in BiH seem to have simultaneously accepted the gendered ethnic logic of the violence while also selectively disregarding its implications in order to continue their lives in the presence of such victims.

Only with time as these children have grown into adolescence have a small number of studies (Carpenter 2007, 2010; Daniel-Wrabetz 2007) and journalistic reports (e.g., Bećirbašić and Šečić 2005; Toomey 2003)[33] appeared that would shed light on these questions based on any empirical evidence, including some limited but revealing interviews directly with such children themselves (Carpenter 2010; Erjavec and Volčič 2010).[34] While this work does report stigmatization of the children and their mothers, there are also stories of support, acceptance, and relatively normal childhoods, particularly, albeit less commonly, where children are raised in more financially secure environments or by mothers with mental health support. There is still much that is unknown about the very complex social and psychological dynamics affecting the lives of rape survivors and the children they bore in relation to questions of stigma, ethnic identities, and gender. Many analysts, however, did not seem concerned with this lack of research, reproducing Orientalist assumptions about patriarchal Muslim culture and uncritically attributing women's or their communities' rejection of children born of rape to ethnic considerations rather than, for example, the father having been a *rapist* and not simply of a different ethno-religious background. Such analyses therefore appear to have concluded on the basis of the rhetoric of rapists and nationalists that the lives of the women and children victims would match the miserable extremes that such discourses threatened (see Jansen and Helms 2009).

Arguing for Genocide

Threats to victims that they would give birth to Serb babies were also taken as evidence of genocidal intent. The question of whether Serb attacks can be classified as genocide is one of the most contentious debates surrounding the Bosnian war (Bećirević 2010; Hayden 2008a, 2008b; Hoare 2010; Nielsen 2013). While acknowledging the meaningfulness of the genocide classification for victims and survivors of mass atrocities, I find it necessary to unpack the variety of assumptions that are masked by the use of this label. I take a similar stance to Christian Nielsen (2013), who argues that while genocide remains an important concept, a "myopic focus" on "genocide or not" (22) is less an analytically productive distinction than an often overused political tool. In this politicized mode, the focus on genocide solidifies the exclusive and timeless approach to ethno-national frameworks and the all-or-nothing logic of competing victimhoods. It also maddeningly implies that other, "lesser," designations applied to cruel and brutal violence, including those condemned by international law, are somehow meaningless or a victory for the perpetrators and their ethno-national group. Here I do not seek to resolve this question—to argue that genocide was or was not committed in Bosnia. Instead, noting the many gray areas involved in genocide judgments, I point here to some of the ways in which assumptions about gender and culture have entered these debates and in fact complicate them (cf. Oosterveld 2009).

According to the UN Genocide Convention, genocide depends on "intent to destroy, in whole or in part, a national, ethnical, racial, or religious group, as such," through acts of:

(a) Killing members of the group;
(b) Causing serious bodily or mental harm to members of the group;
(c) Deliberately inflicting on the group conditions of life calculated to bring about its physical destruction in whole or in part;
(d) Imposing measures intended to prevent births within the group;
(e) Forcibly transferring children of the group to another group.[35]

It has been argued that rape and forced maternity fall into all of these categories (less commonly [a], even though many rape victims were also killed). As the above discussion shows, problems arise in arguing for (e) because this would require classifying children as belonging *either* to the mother's or the rapist's group. As Carpenter points out, "To be forcibly removed *from* the victimized group, the children must be members *of* the group, but if they are members of their group, then births within the group have been facilitated, not prevented" (2010, 107, emphasis in original).

It was also argued that forced maternity by rape reflected a genocidal Serb intent to destroy the group by preventing future births and occupying Muslim wombs (Fisher 1996) with non-Muslim babies.[36] Even though some recognized the discrepancy between the patrilineal notion of making purely Serb babies and the reality of children being brought up as Muslims/Bosniacs, the conclusion was simply that the Serb attackers, but also presumably their victims, displayed an "ignorance of genetics" (139). Clearly, telling victims that a hostile alien was being planted inside them enhanced the traumatic and lingering psychological effects of this form of torture and decreased the likelihood that victims would return to territories now conquered by Serbs. It was thus a highly effective weapon of ethnic cleansing. It is also not surprising that women struggled with the knowledge that their child shared the genes of a man who had violently attacked them, not to mention the additional burdens placed on them by patrilineal and ethno-religious norms as Erjavec and Volčič report (2010). But Serb rapists are reported by survivors to have said many different and contradictory things, including that babies born from rape would be half Muslim and half Serb (Stiglmayer 1994, 132), a statement that Matthew Evangelista (2011, 111–12) takes as evidence that Serb rapists were not in fact ignorant of the workings of genetics. Survivor testimonies also complicate the easy assumptions of Serb intent to commit genocide as opposed to "just" ethnic cleansing.[37] One rapist, for example, reportedly reacted to a victim's pregnancy by saying, "Very good; now Alija [Izetbegović] will have to provide for a Chetnik" (Stiglmayer 1994, 132), thus suggesting a vision of victims and their people *surviving* in the future, just on another territory ruled by Alija, that is, designated as Muslim. Thus, rather than consider pronouncements about making *Četnik* babies as the cruel tactics for intimidating and terrorizing victims that they surely were, analysts arguing for rape as genocide took such threats possibly more seriously than did the rapists themselves.

Gendered assumptions about traditional Muslim society were also explicitly foundational to the ICTY judgment that found the Srebrenica massacre to be genocide.[38] At the trial of Bosnian Serb General Radislav Krstić, the defense objected to the genocide label on the grounds that Bosniac women and children had been allowed to leave the enclave alive. The prosecution successfully countered that, due to the "traditionally patriarchal society" of the Bosnian Muslims in Srebrenica, Serb forces would have known that killing just the men "would inevitably result in the physical disappearance of the Bosnian Muslim population at Srebrenica."[39]

As with the claims about rape trauma and Muslim women, this assertion apparently needed no further explanation.[40] As the judgment itself put it, "It was common knowledge that the Bosnian Muslims of Eastern Bosnia constituted a patriarchal society in which men had more education, training and provided material support to their family."[41] The prosecutor argued that "what remained of the Srebrenica community" was "a community in despair, it's a community clinging to memories; *it's a community that is lacking leadership*; it's a community that's a shadow of what it once was" (emphasis added).[42] The assumption was that the women would be helpless without the men, and that, because of patriarchal norms, they would not remarry and have more children, thus the genocidal effect to the collective. In other words, it was patriarchal tradition, rather than pure mathematics or the inevitable consequences of such traumatic losses, that would prevent the Srebrenica community from bearing future generations. Indeed, several Srebrenica survivors told me that further children would not be born because, as one woman at the Mothers of the Enclaves of Srebrenica and Žepa organization in Sarajevo put it, "we're not going to be whores!" (*nećemo se kurvati!*); since they would not remarry, there was no respectable way to achieve this. But other survivors insisted that remarriage would not be shameful. There simply were not enough available men.[43]

At first glance, the survivors themselves reinforced these notions of patriarchal society by defining themselves and their organizations as mothers and wives of the murdered men rather than families or survivors. Many of them also wore headscarves and rural dress, markers to much of the local population of patriarchal backwardness. Survivors who insisted that widows would not remarry also explicitly appealed to patriarchal tradition. But if the perpetrators had assumed that women from such a "patriarchal society" would be helpless or silent, the women proved them very wrong. Women Srebrenica survivors spoke out sharply and often in the media and directly to high officials, staged public protests, blocked highways, testified at the ICTY, filed numerous law suits, and garnered funding and support from donors and foreign officials (see Nettelfield 2010). They certainly were not without leadership; indeed, at times there were too many organizations of Srebrenica survivors for them to craft a united public voice. Yet they were consistently characterized as rural women, as such doubly out of place in the urban, male political realm and in local hierarchies of civilization also characterized as quintessentially Balkan. In the Federation media as well as everyday conversation, both those who were fed up with the politics surrounding Srebrenica and people sympathetic to the plight of its survivors frequently dismissed the Srebrenica women as manipulated by politicians, that is, men. The only accepted image seemed to be that of the mourning Srebrenica widow/mother weeping over her loved ones' remains, victims looking to state and foreign institutions to provide them with a sense of justice.

Statements stressing the patriarchal nature of Bosnian Muslim society both for Srebrenica and for war rapes were based on real patterns and beliefs. But they might just as well have been explained—and arguments for genocide upheld—without evoking Orientalist images of Muslim rural patriarchy. Indeed, after the Krstić case, another ICTY judgment repeated the genocide classification for Srebrenica but through a less problematic focus on the harmful effects and mental suffering inflicted on Bosniacs in Srebrenica.[44] The "patriarchal society" framing seems to be aimed at eliciting sympathy (or pity?) for the victims and driving home arguments about the particular cruelty of the atrocities and the need to raise awareness, prosecute the perpetrators, and help the victims. They were not meant to be derogatory but were an appeal to innocence in victimhood through images of powerlessness. If the victims as women were powerless, it follows that they were certainly powerless and therefore innocent as Muslims. This made claims about the special vulnerability of Muslim women all the more compelling to those concerned with underscoring Bosniac or Bosnian collective innocence. It is therefore important to understand how Bosniac and Bosnian discourses were gendered.

Gendering Bosniac Nationalism

Gender constructions in nationalist discourses among the Bosniacs share much with the basic logic of Serb and Croat nationalist discourses discussed earlier. The differences lie in the peculiarities of history, geopolitics, religion, and Bosniac nationalist constructions, just as differences between dominant Serbian and Croatian nationalisms were reflected in gendered ways

(Žarkov 2007). While the underlying drive of Croatian nationalism was to legitimize the newly independent state of Croatia, in Serbia the thrust was in defending Serbs from accusations of warmongering and atrocities by proving the eternal victimization of the Serbs. Among Bosniacs and those who supported the newly proclaimed independent state, the argument to be upheld was that BiH was—had always been—a multiethnic country in which members of all ethnic groups were welcome and tolerated and that threatened no one with violence or war.

There was much truth in this claim, but it elided a much more complicated history and present reality. It was also full of ambiguity, due to the overlap between Bosniac nationalism and support for a multiethnic BiH state. This support for multiethnicity was dominated by Bosniacs and others living in Bosniac-controlled areas, but it was never easy to determine what degree of genuine tolerance toward ethnic and religious others or devotion to ethnically blind democratic citizenship were truly at play. Points of conflict between supporters of competing visions for the political and social future of the BiH state were frequently revealed through different narrations of the war and its victims. Notions of gender and sexuality figured in all of these competing discourses.

Unsurprisingly, conservative gender ideals were most commonly put forth by religious nationalists (pan-Islamists) within the Bosniac nationalist party, the SDA, and their close allies among the Islamic clergy.[45] While these factions have dominated Bosniac nationalism, the discourses they have produced must be put into context. They are indicators of the kinds of ideal gender roles and relations being promoted, but I found that they were also vying for dominance with other long-standing versions of modernization and participation in broader global trends that also affected gender relations. Moreover, the appearance of certain rhetoric does not necessarily indicate popular acceptance, even by those who fully subscribed to nationalist paradigms—or even by the speakers themselves—nor did they always result in actual policy measures (see Jansen and Helms 2009). I discuss these elements here to indicate some of the ways in which gender figured in nationalist visions, both as a study in similarity and contrast with their much analyzed Serbian and Croatian counterparts and as a wider context for understanding the gendering of national(ist) victim narratives.

As in Serbia and Croatia, much of the rhetoric about gender for Bosniac nationalism was linked to concern about the reproduction of the nation, if not always ethnically then culturally. Women were cast in the classic role of mothers and nurturers, keepers of the home sphere, tradition, and spirituality. Alija Izetbegović, at the time leader of the SDA, president of the presidency of

Bosnia-Herzegovina, and the grandfatherly figurehead of Bosniac nationalism, summed up his view in a public speech in June 1997, after the male
organizers of the Muslim pilgrimage Ajvatovica, considered both a religious
and a national event, had forbidden women to take part in the walk to the pilgrimage site: "Women make up half of our nation [*narod*]. In the midst of the
war, together they shared with us the burden of wartime misfortune: dying,
starving, and suffering. From them we expect that they bear and bring up a
generation of Bosniacs who will preserve what we have chosen and fight to rid
themselves of what we are not. Such a proud and aware generation cannot be
brought up by humiliated and excluded women."[46] "Us" and "we" were clearly
the male actors of the nation. Women's dignity and right to participate was
upheld, but on the basis of their function as bearers and socializers of new generations of Bosniacs, first and foremost mothers with primary duties toward
the home and family. Furthermore, they had earned this participation through
their suffering in the war, a reminder of the injustice of female victimhood and
possibly an allusion to war rape.

As Duška Andrić-Ružičić from Medica pointed out at the time, Izetbegović's comment was both positive and negative. On one hand, he relegated
women to the role of motherhood and child rearing. But he also chastised the
male organizers of that day's event for excluding women.[47] In Duška's view, it
was better to support the president on this small positive point than attack
him for the more fundamental problem of portraying women as worthy only
for their fulfillment of domestic and reproductive duties, and only in service
to the nation. Indeed, many Bosniac women I met viewed Izetbegović as a
staunch supporter of women and their valuable contribution to the nation.
However, several of Izetbegović's longtime friends and colleagues—religiously
trained men closely associated with the president and pan-Islamist SDA members (see Bougarel 1997)—expressed more extreme and conservative views
about gender as a national/ethnic concern.

A blatant expression came from the deputy reis-ul-ulema (Grand Mufti) of
the Islamic Community (Islamska Zajednica, IZ, the official Islamic religious
institution in BiH), Ismet Efendija Spahić, at an SDA-sponsored ceremony
I attended in a small Bosnian town in July 1997 for the opening of a mosque
that had been rebuilt after its wartime destruction (see Helms 2008, 100–
101). In his speech, Spahić warned that "if miniskirts are worn, the shells will
fall again. If the *Četniks* [Serb forces] don't send them, Allah will find someone
who will." He equated women's dress, demeanor, and religiosity with maintaining social differences and awareness of those differences, thereby suggesting
that failure to remain a separate group and mixing with other groups (Serbs and
Croats), as they had done before the war, would result in renewed hostilities.

This drew on a commonly held view among Bosniacs that Muslims had been too trusting of the other groups during socialism. They had bought into socialist atheism and Yugoslav "brotherhood and unity," abandoned their traditions, forgot they were different, and therefore did not realize they could be targeted and attacked by their own ethnically different neighbors (Serbs and Croats).

Spahić did not mention men's dress, but he did admonish men to attend mosque regularly and to refrain from drinking alcohol (a very popular, male-associated activity). He also advised the audience that a man's honor and worth (as a Muslim) could be judged by looking at his wife and daughters to see whether they covered themselves and how they conducted themselves. Spahić thus brought the responsibility for the maintenance and marking of national essence back to women and their dress and demeanor. He also expressed a common nationalist concern with women's sexuality for maintaining the purity of the nation.[48]

However, most townspeople present for Spahić's speech, Bosniacs who generally supported the SDA and were enthusiastic contributors to the rebuilding of the mosque, shrugged off the cleric's statements as extreme, even ridiculous. They felt he was asking too much, even from the nominally religious, that men give up alcohol and women (especially younger ones) cover themselves and forgo the latest fashions. Indeed, on that hot summer day, even at a mosque ceremony, very few women were covered and many teenage girls wore miniskirts and halter tops, oblivious to the deputy reis's words.

Other Islamists close to Izetbegović expressed a similar concern with ethnic demographics. The reis ul-ulema himself, Mustafa Cerić, talked in an interview about plans to issue a *fetva* (Ar. *fatwa*) calling on Bosnian Muslim women to each bear five children "for Bosnia" (N. Latić 1993). Religious officials also periodically suggested publicly that Muslim men take on additional wives (up to four as per Islamic rules) so as to "take care of" the many war widows who had been left without their men. The population failed to respond, however, except through stories of ridicule that pointed to the fact that these religious men did not themselves have multiple wives, much less five children each.[49] Likewise, the *fetva* never materialized, nor did the birth rate increase (Jansen and Helms 2009).

Still, there were other issues which the IZ and SDA allies apparently took more seriously as threats to the nation. The most notorious was the condemnation of mixed marriages between Muslims and non-Muslims that appeared during the war (summer 1994) in the Bosniac press, especially the pro-SDA weekly *Ljiljan* for which several of Izetbegović's close allies wrote.[50] The debate was sparked in response to the statement by Circle 99, an independent club of Sarajevo intellectuals of all ethnic affiliations, that families of mixed marriages represent a "third nation appearing" within Bosnia. Circle 99 presented this as a positive sign that all ethnic groups could rebuild a multiethnic Bosnia, or "life together" (*zajednički život*) like the coexistence that had existed under Yugoslav socialism, when mixed marriages had reached some of the highest rates precisely in BiH (Dž. Latić 1994; Šantić 1994). Prominent pan-Islamists reacted with appeals to a sort of separate but tolerant policy, publishing repeated denunciations of mixed marriages and the "frustrated" children they produce.[51] In the words of Džemaludin Latić, a close pan-Islamist colleague of Izetbegović's: "Mixed marriages, a kind of banner to a misunderstood life together, are mostly failed marriages, serious conflicts arise from them, the children of such a marriage are frustrated from the beginning, and it would be worth putting a halt to that kind of destructive message. The differences between Muslims and non-Muslims are so great that if we suggest to our young people an alternative way, namely that they marry only those that think like they do, we will more easily build a society without trauma" (Dž. Latić 1994, 40). Scenarios of mixed Bosnian families torn apart by the war were raised as proof that Muslims would do better to stick to their own kind. In these examples, children of mixed marriages were taken to non-Muslim relatives in Serb- or Croat-held areas and "turned into" Serbs or Croats, even baptized into Christianity; others were betrayed during the war by a non-Muslim in-law and ended up in prison camps or dead; and many stories were told of terrible dilemmas faced by mixed families when Serbs, Croats, and Muslims came into conflict (Šestić 1994). The use of the word "trauma" was also loaded, as the concept through which the effects of war atrocities on ordinary people were being described. He thus implied that mixed marriages had had something to do with the outbreak and ferocity of the war.

Another longtime pan-Islamist went so far as to explicitly declare "the evil of mixed marriages" to be "worse than rape": "Even though these rapes [of Muslim women in the war] are difficult, unbearable, and unforgivable for us all, from the standpoint of Islam they are easier and less painful than mixed marriages and the *children and friendships* that result from them" (Spahić 1994, 22, emphasis added). Thus, not only were "mixed" people considered damaging to the nation, but social connections and networks of mutual aid and hospitality between Muslims and members of other ethnic/religious groups were also frowned upon. Women were especially dangerous; as Spahić further wrote, "Every [male] Muslim [*musliman*] in a mixed marriage as a rule was a loss for Islam and Muslims. With girl Muslims [*djevojke, muslimanke*] who have entered mixed marriages, the situation is even more drastic" (Spahić 1994, 22). Women who marry non-Muslims threatened greater harm to the nation than men marrying non-Muslims because, under Muslim patrilineal, patrilocal customs, women move to non-Muslim surroundings, take on non-Muslim names, and bear non-Muslim children. The threat to the nation was clear: if Muslims (Bosniacs), and especially women, did not marry within the fold, the nation would lose them and the children they produced. Moreover, this threat took precedence over the actual bodily suffering and desires of individual men and women, even in the terrible form of wartime rape, otherwise considered a heinous crime against the nation. The mention of friendships used a word (*prijateljstvo*) that also means in-law relations, implying that wider cross-ethnic relationships of the kind that knitted much of Bosnian society together before the war broadened the threat. Further, while a rape victim was forced by the nation's enemies, mixed marriages were entered into intentionally, most threateningly by women—an attack on the nation from within.

There were also signs from Muslim religious leaders of compassion toward women rape survivors and children born of rape (see Daniel-Wrabetz 2007). Early in the war, after the rapes had become known, the IZ in Sarajevo, along with local imams in Zenica and Tuzla, issued statements and *fetve* calling for raped women to be treated with compassion and respect; they were heroines and *šehid*s (Ar. *shaheed*, martyrs to the faith), just as men who had fallen in battle. Citing scripture and religious laws, the imams stressed the innocence of the women and the guilt of the rapists. They expressed dismay over reports of rejection and stigma against raped women and the children some of them bore as a result. Instead, husbands of such women were entreated to "embrace their wives"; bachelors were urged not to consider raped girls damaged in any way and to marry them.

These appeals undoubtedly meant a lot to rape survivors and their families, and were very much appreciated by organizations like Medica.[52] They were also far more compassionate than the positions taken by religious officials of other faiths. At the same time, their messages remained within the ethnic logic of the violence. By definition, *fetve* were only addressed to Muslim believers, although they subsumed all Muslims in the ethnic sense (Bosniacs) into the category of the religious (as the Tuzla message put it, "all of these [raped] women are Muslims, and that means that they believe in God—Allah the Almighty"[53]). Catholics were to heed the messages of their clergy, who in this case were instructed by the pope to encourage raped women to "transform the act of violence into an act of love and acceptance" by nurturing the innocent "new human beings that have been given life."[54] Furthermore, like Catholics, Islamic clergymen were especially concerned with the children born of rape. They explicitly stated that such children were born as Muslims, despite their mixed parentage (and despite the framing of those decrying mixed marriages quoted earlier), and should be raised as such. The Tuzla imam, in a very gentle, understanding tone, appealed to raped women not to kill their babies, as some reportedly did, as this would be the murder of a Muslim for which they would have to answer before God. Instead, the children should be raised in the spirit of Islam and nursed with "Islamic milk."[55]

Government officials made no such appeals for compassion or acceptance, despite the efforts of many of them to appear publicly as devout Muslims. Government and clergy were both ultimately concerned that children born of rape remain in BiH and be raised as Bosniacs/Muslims. During the war, the Bosnian government announced that it would forbid the international adoption of any child born of rape and encouraged their mothers to raise them themselves. Like the clergy, the government did not seem to take seriously warnings from survivor advocates that the babies were for many women constant reminders of their trauma and that very few women wanted anything to do with their children. The children, too, might be more likely to grow up without stigma or suspicion if they left BiH. The government explained that they wanted to avoid the sort of baby market that had careened out of control in Romania after 1989 (see Kligman 1995), but one also suspects that a major concern was to ensure that the babies were raised in the Muslim community rather than being "lost" to the nation. It is in this light that we can understand the publication (Hadžić 1996) of a small book of reprinted texts outlining the evils of mixed marriage, including those quoted above, by religious and nationalist leaders closely allied to the SDA leadership.

We should not be surprised that these conservative, male-dominated religious institutions would discourage mixed marriage, promote motherhood as a woman's sacred duty, or favor the upbringing of children within the faith. It was the influence of such institutions, however, along with the conflation of religion with ethnicity and the silence of secular authorities, that can be seen as reproducing a similar logic of gendered nationalism as those in Croatia and Serbia. In particular, war rapes were understood in the same way by all involved. The message from the Tuzla imam made this explicit. He urged women impregnated by rape to keep their children and raise them in the Muslim community, as a way to "show the enemy that with this crime he did not strengthen his ranks (as it's been said that they wanted), but on the contrary that he has thus strengthened the ranks of the enemy he wanted to destroy."[56] The imam thus countered the logic of the rapists' taunts about producing Serb babies, as discussed earlier, but remained within the paradigm of women as reproducers of ethnic collectivities.

This counternarrative to that of Serb nationalist violence brings us to the place of gendered victimhood in claims to national innocence and moral superiority. They depended on profoundly conservative gender norms that were written into conceptualizations of the nation, its honor, and its collective innocence or guilt. In order to explore further just how this functioned, and, again, as part of the discursive terrain in which Bosnian women's activists operated, I now examine the two main images through which women figured in narratives of Bosniac (and Bosnian) collective victimhood: the female refugee and the raped woman.

Women as (Rural) Refugees

A common media image—both locally and internationally—was that of women, often widows, usually rural and/or religious Bosniac women wearing headscarves, as symbols of (Bosniac) national suffering, and especially evoking innocence and purity. Many such examples can be found that feature women survivors of Srebrenica (Helms 2012), but in order to sidestep for a moment the fraught symbolism of that tragedy, which I will in any case revisit in the course of this book, here I want to examine a typical and fairly unobtrusive example from another region: an article that appeared in the pro-SDA daily *Dnevni avaz* (April 18, 2000, 1), during the period of my initial fieldwork, about the widow and two daughters of a Bosniac Bosnian Army soldier who had been killed in the war in 1992. Their picture appeared both on the front page and on page 9, together with the bulk of the text and the headline "Will the Family of the Hero Safet Hadžić be Evicted?" (see fig. 8). Of the surviving family members, only the widow, head uncovered, and her two daughters, dressed in *hidžab* (Islamic dress),[57] were pictured; the son, mentioned in the text, was absent. A photo of the hero himself appeared in a smaller insert with the caption "Hadžić: fighter for freedom."

In the text, Safet's widow is quoted talking about how he was a good husband and devoted Muslim, while the author stresses that he was a loyal Bosnian patriot. Three of the four subheadings emphasize precisely these points: "He loved people," "The highest [military] honors," and "*Mevlud* in the Švrakino village mosque," the latter indicating that a memorial service would be held for Safet in the mosque in the village from which the family had been expelled when Serb shells had destroyed their house.[58] The fourth subheading refers to the hero's youngest daughter: "She longs for her father" (*Vuče želja za ocem*). Only three when her father died, the daughter is described as prone to crying for her father and craving contact with men. In another part of the text, the widow declares ("with a deep sigh") that she will forget her husband and the good life she had with him "only when I die," and indicates her resignation at their predicament, saying, "But that's the way it is when you are left without your head of household [*domaćin*]." Both the mother and daughter are thus portrayed as

Džemila sa porodicom: Neizvjesna budućnost (Foto: I. Jahović)

Osam godina od pogibije bosanskog heroja

Da li će porodica Safeta Hadžića biti deložirana

Samo kad umrem zaboravit ću Safeta, govori supruga Džemila ● Djeci je najteže ● Žive na Otoci u potpunoj neizvjesnosti

Prije osam godina, 18. aprila 1992. u akciji izvlačenja i preuzimanja municije i opreme iz fabrike "Pretis" poginuo je Safet Hadžić. Rođen je 28. augusta 1952. godine u selu Stragačina, u općini Rudo.

Svoj život Safet Hadžić posvetio je borbi za opstanak bošnjačkog naroda na ovim prostorima. Iza njega ostala je supruga Džemila i troje djece.

Volio je ljude

- Samo kad umrem ja ću svog Safeta zaboraviti. U braku smo bili 17 godina i svakom na dunjaluku poželjela bih život kakav sam imala s njim. Volio je Safet ljude, društvo, uživao je da sazove mevlud, da pozove na iftar - sa dubokim uzdahom prisjeća se supruga Džemila.

Hadžić: Borac za slobodu

izbace na ulicu.

Porodica Hadžić do rata je živjela u Švrakinom u privatnoj kući. Međutim, kako je tokom rata kuća u više navrata granatirana, potpuno je neuslovna za stanovanje.

Vuče želja za ocem

- To je mala kućica na kojo[j]

Najveća priznanja

Safet Hadžić posthumno

Figure 8 "Will the Family of Safet Hadžić be Evicted?" (*Dnevni avaz*, April 18, 2000, 1) helpless and unfulfilled without Safet's male presence. Even the son, not pictured but briefly mentioned, is said to be affected: in the words of his mother, "He's male so he doesn't show his emotions, but I see it's difficult for him."

The photo of the mother and daughters thus reinforces the image of three grieving but pious and pure Bosniac women/girls who have lost a noble, manly, and patriotic husband/father. They have also lost their home and are therefore a reminder of places from which Bosniacs were expelled, territory that is nevertheless asserted here as Bosniac with the mention of the village mosque. Furthermore, as the headline suggests, the women are now once again facing expulsion from their flat. The expelling force is unnamed, though it was common knowledge that intervention agencies, led by the OHR, were enforcing deadlines for evictions to further the process of return of DPs to their original homes. This was a time of intense resentment among Bosniacs toward foreign officials because it was felt that politicians in Croat- and Serb-held areas were not being equally pressured into forcing evictions in their areas so that Bosniacs could return.[59] Many Bosniacs, too, like the family depicted in this article, had no homes to return to, as their houses in villages had been destroyed and few DP families had the money to rebuild (International Bureau for Humanitarian Issues 1998; Stubbs 1999a).[60] Yet who or what was expelling this family was less important than the fact of the irony and injustice of the continued victimization of the innocent family (made up of women) of a Bosniac martyr.[61] The image of the women's purity, piety, and victimhood, coupled with the robust (but kind) and patriotic masculinity of their fallen hero who had fought in defense of his family and home, were made to stand for the predicament of the Bosniac people. Gendered images naturalized and supported a narrative of national victimhood and moral purity, not to mention that they also upheld "traditional" gender ideals. In the most prominent spot, it was the picture of women, reproduced twice, which summoned the association with this familiar narrative.

We should also notice that this family was presented as rural. The mention of the village mosque and allusions to the women's piety placed this story squarely into dominant stereotypes of backward but simple, religious, and patriotic villagers, in the nationalist imagination the backbone of national traditions and loyalty. These were the people who suffered and sacrificed for BiH by bearing the brunt of Serb and Croat ethnic cleansing (no matter that the suffering of cities like Sarajevo and Mostar was equally commemorated in other sorts of national narratives). The pious village woman, as far away as one can get from a political actor and therefore the most self-evidently innocent, stood at once for national essence and national victimhood. This effect was all the more powerful in representations of Srebrenica survivors since they were mostly rural women, too, most of them religious Muslims. There was also an alternative reading from the perspective of anti-nationalist, cosmopolitan urbanites, in which the rural population stood for the epitome of backwardness and primitiveness, not least because of their support for nationalist politics. This ignorance and simplicity, however, did not erase the simultaneous association with innocence even for such urban liberal elites (see Helms 2012).

Women Rape Victims: "I Begged Them to Kill Me"

While reports about wartime rape circulated during the war, it was not as prevalent a topic as one would expect. Medica Zenica engaged the media on the issue quite intensively during the war but local political figures seemed to discuss it mainly because they could not avoid it (Monika Hauser, personal communication, 2012). Bosnian and Bosniac politicians made reference to it in international contexts as a basis for appeals for help from foreign powers, as when BiH ambassador to the UN Muhamed Sacirbey declared that "Bosnia-Herzegovina is being gang-raped."[62] The allusion to mass rapes of Muslim women appealed to the world's pity, but the plea was for help in countering Serb attacks and thus only indirectly for helping women. Even in everyday conversation it seemed that people knew rapes were happening but they were not talked about much. In my time working with refugees during the war, I never heard anyone but foreign visitors mention the rapes. Some refugees confirmed that they knew about them but only when I had gathered the courage to ask.[63] In BiH after the war, I rarely heard mention of wartime rape outside of women's activist circles, and there it was discussed primarily among therapy NGOs and activists where the concern was the well-being of individual survivors rather than wider political meanings.

The publication in 1999 of a collection of nearly fifty women's testimonies of wartime rape signaled the beginning of a new visibility for this topic in the Bosnian public sphere. The collection was titled *I Begged Them to Kill Me: The Crime against the Women of Bosnia-Herzegovina* (Ajanović 1999) and was compiled by the Association of Concentration Camp Torture Survivors of the Canton Sarajevo (Savez Udruženja Logoraša Kantona Sarajevo, or SULKS),[64] with the Center for War Crimes Research. The former was an organization concerned with redressing the injustices of the war felt directly by its members. Its very reason for existing was narrated in terms of this experience and framed in terms of Bosniac and Bosnian victimhood. At the same time, it had an on-again-off-again relationship with the nationalists in power who appreciated the *logoraši* (former camp detainees) for their symbolic utility but had not done much for them materially.

Although *logoraši* are most readily associated with male war victims, the organization decided that its first book of testimonies in a planned series would be devoted to crimes against women (ibid., 14). There was no need to explain that this meant rape; indeed, other kinds of suffering of women are present in the testimonies but are not given the prominence of rape in the essays that frame them, following the pattern noticed by feminist critics of other postconflict processes of transitional justice (e.g., Ross 2003; Theidon 2007). Significantly, in light of feminist critiques of gendered nationalism, the organizers and authors of the introduction reject the image of women as passive victims; they write that raped women should not be ashamed, that they should not be seen as passive objects but "subjects who speak and accuse," and that this book is a step toward the recovery of women's dignity (Ajanović 1999, 14). Indeed, the testimonies in the book are quite powerful and, as Medica activists pointed out at the time, it was very important for the women survivors and for all women that these crimes be documented and validated. It is not this aspect of the project, nor of course the real suffering of the war's victims with which I take issue, but the constructions of gender and nation embedded in the book's overall framing. Here I analyze only a portion of the twenty-three essays and documents by prominent Bosnians, foreign officials, academics, and human rights activists that precede and follow the testimonies.

The primary stress of the book is on the meanings of these rapes for the nation, as part of a wider pattern of *Bosniac* suffering under persecution and genocide, despite the designation "the crime against the *women of Bosnia-Herzegovina*" (my emphasis), another instance of how the overlap between Bosniac and Bosnian narratives creates an ambiguity from which claims to the moral status of both ethnic victim and principled opposition to nationalism can be asserted. Explicit comparison is made to the Holocaust; the texts and drawings interspersed among the testimonies highlight the wider context of ethnic cleansing against Bosniacs (and Croats) by Serbs (and Croats) through pictures of starving men behind barbed wire in detention camps (made famous in the Western press), of mass graves of Bosniacs, of men, women, and children lining up for water and bread in besieged Sarajevo, and of women and children fleeing ethnic cleansing attacks. In all of these drawings, it is made clear that the victims are Bosniacs as signaled by (destroyed) mosques, people praying in the Islamic way, and women in distinctively Muslim headscarves and traditional rural dress (*dimije*). The book's editors assert that Bosniac women made up 99.9 percent of the victims of rape (men are not mentioned) (ibid., 471), and that their testimony "further contributes to the defense of the women of Bosnia, especially Bosniacs" (ibid., 14). Rapes of non-Bosniacs and non-"ethnic" rapes are thus demoted in significance, as are gendered dimensions; the real victim is the Bosniac nation rather than individual women.[65]

Upon closer inspection, the local contributors to the book seem even more concerned with documenting the guilt of Serbs, and, to a lesser extent, Croats. One article by the well-known Bosniac "secular" nationalist (Bougarel 1996; Rusinow 1985) and academic Muhamed Filipović is devoted to a "socio-psychological and anthropological analysis of criminal character, especially of crimes committed against Bosniacs and Bosniac women during the Serb Aggression against Bosnia and Herzegovina" (Filipović 1999). As anticipated from such a title, Serbs are cast as a psychopathic *people*, but gendered male, as a collective "prone . . . to drastic actions such as slitting people's throats, killings with axes or violence against the elderly and women, frequent incestuous relations and sexual abuse of little girls and children" (ibid., 68). Filipović asserts that there is "ethnographic and ethnological" evidence for violent traditions among Serbs, especially because of their pastoralist background, which explains the use by Serbs of types of violence "otherwise inconceivable for normal people" (ibid.). Rape and sexual violence are also explained as a strategy solely used by the Serbs as "a people [*narod*] that has different sexual and family traditions/habits [*običaje*]" (69). The notion of the "dinaric" or "highlander" cultural type as primitive, passionate, and violently patriarchal (Denich 1974; Ramet 1996, 119–22) has a long history in what was Yugoslavia going back to nineteenth-century ethnology and is often understood as applying to Serbs in opposition to urban Muslim traditions (Bougarel 1999; Todorova 1997; Živković 2011).[66] Interestingly, this same logic is used to explain how Croats could have been capable of similar atrocities in the recent war.[67] We are told that "similar characteristics are found also among some (Herzegovinian) Croats, who have an element of Vlah [pastoralist] ethno-genesis in their origins. All of that is what has produced the characteristic variant of Serb-dom in the 19th and 20th centuries" (Filipović 1999, 68).

In case there is any lingering doubt, Filipović concludes that these traditions give us a "picture of the sources of those phenomena which were played out during the [recent] war, and those are sources *built into the social psychology of the Serbs as a people [narod]* (68, emphasis added). This is despite evidence the author himself mentions in the same text, that of the diary of a Yugoslav People's Army (read Serb) officer who complains that some of his soldiers resisted orders to "behave brutally toward their Muslim neighbors" in the area of Prnjavor (ibid.). As feminists have demonstrated in the face of assertions about innate violent and militaristic tendencies in men, if abnormal brutality was "built into" the Serbs, why would there have been a need to force Serb soldiers to commit such acts?

Filipović may offer the most sweeping demonization of "Bosnia's enemies," but the book's introduction is also concerned with the perpetrators, attempting to place equal emphasis on the individual rapists *and their communities*, as it does on women victims. To the women's statement rejecting the notion that they as victims should feel fear and shame, that it is the perpetrators who should feel shame and fear justice, the authors add, "[W]e also want for the communities, the societies that allowed the crime of rape because the women victims were not 'theirs,' not from their own communities, to awaken their collective conscience and accept what the civilized world accepted long ago, to condemn the crime of rape and to cleanse itself of it" (12). As it has been made clear who the perpetrators are, this passage suggests that Serbs lack honor, morality, and are as a group beneath civilization. Indeed, other sections of this text drive this home by asking whether the perpetrators feel shame. Bosniacs, on the other hand, as the victims, are constructed as a people whose morals and feelings "nurtured in us" by "our daughters, sisters, mothers, wives, women of honor" do not allow anyone—"no real 'male'"—to do such a thing: "a true man [*čovjek*] cannot do that to a woman, cannot order others to do that to a woman" (11). Bosniacs are thus elevated to a morally pure state in which men are honorable and strong and women nurturing and chaste, resonating with the Orientalist depictions of female purity discussed above in connection to analyses of wartime rape.

A public promotion for this book in Zenica further confirmed the significance to the book's promoters of the nation, rather than of women per se. Prominent Bosniac intellectuals and politicians, including Filipović, gave a series of speeches about the long suffering throughout history of the Bosniac nation. In often poetic language, they emphasized the honor, purity, and piety of the Bosniac woman, interchanging "woman" with "mother." One speaker, Irfan Ajanović, president of the BiH Union of Concentration Camp Torture Survivors, illustrated this with the "splendid poem" by the twentieth-century Bosnian/Yugoslav poet Skender Kulenović, also printed in the book,[68] the words of a devoted son to his mother, which Ajanović said "paints and represents the Bosnian woman, her patriarchal upbringing, her humble modesty, covered in blushing red *which emerges from the soul of Bosnia itself* and shines onto the pure cheek [*obraz*, "face" or reputation] of the Bosnian-Bosniac woman, showing her the world around her" (emphasis added). He thus tied Bosniac women's modesty and sexual purity to the land itself in a classic equation of women to (national) territory as the objects of (national, male) protection and defense (see, for example, Massad 1995; Mostov 1995; Verdery 1994).

All of the presenters were men, aside from a well-known Bosniac actress who did a dramatic reading of two harrowing testimonies from the book. In condemning the rapes and the war violence in general, Filipović warned that there is evil in humans—"there is the Devil!"—that there will always be violence, "But we can know that such things await us and we can be prepared rather than go along like lambs and leave our mothers, our sisters, and our children, our daughters, our granddaughters, to the bandits and wolves [*hajducima i vucima*]." The formulation made clear that "we" meant the men of the nation, charged with the protection of "their" women and that the evil resided not quite in humanity as a whole but in the nation's enemies, also designated male. The logic was no different from those embedded in Serb and Croat nationalist discourses, or indeed from many other nationalist imaginaries.

Also attending the promotion was a male Bosniac friend in his late twenties who often talked about his conscious efforts to resist nationalist thinking, "not to hate," despite his personal experiences as a victim of Serb ethnic cleansing. He remarked that the presentations had seemed to him like a "call to mobilization," directed to him as a male and therefore potential soldier—"Because I'd be the one to go [to the front], not them or their sons"—rather than an acknowledgment of the suffering of the women victims. "This book doesn't do anything for the women victims," he said as we left the venue, "it offers them no concrete or material help. It's pure politics." Indeed, though the hall was full of men and women members of the local elite (especially those around the ruling SDA), none of the women activists had been invited to the promotion, not even those at Medica Zenica who were well known locally for their years of work with women war victims, especially survivors of war rape, and who were mentioned in the book itself though they had not been consulted.[69] Absent, too, were any of the rape survivors themselves, although most of them did want to remain anonymous. The suffering of the women as gendered subjects was rendered a secondary issue.

Though there was a consistent insistence on preserving the honor and dignity of the women victims, the book simultaneously upheld conservative, traditionalist ideals of womanhood and therefore what honor and dignity might mean. The speeches at the book promotion and the book's poetry, drawings, and essays surrounding the testimonies were saturated with images of female purity, shame, innocence, and motherhood. The title of the book, *I Begged Them to Kill Me*, made clear that rape was to be perceived as a crime of honor after which any decent woman would not want to go on living. This is not to deny that many women experienced rape this way; the title is indeed a quotation from one of the women's testimonies, although there remain other possible meanings of this sentiment for the victims. However, the choice of this statement as the title and the definition of the crime as one against "the women *of Bosnia-Herzegovina*" underscore the idea that these rapes should be seen above all as crimes against women's and thus the nation's honor, rather than individual physical and psychological well-being.[70]

Although the authors were careful to recognize women's agency in speaking out, the absence of these women's voices at the promotion or in the framing essays of the book, indeed in anything except the testimonies of rape, constructed the primary actors as the men who introduced, explained, and framed the women's experiences consistently in terms of "we" and "they." Women's active roles were instead channeled into motherhood and accusations toward the enemy in the name of the nation. Women's suffering and sacrifice was equated with the sacrifices of soldiers fighting at the front lines and of (male) *logoraši* detained as civilians, all actions deemed as part of the struggle for Bosnia and Bosniacs—women who had been detained and raped had resisted the enemy's attempt "to kill Bosnia within [them]," as the book's introduction put it (Ajanović 1999, 14). The women victims are praised for their courage, yet they are expected to *want* to remain silent because of the shame of what has happened to them: "We know that it is very difficult for the tortured women, that they do not happily speak about the crime that has happened to them, about the trauma they feel. We do not insist that the abused women give public statements, that they expose themselves. . . . We just want them to record the truth" (ibid., 12). This could be interpreted as a similar stance to that taken by feminist advocates for women rape survivors such as the activists at Medica who refused to discuss individual women's cases or offer them up to journalists for interviews. Medica's concern was with protecting women from re-traumatization and from manipulation by the press, especially nationalist media (Andrić-Ružičić 2003). However, the overall framing of this book of testimonies points to different motives.

The Biggest Victims

The war thus (re)inscribed a firm connection between gender relations and women's honor on one hand and the nation on the other. The two images of female victimhood—the refugee and the rape victim—continued to dominate representations, both of women in BiH and of the victimhood of Bosniacs and Bosnia. As shown in further chapters, gender and nation were differently privileged in different circumstances but were seldom entirely separable. These categories of victimhood further exacerbated, and were intensified by, existing tensions between the rural and the urban, as well as notions about proper gender roles in society now that religious nationalism was so influential among a population that still believed in certain aspects of socialist gender equality and foreign actors' advocacy of secular, democratic citizenship. Narratives of war victimhood were key to these struggles in the postwar period.

During my research I often heard the claim that "women were the biggest victims in this war" (as in the title of one essay: Belić 1995). Indeed, female victims were very visible, especially the female survivors of Srebrenica and others attacked in ethnic cleansing campaigns. Survivors of sexualized violence were less visible, but the wartime rape of Muslim women was so well known as to add to the sense that women had been particularly victimized. Attacks on women, as on other civilians—a category fundamentally understood as innocent, as opposed to armed males—were a major element that drove the outrage over the Bosnian war. Images of Muslim men, as emaciated prisoners behind barbed wire in Serb detention camps, were also well known; they, too, emphasized the civilian status of the victims, even serving to link these atrocities to the Holocaust. Significantly, however, this was not a sexualized victimhood despite the existence of such violence against males.

What did the term "victim" imply? Take the case of Srebrenica, the largest single crime of the war in terms of the number of people affected. The very visible and mostly female survivors had been treated with cruelty and violence and suffered tremendously through initial rumors that their loved ones had survived, the practical difficulties they faced as refugees without homes or male breadwinners and protectors, and through the ordeal of DNA testing and waiting for years for the results of forensic investigations through mass graves in order to give their men a proper burial (see Wagner 2008). But it was males, including children, who were deliberately killed as such (Carpenter 2006; Jones 2000). Likewise, while women and girls were raped during ethnic cleansing campaigns and many were killed in the process, the intended message of humiliation and genetic contamination depended on most of these victims surviving. This was also the expectation of the population: they knew it was adult men who had to hide from attackers. Men were more vulnerable to killings while at the same time also being seen by perpetrators and victims alike as the defenders of women, children, and the elderly. It was also expected that men would be wounded and killed as soldiers fighting in military formations.

It is therefore not surprising that the overall male death toll of the war was much higher than that of females: according to one comprehensive study, 89.96 percent of the killed or missing were male, 10.04 percent female.[71] Military casualties of course add to this imbalance,[72] but even among the Bosniacs, the one ethnic group in which civilian outnumbered military deaths and the group with the greatest number of killed and missing, male deaths predominated at 86.64 percent.[73] As observers have noted for some time now, modern wars produce many more civilian than military casualties (Kaldor 2007; Nordstrom 2004). The international rules of war, however, continue to define civilian victims as outside the bounds of acceptable warfare; the only legitimate targets are military men. It is these norms that underlie our sense of tragedy and injustice over civilian, and especially female and child casualties. This is also why the dominant images of victimhood in the Bosnian war—of refugee women, raped women, and unarmed men behind barbed wire or murdered with their hands tied as in Srebrenica—have been so effective.

Victimhood in life or death carried different meanings, particularly in gendered terms. After the war, there was no question in BiH that men killed in the conflict were victims, but they were not often the first to be evoked by the term "victim." Those who suffered in survival were the most visible, and survivors were mostly women. At the same time, it was understood—just as the perpetrators intended—that a large part of why female survivors suffered was because their men had been killed or because their capacity to bear future offspring had been ruined. In other words, female survivors were considered victims both because of the pain and hardships of their lives as individuals and because they had been deprived of a life in normalized gender terms. The victim was therefore not merely a murdered man or suffering survivor but the nation, reduced physically in terms of numbers and symbolically by having to be represented by women.

Female victimhood was not only fundamental to imaginings of nation. It also served women's activism through narratives of victimhood on the basis of gender. In claiming that women were the biggest victims of the war, women NGO activists and their donors were not always countering dominant narratives of national victimhood by pointing to the suffering of actual women rather than the collective. There were also ways in which discussions of women as victims underscored notions of national victimhood (see chapter 4). But donors and women's NGO activists were engaged in activities on behalf of women: establishing that women were the "biggest," most deserving, most wronged victims thus underscored the legitimacy of their work, whether it tied in with or challenged nationalist paradigms. In this way, the wartime debates over whether to privilege gender or nation in naming the victim carried on in different guises in the postwar world of donors and NGOs.

3

 # The NGO Boom

Women's Organizing and Foreign Intervention in the Wake of War

The Postwar NGO Boom

During the first few years after the end of the war, NGOs were "springing up like mushrooms after the rain," as it seemed to Šehida, the leader of Bosanka in Zenica.[1] Cynical urbanites joked that any old nobody who could gather the signatures of twenty-nine of their relatives and friends (as the law then stipulated) could become an NGO. While many NGOs were local spin-offs of international NGOs with professionalized staff, there were also many groups of purely local origin. The latter were often a clutch of friends or even just one active person who registered as an NGO in hopes of garnering funding from a foreign donor. Some of these groups were the remnants of socialist-era community clubs, others had started out doing relief work during the war, and still others were coming together for the first time. Cargo cult–like, people all over BiH set up NGOs in hopes that the donations would come pouring in: if we build it, they will come![2] A large proportion of these were women's NGOs.

Much of the hope generated around NGOs reflected the rhetoric of donors and foreign intervention agencies who vigorously encouraged the formation of more and more NGOs as evidence for the growth of civil society and ultimately democracy (Sampson 2003; Stubbs 2007). NGOs and NGO projects were also funded as part of foreign initiatives to aid Bosnian women in response to the publicity over wartime rape and the widespread images of suffering women refugees, especially after the fall of Srebrenica in July 1995. Feminist observers, citing the great numbers of women's NGOs, marveled at the extent of the Bosnian "women's movement." But there were NGOs and there were NGOs: the label masked a range of formations, motivations, conceptualizations, and engagements with communities, donors, and the state.[3] It also hid the differing expectations of donors buried in their calls to build civil society, fight ethno-nationalism, democratize, or simply for BiH to "join Europe." Moreover, "women's NGO" and "women's issues" were terms applied to, and understood as, a wide range of stances and activities, from self-described feminists critical of established gender norms, to those who promoted a "return" to "traditional" women's roles in the patriarchal family, to everything in between. Because foreign donors were virtually the only source of funding available to local NGOs, their demands and policies exerted a profound influence over NGO activities and self-presentations. While groups calling themselves NGOs did not necessarily operate according to the models put forth by foreign actors, most of them tried to shape their activities to conform to ever-shifting trends in donor priorities. Thus, community activities and social outlets for women were described variously as psychosocial aid to traumatized women war victims, legal assistance, interethnic dialogue, work with minority women and returnees, and so on.

In this chapter, I introduce the main activists and organizations I studied in Zenica and beyond in order to give life to this range of approaches to issues of gender, ethno-national, and religious identities that mobilized various expressions of victimhood. I place this profile into the larger context of the NGO and women's activist "scenes," beginning with the discursive and material conditions set by foreign intervention agencies and donors who targeted women and women's NGOs as those who would rebuild society, overcome nationalist divisions, and care for the vulnerable. I then explain some of the disconnects and unintended consequences that arose in this arena, some of them common to other contexts of what has been termed neoliberal "NGOization" and some quite specific to postwar BiH. By taking a broader historical, cultural, and social view than is usually afforded in studies of NGOs, I show how the NGO model both facilitated and hindered local women's rights and gender equality activism. The conditions and paradoxes discussed here set the stage for the chapters that follow, which delve more deeply into the relationship of women's activism to nationalism, the political, and war victimhood, categories that appear here from the very start.

From Wartime Crisis Management to Postwar Reconstruction

While many foreign governmental, non-governmental, and transnational organizations and actors had been active in BiH during the war, the signing of the Dayton Agreement ushered in a shift from crisis intervention to projects and programs geared toward physical, social, and political reconstruction. Dayton had in fact established the authority of foreign-led institutions like the OHR, OSCE, UNHCR, and the rest of the alphabet soup of organizations that descended on BiH starting in early 1996. There were agencies that brought development and postconflict schemes forged in what was known as developing or Third World contexts, those implementing democratization projects throughout postsocialist Eastern Europe, those focused specifically on building political stability or aiding victims in BiH, and various kinds of (feminist and non-feminist) projects aimed at women as the biggest victims of the war.

The focus on NGOs followed dominant trends in Western aid since the 1980s, and especially in postsocialist countries after 1989, of building civil society as a key component of democratization. This was usually described as the sphere of independent associations that mediates between citizens and the state (Carothers 1996; Wedel 2001, 85–122), but in practice, donors focused much more narrowly on local NGOs, placing great importance on their number and distribution (see Belloni 2001; Gagnon 2002; Smillie 1996; Stubbs 1996, 2003). The imperative to strengthen civil society had added layers in BiH: following from the overall goal of undermining nationalist power, the idea of civil society as a sector independent of government control also appealed to foreign intervention agencies and donors as a space where the idea of a unified, multiethnic Bosnian state could be nurtured and put into practice.[4] The emphasis in BiH on opposing the nationalist-led state, however, clashed with other donor-inspired descriptions of civil society as a force that does not oppose but shapes and guides the state. The very concept of NGOs and civil society were therefore sources of confusion and contradictions surrounding the changing role of the state and state-like institutions, and citizens' relationships to these various levels of governance.[5]

Of course, as an alternative to official political structures and with most of the funding and legitimacy coming from liberal Western actors, the NGO sector was a natural refuge for human rights activists, feminists, and antinationalists. The number of participants in the NGO sector was inflated, however, by the incentives of donor funding, however short term and unreliable, in a bleak job market. This financial factor was a major point of suspicion for NGOs' detractors, and the suspicion was often gendered.

Women and women's NGOs predominated in this "third sector" first because it was a new area that was relatively independent from established circles of (male-dominated) power, although it was not lucrative or perhaps stable enough to be of interest to the truly powerful.[6] Social positioning also factored in women's predominance in NGOs engaged in refugee return and reconciliation initiatives: as those structurally and ideologically excluded from the male pursuits of politics and war-making, women more easily crossed ethnicized boundaries of hostility and difference. Moreover, in communities hard hit by ethnic cleansing or male war deaths, women were nearly the only adults left. Dominant conservative notions of gender and women's roles, both locally and among foreign actors, were also key; they were certainly articulated more often, masking the effects of social structure. NGO work converged smoothly with ideas of proper or natural female pursuits, as most NGOs professed to be apolitical and many were also engaged in some form of nurturing work: social service provision and work with children, refugees, and other socially vulnerable categories, including women. It was such notions, typically expressed in affirmative essentialist terms, that were mobilized to promote women's participation in social reconstruction and democratization.

Donor Approaches to Gender and Women

Issues of gender were not high on the list of priorities for the main actors of the "international community." The Dayton Agreement was a case in point: the document makes no mention of women or gender, despite their importance to social and political organization, which Dayton addresses at length (Rees 2002), and despite the global attention to wartime rape (Skjelsbaek 2004, 26).[7] Nevertheless, Dayton also made BiH a signatory to every major international human rights treaty, including the Convention on the Elimination of All Forms of Discrimination against Women (CEDAW), as these were made part of the new constitution (see Inglis 1998). During my initial fieldwork, "women's issues" generally took a back seat to other issues that were seen (by donors and by local male political elites) as more pressing. Over time, many agencies and organizations gradually put in place special gender units and projects, and in the early 2000s the Finnish government bankrolled the establishment of a state-level Gender Equality Agency and entity-level Gender Centers as part of the state apparatus.[8] On the whole, however, intervention agencies were most intent on facilitating refugee return and setting up political and financial institutions that would function in a unified state;

women's rights and gender were prominent buzzwords in NGO and human rights circles but seldom figured in high-level politics.

On the micro level, however, women were turned to specifically, their particular qualities praised and encouraged, through what was often essentialist rhetoric—both traditionalist and feminist—about women as natural peacemakers, and thus the ones to lead ethnic reconciliation and refugee return. Donors addressed existing women's organizations and individual women whom they helped to establish NGOs, in addition to targeting women in politics. Largely due to their gendered position as non-combatants and outside politics, women were in fact in a much more favorable position than men to undertake such reconciliation efforts, and many of them did. The fact that women have dominated cross-ethnic contacts and anti-nationalist initiatives since the war began (Cockburn 1998; Cockburn et al. 2001) was a particular source of pride for these women and one that donors, local activists, and others promoting women's role in reconciliation liked to emphasize.

The donor landscape was as diverse as that of women's activism. Some donors targeted women for the accomplishment of goals having little to do with gender relations, in effect rendering gender inequalities invisible, even naturalized. There were others, however, many of them self-identified feminists, that specifically sought to advance the cause of women's rights or gender equality. These were often smaller, independent organizations formed out of women's and peace movements abroad that channeled funding from their own donors to implement projects locally in the region (Kvinna til Kvinna from Sweden, Medica Mondiale from Germany, and the STAR project from the United States were examples). There were also many individuals within donor and intervention agencies with feminist sensibilities who pushed for varying levels of program commitment to gender equality even when their superiors paid little attention to these issues. Donors and women in the local NGO sector were indeed responsible for many steps toward increased gender equality (see Lithander 2000; Rees 2002; Walsh 2000).

Projects that did address gender hierarchies tended to be designed by development officials working within liberal feminist or Women-in-Development paradigms (see, for example, Kabeer 1994; Visvanathan et al. 1997). They were therefore consciously infused with the language of gender equality and images of women in powerful, decision-making positions. As just one example, an informational bulletin from the US government–initiated, UNHCR-administrated Bosnian Women's Initiative (BWI) fund stated: "The BWI offers opportunities for women in both urban and rural areas of Bosnia and Herzegovina to become *full participants in the economic recovery* of their country and to become *decision-makers and leaders*" (Bosnian Women's Initiative n.d., 2;

emphasis added). It went on to list the "empowerment of women" as one of its key objectives. Like other donors concerned specifically with improving conditions for women, the BWI declared its support for the implementation of major international women's human rights declarations. However, as Erin Baines (2004) shows, the BWI program was ultimately hijacked by the goal of refugee return, which sidelined gender equality issues but appears to have provided a baseline for positive, feminist-inspired rhetoric about the role of women in the refugee return process.

More often, however, and when donor and NGO initiatives were explained to local audiences (typically of local NGO women), the call for women to take part in economic and political processes was bolstered by essentialist rhetoric about women as nurturers and peacemakers—affirmative essentialisms. These were moral claims about women's value to society that relied fundamentally on their roles as mothers and keepers of the home and on gender stereotypes about women's more peaceful and empathetic nature. Whether they represented local NGOs or foreign-funded initiatives, foreigners and locals both tended to reproduce such rhetoric as a way of encouraging local women to take part and, indirectly but perhaps more importantly, for their husbands, fathers, and male political authorities to accept the women's roles. Much in the way that Fox describes for late colonial India (1996; and see introduction), affirmative essentialisms were useful both for mobilizing women in conservative communities and for encouraging more active roles in society as advocated by feminists who hoped that they would have the gradual effect of bringing women further into public and political roles. Thus, while there was a range of immediate donor goals concerning women, for local audiences the message reinforced the primacy of women's domestic roles as wives, mothers, and nurturers, even if it sometimes also argued against dominant attitudes and practices that discouraged women from taking part in arenas seen as public or political.

Geographies of Activism after Dayton

The postwar distribution and character of NGOs was affected by the geography of the war itself as much as by the territorial settlement of the Dayton Agreement, the policies of intervention agencies and foreign governments, and longstanding regional differences within the country. Many postwar women's organizations got their start during the war providing humanitarian and social services, supporting the armed forces, and aiding refugees and other needy populations. Some of these groups were local extensions of projects begun by foreigners who wanted to limit their involvement in the region after the war had ended but also to leave something behind or encourage locals to take "ownership" of the reconstruction process. Because of their wartime origins, many of these NGOs were located in towns that served as refugee collection points during the war, almost exclusively in the Muslim-controlled territories as it was Muslims, the majority of victims especially in the early parts of the war, that foreigners had come to help. Zenica and Tuzla were two such places, while Sarajevo and (East) Mostar also hosted many refugees as well as foreign aid projects despite being under attack for much of the war.

It took some time after the war for major Western donors and intervention agencies to begin operating in the RS- and Croat-dominated areas, although they became particularly active when Bosniac refugees began returning to their homes in those territories. NGOs in Serb- and Croat-dominated areas therefore got started later, with the exception of several local activists who had organized themselves to work on human rights issues or aid to refugees. In fact, as late as 1999, OSCE's democratization section was making a concerted effort to encourage the establishment of NGOs in the most politically hard-line areas of the RS and Croat territories, places they labeled "neglected areas" and targeted for NGO creation as a way of combating local support for separatist nationalisms. NGOs in Serb- and Croat-dominated areas also tended to engage with issues less tied to the war: for women's NGOs this meant

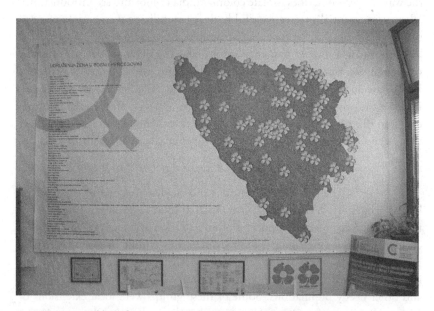

Figure 9 Map and list of partner women's NGOs in Bosnia-Herzegovina on the wall in the office of Žene ženama (Women to Women), Sarajevo. Photographed April 2007. (photo by author)

domestic violence, legal aid to women, combating sex trafficking, and promoting women's participation in formal politics. Women's NGOs in the Bosniac-dominated areas worked on these issues, too, alongside or after the initial focus on war victims.

Women's Organizations in This Study

The organizations I studied were all NGOs in that they were not governmental, but they did not all make consistent use of this label, nor did this rule out their receiving funds or facilities from local governmental bodies. My initial criteria for seeking out groups were that they be made up primarily of women and that they profess, through names or mission statements, to exist for the betterment of women's lives, however defined. In later research, I more specifically sought out organizations of direct war victims, which were much less concerned with women's or gender issues per se and thus did not describe themselves as women's NGOs. However, approaches varied widely even among NGOs that received donor funds for women's rights or gender equality issues. Stances and practices in regard to ethnicity, nationalism, and BiH as a multiethnic state were also tied up in negotiations over the role of independent organizations.

Medica Zenica and Infoteka

As a well-established and self-declared feminist, anti-nationalist organization, Medica Zenica was the NGO that had drawn me to Zenica. It had been established during the war (April 1993) when Zenica was a refuge for mostly Bosniac refugees fleeing ethnic cleansing. Feminists from Germany led by gynecologist Monika Hauser had come here with the goal of helping women survivors of wartime rape at the earliest possible point after their release from detention camps and war zones (Cockburn 1998). Engaging local women psychologists, medical professionals, translators, and others with needed skills and enthusiasm, including some of the war victims themselves and friends and family members of the original staff, the project grew into a women's therapy center offering holistic treatment of various kinds of war trauma through medical, psychological, spiritual, and material help. Outpatient care, including counseling and free gynecological check-ups for all women, as well as abortion services for a time,[9] expanded its reach to the broader community, even traveling to out of the way neighborhoods and refugee centers with a mobile medical clinic. Medica's three locations also provided vocational training, child-care, and a shelter for women trauma survivors, which later housed women fleeing abusive homes as the organization, in local hands since just after the end of the war, shifted its focus to combating domestic violence.

Medica was quite big. It was in fact a major employer and provider of multiple services for women in addition to being a locus of political activism. The main facilities and offices, including the medical and psychological units, residential facilities for clients, a child-care center, administrative offices, and Infoteka (the information and documentation office), were not far from the city center in a rented utilitarian building that had once housed a state kindergarten. A house, owned by the NGO and perched upon a steep hill in a peripheral neighborhood, held vocational training and extra residential space, and a third project with rural refugee women had been established in the town of Visoko, on the road toward Sarajevo. At its peak, Medica employed over seventy women (and a few men as guards and drivers), a majority of them Bosniacs, as in the surrounding population, but with plenty of non-Bosniacs, including several in prominent positions. The organization was accepted by the local authorities but did not participate in the social and political activities of the SDA establishment and was regarded by many in the town as an arm of foreign interests.

The German activists, having formed an NGO of their own in Germany called Medica Mondiale, continued to fully fund Medica Zenica until they gradually scaled back their support beginning during my stay in Zenica in 1999 and 2000.[10] From this point, Medica was forced to apply for donor funding like other NGOs, but they were already quite well networked and known in BiH, internationally, and among feminist circles in the successor states of Yugoslavia. It was the activists at Infoteka, a younger group than most other women's NGO activists, as well as the therapists (the "psycho-team"), whom I got to know the best. These were the most vocally feminist women of the project and those most active in Medica's advocacy work with the public. Infoteka in fact established itself as an independent, feminist NGO in 2009 when it and Medica parted ways after disagreements precipitated by a crisis of funding.

The Association of Women Intellectuals "Bosanka"

As its full name implies, Bosanka (the female form of "Bosnian") saw itself as a group of educated women whose main task was to help other women and their community as a whole through educative and cultural activities. The organization grew out of the wartime humanitarian activities of another women's group called Sumejja (named after the first female martyr to Islam; it had branches in many Bosniac dominated towns of BiH). Through

Sumejja, Šehida, a judge and former teacher, and other urban professional women began organizing language courses and medical-aid teams. Edina, a dentist, volunteered her professional services, often pulling hundreds of rotten teeth each week in exchange for apples from village orchards, which the women then distributed to wounded soldiers in the hospital. In 1994, Šehida and Edina decided to form Bosanka as an organization that would undertake educational activities instead of "just" humanitarian aid as had become the case with Sumejja.

Bosanka was small, with no more than ten active members when I met them, but there had been more previously. These were educated urban women in their late forties and fifties—a judge, several teachers, a school principal, a lawyer, and a few doctors—who felt the burdens of their own privilege in a kind of noblesse oblige toward their less fortunate sisters in the villages. These were the women who most vehemently objected to the CNN images of disheveled, rural Bosnian women "with five scarves on their heads," as Mensura, an active Bosanka member and local assemblywoman put it. "We're not just old peasant women like the world media showed," she complained once when I asked her about the motivations behind her activism, but sophisticated, emancipated professionals with "dignity." It was not by chance, then, that Bosanka's educational seminars, on topics from basic hygiene and health to Bosniac identity and the role of women in Islam, were targeted precisely at village women, that part of the population that had provided the problematic images.

When I first contacted Bosanka members in 1997, I was drawn to them as an organization that promoted Bosniac identity and (conservative) women's roles in the nation. They seemed to me like a perfect counterpart to groups like Medica. They were largely unfunded, operating after working hours on a volunteer basis with occasional funding for short projects or donations of space; they were decidedly local with networks contained mostly within the Bosniac-dominated towns of the BiH Federation. Bosanka members explicitly eschewed the term feminism, said nothing about women's rights or equality, and seemed to advocate and affirm conservative, patriarchal roles for women that supported nationalist agendas such as motherhood and marriage, producing traditional handicrafts, cooking national dishes, nurturing religion, and so forth. Their insistence on their educated, urban identities was not incompatible with this vision but was utterly consistent with patterns typical of their generation of educated women professionals that had established their lives under socialism.

When I returned in 1999, however, Bosanka's village seminars had mostly ceased, though Šehida still talked about organizing another one, or at least taking me to a village to show me an "authentic Bosnian woman," by which she meant Bosniac. In fact, I offered to drive us to a village any time she was free but the trip never materialized. Other members who had been more vocal proponents of nationalist views and affirmations of Muslim identity now had little time for the group. Šehida, whom I saw on a regular basis, continued to operate on behalf of Bosanka but also became more involved in the Bosnian League of Women Voters as it enjoyed a spurt of donor funding. As a result—and I cannot rule out my own unintentional influence through our frequent discussions—her personal views and way of speaking began to change as she interacted with a wider network of women's NGOs, including those from Serb and Croat areas, that advocated interethnic communication and challenged commonly accepted gender roles for women. She was still able to straddle both the worlds of conservative, "patriotic" Bosniacs and of the progressive NGO/donor scene but the shift in her priorities meant that Bosanka activities would never return to the days of educating village girls about Muslim identity.

Naš most

Not far from Zenica's central market, tucked into the space between a socialist-built school, an Ottoman-era mosque, and the huge block of workers' apartments known as the *Kineski zid* or Great Wall of China, were a cluster of narrow streets and private houses, one of which served as the headquarters of Naš most (Our Bridge). Razija, its charismatic leader whose house they used, emphasized that the organization was for "ordinary women," meaning mostly working-class women, both Zenica locals and refugees.[11] Their focus was broadly on social activities and income generation for women, with the idea being that women could help each other out, learn from each other's experiences, and generally become stronger when they banded together. It was therefore a sort of "catch-all" organization (Belloni 2001; Smillie 1996; Stubbs 1996; World Bank 2002); activities ranged from all-women social gatherings, to rug-weaving, sewing, and selling traditionally female handicrafts, to microcredit loan schemes. As one of the administrators told a prospective member who stopped by the office one day, "Any activity that helps women earn some money (*da zaradi koji dinar*) is good. That's why we exist."

At the time of my fieldwork, Naš most had over five hundred members and was rapidly growing, owing to a requirement that women joining a foreign-funded micro-credit loan scheme also join the association. The micro-credit scheme, financed and designed by the American aid agency Catholic Relief Services (CRS), was wildly popular, as unemployment rates, especially for those without higher degrees or elite connections, were very high and ordinary families, many of them headed by women, were struggling to make ends meet. Unlike professionalized NGOs like Medica, Naš most was still struggling to negotiate the world of foreign donors, to learn "NGO-speak" (Wedel 2001; see also Sampson 1996) and how to tailor their proposals to donor priorities. Gradually they had managed to secure foreign funding for several projects, which helped them pay basic operating expenses and stipends for the handful of women who served as regular staff. Still, they were frustrated with the sometimes opaque process of garnering funds, and their membership was overwhelmingly volunteer.

It is difficult to pin down Naš most's stance, even an official one, on gender or ethnic relations. Their focus on helping women survive the postwar economy attracted a wide variety of members. The majority was Bosniac but the group was actively recruiting non-Bosniacs, partially due to the demands of one of their funded projects but also following the general heartfelt conviction that Bosniacs should lead and support a multiethnic BiH society. Non-Bosniacs remained minorities in the group, as they now were in the community in general. And while those women were explicitly welcomed, Razija and several core members also nurtured an interest in the affirmation of Bosniac and Muslim traditions, "especially after Milošević worked so hard to destroy Bosniac identity," as Razija explained to me. But Naš most, she said, was more about "struggling for the rights of women"—only "not the feminist kind" of struggle, she was quick to add, but one that would build "a complete woman—woman as a mother, worker, etc." As among Bosanka members, then, gender issues and women's rights were conceived at Naš most in much the same way they were approached under socialism. Women were to be "mothers, wives, workers," and active in their communities, while taking primary responsibility for the home and the family (Meznarić 1985; Sklevicky 1989a).

Religious Activists

My interest in the intersection of gender and nation led me to seek out women's organizations that specifically catered to Bosniac women. These tended to be religiously oriented—given the political correctness of multiethnicity among both Bosniac nationalists and the Western donor-oriented groups, religion was the only reason any group tended to give for being ethnically exclusive. As I spoke with these women and attended their activities, I was looking for variation in the relationship between religion and ethno-national identity as well as in the ways in which gender was articulated. I was intrigued to encounter two devout, religiously trained women who identified themselves as (Islamic) feminists, but neither of these women was active in women's NGOs specifically for Muslim women. The latter maintained quite conservative views of women's roles in keeping with the form of Islam they followed.

Merjem (Arabic for Mary, mother of Jesus) was one of these conservative women's NGOs in Zenica. Their leader, Ramiza, and most of the core women of the organization were both devout Muslims and members of the SDA. Ramiza and several others wore Islamic dress but more in the colorful prints favored by village woman than the dark, plain urban styles worn by younger religious women. Merjem had been formed as an outlet for older women interested in learning more about Islam and their national identity. Ramiza was clear, however, that their activities were not political because they revolved mostly around religious education and "socializing" (*druženje*) among women (see chapter 5). They organized women's excursions, often to religious events or sites, and frequently joined Naš most in organizing women's *sijela* (social gatherings), especially for March 8 (International Women's Day). Like the women of Naš most, they stressed that Merjem members were ordinary women—"housewives and villagers" in Ramiza's words—not intellectuals like the women at Bosanka or Medica. Indeed, Ramiza did not appear to have thought particularly deeply about the role of women, religion, or ethnicity in society, though other members of the group had very specific ideas.

Merjem had never been funded by a Western donor, nor had they tried to be. They had no office and often met in the coffee house of the local branch of Preporod, the Bosniac cultural society with strong links to the SDA and the Bosniac national movement. During the war they had received funding for various projects from foreign Muslim donors. Throughout my time in Zenica their regular Islamic study classes were financed by local Islamic activists (the Active Islamic Youth) who followed neo-Salafist forms of Islam and opposed the official Islamic Community (see, for example, Bougarel 2003, 2005). The rest of Merjem's activities were self-financed and they remained a locally focused organization that did not speak the language of the NGO world.

Although the women of Merjem seemed proud of their successes despite a lack of regular funding, Ramiza seemed slightly resentful of another Zenica women's organization, Kewser, which, she said, had been financed by "the Iranians." In fact, Kewser's leader and most of its religious members had moved back to Sarajevo when the war ended, and the women who remained in Zenica were no longer an NGO but ran a for-profit daycare center based on Islamic instruction. In Sarajevo, Aiša, Kewser's founder and president (the name is Arabic for source/spring), continued a full program of religious, educational, and social programs for women and their children, including a female choir and the publication of a magazine for religious Muslim women called

Zehra. All of these activities reflected their belief in men and women's innate differences and a distinct division of gender roles whereby women were primarily oriented toward motherhood, the upbringing of their children, and the maintenance of religiously devout households. Unlike most Bosnian women's NGO participants, Aiša did not shy away from describing Kewser's activities as political, yet she also maintained that formal politics and high leadership positions were not a place for women. "The upbringing of children, voting, the economy—all of this is politics, and it's also all connected with ethics and faith," she explained when I interviewed her over coffee. Kewser was decidedly focused on Islam and Bosniac identity and all of its members were Muslims. This had not prevented them from participating in some cross-ethnic dialogue initiatives, although Aiša maintained that Bosnia's ethnic groups would be better off living perhaps nearby but not intermingled together as the dominant sentiment had it.

Refugee Women's NGOs

At several women's NGO gatherings, primarily within the networks of Bosanka's Šehida, and later in multiple visits to their communities, I got to know the main activists of two NGOs of refugee women. While these groups participated in the same donor-sponsored circles that promoted women's rights, democratic values of (ethnic) tolerance, and a multiethnic BiH state, they also had their own very specific local concerns. Namely, both groups were active as Bosniac refugees who sought to return to their original homes now firmly within Serb-controlled territories (the RS). Members of both groups had suffered atrocities at the hands of Serb forces, including their Serb neighbors who had taken part in ethnic cleansing operations. Both groups professed the desire to live again among Serbs. They would not forget, however, and participated in initiatives to remember the victims and prosecute perpetrators.

Srcem do mira (Through Heart to Peace) was started by women who had been refugees in Zagreb working with Žena BiH and allied with Kareta, Bedem ljubavi, and other nationalist women's groups that insisted on the ethnic dimensions of the war (see chapter 2). These were women from around Prijedor in northwest BiH, especially the large Bosniac village of Kozarac. This had been one of the first areas to be ethnically cleansed by Serb forces; community leaders and men had been killed, most of the population had been detained in area camps, and women had been raped, including some of the members of Srcem do mira. At the end of the war, women and what was left of their families had returned to Bosniac-controlled areas of the Federation, living in the houses of displaced Serbs in Sanski Most and other towns close to their former homes, now across the entity border in the RS. When I first met them, they were working to return to their homes; by the end of my 1999–2000 fieldwork, the organization had moved to Kozarac, where its leader Almasa and most of its members had returned, and were engaged in a variety of NGO activities in what was rapidly again becoming a Bosniac-dominated community as it was before the war.

Srcem do mira offered a typical range of psychosocial activities for women, including educational courses, psychological counseling, and seminars in non-violent communication, women in politics, ethnic reconciliation, or whatever was being funded by accessible donor projects. Their office and activity space was at first in Almasa's house but later moved to a large building built on Srcem do mira's behalf, which they called the House of Peace. Typical of many NGOs, Srcem do mira was mostly driven by its leader and her personality. Almasa, a youthful, always friendly woman whose husband had survived the war and whose children were entering adulthood, was well connected among donors, intervention agencies, and other BiH women's organizations like Bosanka and the League of Women Voters, of which she was also a member. The organization also maintained its own connections to groups of sympathetic women in the UK, US, and elsewhere, many of whom journeyed to Kozarac in late May of each year to commemorate the Serb attack on the town in 1992. Almasa also traveled extensively, establishing solidarity with other refugee women's groups, including Žene s Podrinja, the second such NGO I got to know. Srcem do mira's NGO networks did not overlap much with those of Medica and other explicitly feminist and anti-nationalist NGOs. Their relationship to ethnic divisions was in fact troublesome from the point of view of local peace activists and area Serbs, as they often stressed the moral superiority of Bosniacs as victims of the war and the corresponding guilt of Serbs. In terms of gender ideology, they were somewhat typical of the bulk of Bosnian women's NGOs that advocated respect for women and their active social roles but within acceptable limits of dominant patriarchal norms.

Žene s Podrinja (Women of Podrinje) was made up of refugees from the Drina basin in Eastern Bosnia, the area that includes Srebrenica, but was based in the Sarajevo suburb of Ilidža where many Bosniac refugees lived.[12] Zahida, their leader, was its charismatic core. A robust middle-aged woman with grown children, she cut a small-town appearance with her matronly dresses and beehive bun. She was always jolly and welcoming and loved to make jokes, even about herself. She was willing, even more than many of her NGO's members, to reach out to Serb women in her determination to re-create her former life even after her husband had been murdered by Serb forces in the ethnic cleansing of 1992 (see Helms 2010a).

Žene s Podrinja was, even more than Srcem do mira, a "catch-all" NGO that engaged in whatever it could get funding for while also pursuing its goals of return. Unlike Srcem do mira, however, the group boasted several Serb members from Bratunac, the town Zahida was hoping to return to, and in time acquired many more, mostly participants in a donor-funded income generating project. Zahida skillfully adapted her rhetoric to accommodate both donor priorities and her personal goals. As she explained to me, she advised other women's NGOs to channel their activities into "multiethnic work, inter-entity communication," because "that's what's going now" in terms of attracting donor funds. Zahida did not mind the language of feminism or women's rights that she heard at NGO gatherings, although she did not use it much herself. Her views on gender were in line with dominant norms but she was also ready to take advantage of them in order to achieve her goals.

War Rape Survivors and the Women of Srebrenica

In the mid-2000s, two new women's organizations came on the scene, bringing a new visibility to the topic of wartime rape. I describe my research with these groups in chapter 6, reflecting on the figure of the raped woman in contrast to that of the "women of Srebrenica."[13] But they are also interesting for the way in which they related to the world of donors and NGOs, ethnic reconciliation, and women's rights.

The Association of Women Victims of War (Udruženje žena žrtve rata, ŽŽR), established in 2003, by 2008 claimed over 3,000 members in BiH and abroad, all of them women who had survived rape. After it became possible in 2006 to qualify for state benefits as a victim of sexual violence in the war, around thirty men also joined the association. The vast majority of the members were publicly silent; it was the dynamic president of ŽŽR, Bakira Hasečić, who was the most active, including making frequent statements to the press. (In several visits to their office, I never saw more than three or four other women, though these women always changed.) Despite strong rumors that ŽŽR was closely linked to Haris Silajdžić's pro-Bosniac Party for Bosnia-Herzegovina, Hasečić always described the group as "multiethnic, multina-tional, and non-party." ŽŽR members were overwhelmingly Bosniac due to the patterns of the violence, but Hasečić made it a point to mention that they also had non-Bosniac members, including one Serb woman who had been raped by a Bosniac soldier.[14] They also said they were unfunded, although they received many in-kind and cash donations and were provided an office by the local gov-ernment. The office was far away from the city center and inaccessible by pub-lic transport but Hasečić, who was employed full time in an administrative job, had a nice car in which she delivered donations to organization members and traveled to other towns, including her hometown of Višegrad, now controlled by Serbs. Despite constant threats, Hasečić and organization members were active as witnesses in war crimes trials, protesting judgments or political decisions they considered unjust, and lobbying for aid and improved legal status for victims of wartime rape.

The Women's Section (*Sekcija žena*) of SULKS, the association of *logoraši* that had published the book of war rape testimonies, was informally founded in 2001, although its members had been active in the union since its formation in 1996. In 2009 it became an official subgroup of SULKS. The members had all been detained in Serb camps during the war and had thus experienced various traumas, including the threat of rape, but not all had been raped. Still, they became vocal advocates for rape survivors, especially after many of them contributed testimonies to *I Begged Them to Kill Me* (see chapter 2). Members were almost exclusively Bosniac (there were camp-survivor organizations of Serbs and Croats elsewhere). Their primary goal was the improvement of material conditions for their members as well as supporting processes of postwar justice and commemoration. In addition to their advocacy work and participation in war crimes prosecutions and investigations, they were in many ways a typical psychosocial project, offering foreign language and computer skills classes and running an income-generating sewing workshop for women with periodic visits by a psychologist for group therapy. Their funding for utilities and salaries for two office workers came from the Sarajevo Canton Ministry for Veterans' Affairs, and space was donated by the municipality. They were not particularly well versed in "NGO-speak" or project-writing and therefore struggled to secure additional funding.

The two most prominent associations of Srebrenica survivors, generally known as the Srebrenica women or mothers, were Women of Srebrenica (Žene Srebrenice) based in Tuzla and the Movement of Mothers of the Enclaves of Srebrenica and Žepa (Pokret majke enklava Srebrenice i Žepe) based in Sarajevo.[15] The two groups' twin areas of activity were in the search for the missing men presumed killed in the Srebrenica genocide and the quest to bring the perpetrators to justice. They also distributed aid among their members and in general acted as collective support groups. At times the two organizations were rivals for funding or recognition while at other times they jointly and publicly confronted international officials or local politicians with harsh critiques. Like the rape survivor organizations, these groups did not participate in women's NGO circles. In fact, they never saw themselves as women's NGOs. They were made up of women and referred to themselves as such but they were not concerned with the position of women per se.

Women's Agendas, Donor Agendas

In one way or another, many of the areas of tension and struggle with which NGOs and their donors had to grapple revolved around the
concept of the NGO and the way in which it was promoted by foreign intervention agencies and donors. In fact, it is difficult even to write about these
groups without using the very categories that were called into question by local
reception and practice. While foreign intervention agencies tended to label
any independent group an NGO, and every group of women a women's NGO,
everyday understandings of community engagement, organized groups, donors,
and gender underpinned a more complex set of categories used to describe
what "women's NGOs" were doing. I thus explore here more precisely the
meanings and historical-cultural legacies of concepts such as NGO, women's,
and activism.

The NGO as Claim-Bearing Label

Not all local organizations regularly or consistently called
themselves NGOs. In fact, NGO was not a legal category—under the old
socialist-era law, the term was "association of citizens," while a 2001 reform
allowed groups to register as associations or foundations. What the members
of local organizations called their groups, and in which settings, was therefore
telling. "NGO" was, especially for those who had been adults under socialism, a conscious departure from natural speech at first (World Bank 2002).
Under socialism, community-level associations had been organized around
interests like folklore, skiing, chess, or pigeon breeding. Like the socialist-era
women's groups I discuss below, they were at least officially and by reputation
apolitical, though they functioned with Communist Party approval (Andjelic
2003).

From the war period on, "NGO" became associated with foreign funding and other forms of support. It was the groups in these donor circles, where
the ideas of NGOs as the key to civil society and democracy were heavily
promoted, that regularly used this label and that were seen by others as a
new form. It was part of the language of "NGO-speak." But there were other
organizations hopeful of attracting foreign funding for whom the claim to
belong to the "NGO sector" was not only a plea to be included into the ranks
of the funded but also to be accepted and validated—as individuals as well
as groups—as cultured agents of democratic tolerance rather than the petty,
tribal nationalists as they felt the media had unfairly painted them. NGOs
became associated with the West and Europe with all their purported modern
attributes, from cosmopolitanism and enlightened human rights standards to

the material accessories of computers, mobile phones, jeeps, and nice offices (Sampson 2003).

As such the NGO attribution operated as what Dorothea Hilhorst calls a "claim-bearing label" (Hilhorst 2003, 6–8): what people called their organizations conveyed more about their aspirations and desired messages to specific audiences than the actual form of activity. Calling one's group an NGO was meant to signify that one was "doing good" (Fisher 1997) for society. In the Bosnian context, it was also a way to distance oneself from the widely distrusted realm of "dirty" politics, government, and corrupt business dealings. I thus often heard organization leaders say the words "non-governmental organization" rather than use the acronym NGO (NVO in Bosnian), also adding "non-party" and "non-profit" to their list of descriptors, lest their meaning be lost. For similar reasons, it was common to stress the humanitarianism of NGOs as the polar opposite of the political. To be an NGO was to claim moral superiority, an interest in the well-being of others, even patriotism or ethno-national pride, but by no means motivated, like politicians, by personal power or financial gain. Being a *women's* NGO or humanitarian organization only intensified this claim to moral purpose.

"Non-governmental" was also sometimes perceived as a threat by local government officials who interpreted the label as "*anti*-governmental" or, at best, regarded NGOs as irrelevant. It was difficult to shake this suspicion since most NGOs received funds and support from foreign sources, and furthermore operated largely outside of government control, often including an avoidance of taxation. This situation also meant that NGOs were not overly concerned with how they were seen by local officials or even community members (see Henderson 2003; Hrycak 2006; Stubbs 1997). It was only with time, as donor priorities shifted and government authority stabilized, that some NGOs realized a need to cooperate with local governments and started to gain their trust and support.

The NGO label was also less effective among the general population, many of whom were skeptical of foreign-supported NGOs and the locals who worked for them for, it was imagined, enormous salaries. NGOs offering social services such as the free women's health clinic at Medica were evaluated much more positively than those perceived to be pursuing "political" goals like social or legal change (Grødeland 2006), especially when women were involved or established gender conventions were challenged. Medica, therefore, was often praised for its free services to women, especially war victims, but criticized when its leaders appeared in public calling for an end to sexist practices or identifying as feminists. In everyday speech, then, NGOs were referred to more according to their particular character: an NGO offering social services might be referred to as a humanitarian organization, one that ran a youth center would be called just that, and a women's group known to organize women's social events would be called an "association of women" (*udruženje žena*). There was little popular sense of the "NGO sector" as a potential force for collective action or performing a watchdog function on government, as donors advocated.[16] Such language was confined mainly to those NGOs that saw themselves in these roles, their donors, and democratization officials, as well as in media coverage of NGO events.

Aktiv žena: *Prewar Continuities and Organizational Styles*

Even among groups that called themselves NGOs, the model promoted by donors was not always embraced or even understood fully. There was enough vagueness so that every organization could say it was representing the "grassroots" and working to instill democratic values—ethnic tolerance, gender equality, support to democratically elected leaders, and so on. Women's organizations like Bosanka, Naš most, or even Medica could call themselves NGOs for audiences of donors or the other NGOs in donor-funded circles, but in the local community they were more likely to call themselves a women's association. In fact, Medica activists used this as a tactic to avoid the much maligned and misunderstood association with feminism while still staying true to their principles. "Women's association" was a more familiar term but as such it also evoked more familiar modes of women's activities in the community, which were based on longstanding patterns of social organization as well as socialist-era institutions of women's activism.

The type of women's group that most defied donor expectations for political engagement and commitment to gender equality was modeled on the socialist-era *aktiv žena* (women's "active" or auxiliary). Far removed from state-level women's activities that succeeded the more assertive AFŽ of the World War II era, but still under the umbrella of local Communist Party cells, *aktiv žena* groups upheld party policies but strictly avoided "political" issues (Sklevicky 1989a, 103).[17] Instead, operating on a limited local level, they organized charity drives (e.g., collecting toys for poor children), community improvement activities (cleaning up the local park), or women's social events (excursions to other towns or celebrations of March 8). Once the 1990s war started, it took little conceptual or organizational effort for women to mobilize in support of the needy in their midst, including cooking for the army and caring for wounded soldiers. Several groups whose offices I visited in various Bosniac-dominated towns displayed certificates of appreciation from the Bosnian Army for their help during the war. In several places, as with Žene s Podrinja's first incarnation, these wartime groups even called themselves "*Aktiv žena.*" When the war ended, initiatives that did not fold refashioned themselves into NGOs to compete for donor support (see World Bank 2002).

Another important continuity lies in patterns of gender-segregated social activity, according to which it was expected and natural for women to gather together and engage with other women more than in mixed groups (see Bringa 1995; Sorabji 1994). Men had their own male-dominated arenas: politics, business, sports, pubs, the military, and so on. Women had neighborhood coffee visits, socializing at work, and *aktiv žena* activities as acceptable—respectable—venues in which to meet outside the home. These patterns contributed to the establishment of many more women's NGOs as simply groups of women than as groups concerned with changing established gender hierarchies, much to the dismay of some visiting feminist donors and activists. All-women groups were considered the most respectable social outlets for women, both married and unmarried, and were a natural outgrowth of social networks and neighborly relations in neighborhoods and villages.

These patterns were most pronounced in rural areas and small towns or among people from such areas (regardless of ethno-religious background), though there was a range of attitudes toward women's organizing even in larger towns where gender relations had long been considered more equal and "modern" (Denich 1976; Woodward 1985). It is also significant that the majority of the women from more conservative NGOs, especially displaced women and those from smaller places, were in their forties and fifties at the time, of an older generation for which socialist-era patterns were part of their adulthood. Higher education levels, identification with urban or cosmopolitan culture, anti-nationalist political stances, and younger age thus tended to correlate more closely with, but by no means determine, a rejection of the essentialized gender and ethnic differences that accompanied such long-standing social patterns. Such a rejection indeed characterized most members of the small but active group of women's activists, some of whom self-identified as feminists, who explicitly opposed "patriarchal and nationalist" representations of gender and ethnic difference. However, none of these were absolutes; more elements of this ethnically exclusive and patriarchal logic than these progressive, urban activists might have liked to admit often crept into their discourses and actions.

Providing an all-women space was also important for feminist NGOs like Medica and Žene ženama in Sarajevo, but this came from different concerns—these were consciousness-raising groups, spaces for sharing experiences as women in a patriarchal society, or places where women victims of male violence could begin to heal. For Naš most, however, even though it operated in the relatively large town of Zenica, the separation of women's activities that was one of its fundamental principles was envisioned in a more conservative sense. Its members expressed appreciation that this was a women's organization and cited this fact as an advantage in winning the approval for their activities from male family members and even the local authorities. A mixed-sex group would not be respectable. For example, Ferida, an active Naš most member, explained that as a married woman she felt she could only engage in activities outside the home that were seen as legitimate, so that no one would see her as "becoming a whore" (*da ode u kurvaluk*). She told me she was very grateful for the way that this group allowed her a respectable space for activities in the community. As I met representatives of other women's groups from around BiH, I asked them why they had chosen to be a *women's* organization. The majority of those from small towns and villages—indeed in nearly all groups aside from the more Western donor-oriented feminist and human rights organizations—reacted as if this was a silly question: they formed women's organizations because *they* were women. It was the natural, normal thing to do, not least because men and women had different concerns. "Let the men organize their own group," quipped a member of a women's group in a village in northwest BiH when I asked her why they had organized as women. I return to this issue in my discussions of women's relation to nationalism and "politics" in subsequent chapters.

The *aktiv žena* model also lived on in the kinds of activities these groups imagined and organized. A constant activity at Naš most, regardless of the availability of donor funding, was to provide a social space for women in the form of regular women's gatherings, including their elaborate celebrations of March 8, which featured dinner, live music, bingo, and dancing until late in the evening. This was considered a once-a-year break from women's usual housework and family care; at the gathering I attended in 2000, this was reflected in the bingo prizes, which included sets of pots and pans, cleaning gadgets, beauty products, and dishes.

Merjem was a cosponsor of those March 8 celebrations and also organized its own similar gatherings quite apart from its religious activities. Among them was the type of excursion once organized by *aktiv žena* groups for the purpose of getting to know new places in BiH and "exchanging experiences" with other women. As with social gatherings, these trips were considered sufficiently respectable activities, even though they involved travel, because they were only for women. Still, when such an excursion was planned, many of the women would fret beforehand about whether husbands or parents would allow them to go. They scrambled to complete their domestic chores before the big day so as not to offer any reason to be forbidden from attending.

"Exchanging experiences" was also a phrase that Bosnian participants used to describe donor-organized NGO gatherings. Indeed, while there was a strong resemblance to older patterns and conservative gender regimes, these activities also blended into new-style NGO organizing and were mixed with the discourses of multiethnic civil society, human rights, and gender equality being promoted by intervention agencies. The March 8 celebration, for example, included speeches about women's rights and encouragements to vote for women political candidates, although the audience seemed mostly interested in the dancing and other entertainment.

Mixing Styles, Forms, and Meanings

Bosanka straddled these worlds. The educational seminars they had held for village girls evoked even older activities such as AFŽ-run literacy courses from the late 1940s and 1950s, albeit with a much different ideological message. Bosanka also organized social gatherings and excursions with members of other women's NGOs and participated enthusiastically in Naš most's March 8 celebrations. But when Šehida, their president, began gaining more exposure to foreign-funded initiatives and changing her views and way of talking, Bosanka's activities, too, started to change: it was a striking contrast to see "old-style" activities such as excursions and social gatherings become infused with talk about democracy, civil society, and women's rights.

On one occasion, Bosanka hosted a women's organization from another town on an excursion to Zenica. After showing the visitors the main shopping street, the theater, the art gallery in a former synagogue, and the Islamic Pedagogical Academy, nearly all on foot, Šehida had them walk nearly an hour more across town in order to visit Medica, as she considered it important that Zenica was home to one of the strongest women's NGOs in BiH. After this stop, Šehida talked to the visiting women about Zenica women's contributions to wartime survival, aid to refugees, postwar reconstruction, and now to the democratization process. The visitors, who had snapped up Medica's literature on gender-based violence, feminist therapy approaches, and women's rights, were abuzz with talk about the strength of Bosnian women and the things they were doing to make their own town a better, more democratic place despite the failings of the male-dominated political establishment. What looked from the outside like a typical "women's excursion"—an apolitical, unthreatening diversion for a group of married women and dutiful daughters—thus became inflected with the "political" language of NGO projects, democratization, and women's rights.

A similar mix of styles was to be found with the ubiquitous women's knitting projects. One of the first phases of donor interest during and just after the war was psychosocial therapy, as we have seen in several cases above. This usually meant women coming together under the guidance of a psychologist to knit, weave, or sew products they could later sell or use. The idea was for women to discuss their war traumas and find support with each other while engaged in a familiar activity. Foreign feminists often criticized such projects as reinforcing traditional gender roles rather than challenging them (see Walsh 1998). At Medica, however, the Bosnian women defended their therapeutic knitting and sewing workshop as the only way to get women, especially those from rural areas, together to talk and be helped. Such women would never have willingly gone to therapy due to its stigma—they were not crazy, they said.

When Medica's German donor-founders expressed concern that their vocational training in hairdressing, weaving, and sewing reinforced gender-typed professions for women, the Bosnians went further, evoking a feminism of women's entrepreneurial independence. As the coordinator of the training project wrote in Medica's newsletter, these activities "contribute[d] to women's economic independence" and "strengthen[ed] their self-confidence and their self-reliance" rather than reinforcing gender-typed professions:

> We are often asked why Medica, as a feminist organisation, trains the women in "typically female" activities. The reason is that we believe that traditional women's activities neither conflict with feminism, nor with the things feminism fights for and against. These activities simply have to be valued correctly. . . . When women form cooperatives or workshops together and develop an organised system for marketing their products, they are on the way to economic independence. This is why women must not allow their work to be forced into categories which are defined by men. (Zvizdić 1996, 33)

Of course, members of the local community and even the women participants themselves were more likely to interpret such training programs as precisely the sort of occupations suitable for women as the natural caregivers and home-makers of society. But the ambiguity in the two ways of reading the same activities worked to Medica's advantage, ensuring that they would not be seen as "rocking the boat" too much. Organizational forms and activities were thus difficult to read, as conventional assumptions about women's activities could so easily be repackaged in the language of foreign intervention, democratization, and even feminism.

In a similar vein, foreign feminists, including the Germans from Medica Mondiale, also asked the Bosnian women why they were not more "political," a concept I examine further in the chapters to follow. By this they had a different vision of doing politics than did the Bosnians, that is, public visibility,

Figure 10 Bosfam weaving project with refugee women in Tuzla, June 2010. (photo by Peter Lippman)

leading campaigns and protests, and writing letters to the media. In other words, theirs was a different idea of what (feminist) activism meant. "They [the donors] wish we'd bark [*lajati*] in public," explained Duška one afternoon in the Infoteka office when I had asked her and her colleagues about Infoteka and Medica's political work. Infoteka activists saw feminists being "louder" in Zagreb and Belgrade, not only in Germany or the United States, but were convinced that such approaches would backfire in more conservative BiH. They wanted to be more muted, to pursue "feminism the Bosnian way." As another Infoteka activist added, "it's one thing to live here and *stay* here over the long term and it's another to come here for a short time and then go back to your safe, secure country where the rule of law is in place."

Medica/Infoteka and other women's NGOs in their network were in fact working more behind the scenes than out in public view to improve legislation and to change the way local institutions responded to gender based violence. This approach had often been successful: by the early 2000s they had contributed to the passage of stronger laws against domestic violence and marital rape, a state level gender equality law, and to efforts in many municipalities throughout BiH to respond in a more supportive way to women victims of violence. Women's rights activists and feminists would become slightly more visible in public spaces only from the late 2000s with the advent of Facebook campaigns, flash mobs, and a general increase in activities by citizens and civic associations of all sorts in urban public spaces (see Kurtović 2012). Meanwhile, it was some of the most conservative women's groups, the mostly female Srebrenica survivors, who were the most public and vocal, actually demonstrating on the streets during the last days of the war and throughout subsequent years. Their message, however, was not about women's rights or gender relations, and in fact largely reinforced conservative and nationalist gender ideals.

NGOization, Professionalization, and Activism

The contrast between NGOs like Medica and the Srebrenica women's groups highlights one of the fundamental critiques of the NGOization of feminism (e.g., Alvarez 1999; Lang 1997; Silliman 1999), the idea that formalization of feminist activities through NGOs and cooperation with the state has co-opted the movement and hampered the mobilization of a feminist public. On one hand, feminist NGOs in BiH that preferred to keep a low public profile and to get things done behind the scenes challenged the right of feminist donors and supporters to define what women's rights or feminist activism should look like (cf. Murdock 2003). Bosnian feminists like those at Infoteka maintained that they were taking a much more effective course by moving slowly and less visibly, working for long-term change. They were also acting on their conviction that the state had an important role to play, in contrast to neoliberal trends toward the reduction of state welfare programs.[18] It was therefore vital to pursue change on the level of law, public institutions, and state benefits, rather than acting completely on their own but at the mercy of fluctuations in available donor support.[19]

On the other hand, however, Bosnian feminists were in some ways following the neoliberal script that pushes NGOs toward professionalization and institutional approaches, creating dependence on the state and donors and stifling mass mobilization on issues of social justice (Alvarez 1999; Hrycak 2006; Lang 1997; Silliman 1999).[20] Indeed, there were very few Bosnian feminists who operated outside of NGOs or were unsupported financially, however sporadic or unpredictable NGO income could be. The NGO system actually worked in many ways against the notion of citizen action, volunteerism, or social movements, much to the dismay of some donors. In this respect, Bosnian feminists were living up to the models put forth by donors and intervention agencies, including some feminist ones, that encouraged NGOs to become a link between government and society by honing their skills in "policy advocacy." They described this as a necessity in light of cultural norms and resistance to publicly active women, but it also helped that this way of working meant easier access to donor funds and cooperation with state institutions. In fact, at the time of my research, most Bosnian feminists considered this advocacy role to be what made their work public and political in the first place, suggesting that their work did not easily fit into either side of the neoliberalism versus movement dichotomy (cf. Murdock 2003).

There were other structural and conceptual differences in donors' and Bosnians' ways of engaging in activism. When foreign agency representatives talked about how NGOs should operate, they often envisioned Western European and North American models of activism, non-profit organizations, and volunteerism that assumed a level of motivation and commitment to causes that did not necessarily match those of local NGO participants. The disconnect reflected not only the legacies of socialism and apolitical community work but also current economic realities and the way in which democracy aid and the NGO sector have developed in BiH. The starkest example was in the periodic suggestion that Bosnian NGOs might solicit funds or volunteer labor from the local population, an idea that Bosnians dismissed as ridiculous at best and immoral at worst. For an NGO to ask for time or money from an impoverished population that considered NGOs to be overflowing with foreign money was truly beyond the pale. Both foreigners and Bosnians had grown used to foreigners supplying the aid (Belloni 2001). At Naš most, for example, I sensed

Razija's expectation that her group was entitled to sustained funding from "the foreigners," a sentiment that amplified her resentment when they were turned down for specific projects. There were some committed activists who did volunteer their time or continue NGO work through periods when donor money was scarce, but most activists I knew, especially those with dependents, sought to combine activism and employment as the ideal arrangement. The atmosphere was thus a far cry from the *radne akcije* (work actions) that had been organized by the socialist state to rebuild the country after World War II, a comparison I heard made disapprovingly by a few older people who had been drafted (but not so voluntarily) into such activities as youths.

NGO work was thus not primarily thought of as activism in the way that most donors meant it; while many NGO members with a sense of working for social and political change did refer to themselves as activists, many others were simply "NGO women" or female "members"—*članice*. It could not be taken for granted that Bosnians did NGO work out of dedication to a cause, for lower pay or even in their spare time, though few would admit to working in an NGO solely as a job. Indeed, (funded) NGOs offered some of the best paid and most stable work available (surpassed mainly by foreign agencies and organizations). The few who volunteered their time for an NGO tended to be younger people still being supported by their parents (who often hoped that volunteering would turn into paid employment) or older women with grown or no children who, even if employed, found time to dedicate to NGO activities under more of an *aktiv žena* model of social engagement than that of the new-style NGO. In this respect, groups of older women like Bosanka and Merjem were content not to seek donor funding. Especially at Bosanka, they considered their activities as both a charitable contribution to society and a personal social outlet. But the group was a lower priority, as was obvious in the case of Edina, the Bosanka member who eventually abandoned the group so that she could spend time with her new grandchild.

Those employed by NGOs treated it, unsurprisingly, as a job that had to be balanced with one's personal life, which for most women meant also attending to many more duties at home (much like under socialism). They placed limits on how much overtime or travel they might do for their work and especially on how far they might risk their personal well-being by speaking out on political issues or attempting to affect social change. There were definite exceptions to this, but they were few among those who called themselves activists.

This dynamic was intensified at service-providing NGOs like Medica. While there were a dozen or so Medica activists very strongly committed to changing existing gender norms, and even to feminism, including a few who turned down better paid jobs to continue working at Medica, this was not the rule for the nearly seventy employees of the organization working there at the time of my initial fieldwork. Medica women were by no means *against* goals of gender equality; indeed, they all expressed pride in Medica and its special atmosphere of an all-women organization. But this model of women helping women and their children was not so disruptive of traditional gender hierarchies for those who declined to see the work as political. Not all members of Medica had necessarily become or stayed involved out of deep conviction that the patriarchal gender order should be overturned, or that they wanted to devote significant energy to this goal through political action. Indeed, a few even revealed distinctly conservative personal views on gender or distaste for the feminist label under which the organization officially operated.

Medica was a bit atypical for a service NGO, as its feminist roots infused much of its therapy work and especially that of Infoteka. Activists from Medica have also gone on to found other feminist NGOs and to contribute in other ways to the challenging of patriarchal norms in BiH. Other women's NGOs also provided experience and training for individual activists who went on to work for international organizations and in a few cases to bring their feminist sensibilities to that work. Much of this feminist orientation had to do with the history of individuals and the ways in which they embraced a particular feminism through contact with donors and/or activists from abroad. Self-described feminists or politically active women's NGOs were still few in number and concentrated in larger urban centers like Sarajevo, Banja Luka, Tuzla, and Zenica (see Cockburn, Hubić, and Stakić-Domuz 2001). But the mobility and access to information provided through donor circles and the emphasis on NGO creation meant that there also emerged feminist (or feminism-friendly) activists in several smaller towns where one would not have otherwise expected to find them (Helms, forthcoming).

In reassessing her critique of neoliberal NGOization in the context of Latin American feminisms, Sonia Alvarez has conceded that, despite the structural obstacles of the NGO order, Latin American NGO feminists have quietly managed to do some "movement work" toward social change (2009). Further problematizing the critique of professionalization, Murdock argues that NGOs need to be understood in the context of obstacles and possibilities in which they draw meaning from their work, rather than through the question of whether they are "doing good" in some predefined way (2003). From this perspective, we can read Bosnian feminists as having staked out a space of achievement and influence despite the depoliticizing structure of the NGO system and its embeddedness in the political, economic, and social climate of BiH.

However, the general climate of disdain for vocal women with "political" opinions and the widespread rejection of the feminist label in BiH ensured that only the most confident women, usually those with cosmopolitan support networks, publicly adopted such stances. There were several feminist NGOs that put most of their efforts into service provision, their employees often thinking of themselves as social workers, therapists, or bookkeepers rather than activists. The "movement work" by those who did consider themselves feminist activists, even when publicly visible, was easier to present in terms of postwar development and democratization projects rather than as fundamentally or explicitly political.

4

The Nationing
of Gender

Nationalism, Reconciliation, Feminisms

Nationalism: A Bad Word

The political structures laid out at Dayton, now the BiH constitution, and the foreign intervention agencies charged with postwar reconstruction had solidified, in some respects even created, a logic of collective representation, even as the purported goal was to create a stable, multiethnic BiH state (Mujkić 2007a, 2007b). There was thus the constant contradiction of foreign agencies and certain NGOs and local political actors arguing for a civic community of individuals and a break from ethno-national politics even while implementing a political system that bolstered and maintained the power of ethno-national elites (nationalist political parties) (ibid.). Ethno-national logics were therefore unavoidable in politics as well as in many aspects of everyday life, even in the context of efforts to minimize them. Furthermore, ethnicity and religion became co-opted into the meanings and practices of political power, while all other social categories were eclipsed, in local discourses as in academic analyses, by the importance placed on ethno-national belonging.

At the same time, nationalism as such was a negative label. Nationalists were usually found among opposing ethno-national groups; among one's own group were patriots and defenders of ethno-religious traditions and identities (those things the nation's enemies had tried to wipe out or deny). In Bosniac-dominated areas nearly everyone declared themselves to be against nationalism, but the terrible effects they often had in mind were those caused by Serb and Croat nationalisms and the military forces that served them. Indeed, opposing (that) nationalism was in fact a key part of Bosniac and Bosnian collective narratives. There were also those who condemned "their own" nationalists, that is, Bosniac nationalists in the SDA and among its allies, but this usually implied a majority (of Bosniacs) who were not nationalist. In many cases it was difficult to tell whether condemnation of nationalist politics was based on opposition to nationalism, to religious influence, or to the corruption and profiteering that was rife in such circles. Larisa Kurtović (2011) has beautifully captured this ambiguity in her rumination titled "What Is a Nationalist?" through her 2009 fieldwork in a Bosnian town dominated politically by the SDA. It was a setting in which many wanted to avoid the nationalist label or even association with the SDA, insinuating that all its members were just opportunists. Kurtović shows how these uncertainties "create ambiguous forms of politics and personhoods that are at once sites of surrender and room for maneuver in modern day Bosnia" (244).

The moral position, the position of innocence, was to reject nationalist concerns with difference and to claim tolerance of "others," the opposite of what aggressive nationalists had done in the war and continued to do through other means in its aftermath. This frequently entailed narrations of the past that would counter the claims of Serb and Croat nationalists that Bosnians of different ethno-religious backgrounds could not live together and also opposition to foreigners' ideas about intractable ancient ethnic hatreds. I met many Bosnians who passionately recounted a history of ethnic harmony that had only been shattered by Serb and Croat extremists with support from their neighboring "parent states." In smaller towns and older urban neighborhoods there was no denying that ethnic differences had been known and maintained before the war, but as residents of such communities emphasized, differences had been respected and celebrated, especially through the marking of each group's respective holidays. The tropes of a Catholic neighbor sharing Easter eggs and Muslims sharing Kurban-Bajram (Eid Al-Adha, Feast of the Sacrifice) meat with non-Muslims were repeated so often they became cliché. Younger Bosnians, especially in urban areas, often related not having been aware of ethnic differences at all. This was especially true in the town center, where markers of religious observance (e.g., greetings) or ethnic difference that might be expressed in more mono-ethnic neighborhoods like the Muslim *mahala* of Sarajevo studied by Cornelia Sorabji in the mid-1980s (Sorabji 1989, 1994, 2008), were out of place. Tone Bringa (1995) described similar dynamics between villages and market towns, made more dramatic by differences in women's dress in the village. Men, and especially young men, were particularly less "ethnically legible" outside the circles of family and neighbors because many of them went by nicknames that did not reveal ethnic background the way most first and last names did.

There were many for whom ethnic and religious identities were of no concern in their everyday lives and who had difficulty coping with the abrupt changes in social dynamics ushered in by the war (Maček 2009). With incredulity, parents told of their shock when children came home from school during the build-up to the war, wanting to know "what am I?" And much was made by locals and foreign observers alike of Bosnia's relatively high rates of interethnic marriage before the war, especially in the towns (e.g., Donia and Fine 1994; Markowitz 2010).[1] Indeed, it seemed that every family had a mixed marriage somewhere in its tree. Finally, foreigners and locals nurtured the image of Sarajevo as the European Jerusalem, an idea celebrated on mugs and T-shirts sold to tourists in Sarajevo's Baščaršija with pictures of the city's skyline showing the spires of Catholic and Orthodox cathedrals, the Ashkenazi synagogue, and the minarets of dozens of mosques all within a compact area of Sarajevo's center.

All of these accounts reflected established facts and experiences, but they were selective. And while the other extreme—nationalist obsessions with the interethnic killings of World War II (in which deaths among "their own" people were exclusively stressed), or dark retellings of the oppression of religion and thus ethnic identities under socialism—ignored and distorted even more, there were historical facts to fit every picture of the past as they were crafted to justify the politics of the present. Scholars have offered many different views of the history of ethnic categorizations in BiH in support of different perspectives.[2] What is clear from the available literature and my extensive conversations with Bosnians from all parts of the country is that, before the war as after, there was a clear sense of difference marked and maintained among groups (Bringa 1995; Lockwood 1975) and simultaneous coexistence and competition (Bringa 1995, 17–18; Hayden 2002), but also many life contexts in which ethnicity or religion were utterly irrelevant. As Xavier Bougarel writes of prewar BiH, "the words 'tolerance,' 'hate,' 'coexistence,' and 'fear' are all equally applicable. In essence, they are complementary or consecutive rather than contradictory" (1996, 87).

Under socialism, with its attendant processes of urbanization and secularization, such differences had significantly diminished in importance, yet they were still present on the level of everyday life, as anthropological studies from the 1980s show for both village (Bringa 1995) and urban settings (Sorabji 1989). The many stories I was told about prewar life in both towns and villages confirmed this. For example, Milica, an educated woman of Serb background living in Zenica and an Infoteka activist, grew up in another multiethnic central Bosnian town. In attempting to explain to me a different quality "in the mentality of Bosnia" (in contrast to more ethnically homogeneous areas), she characterized prewar life as entailing "a kind of tolerance which means putting up with others." She continued:

> You knew what you could say to whom and what you couldn't, what subjects not to pursue with neighbors of other ethno-religious groups (*nacije*). You tolerated lots of things because you knew it was better not to push. This was especially true in terms of putting your neck out in public and exposing your position, especially in any criticism of the government. And women were especially not used to having deep conversations. . . . Most of all national and religious things were off limits to really probing conversations, which is a good thing I think.

On the political level, however, ethnic categories were not only noted but were also institutionalized, first by the legal categorization of major *narod*s (peoples), which by 1974 also included the newly named Muslim nation, as well as through the power-sharing convention of the "ethnic key" (*ključ*).[3] Ethnicity thus became a major channel through which political power and loyalty were distributed. V. P. Gagnon (2004) has shown how ethno-national divisions and powerful nationalist elites in BiH actually grew out of power struggles among Communist-cum-nationalist elites who eventually hurled Yugoslavia toward destruction and war.[4] Over the course of the devolution of power in Yugoslavia and the violence of the war, ethno-national belonging had become the main support of power to nationalist elites, who in turn used ethnic collectivist criteria to distribute favors and command loyalty through clientelistic networks (see Grandits 2007).

Nationalism and affiliation with nationalist parties thus became the keys to power and position but also became linked to corrupt political and business practices as well as the war violence and a host of other problems. However, the only morally arguable basis for what might be called nationalist positions of intolerance or suspicion toward ethnic or religious others was the war violence. Especially those who had been directly victimized in the war because of their ethno-religious belonging said they were only now wary of difference or mistrustful of ethnic others as a result of the nationalist violence and behavior of those "others." It was also the war violence and especially the large-scale victimization of Bosniacs that made it difficult for many in the Bosniac-dominated parts of BiH to label Bosniac leaders nationalists, particularly when compared to nationalists among Serbs or Croats.

The nationalist label for leaders and parties representing the Bosniacs was also deniable on the grounds that the official position, clearly articulated since the early days of the war, was to advocate a multiethnic BiH where Bosniacs would live side by side with others, even as Islam and Bosniac-ness grew in importance (Hoare 2004).[5] Since the lead-up to the war and after, there had been relatively little direct hate speech against ethnic others or overt acts of discrimination or attempts to drive others from the territories that Bosniacs controlled. There were egregious examples to the contrary but these were generally explained as isolated incidents or those that were committed by criminals and others not controlled directly by Bosnian authorities. There was also the separate term available to describe the ruling political parties: they were "national parties," that is, formed with the stated aim to protect a particular ethnic group's "national interests." It was thus sometimes more palatable to refer to national parties, including the Bosniac ones, than to call them nationalist outright.

There were of course those with no qualms about identifying and criticizing nationalisms among all groups, including their "own." This was especially true among the urban intellectual elite of Sarajevo and other larger towns and included many NGO activists and those working in foreign intervention agencies. This anti-nationalist position advocated a society in which individuals were seen as citizens rather than as members of ethnic groups. At the same time, and often without realizing the discrepancy, proponents of this stance also trumpeted ideas of liberal multiculturalism and the (positive) affirmation of ethno-religious differences that this implied (see Arsenijević 2007; Hajdar-pašić 2008). In other words, efforts to ignore ethno-national and religious identifications, to claim that they did not matter, coexisted with celebrations of ethnic and religious distinctiveness. But these representations often flew in the face of Bosnian realities, minimizing the seriousness of divisions and reinforcing even further the link between ethnicity, religion, and nationalism. Furthermore, because of the ambiguity produced by the overlap with Bosniac nationalism, and especially in light of collective victimhood narratives and the ethnicization of the violence itself, anti-nationalist and multiculturalist positions slid easily into reinforcements of ethno-national difference and assertions of the moral superiority of Bosniacs. Where this fell on the continuum of "good" patriotism to "bad" nationalism was often impossible to determine, but it certainly cannot be said that this production of ethno-national hierarchies was conducive to the overcoming of ethnic divides as represented in romanticized representations of tolerant, multicultural Bosnians. This brings us once more to consider the role of the "international community."

Targeting Women

The goal of foreign intervention agencies and donors to "reverse ethnic cleansing" (Ó Tuathail and Dahlman 2004) and create a functioning multiethnic BiH state made ethnic reconciliation and refugee return major priorities.[6] These were areas in which women predominated, in part because they were the surviving members of communities recovering from ethnic cleansing, but also because they were specifically targeted by foreign agencies and donors through an affirmatively essentialist rhetoric. Many attempts to explicitly recognize and lend value to women's existing roles and/or to advocate their increased participation in positions of power and decision-making nevertheless fell back on essentializing language that celebrated women as more peaceful, less nationalistic, and more prepared for forgiveness than men. Women and women's NGOs were thus looked to as "natural" leaders of reconciliation initiatives.

Figure 11 Houses rebuilt by humanitarian aid agencies for Bosniac returnees, Prijedor area, April 2006. (photo by author)

Figure 12 Visiting Bosniac returnees near Prijedor with members of Srcem do mira, May 2000. (photo by author)

The most romanticized and essentializing versions of such rhetoric completely distanced women from war and nationalism, making them into morally pure, innocent victims of the actions of men. This approach was summed up in the title of US diplomat Swanee Hunt's book profiling Bosnian women of various ethnic backgrounds active in refugee return and reconciliation initiatives: *This Was Not Our War: Bosnian Women Reclaiming the Peace* (2004). As US ambassador to Austria during the Clinton administration, Hunt had used her influence and private foundation to support several BiH women's NGOs in various ways. Her book, a presentation of women she had encountered during her engagement with BiH, opposes male politicians and their war strategies to the suffering and everyday struggles of ordinary women, even as it includes several women politicians and other elites among the profiles. She is also explicit that these women are victims, women in BiH as a group having "suffered far out of proportion to any complicity in causing the conflict" (ibid., 2), but that "they approach the reader grounded in strength" (ibid.). This insistence on women's active roles is an important and common feminist step taken to counter images of passive female victimhood. But in stressing their agency and action within a framework of women as a group, an equally essentializing image is constructed of women as anti-nationalist peacemakers. Having come to know several of the women profiled in Hunt's book, I agree that they have made significant contributions to processes of refugee return, women's activism, democratic reforms, and similar areas. Many also struck me as truly opposing nationalist divisions. At the same time, however, the book includes women allied with nationalist parties and several NGO women whose work and rhetoric often belie a true commitment to (re)building interethnic trust or fully rejecting nationalist logics.

In Mostar several years before the publication of Hunt's book, a collection of women's testimonies with a similar title was produced by Cooperazione Italiana, an Italian NGO funded by the Italian government. The book, *This War Is Not Mine* (Cacace, Menafra, and Miozzo 1996), came with an introduction by the Italian foreign minister at the time, Lamberto Dini, who romanticized women's war suffering and perceived innocence: "Reading the stories of the Mostarian women, the stories of mothers, wives, war widows, one has a strange feeling: *a message of hatred is never expressed* by these incredible and marvelous women" (5, emphasis added). In the same book, Emma Bonino, then the European commissioner for humanitarian aid, made the case that women "can become, in the post-war period, one of the driving forces towards reconciliation and rehabilitation" because, "compared to men, women show a greater inclination towards peace rather than war. They, more often than men, reject ethnic, linguistic, or religious barriers" (ibid., 6). Assuredly, she went on to explain that "they do so for very practical motives: they want to continue cultivating the fields, maintain access to essential goods, and safeguard 'mixed' marriages and families," thus tempering the argument that women are *naturally* inclined to peace. However, the general tone of her essay, and of the others introducing the book, emphasized women's vulnerability, victimization, and innocence. It was a trope I heard repeated over and over in women's NGO circles.

Women were in this way defined not as individuals, but collectively and in terms of dominant patriarchal notions of women and their roles. The excerpt discussed earlier from the Italian book not only talks about "women" but also adds "mothers, wives, war widows." It was not that women in BiH were not frequently mothers, wives, or war widows, but that their suffering was being legitimated through these relationships to men, as wives and mothers (of sons/soldiers). Other common formulations celebrated women as self-sacrificing mothers whose concern for their children was what gave them the courage to cross (ethnic) borders. The evaluation report from another donor, written by a local Bosnian woman staff member (incidentally a woman also profiled in Hunt's book), stated:

> In our working experience, women are much braver than men, and more practical. They always dare what men do not. They are not afraid to go to another entity in order to achieve their goals, to meet people on (the)

"other side." They understand each other, they are clear that people can be only good or bad, and that no other division matters. They do not look at people of another ethnicity as enemies but as people that have gone through the same hardships and trauma. They all know that *all mothers have been equally crying*, and that all of them have suffered a lot. (Savić 2000, 4; emphasis added)

Women were thus assumed to be mothers, their participation in political decision-making called for only on the basis of their continued ties to the home and family.

At the same time, such representations were often mixed with feminist-inflected calls for women's inclusion in positions of power from which they had historically been excluded. In chapter 3, I discussed a statement from the UNHCR-administered BWI program arguing for the "empowerment" of women and their full participation in all areas of society. A report from the same agency, quoting the UNHCR's senior coordinator for refugee women, Rita Reddy, as she addressed a multiethnic meeting of NGO women organized by BWI, started out in a similar vein, noting that despite women's involvement in most sectors of the economy, "their contribution is rarely given due recognition, even by agencies providing funding for postwar recovery" (Bosnian Women's Initiative 1996, not paginated). She then added, however, that "Women, *proved by research studies to be more predisposed to ensuring the continuance of life and promotion of peace than their male counterparts*, must be involved as decision-makers and take the lead in the peace-building processes" (ibid., emphasis added). The assumption that all women are mothers (presently or in the future), and that mothers are naturally both nurturing and concerned with the well-being of society allows for this predisposition to "ensuring the continuance of life" to be connected to an inclination toward promoting peace. At the least, donors seemed to hope that Bosnian women, most of whom in fact were or planned to become mothers, would come to see themselves in this way and to act accordingly.

There was a distinct contrast with the way that donors and intervention agencies related to men and mixed sex groups. While there were also appeals to think of future generations or to give a chance to the purportedly non-nationalistic youth,[7] there was no appeal to men's natural disposition toward peace, connections to family, or the preservation of life. And only occasionally did anyone object to the implication of affirmative essentialisms of women as peacemakers—that all men were thus by nature violent, warlike, and intolerant. Had this been meant seriously, it is hard to see why intervention agencies and donors nevertheless focused the greatest efforts toward postwar reconstruction on the mostly male political, religious, and economic leaders. Women were apparently expected to lead reconciliation only on the level of neighborhoods, villages, and small communities.

The "Nationing" of Gender

Where discourses of nation were often profoundly gendered, in the NGO world of postwar BiH I often found that approaches to gender became "nationed" in many ways. Even when women's organizations strove to focus on issues of gender equality, donor pressures obliged them to integrate concerns about ethnicity into their rhetoric and activities.

As among the population as a whole, nearly every women's organization in Bosniac-dominated BiH (and many in the RS and Croat-dominated areas) professed an aversion to nationalism and a dedication to ethnic tolerance. Among the women I came to know, I never suspected they did not mean this sincerely, but as the politically correct position as well as a donor priority, it was an easy position to take. More importantly, there were many ways of interpreting and rationalizing commitment to multiethnicity and opposition to nationalism. This was brought home to me several times upon hearing certain NGO women mentioned by donors as working toward reconciliation or as examples of peacebuilding when I had seen these women acting in ways that were quite destructive to interethnic trust.

Donor requirements, however, often targeted superficial elements like the ethnicity of NGOs' membership or how involved they were with cross-entity activities. Even Medica had been pressured despite the fact that they were clear outsiders to nationalist circles. Medica linked its anti-nationalism to its feminism and was well connected to networks of antiwar, anti-nationalist feminists throughout the former Yugoslavia, including the anti-militarist group Women in Black in Belgrade (see Dević 2000; Fridman 2006). Within BiH, Medica had long been connected to other women's NGOs from all parts of the country, working on issues of violence against women in a loose network that met periodically to share advice, coordinate efforts beyond their communities, and strategize on how best to deal with their common concerns as women's activists. However, at one point Duška of Infoteka noticed that many of their prospective donors began insisting that every project be funded only on the level of cross-entity (i.e., cross-ethnic) networks or as joint projects of NGOs from different ethnic territories, rather than by individual NGOs. Talking over coffee one day in Infoteka, Duška put this "cross-entity cooperation" on her list of "ridiculous demands the international community has." It had been especially irksome, as she explained, with a project that had brought together women working on Medica's *SOS Telefon* hotline for victims of domestic violence with women at a Serb women's NGO with a similar hotline: "The donors insisted we work together on this, as partners. And, yeah, the program was approved and I'm sure the donors will talk about this as a big success in cross-ethnic cooperation, but in reality we really didn't do anything together." This was also frustrating and insulting for the activists who had long been involved in cross-entity work on their own, not to mention that such requirements had often led to projects that did not meet their potential.

Donor demands for multiethnic membership had also been a problem. Although Medica had always declared itself a multiethnic NGO, its ethnic membership was not equally balanced as some donors seemed to expect. Rather, it mirrored the ethnic makeup of the surrounding community: most were Bosniacs but there were several Serbs, Croats, and women of mixed background at all levels of the organization. They had even come under fire from Bosniac nationalists for having non-Bosniac women as visible leaders of the organization. But their reputation and excellent working relationships, even close friendships, with activists in Serb- and Croat-controlled areas of BiH, as well as in Serbia and Croatia proper, did not satisfy some of their donors, who suggested they diversify their membership by ethnicity and were forcing cooperative projects with NGOs in the RS and Croat areas. Duška, incidentally of Serb background, exasperatingly argued, "But Medica is concerned with doing its work, with helping women, so let the ethnic makeup be like it is." Dženana, a Bosniac Infoteka activist who had worked with many other NGOs throughout Bosnia, likewise complained about organizations that keep members of other ethnic groups around just "for decoration."

Such pressures took away from the effectiveness of NGO work.[8] Instead of hiring people with certain skills that were needed, such as an accountant or a psychologist or a cook, NGOs spent time trying to recruit members by ethnicity. "Multiethnicity looks great," Dženana said, "but this loses its real value, the positive picture it could have . . . Instead it's something forced." Medica had solid proof for donors that they were committed to multiethnicity, but they often had to go through this before they could get on with their work on behalf of women. Things were not as easy for mono-ethnic NGOs, especially those organized around religious identity.

Gender, Ethnicity, and Religion

Western donors and international community representatives consciously evaluated local NGOs on the basis of how nationalist they were. The two main feminist donors working in the country at the time of my initial research were perhaps the most insistent on a non-nationalist stance from any women's group they funded.[9] In fact, they were stricter on this criterion than on how feminist a group was. With feminism as much if not more of a dirty word as nationalism and interpretations of both these "isms" varying widely, neither was an easy judgment to make.

Groups with mono-ethnic membership were usually suspected (by many locals as well as donor representatives) of nationalist tendencies—were that not the case, the reasoning went, members of other groups would feel comfortable joining them. Donors tended to fund mono-ethnic groups only if they belonged to what were now ethnic minorities in places dominated by another ethno-national group, like the mostly Croat women's group Antonija in Bosniac-dominated Bugojno; or if they were refugees expelled through ethnic cleansing and now aiming to return to a place dominated by another group, like Srcem do mira (Bosniac women who returned to the RS). A largely mono-ethnic NGO like Naš most could either "grab" ethnic others in response to donor demands for mixed membership or, as Žene s Podrinja's leader told me she advised other all-Bosniac NGOs to do, they could "go for multiethnic cooperation" in order to show their dedication to interethnic reconciliation (and, as noted in chapter 3, as a way to appeal to donors).

This situation was an obvious obstacle for organizations like Bosanka, an all-Bosniac group in a majority Bosniac town. The group's core members were not very savvy about securing donor funds, but they had also been allied with an umbrella group of women's NGOs that had the reputation of being Bosniac nationalists and included another group called the "Muslim Academic Club, Bosanka." The Zenica Bosanka did not have "Muslim" in its name (it was simply an "association of citizens"), nor did the name Bosanka indicate ethno-national affiliation—they had not called themselves Bošnjakinja after all—and so the group's members complained that it could not possibly be seen as nationalist or unwelcoming to members of other ethno-national groups. Yet its name indexed a similar kind of Bosniac overeagerness to profess loyalty to the BiH state as a multiethnic place as that detectable in some Bosniac nationalist discourses. It was not the sort of name usually chosen by successfully funded women's NGOs, which tended to avoid references to national identity and often stressed only female identity.

Associations of religious Muslim women were even more readily seen as nationalist and ignored by Western donors and intervention agencies. To be sure, many of these organizations did tend to engage in the kind of affirmations of Bosniac-ness that put non-Muslims off. Many more were not interested in Western funding, existing without or seeking funding from "Eastern" donors, that is, those from Muslim countries or Islamic organizations interested in solidarity with fellow Muslims and usually also in spreading and strengthening the faith in certain forms.[10] This was evident in the lack of standard NGO-speak that peppered the self-presentations of other groups, whether funded or aspiring to be funded by a Western donor. Even "NGO" was not used, although they fit the definition as well as other groups did; they generally called themselves "associations" (*udruženje*) and operated more in the tradition of local, apolitical *aktiv žena* groups. In my conversations with leaders of several of these associations, it was clear that they did not aspire to be part of Western-supported NGO initiatives, or to receive funding from anyone who "would impose conditions on us that we could not meet," as the president of Kewser explained.[11] The worlds of religion and of NGOs seemed to be like parallel universes existing in the same space.

Or more precisely, religion and Western-supported initiatives were unconnected when the topic was gender or women. During my initial research, western donors and agencies did sponsor organizations and projects focused on inter-religious dialogue in which women participated, but seldom was gender a topic of discussion in such circles. Among NGOs, intervention agencies, and donors working on women's issues or gender equality, religion was generally seen either as a private matter or negatively, as a conservative force opposed to women's equal participation in public life or decision-making positions, much as in the treatment of religion in the critiques of gender and nationalism in Serbia and Croatia. Moreover, openly religious women, especially those who wore Islamic dress (*hidžab*), were seldom seen at such women's gatherings.[12]

In fact, the appearance of "covered women" sometimes provoked uneasiness. They were associated with the strand of Bosniac nationalism that promoted a bigger presence of Islam in all spheres of life including politics, and with even more conservative, "fundamentalist" kinds of Islam that secular urbanites found especially disturbing (Helms 2008; see also Ghodsee 2009; Navaro-Yashin 2002). Despite many expressions of respect for believers, there were activists and donors who saw nothing redeeming for feminist or women's rights politics in ethnic affirmation and especially in religion, which they saw as inherently based on patriarchal gender ideologies. Further, the ideal of a multiethnic, civic BiH meant a secular public sphere, the understanding of which was tied to the way public behavior had been governed under socialism. And except when a person's sincere faith could be vouched for, there was suspicion that outwardly religious people had only adopted such practices for political or material gain. Outward markers of religious devotion were therefore less welcome. Devout, *hidžab*-wearing women complained that liberal, urban Bosnians as well as Western foreigners (i.e., precisely the bulk of the NGO crowd) expected them to be close-minded, uneducated, and nationalist; they elicited surprise when they revealed their knowledge of English or made critical remarks about political issues.

Religion and ethnicity were thus conflated with nationalism, just as they were in nationalist discourses themselves. And gender issues remained confined to the world of NGOs, academia, and pockets of political activity and state institutions. In her critique of radical feminist positions expressed in Serbia during the Bosnian war, Dubravka Žarkov points to the ramifications of their insistence on gender as *the* explanatory category for understanding the war violence in Bosnia. Because this formulation stressed female victimhood on the basis of their gender only, it became impossible to conceive of women who were at the same time also ethnic. Žarkov thus reasons that:

> Instead of asking why and how all the politics in the region was reduced to identity politics (in this case—nationalism), and how ethnicity gained the privileged place therein, many feminists simply surrendered ethnicity to nationalism. Consequently, ethnicity and femininity were either collapsed into each other or were totally separated. This further meant that ethnicity was granted meaning *only in the context of hatred and violence, and only as a collective identity* (which is in many ways surprising considering the general feminist concern with personal experiences). (2002, 66, emphasis in the original; see also Žarkov 2007)

In the same way, meanings attached to religion in BiH were surrendered to nationalism. Instead of reclaiming religion and ethnicity by considering how they might find a meaningful place in women's lives without contributing to oppressive social structures, women's NGOs and their donors had effectively left them to the nationalists.

There were a handful of religious women interested in feminist critiques of Islam, some of whom had begun modest initiatives to address the issue. One, Zilka Spahić-Šiljak, a trained mu'allima and self-professed "feminist, but an Islamic one,"[13] later became much more publicly active on this front. After completing a doctorate in gender studies, she published several illuminating studies on gender and religion (e.g., Spahić-Šiljak 2007, 2008, 2010, 2012; Spahić-Šiljak and Anić 2009), and increasingly took part in donor-sponsored initiatives on both religion and on gender where she made clear her feminist critique of the practice of all BiH religions, including Islam. Spahić-Šiljak's efforts were in fact central to later efforts to interrogate the position of women in religious communities and their relationship to politics, efforts that bridged academia and the NGO sector (see Raudvere 2011).[14] However, religion remained low on the list of priorities for women's NGOs in general.

Women's NGOs, donors, and intervention agencies in BiH that professed to be working toward interethnic harmony and a liberal, civic democracy were not the radical feminists critiqued by Žarkov. But their positioning of women as victims of male-associated forces, here not only nationalist war violence but also nationalist and religious politics among "us," had similar effects. Reclaiming ethnicity and religion for women's activism or reconciliation initiatives apparently threatened to disrupt the easy dichotomies of peaceful, tolerant, but powerless women as victims of religious nationalisms directed by men. To acknowledge that some women participated in, even cherished, the maintenance of ethnic and religious identities required the decoupling of ethnicity and faith from nationalism, religious authorities, and politics, something that the women's NGO scene was reluctant to do. This reluctance, I argue, came not only from the liberal constructions of the public and secular society being promoted by intervention agencies, donors, and many NGOs but also from affirmative essentialist notions of women as unimplicated in nationalist power, which underscored their arguments to a skeptical public about why women and "women's issues" should be taken seriously at all.

Women and Ethnic Boundaries in Practice

In the hands of Bosnian women's organizations, affirmative essentialisms came in different versions from the dominant narratives promoted by donors, but they shared the function of underwriting various claims to moral superiority. The simple dichotomous framework attributing goodness and innocence to victims, women, and ethnic selves, as opposed to the responsibility and evil attached to those in power, men, and ethnic enemies, allowed for the construction of new narratives that combined these elements in novel ways while remaining within the broad framework of intervention policies. What was more, the overlap between Bosniac nationalism and support for a multiethnic BiH allowed for the coexistence of many different approaches to gender and nationalism under one umbrella of tolerance. Under scrutiny, such pronouncements did not necessarily deviate very far from those of conservative, essentialist nationalisms. This becomes visible through the ways in which women's activists' professed commitment to ethnic tolerance, support for a multiethnic BiH, and women's rights advocacy—major bases for claims to victimhood—were narrated and put into practice. The rest of this chapter examines several such moments in the lives of women's activists from different perspectives.

"Women Started This War"

After hearing over and over about women having had nothing to do with nationalism and war, Emira's assertion that "women started this war" was a jarring statement. Emira was the leader of a mostly Bosniac NGO in a Bosniac-dominated provincial town that organized socializing and income-generating projects for its mostly working-class and rural members. This group existed in the margins of donor- and intervention agency–supported initiatives, but Emira was well aware of the dominant messages being sent there and that her statement was provocative. Seeing my shock, she explained:

> I don't mean women are guilty for the war in the sense that they wanted war, but because they didn't think about the consequences of their talking. They only thought in the short term. Definitely the ideas from Yugoslavia [i.e., Serbia] were behind the war. But in Bosnia it was purely this provocation [*prepucavanje*] between women and their neighbors. . . . If something starts up, some trouble, who is it that runs around gossiping, talking, getting people riled up? I'm not talking about in public life but within the family and we know that's the main cell of society. When it all bursts then women return to their role and the men go off to fight the war. With men it's guns and cannons; with women, talking and blabbing.

Instead of being passive victims of male nationalist politics and violence, Emira had women playing an active role in stirring up ethnic hatred. Still, their activity remained a reaction to "ideas from Yugoslavia" (that is, Serbian nationalism), and was confined to the private sphere of the family and the neighborhood, proper places for women, rather than the truly culpable arenas of nationalism and politics. Her portrayal relied on the more conservative divisions of gendered public and private spheres shared by much of her group's members. The public, outside the home and neighborhood, was still coded as political and male, but responsibility for nationalism and war was now spread between the public and private spheres, between men and women.

Fikreta, the outspoken leader of a group of Bosniac women refugees, now returnees, that had successfully led the return of much of the population back to their hometown in the RS, had a similar perspective based on women's presumed roles as mothers. In a long conversation one evening in her living room, she explained that even though it had not been women who had "raped, killed, and burned" in the war, they nevertheless shared a degree of guilt, "through their role in upbringing. . . . Women give birth and raise and feed children. So men aren't the ones most guilty for that." In fact I heard this often from activists with more conservative views on gender. In the words of Amila, an activist with a small women's NGO in Sarajevo made up mostly of Bosniacs, women should be held most responsible for "nationalism and war" because "they are the ones who bring up the children. If they don't teach their children tolerance, but instead obsession with the past, prejudice and intolerance, those kids, especially boys, will turn out that way." Fathers, schools, and the rest of the social environment were not insignificant, she acknowledged when I questioned this, but she insisted that the "biggest impact comes from a mother's early upbringing."

Amila's terminology echoed a common distinction between the "tolerance" of Bosniacs based on their general support for a united, multiethnic BiH, and "obsession with the past," a clear reference to the importance in Serb nationalist ideology of World War II massacres of Serbs, Ottoman domination, and the great loss at the Battle of Kosovo Field in 1389, which were often evoked in justifications for Serb hostility and attacks against Muslims (Čolović 2002; Dragović-Soso 2002; Jansen 2003). Fikreta continued in a similar vein about women's roles in guiding children: "Women have the chance to form a person who won't kill but will love—they can sow love rather than death . . . So don't give them violent models, give them something positive to strive for."

Respectability and Benevolent Patriarchy

These models also extended to women's behavior toward their husbands; when men used violence it was because their wives demanded that they be "strong and protecting" while women with "a broad perspective . . . would never live with violent men or let their sons be that way." As Fikreta explained how this worked, it became clear that these two types of gendered behavior corresponded to ethnic differences: it was Bosniac women who sowed love and tolerance, "but among the Serbs, their wives/women [žene] simply bring up their children this way [encouraging violence] and they find those kinds of husbands."

Fikreta continued in the mode of "us" (Bosniacs, Muslims) and "them" (Serbs), explaining that "Serb women learn they should raise their sons for the military and for the state, but we're brought up to think of family and the home as the most important things in the world." Echoing the culturizing generalizations of the book of war rape testimonies discussed in chapter 2, she claimed that Serbs did not value family in the same way, concluding piously, "For me, children are more important than any state."[15] In this way, she (re)-produced a moral hierarchy of ethnic difference centered on women's roles as mothers and wives: Serb women were responsible for nurturing a culture of violence and death, allegiance to the state, and (Serb) nationalism. The morally right position, and the Muslim pattern, was to dedicate oneself to the family, away from the state or politics, especially for women.[16] When women did get involved, as Fikreta and the members of her organization had, it remained respectable if the goal was to call for peace in the name of protecting their children. But, in her telling, Serb women had crossed the line by publicly cheering on the (Serb) army, by definition then supporting military violence (the possibility that those women might also have felt they were acting out of concern for their families' safety was apparently unthinkable). They had become political, precisely the opposite of respectable women.

Emira, after speaking of women's guilt for "talking and blabbing," was also clear about which women had done this, pointing to incidents during the war when Serb women had lain in the road to block United Nations troops from delivering humanitarian aid to non-Serb populations. As Emira stated, "the dignity of Bosniacs doesn't allow this kind of display." Her concept of ethnicity, however, was reduced to religious identity:

> Emira: In Islam it's the stove for women and politics for men. Look at where [Slobodan] Milošević's wife is. And then look at Alija's [Izetbegović] wife.
> EH: She's nowhere to be seen.
> Emira: Exactly. You don't see women in politics among the Bosniacs. But look at the Serbs. Look at Mira Marković and Biljana Plavšić and others. They had lots of women in politics. Women have lots of influence.[17]

It was traditional, patriarchal gender roles that elevated Bosniacs to a higher moral plane above Serbs, whose women were "too visible" in politics. This was a surprising formulation coming from Emira, who was usually going on about women as workers (*radnice*). She did not exactly see women's ideal role as chained to the stove, nor did she live that way—she once showed pleasure in having her grown son make and serve us coffee while she sat chatting with me, the usual male role.[18] It was, however, an effective simplification for pointing to a supposed collective failing of Serbs.

Although Emira and Fikreta belonged to a circle of women's NGO activists that often called for increased participation of women in formal politics, these narratives suggest that women's association with politics still carried a stain of suspicion, especially where politics were equated with nationalism, at least the nationalisms of ethnic others. Their accusations were selective; they pointed to the most nationalistic Serb women and ignored several highly placed (yet not as prominent) Bosniac women politicians, as well as non-Bosniac women active in politics who were outspoken in opposition to nationalisms and the war.

Their involvement in NGO activities had also made them acutely aware of Orientalist depictions that cast negative connotations on the sort of patriarchal values in which they placed their positive picture of Bosniacs. Fikreta, for example, was careful to distinguish between a benevolent patriarchy practiced among Bosniacs and a violent one nurtured by Serbs (for details, see

Helms 2010b). Among the Muslims, she said, going back to a timeless, rural past, "men didn't dominate, they were actually victims," having to perform heavy labor while women got the lighter jobs. Things had changed now, her own very assertive and public activity showing that she, like Emira, was hardly confined to the house under male control. But her image of the past lent an eternal, natural quality to differences between Bosniacs and Serbs as peoples in the way that time and gender frequently figure in nationalist discourses (e.g., Chatterjee 1989; McClintock 1993; Yuval-Davis 1997). This was a clear moral hierarchy of difference between Bosniacs and Serbs, one that preceded the atrocities of the war, thus reinforcing the general belief in essential ethno-national differences.

In the picture Fikreta painted, it was crucial that Muslim men were gentle, noble, and respectful. They were selfless, even victims, sacrificing themselves in their shouldering of the "hardest, most dangerous jobs" and inherently not aggressive or violent. There was no coercion involved in their authority. It followed then that when Bosniac men went off to fight, it was out of duty to defend their homes and families, not out of any violent tendencies. Further-more, from Fikreta's earlier statements, Bosniac women were to be thanked for bringing up their sons in this peaceful, tolerant manner, in direct contrast to the aggressive and violent ways of Serb mothers, which produced the war-mongering nationalists and genocidal warriors who had violently forced Fikreta and her neighbors from their homes during the war.

Thus, some activists who were held up as, and themselves claimed to be, peacemakers and advocates for women's rights, at the same time expressed pro-foundly conservative, patriarchal gender ideals as well as notions of inherent cultural differences of ethnic groups, their own group being morally superior. Their statements implying the inherent peacefulness of women actually turned out to oppose that view by implicating *Serb* women for the outbreak of war. Lest the point be lost, one Bosniac women's NGO had T-shirts made that read "World peace starts right here. I will not raise my child to kill your child." In addition to implying that all women were by definition present or future moth-ers (since the T-shirts were to be worn by women), this slogan also suggested that there were *some* women-mothers who *would* raise their children to be kill-ers. Just who those "bad" women-mothers were was well understood when the Bosniac women wore them on a trip to Srebrenica through a hardline Serb area in the period before Bosniacs had begun to return. Those whose children grew up to kill or whose husbands joined nationalist causes—and here this was generalized to include all Serbs—had clearly failed in their *gendered* roles—as mothers and wives. This was a far cry from female solidarity across ethnic lines as portrayed and called for by many donors, women's activists, and feminists.

Talking across Ethnic Divisions

With such a view of ingrained ethnic difference between respectable, peaceful Bosniacs and violent, nationalistic Serbs, how could organizations like Fikreta's be working on reconciliation as they claimed? And why look to (Serb) women as the key to reconciliation if they were so aggressive and nationalistic? The availability of donor funds for projects on reconciliation was certainly an incentive, but so was the determination of these women to return to their original homes and reestablish their previous lives, even if it meant living again alongside Serb neighbors. Elsewhere I have written about how reciprocal neighborly relations and the kinds of notions of separate women's and men's activities described above figured in reconciliation initiatives among returning refugees like those in Fikreta's organization (Helms 2010b). Here I focus on how groups that adhered to such ideologies of gender and ethnic difference made use of the affirmative essentialisms of women as peacemakers that circulated in the NGO scene. I contrast these groups with (mostly) feminist NGOs who pursued different sorts of work across the ethnicized internal borders of BiH. I offer these portraits as two extremes along a range of approaches to gender and ethnicity among BiH women's NGOs in order to illustrate the dilemmas and implications posed by affirmative essentialist constructions of women as peacemakers and agents of reconciliation.

These NGOs participated in, and were therefore familiar with the language of, both ethnic reconciliation and gender equality projects supported by intervention agencies and donors. Different aspects of their dominant constructions were mobilized for different purposes and different audiences. Given the sensitivity and starkly different competing narratives about the character of the war and collective victimhood, activists made constant tactical decisions about what to mention and when, or what Cynthia Cockburn has described for feminist activism across ethnicized and militarized divisions as "crucial choices about silence and speech" (1998, 262). Staying silent in these circumstances enabled certain kinds of work across ethnic divisions but also left many issues unexamined.

As we saw above, activists like Emira or Fikreta easily accommodated affirmative essentialisms of women as peacemakers into notions of men's and women's separate spheres, even if only considered in terms of the ethnic self (Bosniacs in this case.) Women, at least "our" women, had not been responsible for the war or nationalism as those belonged to the "political" world of men. Women were logical peacemakers because they were the ones who had to reknit the community together through coffee visits and neighborly reciprocal aid. A delicate balance was required, especially in public meetings of NGOs and donors, as I witnessed when I accompanied the members of another refugee women's organization for a meeting of NGOs and donors in the area to which these women were hoping to return.

Žene s Podrinja, as introduced earlier, was an NGO of mostly Bosniac women refugees working to return to Srebrenica and nearby towns in the eastern RS. Members of this group had ample reason to be bitter toward local Serbs. They had all lost husbands, sons, and other loved ones and had been forcibly expelled, either during the ethnic cleansing campaigns of 1992 or during the 1995 fall of Srebrenica. In fact, many of the members were too bitter to consider "reconciliation" or even return to the region. Their president, Zahida, disagreed and was determined herself to return.

It was not that she had not also suffered. Zahida had been expelled from Bratunac after her husband was murdered and was not going to forget what had happened. She assured me she made this clear to local Serbs, saying, "Don't think we're fools that we don't know what you did, *what you women did to us*. We all know that our men were killed, that we were kicked out of here without firing one bullet. We know what you did but we didn't come to talk about that" (emphasis added). She addressed Serb women specifically because, as she explained, it was natural. These were the separate gendered spheres she was used to from her life in small town, semi-rural neighborhoods: men had their spheres of activity and women had theirs.

As she continued, it was clear that she felt she was on morally superior ground: "Muslims are returning with heads held high. We don't have blood on our hands, we didn't do evil to our neighbors, but we want to have a life like we had before. Those who bloodied their hands are afraid that we'll want to return to them what they did to us but we won't. Our faith doesn't allow it." This was an essential superiority that stemmed from Bosniacs' religion. Like Emira, Zahida was equating religious identity with ethnicity, but unlike Emira she came from a community where nearly all Bosniacs were also practicing Muslims. Zahida's attitude also rested strongly on the feeling, shared by many Bosniacs, of moral superiority as victims of Serb attacks. She thus made similar generalizations to Fikreta's about the essential nature of Serbs and Bosniacs, for example stating, "We [Muslims] were illiterate about war but they [Serbs] learn it from birth." This was again the argument that Serbs had secretly wanted and planned the war behind the backs of the unsuspecting and innocent Bosniacs. But at other times she insisted on differentiating between all Serbs and "*Četniks*" (as some of the members of her NGO failed to do) and insisting that there were "good people" in the RS with whom Bosniacs could talk: "Those people who weren't for [nationalist] politics, the politics that got implemented, are now suffering." Indeed, several such Serb women were members of Žene s Podrinja and wholeheartedly supported the process of Bosniac return.

Zahida chose her words carefully in front of Serbs, not emphasizing her sense of moral superiority too much because she was serious about reestablishing a life in Bratunac. Making a distinction between women's and men's spheres was crucial to this strategy. So were "choices about silence and speech." At the meeting I attended with Žene s Podrinja members in Bratunac in the fall of 2000, Zahida made every effort to prevent the discussion among Bosniac and Serb NGO women from the region from revealing the extent of their mutual mistrust. She wanted simply to have Bosniac and Serb NGO women meet and to solicit promises from donors to support the Bosniacs' return and general initiatives to jumpstart the moribund economy. "We just need better economic conditions, factories, and then things will calm down very quickly," she explained to me as we traveled to the meeting—"things" being the lingering mistrust and bitterness a majority of Bosniacs and Serbs felt toward each other as groups.

Participants gathered in the Hotel Fontana, the same building that Serb forces had commandeered during the war and where several tense meetings had been held with Dutch peacekeepers, Bosniac representatives, and the Serb general, Ratko Mladić, in July 1995 just before the slaughter of Bosniac men from Srebrenica began, a fact that was not mentioned but that must have been on the minds of the Bosniacs especially. The meeting was organized as a series of short speeches. The speakers, mostly Bosnians, came from donor and intervention agencies and other women's NGOs from Bosniac-dominated areas of the Federation, including Almasa of Srcem do mira. (Zahida later explained in response to a Serb woman's objection that they had asked for speakers from the local community but that none had volunteered.) One American woman from a donor organization addressed the gathering through an interpreter, who the rest of the time provided translation for the table full of foreign donor representatives (the main target audience). The one Serb presenter was a Bosnian member of Women in Black Belgrade. She spoke in that organization's characteristic feminist, anti-militarist vocabulary, critical of both nationalism and patriarchy, which was not well understood by most of the small-town and rural women she was addressing. Several more presenters dealt with refugee return and reconciliation. They spoke of wartime atrocities, naming several places associated with Bosniac suffering in their accounts of what women had endured, and a few talked about responsibility and justice, but the main focus soon shifted to "neutral" issues like the economy and women's under-representation in politics. Zahida and the facilitator, a young Bosniac woman who regularly did freelance work for international organizations, repeatedly urged the participants to stick to "concrete proposals" and plans for the future.

Running through the speeches were versions of affirmative essentialisms: women had common interests that transcended ethnic divisions; they had all suffered a lot, especially as mothers; their energy and determination to provide for their children would contribute to the revitalization of the economy.[19] As the facilitator put it, "This means we know that women, with their work together and support of one another, can really do things and to contribute to the development of civil society and the normalization of relations, and with this means also reconciliation and living together [suživot]." Such appeals were clearly meant to project a positive sense of unity that would transcend ethnic divisions.

Yet even in these rosy declarations, the speakers indicated their awareness of the mistrust among the women of the region they were visiting, and that most Serbs and Bosniacs held radically different views on what had led to the need for return in the first place, that is, the war. After having talked for several minutes about women's NGOs' efforts to increase women's participation in politics without mentioning nationalism or even national parties, a Bosniac NGO leader from another part of BiH added: "At the end I wish to convey a message to all women and mothers of BiH that they are an important factor in maintaining the peace in this region. We need to bring up children in the spirit of tolerance, in valuing those who think and believe differently and not in the spirit of hatred and intolerance." Like the narratives described above, at first glance, this was a representation of women as mothers and an invocation of the woman-as-peacemaker image. But she did not say this was the way women were but talked about what they should ideally be doing. It was hard, especially in the polarized atmosphere of Bratunac but also given common notions of peaceful Muslims and militaristic Serbs, not to understand this as aimed at Serb women.

As everyone was aware, the audience was full of women members of Žene s Podrinja who had lost most of their male family members in Srebrenica or in Serb ethnic cleansing campaigns of 1992. A few of the presenters, including a human rights activist from Sarajevo, had explicitly talked about genocide, a clear reference to Serb crimes against Bosniacs at Srebrenica and elsewhere (this was before the ICTY genocide judgment on Srebrenica). At the same time, the Serb women in this area had also suffered great losses at the hands of Bosniac forces and desperate civilians from Srebrenica who had attacked Serb villages, killing both soldiers and civilians in their attempts to expand the enclave or to find food (see, for example, Duijzings 2007; Sudetic 1998). As the speeches gave way to free discussion, the Bosniac and Serb women, in the framework of invoking the suffering they had endured as women and mothers, began to take turns mentioning sites of wartime atrocities and suffering of their own ethnic groups while others muttered to themselves in the audience about who, in ethnic terms, had been guilty for what and who had suffered the most. The speaker from Women in Black appealed to the audience to recognize and come to terms with "our own Auschwitzes." But the women continued to speak about the "Auschwitzes" in which members of their own ethnic group had suffered rather than where they had been perpetrators as the speaker had meant.

There was thus a sort of competition of victimhood between the two groups, expressed through the identification with motherhood, which was invoked as an argument against the possibility of guilt for the crimes that had been committed by members of their own ethnic groups. After Almasa had delivered a plea to bring to light all crimes against everyone, suggesting that this was difficult "especially if you felt any guilt yourself," a Serb woman from Bratunac responded emotionally: "It hurts me a bit that you asked us, maybe unconsciously, to admit guilt for 1992. We're victims, too, not killers as you portray us. If that were true, my child would have a father today." Her appeal to innocence and victimhood were thus explicitly tied to motherhood and widowhood. How could Bosniacs accuse Serb women of complicity for the expulsions, killings, even genocide, when they themselves were victims?

The framing of women's solidarity as peacemakers was thus rapidly failing. The American donor representative attempted an intervention that remained within the framework of gender essentialisms, pleading, "I'm here as a woman and foreigner bringing you a warning from the world. Where women are weak, evil is strong. You have a chance to make peace and a future here, but you need to take pain, suffering, and loss and turn them into glue which will bind yourselves together as women." No one paid much attention. It was far past lunch time and the participants were eager to get to the buffet table visible in the next room. The organizers pressed the meeting to a close. Zahida explained afterward that she had deliberately not stopped for lunch even though it was late, "so that there wasn't time for things to go too far." In fact, things could have gone a lot further, as I discovered in the car ride back to Sarajevo with Zahida and several other members of her group (Helms 2010b).

Still, Zahida and her closest allies, including the three Serb women members of the organization who still lived in Bratunac, seemed quite satisfied with the meeting. They knew that their goal to facilitate Bosniac return would take time. The process of reestablishing contact had begun and the donors were aware of their intentions. Indeed, over the following few years, Bosniacs began to slowly return to the area under strong political pressure and monetary aid from intervention agencies. None of these women were worried about the tensions that had come out, even though they had tried to keep them hidden.

There had still been the appeal to women's solidarity, which, combined with women's claims to being apolitical and simply the fact of their being women, had facilitated their efforts on all sides.

"Strategic Avoidance"

A different sort of women's solidarity was mobilized by the network of more critical women's activists in which Medica participated—critical in the sense that they strove to oppose both nationalisms and the sorts of dominant conservative gender norms upheld not only by ruling elites but also by groups like Zahida's or Fikreta's. These were NGOs engaged with lobbying for more gender-neutral laws and procedures, with combating domestic violence, and with promoting not just women in politics but women who shared their aims for a more equal society. I refer to this group as feminist-friendly since many of them embraced the term and none of them distanced themselves from it when asked. However, they did not all readily identify themselves this way. What they shared was a challenge to patriarchal practices and ideologies in a way that agreed with much feminist critique, including that of the self-described feminists in BiH. As part of this feminism or critical stance on gender issues, the NGOs in this network also considered themselves anti-nationalist and took pride in working with each other across ethnicized borders. As NGOs and for the most part as individuals, they all went against the dominant politics of their communities. Maintaining regular contact across ethnicized borders was part of this.

As women, they had been able to cross the erstwhile front lines of the war much sooner after the signing of Dayton than men could or did. In those early days, even though freedom of movement had been declared and peacekeeping forces had been deployed to ensure this, most of the population did not dare to cross these lines. Little was known about conditions on the other sides and there had been a lot of disinformation.[20] In many areas, older (married) women acted as scouts, testing the waters in territories of different ethnic control for the rest of their families (when there were surviving men at all who might have gone). When I lived in the divided (Croat-Bosniac) city of Mostar in the summer of 1996, just a few months after the end of the war, it was common for women to cross the ethnic boundary to the other side of the city where they no longer "belonged." When there was some errand that could not be accomplished on one's "own" side of the city, a woman would typically be the one to cross to the other side to get it done. Unless they were wearing visible markers of religious belonging—Islamic *hidžab*, a nun's habit, a large cross or crescent moon—women could not be distinguished by ethnicity. But men crossing the boundary—and especially younger men (of fighting age)—

were more likely to be recognized by former neighbors or acquaintances or challenged by police or local thugs and risked violent assault if they were determined to belong to the "wrong" ethnic group.

Women's activists were indeed the first to begin crossing what was now the inter-entity border line. Several cross-entity meetings were organized within the first six months after Dayton. Donors were the initiators and guarantors of safety, but as some of the participants later pointed out, the women invited all came, crossing from the Federation to the RS and from the RS to the Federation. Azra, a Bosniac Medica activist who had been in her early twenties at the time, remembered her intense fear as she traveled in March 1996 to Laktaši, a small town north of Banja Luka, for a meeting with the women's group Duga (Rainbow), which also worked with women war victims. She only stayed, she said, because of the presence of Western donor representatives and of the familiar faces of feminists from Belgrade and Zagreb who kept the meeting focused on women's issues.[21]

That summer, a large women's NGO meeting was organized in Sarajevo by the women's group Žena 21 with the backing of US diplomat Swanee Hunt.[22] A few women from Banja Luka, the largest town in the RS, who were just forming their own NGO, United Women (Udružene žene), which would later become close allies with Medica, decided to go as they had also ventured to the Federation for several other women's NGO meetings that year. In discussions with me in their NGO office in June 2000, they recalled what it was like. Banja Luka and all Serb-held territories had been under a strong media blockade during the war. Almost no foreign humanitarian organizations had been active there, there was no contact with feminists from Serbia or Croatia, and foreign journalists were few and far between (in stark contrast with Muslim-dominated areas, especially Sarajevo or Mostar). Most of the information they had about what things were like in the "Muslim" parts of BiH came through the media controlled by Serb nationalists. In general, though, the existence of non-Serbs and even of a state called Bosnia-Herzegovina was pointedly ignored. This was the Republika Srpska.[23] Common café items like Turkish coffee, which was called Bosnian coffee in most of the Federation,[24] had been renamed Serbian or local, "domestic" coffee (domaća kafa) as part of the effort to make the reality of a Serb political territory stick.[25] By 2000 the atmosphere was changing some. United Women activists were already noticing that one could freely use the Latin script again instead of only Cyrillic. The ethnic composition of the RS was changing, too, as some Bosniacs and Croats were starting to return to their former homes. But back in 1996, Sandra explained, crossing what was now the inter-entity border line was seen as "some sort of national betrayal."

Nevertheless, or in spite of this, Sandra could not wait to cross over. She was of mixed Serb-Croat parentage and, typical for an urban Bosnian, had members of all of Bosnia's ethnic groups in her extended family. Some of her relatives lived in the Federation and she was anxious to see them and to see for herself what things were like. Her colleagues Vera and Tanja felt the same. Given where they had come from, however, it was fairly off-putting to attend the Žena 21 conference in the House of the Army (*Dom Armije*), which now referred to the Bosnian Army, from the RS perspective the enemy. Symbols of Bosnian patriotism—to its supporters the denial of Serb nationalist separatism but to the Banja Luka women symbols that had been co-opted into Muslim nationalism—were everywhere. What was more, the keynote address was given by Alija Izetbegović himself, leader of the enemy forces and a symbolic figure of religious Muslim nationalism. Sandra saw this as out of place since "this was not a political meeting but a meeting of women who declared themselves non-political." Tanja found it insensitive to them as guests who after all had been willing to cross the border in the first place. There were other women's groups more supportive of Serb nationalism in the RS who even in 2000 had not traveled to the Federation much less would have gone in 1996.

Still, as the Banja Luka women mingled with those from the Federation at that 1996 conference, they found other women they could talk to, including those from Medica's Infoteka. As Sandra explained, "There are lots of similar women in the NGO sector and we found each other. We realized it's impossible to live separately—we're so intertwined with each other. And we weren't guilty for the whole war. Simply, no one even asked us women [*nas ženama jednostavno niko nije ni pitao*]." They found common cause with many of the Federation women and had built effective cooperation with them on what united them: "women's issues and alternative politics," in other words their opposition in each locality to the ruling elites and their corruption, nationalism, and sexism.

United Women and Medica shared a specific focus on combating violence against women (although crucially this did not include wartime sexual violence, a distinction I take up in chapter 6). I witnessed many instances of cooperation between the two NGOs, both bilaterally and in larger groups of similar-minded women's organizations. As individuals and as NGOs, they had achieved a great deal of trust and cooperation, indeed real friendships, across ethnic divides, which they put to work on a variety of initiatives to benefit women. They counted on each other as allies.

Members of these groups as well as other women's NGOs from all parts of BiH were present at the round-table meeting, "Obstacles and Advantages in the Struggle for Equal Rights in the Third Millennium," organized in Banja

Luka in March 2000 by United Women and the Banja Luka office of the Helsinki Citizens' Assembly (an NGO dominated by women that often participated in feminist initiatives and worked closely with United Women). As at most such meetings, issues of ethnic politics—confronting the past, reconciliation, or debating the future of the BiH state—were never direct topics, despite the consensus in opposing nationalists and supporting refugee return. Discussions at meals and coffee breaks were different, however. There I witnessed conversations that never could have taken place a few years earlier. One night over dinner, at a table full of Federation women, two women from Banja Luka joked about their having had to register for the draft when the Bosnian Serb Army was short of men. Another told a story involving her husband's experiences in the Bosnian Army, the very troops against which the husbands of the women across the table had fought. Two women from opposite sides of the Bosnian-Croatian border figured out amid friendly laughter that the husband of one had been helping to shell the enclave town where the other woman had been trapped during the war.

It was safe to discuss this first of all because these women had gotten to know each other and their respective political commitments well. But this also depended on their positioning as women talking to women: persons not seen as combatants or political decision-makers. Their underlying assumption, which they also often articulated, was that none of the women had wanted the war, that everyone had suffered, and that their husbands and sons had had no choice (being males) but to serve in the army where they were living. It was accepted, in other words, that neither the women nor their family members were nationalists or had any sympathy for the chauvinistic ideologies that fueled the war or the violence that ensued—"No one even asked us women."

When I asked them later and separately about this dynamic, however, members of both Medica and United Women admitted that they avoided probing too deeply. They did not want to find out anything that might compromise their working relationships. At Infoteka, Duška explained, "If the husband of one of the women in another organization was in another army from mine, well, if I think about that, it can only hinder my work." United Women leaders had a similar explanation. In Sandra's words, "No one would have talked about those things in 1996. Now we know each other. Now we can agree to disagree." Tanja called their careful selection of terminology, topics, and approach "strategic avoidance" (*strateško zaobilaženje*).

I had seen evidence of this in many meetings among this group of women's NGOs. As critics of dominant politics, these were not women who spoke in nationalist terms or displayed attachments to ethnicity. But there were issues they knew they disagreed about, especially on how to characterize the war or the Dayton Agreement that had established the current political structure they were all trying to reform. Many of the activists from the Bosniac areas of the Federation expressed the dominant characterization there of the war as aggression on Bosnia-Herzegovina as an internationally recognized sovereign state by military forces from neighboring states. Likewise, many women from the RS adhered to the dominant viewpoint in their entity of the war as a civil war between ethnic groups in Bosnia that could not agree on how to react to the dissolution of Yugoslavia.[26] But at meetings of this network, I generally only heard reference simply to the war (rat).

Discussions of war events and the past were of course part of what these women were avoiding, but even so, attitudes about the war were relevant, as they carried implications for the way BiH should be structured (or not) in the future. Particularly touchy was the question of the entities. Many in the Federation felt that the RS had been founded on the basis of ethnic cleansing and was therefore illegitimate. They favored the abolition of the entities and ethnic control over all territories so as to allow for the equal treatment of all BiH citizens throughout the whole territory of the state and to neutralize nationalist separatists' power to obstruct the functioning of the state. The entity structure was posited as a mistake in the Dayton Agreement. Many RS Serbs, however, felt that Dayton was flawed because it had not provided for a *third* entity— for Croats. The leaders of United Women were sympathetic to this view. While they supported a multiethnic BiH state, they saw a value in maintaining the RS as an entity, as it provided a certain level of security for many Serbs who, still in the mode of ethnic-group-as-power-block thinking, were wary of being "ruled by" the more numerous Bosniacs. The women in this network, therefore, tried not to delve into their reasons for complaining about Dayton, just as they avoided other linguistic and symbolic cues that might be perceived as threatening by the women from other entities and ethnic groups.

Back in Zenica, Azra was at first upbeat about the level of cross-entity cooperation among women's activists, especially because she had witnessed such an improvement from the first meetings in 1996. "Now," she said in an interview over coffee, "we have real common ground." In qualifying this, however, she confirmed the tactic of strategic avoidance: "But there still isn't much talk about nationalism. It's like we've forgotten. You get the feeling that everyone is staying silent. Maybe this is to avoid getting into arguments, to avoid any kind of insults. No woman likes war and we all see that we have to live together and live with what happened." Despite the implications of underlying disagreements, Azra concluded her assessment with a gesture to female solidarity in the mode of affirmative essentialisms. Rather than finding the explanation in these women's shared commitments to feminist critique and alternative politics and thus pointing out that these were particular women working hard to bridge political divides, Azra invoked a common stance based on shared womanhood.

This came just a few minutes after she had passionately described to me the harrowing experiences of Nedim, her boyfriend at the time, a Bosniac who had been doing his mandatory service in the Yugoslav People's Army in 1991 when the war broke out in Croatia. He had been sent to Vukovar in eastern Croatia to defend Yugoslavia, he thought, from dissolution. Instead, he encountered "real Četniks" who sported Serb nationalist regalia and asked what a guy with his (Muslim) name was doing there in their fight to help Serbs in Croatia "cleanse" and claim territories for themselves. Sensing that he was in danger, Nedim had fled back to his hometown in Bosnia, only to be attacked and put into a camp (logor) a short time later by Croatian nationalist militias trying to "cleanse" the area of Muslims. Azra's boyfriend clearly did not like war and had not supported offensive actions or violence. In fact, he was one of the most non-confrontational people I knew in Bosnia, male or female. Yet Azra's appeal to the essentialist binary, "no woman likes war," implied that men, also as a group with essential qualities, did.

Azra's point in relating Nedim's experiences had been to explain how she and others in "the area with Bosniac majority or however you want to call it" could freely cross into the RS or Croat areas because they had not attacked their neighbors. Nedim, back again in his hometown after several years as a refugee, had recently encountered on the street one of the Croat guards from the camp he had been in. The man had said hello and Nedim had greeted him back. Azra told me she had asked Nedim why he had acknowledged the man and Nedim had said he had nothing to hide or be ashamed of, "so why not answer the guy, let him think about what he's done?" The conscience and "face" (obraz) of people like Nedim had remained clean, which gave them "a sort of moral satisfaction because they know they are innocent." It was clear, therefore, that the implied aggression of men in Azra's narrative, as in Fikreta's, referred chiefly to men in nationalist militaries, that is, Serbs and Croats fighting for ethnically pure territories.

Azra wondered about the Serb women activists in their network and why they could not see that the war had been aggression incited by the Serbs. "They are afraid to think this way because they or those close to them did those things during the war," she concluded. But she did not single anyone out individually and she and her colleagues still counted the women activists in their feminist-friendly network as close allies in their work on gender equality and combating violence against women. The women in Banja Luka were aware of these suspicions but also spoke in generalities. They saw their differences with Federation women as irrelevant to the job at hand and they resented the assumption that because they had stayed in a town that was largely ethnically cleansed and became ruled by Serb nationalists that they shared that guilt. Tanja was ready to leave these issues untouched:

> We can work great together. But if they say we have to first say who the aggressor in the war was before we can talk about anything else . . . why? What does that have to do with the job we are trying to do? I stayed here throughout the whole war and witnessed the loss of my friends, non-Serbs. But if a woman from the Federation wants to call me aggressor, then fine if that makes her feel better. I don't know, I wasn't shelled myself. I don't hate her.

Fortunately, it did not come to such challenges among this group. And the suspicions and different positions these activists worked hard not to expose were ultimately not rooted in essentialist views of collective ethnic cultures but were shaped by the geographies of war and postwar politics. After all, not all of the Federation women were Bosniacs, or the RS women Serbs. As Azra made clear, she located the sense of innocence among people in "the area with Bosniac majority or however you want to call it," in other words those of any ethnic background who had stayed in the Federation and were attacked by Serb (and Croat) nationalists.

The women in this network were unusual in their commitment to challenging patriarchal norms and entrenched institutional practices that kept women in marginal and vulnerable social positions. They stood out as opponents of most aspects of dominant politics in their communities, which closed many doors to them and even put them at risk, especially in places governed by separatist nationalists as in the RS.[27] Receiving funding from foreign donors did not help their reputation in this regard. This critical stance and openness to difference was the first condition for their successful cooperation, but it was also crucial that they were able to build their positioning as women with all the implied positive characteristics that went with popular essentialist notions: women were uninvolved in politics and war, they carried no guilt and were more open to cross-ethnic communication. Working on problems like violence against women allowed them to both avoid disagreements on "ethnic" issues and to suggest in public representations that because they were women working on "women's issues," they were not political and therefore not threatening. At times this was an important strategy toward skeptical local authorities, but it was just as often a rhetorical device that peppered conversations among the activists themselves, especially when political differences threatened to emerge. Reminding each other of the reality of women's general absence from positions of power was a way of reassuring each other of their mutual unimplicatedness and innocence so that they could get on with other work.

Testing Feminism 1: The NATO Bombing of Serbia

In the time I spent with Medica Zenica, I witnessed many encounters with foreign feminists, often donor representatives, whose questions to the women of Infoteka about their relationship to feminism would always elicit eye rolls and knowing glances at each other around the table. Here we go again. . . . Then one of them would patiently and earnestly explain the situation. They were feminists, but "in a Bosnian way."[28]

There were various aspects to this question. Here I want to consider the assumptions about nationalism that came with the label of feminism. For Medica, their feminism was inextricable from their ties to feminists abroad. First of all, the founders and original funders of Medica had come from Germany and given the project its overtly feminist face, although, as the Bosnians and Germans involved all acknowledged, there had been little discussion of what this meant exactly aside from the fact that this would be a project focused on helping women. Perhaps more important for individual Medica activists' sense of feminism, however, had been their sustained interaction with feminists from Zagreb and Belgrade. Several of the women from Medica had in fact attended various training sessions organized by the Croatian and Serbian feminists, including a feminist summer school led by activists from Women in Black in Belgrade.

This feminism was explicitly anti-nationalist and anti-militarist, having been formulated in opposition to the war violence and to the consequences for women of newly powerful traditionalist nationalisms in Serbia and Croatia. It was thus logical and easy for the Bosnian activists to embrace these principles, positioned as they were as advocates for female victims of those nationalist projects. When the Serbian government began to crack down militarily on Albanians in the contested province of Kosovo in the late 1990s, Medica women easily joined Women in Black in Belgrade in condemning the militarism, nationalism, and racism of the Serbian government (see, for example, Women in Black 1999). But these positions were challenged when Serbia itself became a target of NATO forces in the spring of 1999.

The atmosphere in the Bosniac-dominated areas of BiH was decidedly pro-NATO. When the bombing began, I was in Sarajevo where I witnessed the euphoria of people who had spent four years under a brutal Serb siege, for which they held the Milošević regime substantially to blame. The house where I was staying was perched on the hill to the east above the city center.

We could see and feel NATO bombers flying directly over our heads on their way to Serbia. My Bosnian host, a man my age who had survived the war as a Bosnian Army soldier trying not to get sent to the front lines, spent hours watching BBC coverage of the crisis, waving his fist at the television and chanting for my benefit, but only somewhat tongue-in-cheek, "Bomb them! Bomb them!" When I visited the leader of a Sarajevo women's group in her home to celebrate Bajram (Eid al-Fitr), she was also watching coverage of the bombing. She told me how glad she was that NATO was doing this. Everywhere Sarajevans were toasting the bombers for taking the only steps that could stop Serb forces in their attacks on Albanian civilians, steps that many felt had finally brought the Serbs to the negotiating table in BiH and that should have been undertaken much earlier to save more Bosnian lives. The only people I could find who shared my uneasiness about NATO's militaristic intervention and its imperialist implications were a few other foreigners and a handful of Serbs, only some of whom were equally concerned about the plight of the Albanian population. To be sure, many Sarajevans of all ethnic backgrounds voiced unease with the way NATO was handling the situation, especially when it began bombing less obviously military targets. No one raised objections publicly, however.

A similar atmosphere prevailed in Zenica and other Bosniac-majority towns.[29] It was easy to understand that the Medica women of all ethnic backgrounds, who had worked so closely with or were themselves victims of Serb ethnic cleansing campaigns, would be happy to see the Milošević regime punished. Still, given their solidarity with Women in Black, their general stance against war and nationalism, and their concern for civilian populations, I wondered, would Bosnian feminists be critical of the NATO bombing?

It is not that feminists in Bosnia claimed to be pacifists. Even Alma, a former member of Medica and the leading Bosnian activist for the rights of conscientious objectors, did not oppose military action in certain circumstances. After having helped to organize peace demonstrations in Zenica at the beginning of the war, she had enlisted in the Bosnian Army. As she explained to me during one conversation:

> I did this purely to fight to defend my country, my family and friends, literally to defend Bosnia. This is how I saw it and I'm still sure that the ideas I went off to war with were pure and honorable. Yes, pacifists said to me that it did no good, that violence was wrong. I didn't like holding a gun, none of us did, and we just hoped we didn't have to use it on anyone. But in those conditions, when you are attacked, it's ridiculous to talk about nonviolence and pacifism, especially in the kind of conditions like in 1992.

Alma was one of the most critical feminists I had met in BiH. She was acutely aware not only of sexism and nationalism but also of racism, social injustice, heterosexism, classism, and was critical of state and corporate power on a global level.[30] She, like other Bosnian feminists, including those at Medica, supported Women in Black and their principled stand against militarism and violence. In fact, my conversation with her took place at the annual Women in Black meeting, which had to be held that year in Montenegro due to the bombing and the political situation in Serbia. Alma, Infoteka activists, and other Bosnian feminists had all made the long journey through hostile border crossings in order to show support. I was therefore somewhat shocked when Alma said she supported the bombings. Seeing my surprise, she exclaimed, "I've waited eight years for someone to bomb Milošević!" After having suffered so much during the war at the hands of Serb forces, the point for her and for many Bosnian feminists was that action be taken against Milošević and Serb nationalists to prevent the atrocities they encouraged or perpetrated.

It was not that Bosnian feminists had lost their critique of nationalism's gendered effects, nor would they turn against their activist allies. Sarajevo feminists provided shelter to several Serbian women activists and male conscientious objectors who had been threatened for their outspoken opposition to Serbia's actions in Kosovo (see Fridman 2011). At Medica, there was no consensus. Most of the women in Infoteka had cheered the bombing as Alma had. They kept in touch with their Serbian feminist friends by phone, even if also to tease them with the Bosnians' notorious black humor about how it felt to have bombs raining down on them. They offered the Serbian women advice on how to survive in a bomb shelter, conveying both sympathy and concern, but also a reminder that Bosnians had been through a worse situation and for much longer.

A few Infoteka activists had not shared in the euphoria. Their American volunteer opposed military solutions on principle but, like me, she found it difficult not to empathize with expressions of relief from those who had lived through the war. Duška expressed a similar stance when I asked her about it later. She said she understood everyone's joy after all they had suffered during the war at the hands of Serbs, but she could not support the bombing. She was "really torn," she said, because "part of me was really sorry for people there [in Serbia] but the other part of me thought, eh, screw it. Let it be" (*E, jebiga, neka*). Though it troubled her, it was not high enough on her list of concerns to risk articulating this, perhaps also because her criticism might be read as affinity with Serb nationalism since she herself was of Serb background. One other activist of Serb background had voiced some opposition but only around Medica, and was never able to draw anyone into critical discussion. In any case, Medica issued no public statements on the bombing.[31]

In fact, no women's group in BiH said anything in public about this event. I had attended a meeting called by the Bosnian office of the OHCHR (Office of the High Commissioner for Human Rights) to discuss how to voice opposition to NATO's actions in Serbia and Kosovo. In addition to the foreign women present, three women's NGO activists from the Federation and two from the RS had come, all of them passionately opposed to the bombing out of feminist and anti-militarist principles. But the initiative never got off the ground, presumably because of lack of support, and the moment passed.

It was common among self-described Bosnian feminists to say that the war had made them a feminist. Seeing the gendered effects of nationalist violence firsthand and knowing they themselves might have been attacked or raped, too, because of their names and presumed ethnic identity, or even experiencing these things themselves, had led many activists first to humanitarian work and, through this, to feminist activism. These trajectories were quite individual and contingent. Often a feminist stance had been built through personal friendships with feminists from neighboring countries or farther afield and was then brought to relate back to the situation in BiH. There was plenty of discussion and agreement on topics that were central to these activists' work—domestic violence, sex discrimination, women's political representation, and so on. But since any deep engagement with issues of ethnicity and nationalism tended to be sidestepped in women's and feminist activist circles, there was no common position or sets of positions vis-à-vis nationalism as a general phenomenon rather than one associated with particular nations, particularly when associated with a hostile nation.

Gordana was a Serb from Sarajevo who had become a feminist activist during her years as a refugee in Belgrade where she became a member of Women in Black. As a Serb woman protesting Serbian nationalism, she had cut her feminist teeth opposing a militaristic nationalism that claimed to act in her name rather than excluding and attacking her. When she returned to Sarajevo after the war, she, along with two veterans of Medica, had helped to establish a new feminist NGO that would maintain a sharp anti-nationalist and anti-militarist feminist stance. In 2002 Gordana told me of her recent visit to Kosovo where she had been disappointed with many of the Kosovar Albanian women activists who, she said, were "not critical of their own people." Now that Serbian troops had been forced out and Kosovo was being run by Albanian politicians under a UN protectorate, Gordana had expected Albanian women's activists, especially those who declared themselves feminists, to be just as critical of Albanian nationalism and military campaigns as they had been of their Serbian versions. For her, the categorical opposition to nationalism and militarism were part of being a feminist.

Of course, there was a difference between Serbian nationalism and (leaving the case of Kosovo aside) Bosniac variants. In BiH, the (gendered) effects of Bosniac nationalism had been less visible and, most importantly, not nearly as deadly and devastating as those of Serb and also Croat nationalisms. Location and outwardly perceived identity thus created differences in the possibilities of political opposition, something Milica noticed when considering Medica's work in relation to that of feminists elsewhere. In Belgrade, even though they were villified, feminists openly protested the Serbian regime that had sponsored and fueled the war in BiH. But Medica was unlikely to take on such a public role, not only because they had started out keeping a low profile in order to protect the women they were helping, but also because of their position in relation to victimhood. As Milica put it, "Bosnia is in a different position from Belgrade—Bosnia is the victim of the war so it's harder to stand up to the powers that be here. . . . Here it's hard to criticize those in power because they're held as victims, heroes. For example, talking about domestic violence is very difficult. Who are the perpetrators? Local men! But they are the heroes of the war, our defenders and saviors." It was more acceptable to point to the gendered workings of power when the perpetrators were ethnically "other" men, but the politics of victimhood resisted applying a feminist critique to gender regimes "among us." There were few issues that would not be read through assessments of the war, understandings of ethno-national divisions, or, in short, collective victim narratives of various kinds.

Testing Feminism 2: Wartime Rape

Another incident illustrates the difficulties of reconciling collective victimhood with feminist critiques of nationalism and to Medica's identification with the anti-nationalist feminisms articulated in Belgrade and Zagreb. In 2001, on the occasion of the conviction of a group of Serb men for the rape of Muslim women in the eastern Bosnian town of Foča,[32] Gabriela Mischkowski, a feminist historian and co-founder of Medica Mondiale, published an opinion piece in a German newspaper asserting that rape in the Bosnian war was nothing new.[33] Aimed at a German audience, the editorial argued that the systematic and mass character of rapes of Muslim women by Serb forces did not constitute proof that rape had been a Serb "war strategy." Orders "from above" had not been necessary; the rapists had acted "from below" according to a shared patriarchal script that treats women as the spoils of war and symbols of national honor. In Bosnia, those involved had not needed orders to understand that rape would be a powerful weapon of ethnic cleansing. Mischkowski's goal was to force an acknowledgement in Germany that rape happened in all wars—she also mentioned rapes by Japanese and

Soviet troops in World War II—it was not a uniquely Serbian crime or "Balkan" atrocity. She was arguing for international standards of prosecution and for militaries to take seriously their powers to stop such behavior in their soldiers.

Read by some activists in BiH, the editorial apparently attacked a core pillar of their sense of morality and purpose in their work on behalf of women war victims.[34] An outraged human rights activist in Sarajevo who worked closely with Medica sent the organization a translation of the German article. At Medica, a small group of women vented their indignation, which was exacerbated by a sense of betrayal: as a key leader of Medica Mondiale, Mischkowski had spent many months at Medica Zenica in the early days of the organization and was considered a close friend and ally by the Bosnian women. An incredulous response was drafted, signed by nearly all members of Medica Zenica, and sent to Germany after being translated. In contrast to Mischkowski, these women insisted that the rapes had been systematic and ordered from top Serb military leaders as a weapon against Bosniacs and BiH. To suggest otherwise, they said, was to equate the victim (i.e., the Bosniacs) with the aggressor (i.e., the Serbs). They were perhaps most bothered by Mischkowski's argument against concepts like "genocidal rape" and "rape warfare," which she said had been manipulated to serve the interests of Bosniac and Croatian propaganda. Turning the tables, Medica's letter accused Mischkowski of succumbing to "Serb propaganda" and betraying the Bosniac women victims of these brutal crimes.[35]

In fact, Mischkowski's article had specifically mentioned the way in which local and foreign media had taken up the arguments of Croatian "nationalist feminists" and their allies in the United States and elsewhere (as discussed in chapter 2). And it was precisely the opponents of the nationalist feminist camp, the "anti-nationalist feminists" in Zagreb and Belgrade, with whom Medica had always allied itself. Isolated in BiH by the war, Medica Zenica had not been part of the debates in Zagreb but had built close relationships with the activists in the anti-nationalist camp. Once or twice in Infoteka I had heard the women mention their differences with BiH women's groups like Biser and Žena BiH, precisely because of differences over how to characterize wartime rape.[36] They had been careful to emphasize the gendered dimension of the crime and to place their focus on helping women victims heal, to become survivors. In retrospect, it had only been a few of the most critically anti-nationalist and feminist of the Medica activists who had stressed this positioning. Some of them were no longer with the organization in 2001 to react to Mischkowski's article. And although there were also Bosniacs among this more critical group, several of those who were wary of strong assertions of Bosniac victimhood also happened to be women of Serb or Croat background. It was more difficult for these women to voice their dissent even though they, like the Bosniacs, positioned themselves as pro-BiH and against the especially destructive nationalisms of separatist Serbs and Croats. When the issue was the victimization of Bosniacs, the non-Bosniac women felt it would be better not to voice any critical remarks.

Things were complicated and emotionally charged. At Medica I had also heard other activists—sometimes the same ones who insisted on the gender dimensions of the war rapes and who solidly allied themselves with the anti-nationalist feminists in Zagreb and Belgrade—draw a distinction between rapes "on all sides" and a systematic, planned campaign by Serb forces. Indeed, for Azra, this view of rape was for her a reason to insist on innocence of Bosniac and pro-BiH people. Azra was not an instigator of the response to Mischkowski's article, but it was sentiments like hers that had prevailed in this incident. The few dissenters were disappointed with the way the response had unfolded. As one of them put it later, the supporters of the response letter had just reacted "with their gut" instead of engaging in a reasoned discussion.

Medica's focus on healing women war victims and later on domestic violence had apparently allowed its members to avoid a discussion of its precise stance on the nature of the violence. Perhaps this was unnecessary for getting their work done, just as discussion about the nature of the war itself would have placed unnecessary obstacles in the way of the cross-entity work engaged in by Medica, United Women, and the others in that feminist-friendly network. As Medica now focused on other issues and as wartime rape had not been debated or even much discussed in public by that time, there were few chances for these disagreements to emerge and endanger established relationships. Indeed, as the objections to the Mischkowski's article were directed at the author, Medica's relationships with Zagreb and Belgrade feminists who had articulated similar stances could remain intact without opening up potentially divisive issues. These activists could continue their cooperation on the basis of a common opposition to gender-based violence, of which the main perpetrator was "men." There was no need to specify *which* men were meant.

5

 Politics Is a Whore

Women and the Political

A young woman is hanging out by an SFOR [military peacekeeping] base in Sarajevo practicing the world's oldest profession. An older man from the community comes to her and says, "Why are you doing this? You're young and fit, you're a Bosniac—surely you can find other things to do. Why didn't you choose instead to get an education?"

    The girl replies, "I have an education. I graduated from university."
    Old man: "Well, there must be another job you can do."
    Girl: "But I'm not a member of the party."
    Old man: "Why don't you join the party?"
    Girl: "Are you kidding, my mother barely let me do *this*!"

                                          Joke recorded in Sarajevo, 1999

The Trouble with Politics

"I don't have anything to do with politics!" Halima quickly shot back as soon as the word "political" had come out of my mouth. I had started to ask her how she saw her work as spiritual counselor to women victims of gender-based violence at Medica. After all, Medica declared itself a feminist project, and this was a label that was generally viewed by Bosnians as "something political." Halima herself did not shy away from the feminist label and even embraced it. She had also just finished telling me how she always tried to convince women of their social worth and that they had the right to be heard, that they should demand their rights and "use their brains." They did not have to blindly obey men, she told them, including men in positions of authority such as at the Islamic Community, where she also worked and often challenged interpretations of Islamic practice that enforced male dominance. As we talked about what politics might mean, Halima eventually said that her work did have a political aspect in terms of promoting social change, "if you broaden it like that," but she stressed again that she was not connected in any way to politics in the sense of parties and government.

At the many NGO meetings I attended, I heard activists from all parts of BiH introducing their organizations and activities as "humanitarian." They stressed their independence from political parties and, as discussed in chapter 3, often emphasized that their groups were "non-governmental, non-party, and non-profit," as if countering unspoken accusations that they pursued their activities out of personal or financial "interest" (*interes*). Such disclaimers were widespread, and not just among women. Even when ordinary people joined or volunteered for a powerful party, it was often assumed to be based on material rewards rather than (purely) out of ideological conviction. Speaking at least for the urban, educated population, Ermina at Infoteka argued that political parties and elections left a bad taste in Bosnians' mouths because multiparty elections had only been introduced in 1990 and it was the politicians elected then that soon brought the country into war. Since then, the media had been full of reports of political corruption, collusion with war profiteers, even exposés of how politicians were themselves the war and postwar profiteers, enriching themselves using the power of their positions and networks (see Helms 2006). Few people had any sense that politicians were doing them any good. Rather, it was the politicians who were obstructing the (re)establishment of peace and prosperity. Of course, there was no consensus on *which* politicians were guilty of this obstruction when it took on ethnic overtones, as there was a tendency to regard the politicians representing rival ethno-national groups as worse nationalists than one's "own" politicians.

The question of politics was thus a troubled one, especially for women. It was a catch-all for everything that had gone wrong in BiH in recent years—chauvinist nationalisms, war, corrupt politics, and the ethically questionable profiteering of the new business class. I was often given this one-word response—"politics!" (*politika!*)—along with gestures of helplessness and exasperation, as an explanation for the war, or indeed any pressing social or economic problem BiH was experiencing (see Kolind 2007). Politics (and politicians) had in fact been distrusted by much of the population since before the war as a realm of self-interested maneuvering, dirty deals, and public lies. As I was told over and over, politics was a whore (*politika je kurva*), the ultimate immoral figure and a metaphor for a host of gendered implications. For everyone but especially for women, then, it felt much more comfortable to be doing "humanitarian work."

At the same time, the NGO as a new form of social organization was being promoted as a link between society and the state, or in other words, between the private and the political. As we saw in chapter 3, foreign donors and intervention agencies were not always consistent in their explanations of the role of "civil society" or NGOs; nor was there consensus among NGO activists as they endeavored to explain their roles to themselves, their fellow NGO members, or the larger public. Refugee return and ethnic reconciliation, where women's NGOs had been encouraged to play a leading role, were profoundly political activities even though this was seldom acknowledged. Still another part of expectations for NGOs was for women's rights organizations such as Medica Zenica to engage in public advocacy and lobbying of lawmakers and government officials on behalf of the members of society they purportedly represented, that is, women. This explicitly political engagement was being touted as a hallmark of true democracy after Western (ideal type) models. Engaging in politics was therefore being put forth as a legitimate, moral enterprise, especially for women, whose political participation would help to ensure a more complete democracy. For similar reasons, and as part of the same foreign-led democratization project, in 1999–2000, women were being strongly encouraged to enter into formal politics, the heart of the morally corrupt and male space of *politika*. Propelled by foreign actors and local women's NGOs alike, women were being recruited and trained to occupy the new spaces that had been reserved for "the minority gender" in a new gender quota rule that had come into force in 1998.

Although some of these positive arguments about political engagement were taken up by the women I met, for the most part they attempted to distance themselves from *politika*, once again claiming a sort of collective victimhood status in order to avoid any suggestion that "women" bore responsibility for the evils produced by the political sphere—nationalist exclusions, war violence, corruption, and theft, and a variety of other injustices that led to poor quality of life for most of the population. As women positioned themselves in opposition to nationalism, they also played on and reinforced the construction of "politics" as a corrupt male arena. Paradoxically, this positioning was often mobilized in support of women's claims to legitimacy as *public*, even *political* actors. This was another way in which women activists made use of representations of women as passive, unimplicated actors (victims) in order to be accepted as *active* social agents.

This chapter shows how those representations were constructed and enacted, and how women NGO activists and those directly engaged in party politics attempted to resolve the dilemmas that arose without compromising their claims to moral standing. I argue that these dilemmas were resolved first through strategic use of affirmative essentialisms and then, especially for women directly involved in the political system, by a temporal distinction between a corrupt male politics of the past and present, and a more just and honest politics of the future, made possible by the participation of women. These framings, I argue, were helpful in building acceptance of women in political pursuits but did little in the short term to change dominant ideals of women as the pillars of the family.

Further, in addition to showing how politics was gendered, I aim to turn the analytical lens around to consider how attention to gender dynamics sheds light on areas of political and social contestations more generally. Discourses and practices of the political inevitably invite distinctions between what is political and what is not, the not-political being understood variously as the private or the domestic. The dichotomies thus produced are classically gendered and profoundly embedded in the historical developments of the dominant models and ideologies that circulate in postwar BiH, that is, liberal capitalism and democracy (e.g., Fraser 1997; Pateman 1988) as well as socialism (Gal 2002; Gal and Kligman 2000).[1] At the same time, due to the naturalizing force of gender associations (Scott 1999; Yanagisako and Delaney 1995), their mobilization calls attention to areas of uncertainty and contestation over the boundaries of the political and the public with the domestic and the private, or, as the case of postwar BiH especially brings out, the socially immoral with the moral. In other words, gender and gendered metaphors become ways of naturalizing and making sense of the uneasiness produced over what is political or public and what is not.

In this process, affirmative essentialisms are again crucial. Positive representations of women's qualities and virtues were contrasted with equally essentialized and characterized constructions of men and male-dominated spaces, the very places from which the evils of war, nationalism, and political corruption had come and now the places that women were proposing to "clean up."

Politics as Male

To understand women's relationship to the political, it must first be observed that "politics" was most often understood as the formal sphere of political parties, government power, and elections. This was the politics seen as dirty and corrupt but it also tainted any conceptualization of the political, as my conversations with Halima and many others brought out. Women activists attempted to deny a relationship to politics in both these senses, but especially the former.

A second point is that women as a group had *not* been among the politicians, government officials, or military leaders who led the country to a disastrous war. Even during the Yugoslav period, when official state policy encouraged women's participation in the institutions of self-managing socialism, the percentage of women in the Assembly of the Republic of Bosnia-Herzegovina stood at 24.1 percent, with 17.3 percent women in the republic's municipal assemblies.[2] A few exceptions offered at least some models of female politicians: several female partisan veterans served in the top party leadership and Milka Planinc became the first and only female prime minister of Yugoslavia from 1982 to 1986. But overall, politically active women were mostly concentrated at the lower levels and women's Communist Party membership (a prerequisite for getting elected) remained at much lower levels than men's (Massey, Leach, and Sekulic 1997; see also Ramet 1999).[3]

With the demise of socialism, women's participation in politics fell drastically as it did in other parts of the postsocialist world (Gal and Kligman 2000; Rueschemeyer 1998; Watson 1993).[4] In the first multiparty elections of 1990, the percentage of women in the BiH Assembly fell to 2.92 percent (seven women out of 240 delegates) and to 5 percent (315 out of 6299) in municipal assemblies. In the first elections after the war (1996), percentages of women in state and entity-level Parliaments remained below 5 percent, with only one woman elected to the state-level House of Representatives. There was

Figure 13 OSCE poster promoting women candidates: "2000 Women in 2000: Almost 2000 women are candidates for the local elections 11/11/2000. Look for them on the open lists." (photo by author)

Politics Is a Whore

again one high-level exception: Biljana Plavšić of the SDS was the Serb member of the three-person collective presidency of BiH in 1990 and after the war, in 1996, she was elected president of the RS. Like Planinc, however, Plavšić was a rare example. Percentages of women in politics remained very low in BiH until 1998 when the OSCE, with the support of local women's NGOs, pushed through a series of quota rules for women's representation on party ballot lists. This was accompanied by a sustained effort on the part of OSCE and other intervention organizations to encourage and train women to run for office and to urge voters to vote for them. Only then did women's presence in formal politics increase again, this time to 18 percent (Ler-Sofronić 1998).[5]

Despite the rise in women's participation levels, however, politics continued to be seen as the realm of men where women had no place.[6] While women's images were used in the media and public space to convey political messages, they were typically of anonymous women standing in for certain social categories or metaphorical associations. In contrast, male politicians appeared as specific individuals. This contrast was summed up in the SDA campaign billboards placed around Sarajevo before the 2000 local elections that pictured male politicians standing confidently in dark suits and ties, each labeled with their full name, beneath the slogan "Vote for Your Own People/Men" (see fig. 14). At the same time, another set of billboards featured anonymous women

Figure 14 SDA local elections, 2000, campaign billboard: "Vote for your own people/men." (photo by author)

as symbols of a "beautiful Sarajevo" (Helms 2008, 102–3) (see fig. 15). Taken together, the ads reflected the common assumption that it was men who would be doing the job of politics.

One might object that the word used in the posters of men was *ljudi*, plural of *čovjek*, which means both people/person as well as the universal men/man (see Iveković 1997, 98). While ostensibly neutral, in practice, it was often assumed to refer to men, leading to the common clarification of "people—and women" (*ljudi—i žene*) when women were explicitly included. This raised particular difficulties for women's activism in general but especially in relation to politics. One political party poster in Zenica in 2000 listed the "rights of man" (*prava čovjeka*) the party promised to uphold, but felt the need to add a specific call to women: "Woman! You are also a man/person!" (*"Ženo! I ti si čovjek!"*). *Čovjek* was also understood as referring to the regular person, a decent guy, or human being who was afforded all the conditions to live a dignified life. The Social Democratic Party (SDP) offered itself as a multiethnic and non-nationalist party that also promoted women and youth and indeed counted many prominent female politicians in its ranks. Its campaign posters for a later election promised, among other things, "equal rights" using a phrase often associated with women's activism while also touting their platform as *za čovjeka*, "for the person/man," implying that citizens under an SDP government would

Figure 15 SDA local elections, 2000, campaign billboard: "For a Sarajevo as beautiful as Sarajevan women." (photo by author)

Politics Is a Whore

be treated with dignity (see fig. 16). The terminology left it somewhat unclear, however unintentionally, whether women were to be included.

On the level of practice, the understanding of politics as not only a male realm but also one of prestige and power (despite negative popular assessments) was made abundantly clear when the question of women's effectiveness as politicians arose. In a telling example, delegates at the opening session of the Federation Parliament in early 1999 were deadlocked after having elected a Bosniac (from the dominant Bosniac party, the SDA) and a Croat (from the main Croat party, the HDZ, Hrvatska Demokratska Zajednica or Croatian Democratic Union) for two of three executive Parliament positions. When the leading Bosniac politician, Ejub Ganić, suggested that the third post be given to a woman, the delegates burst into laughter.[7] The few women representatives present chuckled nervously but said nothing and when the laughter died down, Parliament got back to business and elected a man for the post.[8] Despite the serious political differences between the two ethnically based parties, they were in perfect agreement that the only serious candidates for positions of power were men.

One man I knew in Zenica, Mirza, revealed these assumptions in a different way when, stopping in the street to chat, he began to complain about the corruption of the politicians in power. Knowing from previous conversations

Figure 16 SDP elections poster in downtown Sarajevo, 2008: "For the person/man: Equal rights, At the workplace, On a European path." (photo by author)

that I was interested in women's political participation, he declared: "I'd love to see a woman win at the top of the canton. This would show those asshole— if you'll excuse me—politicians who go around acting all important, you know those manly [*muškobanjasti*] ones all pumped up [*sve napumpani*]." He swelled out his chest and arms to demonstrate. "They act so important. But if the voters picked a woman over them, that would put them in their places. [It would say to them,] We'd rather have a *woman* in office than you!" Mirza was eager for me to recognize him as a cultured, enlightened male who supported women's participation in politics and who was morally offended by the corruption of the politicians in office—above the "primitive," Balkan fray. The way he expressed this, however, revealed not only an unquestioned association between powerful masculinity and politics but also the presumption that choosing a woman over a man should be a big insult. Because political positions were seen as male entitlements, electing a woman was a fit punishment for corrupt men and their male-dominated parties. Proper urban masculinity of the kind to which Mirza aspired (or at least what he imagined would impress a "Westerner" like me) opposed itself to the "primitive" Balkan macho types who, in this view, tended to overdo their masculine performances, "acting important" and "manly," "all pumped up" (see Helms 2006). Still, a male politician could apparently remain properly masculine and exercise authority and power in an ethical way without taking on feminine qualities, similar to what Jessica Greenberg (2006) identifies as the "new democratic masculinity" in post-Milošević Serbia. Association with the feminine remained an insult, in Mirza's view, to men who had failed to properly do "their" job—as political leaders and as men. But it was still a job for *men*.

Politika je Kurva

If politics was a male realm, it was not a place for women, especially not respectable women. First of all, women were presumed to lack the "male" qualities necessary for politics—an air of authority, confidence in public speaking, wisdom and knowledge about the wider world. Certainly many women were not as proficient as men in the particular ways of speaking and wielding authority customary in a male-dominated arena. But the mere fact of their being women and presuming to operate on par with men was seen by many as a threat to the very masculine authority of the male politicians. Women politicians participating in women's NGO meetings told stories about how some male politicians regularly questioned and scrutinized them, even humiliating and excluding them from important discussions. (But they made a point to stress that they also had "normal" male colleagues who appreciated them.) Sabina, a woman in her midthirties who was a member of the Federation House of Representatives, told me in an interview in September 1999 that when she had first been elected to Parliament, the men in her own party "questioned my abilities, my authority and knowledge." Later she told a gathering of women activists about a man she knew who had complained, "If I had known my wife would go into politics I wouldn't have married her. A woman talking on the same level as a man about politics?! And being gone from home so much?!" Her audience nodded in recognition.

Women's absence from home seemed to be the real problem. It was not that they were not accepted in the public realm of paid work, even in positions of authority. In fact, as had been well established since the socialist period, urban women were expected to work and to contribute to the family budget (Denich 1976, 1977; Woodward 1985). This was all the more important in the difficult postwar economy when jobs were scarce, pay was low, and many women had become their family's sole breadwinner because their husbands were unemployed, sick, or had been killed in the war. But for a large majority, including most of the women's activists I met, women's primary role still lay in caring for children and households. Only when those roles were fulfilled, regardless of a woman's educational achievements or position at work, could she be considered successful, as Lidija Korać, a prominent female official, declared during a TV talk show on women's position in society in the summer of 2006.[9] Her statement was received by the (male) moderator as uncontroversial. Only a handful of feminist activists objected publicly, while many women activists I talked to at the time said with resignation that this was unfortunately still the majority opinion in society.

Working women were frequently absent from their jobs when they had to care for sick children or elderly parents. They carved time out of their working hours to bring children to school, obtain medicines from the pharmacy, or shop for food or household items. Men also took advantage of relaxed norms at work to pop out for personal reasons, but they were more likely to be meeting friends or colleagues for coffee than running errands for the family. These latter tasks were widely seen, first of all by many women themselves, as women's responsibility, although men also took on errands when instructed by their wives. (These patterns and norms of course did not always apply and there was some indication that they might be shifting; I knew plenty of younger urban couples who shared domestic duties and child-care more evenly.) Women were therefore able to maintain paid work while fulfilling their domestic duties. But their success in balancing these roles meant that women did not have much extra time for themselves or for earning promotions and higher pay at work. They also relied on their working in relative proximity to their homes and their children's schools.

Women's engagement in formal politics was not merely a logistical problem, however. After all, politics was a whore. Men were its legitimate actors but the realm itself was female—a disreputable, immoral one. "She" enticed and corrupted men, compelling them to engage in immoral acts. Politicians themselves were cast as prostitutes who sold themselves and their moral principles for personal gain. But male politicians did not lose their masculinity by participating in politics. Indeed, they engaged in some of the most quintessentially masculine arenas: the public and the political. Masculinity, or virility, was in some ways enhanced through a man's association with a "whore," through the sexual double standard (see A. Simić 1983). Thus, politics as a whore did not feminize or emasculate male politicians so much as point to the corruption and immorality of their profession. Mirza, the man who complained about corrupt male politicians, took pleasure in referring to government functionaries (*funkcioneri*) as "*fuksioneri,*" a play on the word *fuksa,* or loose woman. In other words, politicians were to be accorded as much respect as a whore. They were still men, however, with a chance to redeem themselves as politicians and as men by wielding their power responsibly.

Women, on the other hand, were doubly suspect as political actors, both for entering this contaminated realm and, on a personal level, as it cast suspicion on their sexual reputations. As we saw in chapter 3, women who spent too much time away from home, especially in places where there were men and that were not connected with their domestic or work duties, could fall under suspicion. To be a politician, one had to travel around the country meeting strangers and staying in hotels or stay late at meetings and parliamentary sessions. The higher up the position, the more demanding it was on a politicians' time and the further away they might have to travel. And since most politicians were men, it meant spending lots of time among non-kin males. Thus, Sabina, the Federation MP who was the mother of a small child, was asked with incredulity how her husband could "let" her get involved in politics. And Monika, an outspoken nineteen-year-old political activist and candidate for the Zenica municipal assembly, told me that her boyfriend was now resigned to her involvement in politics but that, "at the beginning he would make [critical] comments, he thought it wasn't right. You know, they say politics is a whore so a woman in politics is therefore a whore."

The most respectable position for a woman, therefore, was that of wife and mother. But since these roles carried considerable demands, a commonly voiced opinion was that women should not get involved in politics until they had raised their children to adulthood. Women could thus participate but would remain peripheral actors, unable to build up seniority and alliances the way male career politicians did. Many politically active women themselves took their motherhood responsibilities into consideration when deciding to get involved. For Hajrija, a former member of a women's humanitarian organization and a trained Islamic teacher who counseled women at the Islamic Community, the minimum age was forty-five because "women are needed by their children until then." While there was no question for her that women should be employed to ensure their financial independence and therefore autonomy from men, she was firm that "there is more value in bringing up their children than there is value to society by what [women] can do in public life." Hajrija represented more conservative, religious views, but popular secular views were not much different. On the same 2006 television talk show cited above, another woman politician argued that women should participate in politics but only before marriage or after their children had grown. If a woman's children do not turn out well, she said, then it is mostly because she has not fulfilled her role properly. Engagement in politics would apparently take too much away from this important role.[10] Their participation was furthermore less disruptive at a later stage in life, generally past reproductive age. Being away from home so much and in the company of "strange" men was no longer as much of a threat for such women, their married male colleagues, or their own husbands.

Being unmarried and/or childless did not always make women fit for politics either, even when they were past childbearing age, as the many remarks I heard about two prominent single women politicians attest. One was Amila Omersoftić, the well-known former director of the state television firm who had left a high position in the SDA to form the Women's Party. An acquaintance told me she was "in politics because she doesn't have children or a family. She has nothing else to do so she decided to meddle into politics." At the same time, she had her admirers and was an important inspiration to the women who joined the Women's Party. Biljana Plavšić, the only woman politician to have served in a major office in BiH in the post-Yugoslav period (and the only prominent woman to be convicted of war crimes), was also derided for not having children or a husband. In fact, Bosnians of various political orientations I talked to found reasons for her failings—her Serb nationalism and support for violence against ethnic others—precisely in the fact that she was unmarried and childless. Maybe if she had a child, people reasoned, she would have thought twice about encouraging ethnic hatred and supporting war. At the least, she would have considered the consequences of sending a son to fight (in imaginings of respectable motherhood, the child was apparently male).

These views were contested, not least by women's rights activists, but also by the many "respectable" women (wives and mothers whose children were in some cases still small) who had begun to respond to initiatives to increase women's participation in formal politics. Various kinds of women activists, too, were making their voices heard in political arenas, even if their activities tended to be limited to social policy, war victimhood, and issues delineated as affecting women or children. International intervention agencies also played a role in attempts to reshape the meanings of the political for women.

Promoting Women in Politics

The need to increase the numbers of women involved in formal politics became a major focus for donors and NGOs during my research in 1999 and 2000. For feminists and women's rights advocates, whether Bosnian activists, feminist donors, or concerned individuals working for foreign intervention agencies in BiH, at issue was women's access to power. A refrain often heard at women's NGO meetings was that if women were not present in decision-making positions, it would be difficult to change the legal structures and practices of governance that reinforced women's second-class citizenship. Discussions on the role of NGOs and initiatives to promote cooperation between women NGO activists and women politicians (of which the OSCE was a major promoter) had placed "women in politics" firmly on the women's NGO agenda. Although there were different ideas of what a women's agenda should be, even those who stressed women's roles as the pillar of the family argued for women's political participation. For example, Amila Omersoftić, the Women's Party leader, appeared in a televised debate among women candidates in the run-up to the November 2000 general elections talking about women's responsibilities in the home and toward children as "issues important to women," despite the fact that she was herself unmarried and childless. She also argued that women needed to be in Parliament because of these issues and asked rhetorically, "When have you seen a man get up and initiate something about women's rights?" implying that "women's rights" were about home and family.[11]

The most active programs promoting women's political engagement were initiated and run by women's rights advocates working for foreign intervention agencies or donors. Such initiatives followed a dominant liberal or social democratic approach to women's rights for which women's political representation was a key component. There were other reasons for the attention to this issue, however, starting with the general goals of foreign intervention agencies at the time of my initial fieldwork. As with every election since the end of the war, the spring local elections and autumn general election of 2000 were viewed by foreign officials as a chance to vote the ruling nationalists out of power and end their obstruction of a functioning, unified state. Although foreign agencies, and especially the OSCE as the logistical organizers of the elections (Coles 2007), were supposed to be neutral, their hopes were often blatantly promoted, as in the OSCE's voter registration campaign slogan, "Vote for Change" (*Glasajte za promjenu*). The message was not lost on anyone, least of all the nationalist parties in power who complained that the "foreigners" were working against them (and therefore against each of their nations).[12]

Promoting the candidacy and election of women therefore coincided well with the larger goals of promoting "change." This was because foreign agencies and donors also saw women, as well as youth, as forces for change, representatives of a different approach to politics. As a rule, both groups had been excluded from positions of political power, but they were also both represented as essentially anti-nationalist and morally pure. In an OSCE campaign to mobilize the youth to vote for the November 2000 general elections, both females and youth were used to convey this message through a widely distributed song and music video by three young female pop singers, each from a different area of ethno-national control, singing "Grab hold of your destiny! Why always play the same song when you can choose (vote)?" (*Zgrabi svoju sreću! Zašto uvjek istu pjesmu sviraš kad možeš da biraš?*).[13]

When it came to women, foreign agencies and donors mobilized a familiar set of essentialist representations. In the construction of women as peacemakers, anti-nationalists, and mothers whose first concern was for the future of their children, they were morally superior, noble victims of male-led war who were more willing to compromise and to communicate with members of erstwhile enemy ethnic groups. They were thus particularly targeted to carry out projects of ethnic reconciliation and refugee return—two profoundly political processes—even while being described as apolitical.

My sense was that there was an element of the strategic in these representations on the part of foreign actors, in that they were keen to identify with and encourage Bosnian women to get involved in building a better postwar society. They were also eager to find locals who might counter the corrupt and obstructive tendencies of nationalist party (male) politicians in power—in essence, anyone new. However, this strategic element was unstated and may have often been unconscious, as notions of women as mothers, as peacemakers, or as more concerned about the common good than men—or conversely ideas of men as self-centered, greedy, and violent—coincided easily with commonsense ideas about gender held by nearly everyone who came to work in BiH. What was more, those presenting foreign-funded projects to local audiences were frequently Bosnians themselves. They were quite aware of how to make their audiences feel good about themselves and their abilities without appearing radical by challenging entrenched gender hierarchies. At the same time, promotion of women as political actors in such an affirmative way could seem progressive and feminist.

Since the politicians obstructing reforms and promoting nationalist agendas were by and large males, women, as anti-nationalist peacemakers, represented a promising force for change. In an OSCE-produced television spot celebrating and promoting women in politics, "In Her Own Name," which aired on International Women's Day in 2000, Mary Ann Rukavina, director of the OSCE's Women and Politics program, voiced the optimistic note that the increase in women's political participation that resulted from the new quota rules could be seen as paving the way for "a new politics, a politics led by women which is a women's politics." Female politicians were then shown extolling the successes of the OSCE program, which had brought them together across party and ethnic divides to enter into dialogue about common issues, something male politicians had never come close to doing.[14]

A similar message was conveyed by an OSCE representative at an OSCE-sponsored gathering of NGO and political party women in the town of Ljubuški on September 7, 2000. The regional OSCE representative, an older, American man, told the gathering that the international community supported increased participation in political life by women because "women . . . typically bring up issues that go beyond 'who's a better Serb, Croat, or Bosniac.'" He implored the women present to encourage voters and the rest of their parties to concentrate on issues such as "the economy, jobs, education, and health care" rather than those of national identity. This was also the OSCE's and other international bodies' hope for male politicians, but when addressing men there was little talk of families, loss, and victimhood, or tapping into natural tolerance. Women were assumed a priori to be uninterested in national(ist) agendas and were being encouraged to think of themselves this way.

If Women Had Been in Power, There Would Not Have Been a War

Many politically active women embraced this mode of representation, not least because it aligned easily with commonsense notions of gender difference. When Šehida of Bosanka, through the Bosnian League of Women Voters (Liga Žene Glasača),[15] held a public forum in Zenica for the presentation of female candidates in the spring 2000 local elections, the theme of the event was "Votes for women: A force for change." Both the league and the candidates themselves were promoting women as new faces who would change the dirty nature of politics. Neatly dressed in colorfully feminine suits and scarves as befitted educated working women, they highlighted women's "more refined" ways of relating to others, their down-to-earth, practical nature that would help them pass useful laws and keep a measure of civility in political rhetoric. Women were an antidote to the two complaints that voters, like the "internationals," had about the ruling nationalists: corruption and nationalist warmongering.

I repeatedly heard Bosnian women (and a few men) state that, if women had been in power, there would not have been a war. In the OSCE television special mentioned above, Irena Soldat-Jovanović, a parliamentary representative from the SNSD party in the RS, lamented women's virtual absence from politics just before the war, asserting that "had women had a higher degree of participation in 1991, maybe it would not have even come to this war, maybe we would have found, in some peaceful way, a compromise in which women were very prominent, and through which the family would be preserved." Later in the same program, Mevlida Kunosić-Vlajić, a politically active NGO leader from the Federation, explained why she found it important to support increased participation of women in politics: "I don't believe that a woman would make the decision to go to war."

The OSCE program was in fact a parade of Bosnian women active in NGOs and political parties describing the successes of women's joint political initiatives (especially those of the OSCE) in affirmative essentialist terms. An HDZ parliamentarian stressed women's willingness to "erase differences" across party and ethnic lines in order to get things done in a way that men would not. Soldat-Jovanović further praised women's reasoned approach "with arguments," contrasting them with men's ways of attacking and insulting their opponents. On many other occasions, women from a variety of political orientations claimed to have their own unique "female diplomacy,"[16] to be interested in dialogue and a greater good. According to Sabina, the Zenica MP from the SDA, "Women are more honest, have more soul, and are more open in conversation. They're not as arrogant. It's easier to communicate with women." "Bosnian women have a better feeling for justice," claimed a woman member of another party at a women-in-politics gathering, "so women would be more honest. They *are* more emotional, but this is good. They will have more feelings for others." These characterizations implicitly, and often explicitly, portrayed men as incapable of dialogue or compromise, more interested in personal gain and in one-upping their fellow male politicians. "Men are constantly insulting and degrading each other in public, in the Parliament," asserted a woman candidate in a televised debate with other women candidates. Another debate participant agreed: "Women always put general interests first, common interests, while men are in it for personal interests."[17]

When I attended the Zenica session of "Women Can Do It!" (*Žene to mogu!*), an OSCE-sponsored training session for women interested in political engagement, the Bosnian facilitators, women I knew thought of themselves as feminists, sketched a similar picture. They were working from guidelines drawn up by OSCE, which had adapted the program from a Norwegian model,[18] but they were adding in a lot of their own touches, doing their best to connect with and convince the local women participants, some of whom were only passive members of their parties and had been sent to be "trained" as the parties' fulfillment of the OSCE's invitation. The nodding heads and expressions of agreement among the participants throughout the day-and-a-half-long session showed that the facilitators were tapping into a common way of viewing gender differences. After some introductory lectures, the group, given the task to list "female and male ways of working in politics" came up with the following, which they wrote out on the flip chart provided:

Men	Women
attack/defend	we communicate and cooperate
not listening to others	listening, prepared to work together
conflicts for power	women just want equality, not to dominate
prone to intrigue, conspiracies [made in] all-male circles	solidarity
race for prestige	just want to oppose discrimination
competition, rivalry	want to be able to fulfill everyday needs

What we have in common
camaraderie (*drugarstvo*)
unity
warmth
friendship, understanding
support

Despite this polarizing picture, which was perhaps an inevitable outcome of the way the task was framed, the facilitators were careful to prompt the participants to think about what men and women had in common since, in the end, they were trying to encourage women to dive into this arena of self-centered, bullying men. Later in the session, the participants were asked to practice. The facilitators divided the group into "men" and "women" and had them role-play a political party meeting at which the women argue for the nomination of a woman to a top post. The "men" were extremely rude, cutting the "women" off, brushing over their suggestions, and declaring that everything had already been decided last night in the pub. Making it obvious that they were trying to take up as much space as possible with their bodies and gesturing wildly, the "men" acted impatiently, finally saying they were in a hurry to finish because "the game is starting soon!" The "women," standing primly with folded hands and waiting to be allowed to speak, had little success in convincing the "men," who were playing their roles a bit *too* well. Everyone was familiar with the failings of the (male) politicians in power, including the boorish way in which they related to others. The male professor who had opened this training session—the husband of one of the facilitators and a man I'd known to describe himself as modern and enlightened—had summed it up when he suggested that this program should really be called "Men Can't Do It!" (*Muškarci to ne mogu!*). It was up to women, he said, to put things right.

Talking about it later over coffee in Infoteka, Dženana, a self-declared feminist in her twenties, was annoyed at this kind of suggestion but recognized it as common. "This is still the expectation of society," she lamented. "Women smooth out what men have messed up." Whether it was politics itself or the mess that politics had made of society, women were still placed in the role of mother.[19] But this was precisely the reason that many felt women should now engage in politics. As one of the "Women Can Do It!" facilitators explained, "we women always see things in perspective because of our children. We think about the future and how our kids will be instead of dealing with the past like our politicians."[20] It was the moral, respectable position of the mother—a mature woman with grown children—that would now "save" politics and society. On Zenica local television around this time, a male candidate from a small, unsuccessful opposition party was seen as quaint and a bit ridiculous, though absolutely right, when he declared as part of his platform: "I advocate the equal participation of women in politics . . . because women have endured the trials of giving birth and raising children for eighteen years until they are adults. If they don't know something about life, who does? Women, mothers, know the needs in society." Women were, almost by definition, mothers, and "motherhood was and has remained the strongest argument for women to engage in politics," as a member of the Women's Party put it in addressing the participants of "Women Can Do It!"

Of course, motherhood was more than just a strategic image; many women, perhaps the majority, identified strongly with it. At the OSCE training session, one woman who was already known locally for her political candidacy voiced a word of caution when the group expressed rejection of the idea that women should not be in politics because they have duties at home: "We have to be careful not to fall into this trap when we argue against women's role as caring for the children and the house. We can't leave this up to a helper, babysitter, etc., if we want our children to have the proper upbringing." A few members of the group objected that fathers should do more but this woman insisted that the job could only be done by women.

It must also be acknowledged that the complaints from women parliamentarians about the self-interested and bullying behavior of male politicians were based on all-too-real experience. Indeed the bullying "men" politicians in the role-play knew just how to play their parts and elicited much laughter of recognition from their audience. Likewise, experiences of women finding common ground and communicating and acting across ethnic and political boundaries were vividly real. But despite the social and cultural reasons for this, the explanations typically given for this reality tended to rest on precisely the kind of associations that bolstered the situation, that is, essentialist constructions of women and their nature. In fact, according to Sabina, the Parliament member quoted above, despite what she said had been skepticism about women politicians' joint initiatives, in the end "it was shown that women understand each other very well even without opening their mouths." Female solidarity, for her, was more instinctual than a question of will.

Using Essentialisms Strategically

As with Dženana, there were those women activists and a few politicians, mostly those who identified as feminists, who were critical of such essentialist representations of gender. Again, it was Dženana who complained about how other women's NGOs tended to put forth "that picture that men make war and women make peace—that really annoys me." Her colleague Duška also shook her head at such depictions. She regularly got into debates about gender hierarchies in society with friends, local officials, visitors, and even for a time a group of young, mostly male, participants in an early Internet forum, and always stressed the way common ideas about women's and men's "natures" was socially constructed. Most of the members of Medica and the other self-described feminist activists generally refrained from reproducing essentialist dichotomies. Yet they were careful about how far they drew out their critiques when speaking in public forums or even to certain donor representatives (in the same way that their feminist critiques were emphasized when speaking to other feminists). There were benefits to being seen in the affirmative light cast by such representations.

NGO Work as Humanitarian

NGOs in general, but particularly women's NGOs, were judged in their communities by their ability to perform "humanitarian" services for others. As we saw in earlier chapters, this standard was based on understandings of women's community engagement forged in the socialist era (the *aktiv žena* model), solidified during the war, and reinforced in the postwar period by the promotion by foreign intervention agencies of the NGO as a depoliticized vehicle for the provision of services no longer provided by the state. This presented both an opportunity and a dilemma for women's organizations conscious of the political nature of their goals. On one hand, they were able to retreat into claims of apolitical humanitarianism and "women's issues." On the other, such a position in some ways reinforced their political marginalization. When these NGO women took a more political stance—expressing their opinions in public, demanding legal changes, or insisting on increased participation by women in the formal political sphere—they were more likely to be derided in the same gendered terms as women politicians were, dismissed as unqualified, nosy women meddling in an area where they did not belong. Several people outside of NGO circles told me that NGO women who were engaged in political, especially feminist, issues were "just sexually frustrated women with bad marriages" or that they only "sit around and gossip over coffee."

I also heard people dismiss the public statements of women activists as unqualified, "talking off the top of their heads" (*govoriti na pamet*) because, they said, the women do not hold government functions, academic posts, or other positions of authority normally associated with male public actors. (Such empty talk by men, usually delivered in an authoritative, even belligerent manner, was frequently singled out by those critical of typical "male" behavior in politics, though here it was most often termed *pametovanje*, something between lecturing or being a smart ass.) Although some male NGO leaders were also dismissed as greedy tools of foreign donors who did not represent grassroots opinions, they were not derided in the same gendered terms as were women. Women's offense was presuming to act within the public, male sphere on issues of political importance, whether they had the right qualifications or not.

One acquaintance in Zenica, a middle-class educated woman not involved in NGO work, complained to me that the "humanitarian services" of Medica were good, but that the women working on political issues there "don't do anything. They just act important and pocket foreign money." Activists and NGOs earned respect when they offered free aid or services to those in need, but not when it seemed that their work was political. For NGOs, engaged as many of them were in public pursuits, the way to distance themselves from the political was to be "humanitarian," to stress the *non*-governmental part of the NGO label, or to eschew this label altogether in favor of more neutral terms like association. In general, calling one's organization humanitarian was used to claim moral superiority, an interest in the well-being of others, even patriotism or ethno-national pride, unmotivated, in contrast to politicians, by personal power or financial gain. To call oneself a "women's NGO" made possible a strengthening of this claim, especially if motherhood was also stressed.

Women of Srebrenica

The most visible example of such positioning, indeed the most visible organizations of women in BiH public space at the time of my initial fieldwork, were the groups of Srebrenica survivors, commonly referred to as the women or mothers of Srebrenica. As victims of the biggest massacre of the war, one that had been officially labeled genocide and one that held a key place in Bosniac narratives of identity (Duijzings 2007; P. Miller 2006), theirs was in many ways the highest order of moral claim in the Bosniac and pro-BiH communities. At the same time, however, they were often treated with disdain as rural women from a notoriously "backward" part of Bosnia. It was common to hear those who claimed cosmopolitan identities assert that these rural women were being "manipulated" by (male) politicians, or worse, that the women themselves were involved in politics or corruption. For such a political issue as Srebrenica, this might seem a surprising complaint. But as their popular image was as rural women with little education, they were the polar opposite of legitimate political actors. Moreover, their visibility was based on their victimhood. Any "political" engagement threatened to taint the innocence required of victims as national symbols. It was thus incongruous that these women would be acting, even forming political alliances, on their own behalf.

The organizations, consciously or not, played into these associations, emphasizing their roles as mothers and wives, now widows. They specifically stated that they had no ties to politicians and their banners used in public protests typically emphasized motherhood: "Mothers ask, where are the missing from Srebrenica?" and "Srebrenica Mothers want the truth." They kept their focus on the identification of their loved ones' remains and on bringing to justice those responsible (not only Serb forces but also foreign actors). All the groups had "women/wives" (žene) or "mothers" in their names, despite the membership of some men, most of whom had been children when the town fell. One of the two most prominent such groups, "Women of Srebrenica" (Žene Srebrenice) based in Tuzla, was emphatic that, as they put it at the top of their website homepage, "our task is not a fight for women rights" [sic], but the search for (the bodies of) their missing family members and the campaign to bring their killers to justice.[21] The other major organization, based in

Figure 17 Memorial marker at the Potočari Memorial Complex, as in English on its other side: "In the name of God the Most Merciful, We pray to Almighty God, may grievance become hope! May revenge become justice! And mothers' tears may become prayers that Srebrenica never happen again to no one anywhere!—Reis-ul-ulema, Srebrenica Prayer, July 11, 2001." Photographed July 2007. (photo by author)

Figure 18 One of Women of Srebrenica's demonstrations held on the 11th day of each month in central Tuzla to call for justice and recovery of the remains of the dead. They hold pillowcases upon which they have embroidered the names of their missing loved ones. Photographed September 2008. (photo by author)

Sarajevo, was "The Movement of Mothers of the Enclaves of Srebrenica and Žepa" (Pokret majke enklava Srebrenice i Žepe), and a third group called itself "The Association of Mothers and Sisters of Srebrenica and Podrinja" (Udruženje majke i sestre Srebrenice i Podrinja), even though it was headed by a man. Just as plausible a term might have been "families" or "survivors." However, when, in the summer of 2005, I asked members of these groups about this choice, they responded impatiently that this was natural since *they* were all women and mothers, and that the suffering of the mother who has lost a child was the worst of all.

The stress was thus on female familial roles far removed from anything political (i.e., private and domestic), and which bolstered images of victimhood by calling attention to the emotional and family bonds the survivors had with those who had been killed (see Helms 2012). This emphasized not only their non-involvement in politics but also that their engagement was not about them but about their loved ones, a stance more befitting a self-sacrificing mother than a purportedly self-interested politician. This was less a strategic choice, however, than a commonsense plea. The fact that most of the survivors were women and children, and indeed that the groups were mostly led by women, made any other positioning unthinkable. Apparently it was not only unthinkable for members of the organization: of the hundreds of journalists, investigators, academics, foreign students, and other visitors who had passed through their office, the leaders of Žene Srebrenice said I was the first to ask them why they called themselves "women."

The Srebrenica organizations drew moral standing from their being recognized as victims, a recognition that was strengthened by their being women, since women, and especially mothers, are by definition civilians and thus illegitimate targets in war. Somewhat paradoxically, then, they were acting as female victims in the male-associated space of the public sphere on an intensely political issue based on the loss of male loved ones who had been the *ultimate* victims, since it was they who were actually killed. This contradiction illuminates the dual categories of victimhood as differentiated by gender: the purest male victims were dead (see Čolović 2002; Schäuble 2009a), but female victims evoked the most sympathy when alive and continuing to suffer, in this case suffering the loss of male breadwinners and protectors and of male children to signify their worthiness as mothers in a patrilineal society. Since they did face various forms of resentment and prejudice, even though the population generally did see them as true victims, it was all the more imperative that they be seen as embodying a category as innocent and unimplicated as possible, even as this paradoxically facilitated their being more effective political actors.

Women of Podrinje and Kozarac

In late summer 2000, when I asked Zahida, the leader of Žene s Podrinja (Women of Podrinje), a group that readers will recall also included many Srebrenica women, why her organization only worked with women in the towns they wanted to return to, she looked at me as if I was asking the obvious. "We *have* to work with women," she explained, "Because *we* are women. If we tried to talk to the men there, then it would be political." In chapter 3 we saw how notions of gender-segregated spheres informed understandings and practices of women's community activism. Zahida's NGO was a prime example of this, as her answer reveals, but she also showed that she was consciously using ideas of women as apolitical to her group's advantage. "Yeah," she told me with a note of sarcasm and a big grin, "we supposedly [*k'o fol*] aren't political."

In working for refugee return, Zahida's NGO was engaged in one of the most fraught political questions of the time. Indeed, return to this part of the RS looked all but impossible at the time due to the fierce opposition of Serb politicians (and much of the population) who now controlled the area. On the opposite side of BiH, in Kozarac, Srcem do mira was also working toward return, a process that was already underway in 2000. Like Women of Podrinje, Srcem do mira explicitly called their activities humanitarian, stressing that they worked only with women rather than "meddling" in the male world of politics. As in the sharp ethnic divisions constructed by the gender narratives discussed in chapter 4, Almasa, the leader of Srcem do mira, opposed her group's "humanitarian" activities to what she said was the more "political" nature of Serb NGOs operating in her area. For her, "political" activity by women was morally suspect.

These formulations were unsurprising given that these were groups of women from small, semi-rural communities where notions of gender-separate spheres were much stronger than among urbanites. But their strategy was also somewhat effective politically, precisely because women were seen as less threatening or politically consequential, and because they actually did lack power in the formal political realm. Both groups were able to quietly circumvent the spotlight without putting the public reputation of (male) officials directly on the line. Since 1998, Srcem do mira had been instrumental in the reestablishment of a viable Bosniac community in and around Kozarac. Ethnic relations there were far from smooth, but their goal of return was achieved against great odds and they continued to successfully push for improvements in their community. Žene s Podrinja succeeded in October 2000, after several years of effort, in holding the cross-ethnic meeting in Bratunac discussed in chapter 4. Bratunac was one of the most politically hardline towns of the region in terms of opposition to non-Serb return. There, only a few months before, stones had been hurled at Zahida's group and other women to prevent them from entering and continuing on to nearby Srebrenica.[22] The women were continuing to work to achieve their return and to improve communication with their onetime Serb neighbors.[23]

This quiet circumvention of public, political channels also drew on popular notions of hidden female power, what Andrei Simić long ago termed the "cryptomatriarchy" of the family sphere (1983), which was here evoked by women politicians when describing women's skills in "lobbying" to get things done. Women's activists who adhered to this more "traditional" idea of female domestic power hoped to use this channel to accomplish their *political* goals in a particularly clear instance of the blurring of the boundaries of the political and the private. Zahida explained how she envisioned this helping her achieve her goal of holding the Bratunac meeting. "Women can do a lot," she said, "Someone once asked me why I'm doing this through women and not through politicians. I said, 'Today we'll meet and I'll say what we want. You're married to the mayor and you'll lay in bed tonight and tell him that we want to meet in Bratunac and you'll convince him to do it.' It's much easier through women." By setting this scenario in the marital bed, Zahida implied a rare acknowledgment that women derived power, in this case another sort of indirect, hidden power, through their sexuality.

She also unquestioningly assumed the general category of "politicians" to be male and opposed it to the category of women, although the mayor was in fact a man. This formulation was an advantage, however, as she further argued that "women can make better progress, exactly on this path to reconciliation. The authorities didn't think we'd be able to do too much in Bratunac, and now when they see how much we're doing, they can't do anything [to stop us]. . . . They didn't imagine—[they said] 'Well, so what? There's a couple of women there, what can they do?' But we criticize power (*vlast*) and politics. But hey, we're not politicians!!" Zahida delivered this last sentence with a big grin on her face and a twinkle in her eye. She was quite aware of and pleased with the way she was playing with other people's assumptions about women's political insignificance in order to achieve her very political goals. In fact, she went on to explain that with goals of returning to their prewar homes, they had no choice but to deal with politics and "the darkest, worst politicians." Since politics was a whore (*kurva*), this meant they would have to "prostitute themselves [*kurvati se*] with her sometimes."

Even while Zahida and some other women's NGO activists freely admitted the political nature of their activities to me and to each other, they did not mention it in public forums. Instead, as we saw with the Bratunac meeting, they stressed female solidarity based on motherhood and respectable family roles. At the same time, this strategy would not be successful on its own, which is why both Almasa and Zahida also worked the other channel of influence available to them as NGO activists: foreign agencies and donors. In fact, it was due to foreign pressure and deals with RS politicians desperate for economic assistance that return to both areas was ultimately allowed in greater numbers. In other words, the most significant changes were ultimately achieved on the male-dominated level of formal political structures. Still, the women's influence on this process, both through local politicians and with foreign actors, had depended on their construction as apolitical women.

Feminists at Medica Infoteka

Consistent with her feminist stance, Duška at Medica Infoteka was irritated at suggestions like Zahida's that women should influence reconciliation through husbands and other men in positions of power. Instead, Duška insisted that women be active in their own right. As she put it in one of our conversations in late 2000, "When all is said and done, it's better to be in the margins than not at all on the page! At least you have a chance at getting into the text that way." Duška's metaphor pointed directly to the effective marginalization of women from the formal political sphere created through the use of affirmative essentialisms of women.

Despite these criticisms, however, Medica activists and other like-minded, self-professed feminists approached gender essentialisms strategically. Because of the public wariness of politically active women, they were careful about how they presented themselves in public, especially about when and how they used the term "feminism," a term understood as political and threatening. Medica activists knew what my interactions in the community also confirmed, that associations with feminism would only hurt their reputation. The organization was known and respected for having "helped raped women" during the war but now when activists appeared in public talking about the need to support women victims of domestic violence, many in their audience balked. As I was told by several Zenica residents, the Medica women were being too feminist, too political. "Feminism" here was meant as a condemnation. (Domestic violence, though generally condemned, was in any case something that many felt, along the classic reasoning, should not be exposed to public scrutiny; it was a private matter.) At the same time, a small minority of self-styled urban intellectuals I knew condemned the Medica activists for not being political *enough*—for this group, most of them men, "real" feminists would be out protesting in the streets and being much more vocal about their feminism. As Dženana observed about Medica's public activities, "People think it's too much but in fact it's not enough."

Medica feminists were in many ways mediators engaged in translation of ideas perceived as coming from outside the local (Gal 2003; Lendvai and Stubbs 2007, 2009; Merry 2006a). Sally Engle Merry (2006a, 2006b) calls attention to the important role being played by such activist-translators in the "vernacularization" of human rights ideas like feminist campaigns against domestic violence, but also to activists' vulnerability to political manipulation or charges of betrayal, as Medica activists were acutely aware. Having to strike a balance between effective advocacy for social change and the risk of rejection and condemnation, they took strategic advantage of affirmative gender essentialisms to some degree when they did not object to their activities being publicly characterized as apolitical and humanitarian, or when they were included in descriptions of nurturing, peacemaking women. This only bolstered their sense of moral purpose as women helping women, not to mention their public image.

One example was the cross-ethnic cooperation among Medica and other feminist-friendly NGOs discussed in chapter 4. Even those activists who were most critical of essentialist and traditionalist representations of women's roles easily fell back on the narrative that they were women tackling "women's issues," a phrase that most Bosnians, sometimes including the activists themselves, would read as issues that were not "political." Of course, their initiatives to fight violence against women, one of their main topics, were inherently political as they involved campaigns to reform legislation and institutional practice around gender-based violence. And their very cooperation across ethnic lines was political. They did it out of principle; strategic avoidance was their way of ensuring that this work could happen, and happen effectively (see Cockburn 1998). But the emphasis on their identity as women ensured that these ultimately political acts would not be scrutinized as much by local officials with opposing agendas, as well as facilitating their own communication.

At Medica, activists consciously tempered their public statements so as not to appear too "aggressive" or "feminist," that is, political. Duška was strategic about how much the public could take, as she explained to me one day in Infoteka:

> The best way to proceed here at the moment is to be un-aggressive. We can be aggressive but not too often and in small doses. When I feel, in my mild approach that someone is really listening to me, then I come into conflict with them, irritate them, and then go back down to being mild and gentle, to bring things to a level of rationality, to make them think and not just dismiss me. It's hard—how do you say something like, every man is a potential perpetrator of violence [*nasilnik*], which I do believe. You can see it in every man that he sometimes gets frustrated and is tempted to use violence. But this isn't because he's a man, it's because it's been served to him all his life. But how to say that all at once to someone [who's never thought about it]? . . . I can speak in public and publicly say I'm a feminist and all that, but if I get into a situation and I feel the word "feminism" isn't appropriate, that it won't be understood, then I don't use it.

On numerous occasions, I witnessed discussions that Duška and other Medica activists had with various community members in which they employed precisely this tactic, emphasizing a view of gender as a social construction that could be subject to change. I actually did not hear the word "feminism" much except by their detractors who used the label in a negative way.

As we saw in earlier chapters, Medica activists distinguished their feminism from what they saw as more radical and more vocal versions in Western countries and even in neighboring Serbia and Croatia. Part of their "feminism the Bosnian way" meant toning down their public rhetoric and using other channels of political action than those that were readily visible in the media or on the streets.[24] Duška was particularly enthusiastic about the strategy they were pursuing with their initiative to train local officials in public institutions to be sensitive to the needs of victims of gender-based violence (see Helms 2006). They could see concrete changes happening on the level of laws, protocol, and institutional practices in ways that would better support women victims of violence. They were rightly proud of their success in this area, especially after the deeply impressed response of their visitors from Medica Mondiale, who said they had never accomplished something like this in Germany even after twenty years of the women's movement. In the long run, the Bosnian activists hoped, there would also be changes in social attitudes and behaviors in this realm. Their strategy was to pace themselves. This was why, they explained, they approached their task in a quiet way, behind the scenes.

In this strategy of bypassing visible channels, Medica's approach was perhaps not as different from Women of Podrinje as Duška made it seem. Medica and other similar women's NGOs did work behind the scenes with the politicians and state officials already in power. The difference was that they did not do this out of a sense that "women" belonged only or primarily to the domestic sphere and were separate from "the political." Instead, they saw their role as members of the NGO sector, of civil society, as a link between the state and society. Putting pressure on state officials and advocating change was precisely their role as political actors in the liberal democratic model. Being women was important, especially since their activities centered around women as victims of gender-based violence, but they were in fact engaging in public action on what was considered a deeply domestic and private issue.

Recall, too, from chapter 4 how domestic violence took on additional political weight in BiH. Medica's activism on the issue of wartime rape usually met with support in the Federation, since the crime was part of the larger narrative of Bosniac and Bosnian victimhood. But domestic violence turned the narrative around: women were still the victims but the perpetrators were local men, "the heroes of the war, our defenders and saviors" as Milica had put it. To her, Medica's move into combating domestic violence was another reason it could not be more vocal, more political (in contrast to a group like Women in Black Belgrade); it was harder to criticize those in power since they represented a group seen as both victims and heroes/defenders.

Domestic violence was nowhere supported, but many played it down or justified it in individual cases as an inevitable reaction by men to the hardships and traumas they had endured in the war, added to the humiliations of unemployment and the inability to fulfill their breadwinner role in the difficult postwar, postsocialist economy. When Medica argued for support to the victims of domestic violence, offering shelter and counseling at their facility for victims and their children, many in the community interpreted this as an attack on the male abusers, even a conspiracy to get women and girls to now refuse to obey their husbands and fathers. With such conclusions being drawn, Medica could not afford to be seen as feminist (i.e., against men) or as women "meddling" in politics. An image of apolitical, nurturing women advocating for victims in need was much more productive in this sense.

Women in Politics: Ikebanas with Boots

Since there was little room between the dirty, unscrupulous realm of the political and the morally pure, nurturing, realm of the domestic, how did women active in the formal sphere of party politics position themselves? Claiming non-involvement in politics was obviously not an option. A different set of affirmative essentialisms was thus mobilized.

As a result of the new quota rules and donor-led initiatives, women were appearing more and more as party members, candidates, and elected officials. Advocates were pleased but some worried that the sudden increase would render women little more than cosmetic dressing—an *ikebana*, after the Japanese flower arrangement—for the table where men continued to call the shots. As one of the facilitators at the "Women Can Do It!" training told the participants, once they got to Parliament, they could not be silent. "If you are," she said, "they'll think you're a good *woman* but not a politician. You'll just be an *ikebana*." A politician had to be confident and effective, to speak with authority and get things done.

A woman could master such skills, and many had. But this sparked anxiety about the need for women in politics to "remain women." Women had to walk a constant line between being taken seriously as politicians and being perceived as unfeminine or "some sort of feminists."[25] At the Zenica presentation of women candidates on the eve of the 2000 local elections, one candidate who led the cantonal list for one of the smaller parties tried to quell women's fears. "Don't just use the refined influence of women over men—sons, brothers, husbands," she told them. "Startle them. Go for real male behavior—you won't lose any of your femininity that way." Later, over coffee, she explained that she never expected women to "turn into men," since women had their own innate ways of relating to people. The most effective way was for women to behave, "not like a real man with boots but as a person with opinions." Here was an area of blurriness between the femininity required of women's private roles and the professional, confident manner needed for success in politics.

The dilemma was reconciled in several ways. First, they dressed the part, wearing serious suits—skirts or pants—but often in pastel colors and almost always with a colorful scarf, jewelry, makeup, and hair styles that took time and effort to achieve. Heels were a must but they were not too high. Younger women dressed more informally but, as was true not just in politics, I often took women in their thirties to be much older because of their matronly appearance. It was important to emit a serious tone but a feminine one at the same time. Striking the right balance was a matter of contention, however. Velida, a woman judge who was active with the League of Women Voters, complained strongly to me and a fellow activist about the public persona of politician Senka Nožica on the grounds that she was *too* refined and feminine. "Bosnian women aren't like that," Velida observed. She didn't want a "male model" like Margaret Thatcher, but Nožica was too delicate and elite to represent the average Bosnian woman who was "tough and direct and practical," in Velida's words. This surprised me somewhat. I could see her point with Nožica's style of dressing and educated manners, but this candidate had built her reputation as a very tough defense lawyer who was quite outspoken in the media, positioning herself and other female politicians as not just in the minority but creating "incidents," shaking up the male political system—in a good way.[26]

Velida's concern was that women politicians be "still feminine but effective," in an arena where being too feminine was clearly a handicap. But they had to be sure they would remain *respectable* women, there to civilize the heretofore dirty realm of the whore. As such, positioning themselves as mothers and homemakers was most effective. Women's abilities managing the home, especially in dealing with children, husbands, in-laws, and neighbors, were cited as good training for women to be successful politicians: "We know how to rule/take charge [*vladati*] because we do that at home, too," declared a prominent leader in the Women's Party to a group of fellow advocates of women's political participation. They thus extended skills seen as belonging to the private sphere to the public sphere tasks they hoped to perform. At a League of Women Voters round table when she was standing for election, Senka Nožica argued that "women are naturally responsible because of our duties toward our children. There are so many small details we have to think of and take care of, and we have no choice, we have to do these things. They are things that can't be put off, they have to be done every day. We can't stay in the *kafana* [café-bar] for another drink like men can." The *kafana*, like politics, was a place for men and profane (immoral) women—out of bounds for respectable women (A. Simić 1983; Cowan 1991). Women had no time for such immoral pursuits because they were busy with the far more noble nurturing tasks of maintaining homes and children. With this one image, women's respectability was shored up while it was also implied that women would be more honest, conducting politics in the Parliament and party offices during the day rather than cutting deals in the pub after hours.

Another common narrative was aimed at countering the notion that politicians were only out for personal gain. Women expressed their motivation for getting involved in politics as an outgrowth of the extraordinary conditions of the times. The war had forced politics into everyone's lives in a way they could not ignore. With this claim, women infused their actions with a sense of moral duty, denying and excluding the possibility that they had had any preconceived aspirations for personal power or engagement with the disreputable realm of the political. As one woman candidate put the frequently stated assertion, "I started engaging [*baviti se*] in politics because politics was engaging with me!"

More explicitly, others cited injustice, by which they meant the abuses of the war and the economic inequalities of the postwar period, products of inept, corrupt (male) politicians. When I interviewed her in November 1999, Edisa, a member of the Zenica Cantonal Assembly and a DP who had fled to Zenica when her town was ethnically cleansed, explained:

> I didn't choose politics, politics chose me. Politics started messing with my life. People/men (*ljudi*) in politics, that is, people making decisions in the name of others. It was a reflex for me to get involved—to defend myself. . . . Now I'm in politics *out of need* because some other people took my life *and the lives of my family* and threw it in the air like a leaf into the wind. Our lives are now without security. I don't mean physical insecurity but the ability to plan for the future for us *and our kids*. (emphasis added)

This was a time of crisis that warranted extreme measures in which the normal rules of social organization could be bent. Things were so bad that even women were feeling the need to get involved in politics.

What was worse, even those politicians in power who were supposed to be protecting the people were widely seen as incompetent or simply uncaring because they pursued their own personal interests as typical men. Amela, at the League of Women Voters presentation of female candidates mentioned earlier, explained why she had entered politics:

> For years I thought that a woman like me, a doctor by profession who does a highly sophisticated job and also a mother and wife, has no need to enter into politics as a classic male pursuit. But when I saw what kind of jerks [*kreteni*] were passing certain laws, which led to certain changes and brought me and those closest to me into the situation where we have to endure hardship because they're either not responsible or not intelligent, then I decided and I said I'm not going to just talk at home or over coffee . . . I decided: I'm going [into politics].

Amela made it clear that she was a mother, a wife, and had a responsible job (one in which she helped people, no less—a humanitarian profession). In other words, she had been living up to her role as a respectable woman. It was the men, as those responsible for politics and government, who had failed to live up to the duties of *their* gendered roles as defined in this view.

Almost without exception, politically engaged women thus took pains to justify their extraordinary involvement by pointing to markers of their respectability *as women*: roles as mothers and wives and properly feminine individuals. They emphasized that their concern for these "private sphere" duties was what had motivated their engagement rather than any bid for personal status, power, or gain in the model of the egocentric male politician. What made these strategies possible, and what distinguished them from most representations put forth by NGO women, was the temporal distinction they implied between politics of the past and present—immoral, corrupt, destructive—and a more hopeful politics of a future in which women would be present in much higher numbers. Women's presence would "clean up" the realm of the whore, neutralizing its ability to threaten women's image as moral and legitimate actors. It was thus important to stress that women had not been involved in politics before this, that politics had "traditionally" been a male realm, in other words, to maintain the gendered dichotomy of male politics and female domestic roles.

Tool or Trap?

Because of (urban) women's significant presence in higher education and employment outside the home, many Bosnians, both men and women, insisted that women had been "emancipated," that they were equal in all respects (just as socialism claimed to have achieved). But very different expectations and standards were employed for women as compared to men, heavily affecting their choices and possibilities as political actors. Gender was once again a major way in which the divide between public and private, or the political and the domestic, was marked, while these distinctions were fundamental to the kinds of claims that might be successfully put forth. In order to "remain women," women felt compelled, and were expected, to maintain and emphasize their private sphere roles as mothers, homemakers, and wives. Indeed, through affirmative essentialisms, women celebrated these roles and proposed to carry them into the public sphere of politics. In other words, they pushed the limits of female political engagement but did so through idioms that reinforced women's primary responsibility for the family and maintaining

Politics Is a Whore

sexual purity. They thus did more to challenge notions of politics than notions of womanhood.

Affirmative essentialisms were therefore both an effective tool and a potential trap. They facilitated women's entry into the political arena but only in a limited way. They also reinforced a gender order in which women bore the responsibility for domestic duties and men continued to hold the top power positions in society. Likewise, the rhetoric and practices of intervention agencies and donors also reproduced affirmative essentialisms of women, presenting a paradox for the women they targeted. NGO women were charged with accomplishing highly political goals like reconciliation and return, while the images used to mobilize them effectively marginalized women from the circles of real political power.

Even initiatives to increase women's participation in formal politics in many ways constructed women as less significant political players. In the near-term, portrayals of women as (morally respectable) nurturers and outsiders to politics were helpful in getting women elected by voters like Mirza who were fed up with corrupt "politics as usual." They were unhelpful, however, in allowing women to be taken seriously as politicians. They encouraged women's equal participation in politics, as in civil society, but with the message that they should do so in the guise of their home-sphere roles of mother and natural peacemaker, the one who cleans up messes. In most parties, men continued to hold the vast majority of decision-making positions and to shut women out of their own party processes, expecting women parliamentarians to stay silent and vote as the male leadership instructed them. "Real" politics, therefore (where the messes were made), remained the realm of men. Furthermore, affirmative essentialisms of women constructed *men* as nationalistic, self-interested, and corrupt actors, which, given that they continued to dominate in politics, did not bode well for the future of a democratic, united, and multiethnic BiH.

Nonetheless, these representations resonated strongly with women themselves. Even those who were critical of such portrayals, like the feminists at Medica or the facilitators of the "Women Can Do It!" training workshop, took advantage of their power, especially when dealing with the local public. This was a practical, effective, and often conscious strategy in the moral and political climate of postwar Bosnia that ended up serving a variety of ideological positions on gender.

Most significantly, there was more legitimizing power in narratives that emphasized distance from those who wielded power and from responsibility for the many ills now plaguing Bosnian society. Women were thus drawn to, and indeed identified with, a position of victimhood. This victimhood took only certain forms, however, forms that retained a measure of respectability in ways that women could reasonably claim, such as in the figure of the self-sacrificing mother. Conspicuously absent were identifications with the most politicized forms of victimhood, those of direct war victims. In the next chapter, I turn to consider perhaps the most notorious and notoriously gendered category of war victimhood, that of wartime rape.

6

Avoidance and Authenticity

The Public Face of Wartime Rape

Representation is always an usurping of the status of victim; the silencing and censoring of the real victim.

Biljana Kašić (2000, 275)

Niko ne voli žrtve.
(No one likes victims.)

Besima Borić, SDP politician and war victim advocate

Teddy Bears of Peace

November, 2005: The cobbled lanes of Sarajevo's Baščaršija teem with pedestrians. Foreign delegations and increasing numbers of tourists admire the Ottoman-era architecture and browse shops full of local handicrafts. Locals drink Bosnian coffee and eat baklava on the "sweet corner" of cafes or grab *pita* or *ćevapi* for lunch. On the main thoroughfare is a former Ottoman inn, Moriča Han, the courtyard of which once stabled guests' horses but is now filled with Oriental carpets for sale and a café favored by young women in Islamic *hidžab*. Away from the commotion, up the steep wooden steps and down the dark, drafty corridor, are two rooms occupied by SULKS, the organization of mostly Bosniacs who were detained during the war in Serb-run camps.[1] In one of the rooms, some of the women members sit behind a handful of sewing machines putting together teddy bear puppets for a company in Germany that sells them as "teddy bears of peace." Film director Jasmila Žbanić has helped to set up this scheme as a way to do something for survivors of wartime rape, the subject of her film *Grbavica*.

The women are mostly refugees (IDPs) from Eastern Bosnia or peripheral areas of Sarajevo, unemployed and living with extended families in temporary housing. The youngest are in their thirties, but several are older with gray hair and stories of grandchildren. They work like a factory assembly line, each doing a particular bit, chatting, joking, and sharing their troubles with each other while they work. A portable heater barely keeps them warm. When I visit the following summer it is warm and stuffy. In all weather they keep each other well supplied with *fildžani* (demitasse cups without handles) of Bosnian coffee. Making teddy bears, they can each earn about five convertible marks (KM) per day, which, as they pointed out, is just enough to cover their transportation to town and some coffee or lunch while they work.[2] They are mostly there for the companionship, to have something to do, and in hopes that the contacts they made at SULKS might turn into some form of aid that might improve their disrupted lives. Periodically, the organization arranges for a psychologist to come talk with them as a group, but the sewing itself is conceived of as psychosocial help for traumatized war victims. And the women all say they feel more comfortable with others who went through similar ordeals. Many, but not all, of the women are survivors of wartime rape.[3] All of them endured the terror and uncertainty as camp prisoners in war, including the fear that they would be sexually abused. Most were also expelled from their homes, lost husbands and other loved ones, and witnessed others being tortured and killed. But their immediate concerns are now with securing adequate housing for themselves and their families, schooling their children, and treating illnesses with their meager and unsteady incomes.

Many of the women have testified as protected witnesses in war crimes trials, both at the ICTY and at the Bosnian War Crimes Chamber. They are used to visits by foreign officials, war crimes investigators, journalists . . . and academics. When I drop by for a visit in late 2010, they have stopped making teddy bears—the company did not want them anymore—and are now sewing handbags and slippers that they hope to sell to visitors. I buy a few pairs of colorful hand-knitted socks priced a bit higher than in the gift shops of Baščaršija. They tell me how things have been going since my last visit and ask me about my life. We are interrupted by a female French journalist with a Bosnian translator, also a woman, and a male Czech photographer who smiles and shakes everyone's hand in introduction. The journalist wants to know about the organization and the women's lives. After Binasa imparts some basic information about the group, she turns to the rest of the women. As if they know what the journalist wants, each in turn tells her own war story, patiently waiting for the translator every few sentences.

Even though there are moments when they choke up, finding it difficult to speak, I can sense they've told their stories many times before. Zehra, an older woman sewing a skirt she can wear while working in her vegetable garden, is eager to speak. She pipes up in a loud voice from behind her machine and begins to matter-of-factly relate her experience of expulsion from her Eastern Bosnian town. While she and her children were released after some time from a Serb detention camp and sent across a minefield to the Bosnian Army front lines, her husband and other Bosniac men were burned alive by Serb forces. She points out that she's shaking as she relates this but that it's important for her and the others to talk "so that history does not forget." Zehra freely explains her current economic woes. In addition to her husband's pension of 300 KM per month, she also gets 100 KM as a civilian victim of war. "I wasn't sexually abused so I get only 100 marks," she says matter-of-factly. In 2006 rape survivors were granted status as civilian war victims, entitling them to monthly state benefits of up to 513 KM.[4] A few of the women in the room have established eligibility. They, too, tell their stories, stating the fact of their having been abused (*zlostavljana*) only briefly within their larger narratives of loss and pain. A few break down crying and are comforted by the others.

As explained in chapter 2, the women rape survivors from SULKS had provided testimonies for the book *I Begged Them to Kill Me*, a co-publication of the Bosnia-level Union of Former Concentration Camp Survivors. It was after this that the women's section (*sekcija žena*) had become active and visible in public, in part as a reaction to the way in which their stories had been packaged and presented by the mostly male organizers. When I first made contact with the women's section in 2005, the leader at the time,[5] Alisa Muratčauš, defended the men of the Union but said that women victims needed to take control of how they were represented in public.

It was very important for her and her organization that victims speak publicly about the crimes committed against them. This was not so simple, she explained, given the strong "patriarchal roots" of Bosnian society and the ways in which even sympathetic listeners, even other victims themselves, reacted to "raped women." "We all carry a bit of the guilt," she said. Indeed, even though the women in the sewing workshop were clearly used to telling their stories to visitors and did so consciously so that "our pain is known" and not forgotten, as one of them put it, the act of speaking remained an ordeal, part of the burden of their experience.

At the same time, without making known what they had been through, there was little basis for their pleas for help—from the state, from foreign humanitarian organizations, or from any visitor who might buy the bags and slippers they sewed. Unemployment was staggering, much of the population was impoverished, and nearly everyone, especially in this city that had endured nearly four years of siege, was scarred in some way from the war. Spurred on by these urgent needs but also by the desire that their suffering be socially recognized, SULKS had joined other women's activists in successfully campaigning for state recognition of those who survived sexualized violence as legitimate victims deserving of society's help. This was a major achievement, but it only applied to survivors with legal residence in the Federation. The Union and other groups still advocated a state-level law on victims of torture that would extend recognition and the rights that went with it to all camp survivors in all parts of BiH. This required agreements and financial commitments across ethnicized borders, something that Bosnian politicians were notorious for obstructing.

This chapter is about the public life of women victims of wartime rape: the figure of the rape victim, the survivors themselves, the role of state institutions, and the face of women's activism around the topic. We saw in chapter 2 how wartime rape figured in ethno-national narratives of the war and of collective identities. Bosniac religious and nationalist leaders called for compassion toward the victims but did not challenge the profoundly patriarchal interpretations of the meaning of the rapes and their connection to nationhood. We also saw that debates over how to interpret this violence became a highly contentious issue among women's activists and feminists both in the former Yugoslavia and internationally. And in chapter 4 we saw how briefly exposed disagreements over how to characterize the rapes raised questions about Bosnian feminists' relationship to nationalism.

But where were the victims themselves? What was being done for them by those in power who professed to care about them? What were their lives like? And what did activist initiatives on their behalf say about women's relationship to nationalism? Would activists take up the arguments about gender and nation made during the debates that had split women's activists and feminists during the war? These were some of the questions that had driven my initial interest in women's activism after the war in BiH. But apart from the fact that many women's NGOs had been founded or funded at least in part as a response to wartime rape, local activists and NGO workers were mainly concerned with other issues. Even Medica, founded explicitly to help women rape survivors, had moved on to domestic violence as the focus of their work, although they continued their engagement with the topic of wartime rape and with the survivors they had treated. As I completed my research in 1999–2000 and as I noted in the dissertation that came out of it, despite their positioning themselves in various ways as victims, Bosnian women's activists in all their diversity made surprisingly little out of the most notorious female victim figure, the war rape survivor. In fact, the topic almost completely disappeared from public discourse in the immediate postwar years.

In hindsight, the publication of *I Begged Them to Kill Me* in 1999 (and another similar collection the same year[6]) and the subsequent formation of the women's section of SULKS marked the beginning of a new visibility for wartime rape and its victims. Over the next few years, wartime rape slowly became more present in public discourse in the BiH Federation. Verdicts were announced in several ICTY war crimes trials in which rape was among the violations prosecuted, including the notorious Foča trial judgment of 2001, which focused on rape as a war crime. In 2003 another organization, the Association of Women Victims of War (ŽŽR), was formed and began, through its leader Bakira Hasečić, to make its voice heard quite often in the press. Medica and other women's NGOs were also increasingly vocal on the topic. Much later, the UN Population Fund (UNFPA) and Amnesty International would raise the public profile of the plight of war rape survivors even higher, engaging local activists who had dealt with the issue for much longer.

Intrigued by these developments, I undertook new research in several trips during teaching breaks in 2005–7 and after. I wanted to observe how wartime rape was being handled in public discourses, what stances women's activists were taking toward it, and how this new visibility was being related to the other gendered victim images I had observed previously. I focused on the campaign "Za Dostojanstvo Preživjelih/For the Dignity of Survivors," mentioned in the opening to this book. This was a campaign led by Medica together with other NGOs, victims' associations, and sympathetic politicians and government officials to achieve official recognition of rape survivors as civilian war victims, a status that would make them eligible for a small state pension and other benefits. The involvement of Jasmila Žbanić, director of the film *Grbavica*, and the success of the film gave a boost to the Dignity campaign and prompted renewed attention to the issue of wartime rape and its survivors. An amendment to the Federation law recognizing sexualized violence victims' rights to benefits was finally passed in the spring of 2006.

This research took me back to Medica and some of the other women's activists I had known over the years, but I also got to know new actors, especially those of the victims' associations mostly headquartered in Sarajevo.[7] Because the initial campaign was limited to the Federation and because the majority of the war rape survivors were Bosniacs, this chapter focuses even more than the preceding ones on Bosniac-dominated areas and the politics of nation, state, and gender in that community. The Dignity campaign and the process leading up to the passage of the amendment brought out the lingering stigma against rape victims and the tensions created as women's organizations and state institutions struggled between the political value of such victimhood for the nation, the concrete needs of actual survivors, and the politics of authenticity over who had the moral right to speak for women victims. Ultimately, I argue, the discourses and silences of activism by and on behalf of rape survivors exposed the enduring power of national narratives of collective victims and perpetrators to dictate the way in which sexualized war violence is understood.

The Stigma of Rape

Writing about another incidence of war rapes by Pakistani soldiers during the 1971 war that created an independent Bangladesh, Nayanika Mookherjee (2006) reveals the problems that public acknowledgment of rape posed for women survivors even twenty years later and in a context in which they had even been declared "war heroines" by the Bangladeshi government. When three women survivors allowed their pictures and names to appear in the newspaper as war heroines, they and their husbands were met with scorn in their home village for making explicit the public secret of their rapes. Bosniac-dominated areas of BiH presented a similar context in which rape survivors were publicly valorized as symbols of national victimhood and of the barbarity of the enemy, even proclaimed *šehidi*—martyrs—by some. Feminists and women's human rights organizations had also helped shift the view of rape toward understanding for the victims (Andrić-Ružičić 2003). As a group, women rape survivors were mostly spared the moral suspicions often cast upon victims of "normal, everyday" rape and many people professed sympathy for the victims when the subject was raised.

However, few people I encountered outside of women's activist circles actually knew any survivors or were aware that they did. When they did appear, women survivors seemed to cause unease, even among sympathetic observers. Back in 1999, a Bosniac male friend in Zenica who lived near one of Medica's residences assumed on the basis of Medica's reputation (as working with raped women) that the young women he saw coming and going from the building every day had been raped. In fact, they were not rape survivors but refugees from Srebrenica for whom Medica was paying for schooling. Nevertheless, my friend challenged their status as victims, saying, "They don't look like raped women—they're always giggling and smiling and going out [*izlaze*, implying with boys/in mixed company]." "Raped women" were apparently expected to remain grieving and isolated for the rest of their lives, ruined for any further contact with men, or indeed with society in general.[8]

A similar notion was suggested by public initiatives that seemed, at first glance, to convey support for rape survivors. It was very important that local imams in Zenica and Tuzla had called for compassion toward these women, or at least the Muslims among them as the majority of victims. Just after the war, other Muslim religious leaders referred to women war rape survivors as *šehid*s, or martyrs to Islam/the nation.[9] This designation, though intended to valorize sacrifices made for the nation, effectively declared these women dead as (respectable) women, as *šehid* was most commonly a status conveyed upon soldiers killed in battle. Rather than their lives, the women had sacrificed their respectability and moral integrity, though conceptually, under the rubric of *šehid*, there was not much difference.[10] Several years later, a man at a Sarajevo round table discussion on women and war declared to a stunned audience of local feminists and intellectuals that such women should not be referred to as raped but as women who had "martyred their reputations"—*ušehidile su obraz*.[11] Indeed, the idealized figure of the woman war rape victim (in BiH as in countless other contexts) was one who had been killed or who had preferred death over "dishonor," as in the book title *I Begged Them to Kill Me*.

Notions of honor also underpinned the common assertion that rape was especially difficult for Muslim women, Bosniacs. I heard this from many people in the Bosniac areas, including women's NGO activists, with the notable exception of the women at Medica and some of the other self-declared feminists. As noted in chapter 2, Medica's experience had shown no evidence that Bosniac women had a harder time coping with wartime rape or were more likely to be rejected by husbands or other family members. Still, even maintaining this view, there were activists at Medica like Halima who stressed that Serb and Croat rapists had had in mind "the role of the Bosniac female [*Bošnjak-inja*], Muslim women in the family" and the expectation that a Muslim girl "enters marriage as a virgin." As members of the same society that considered Muslims more deeply patriarchal than other groups, the rapists had operated on the assumption that rape would deal an especially hard blow to Bosniacs. Survivor association activists like Alisa Muratčauš also recognized the "attack on women" but placed more emphasis on the "patriarchal roots" of the Muslim community and the fear of Bosniac women, the vast majority of the victims, of telling their families that they were raped since "their husbands are from the Balkans. They're afraid of [hearing] that [question], 'ah, are you sure you didn't give [him] a reason [*Ah, da nisi dala povoda*]?'"

There was an oscillation between stressing "patriarchal roots" throughout the former Yugoslavia and the specificity of Muslim culture where within living memory women had been secluded and veiled in order to protect their sexuality. Ziba, one of the leaders of Žene Srebrenice in Tuzla who talked to me in 2005 about rape among their members, also qualified her statement that rape is "shameful and humiliating" for all women—it was so "especially for Bosnian women." When I asked for clarification she said she meant Bosniac, Muslim women since "maybe non-Muslims are more ready to talk about it." But she did not claim any experience with non-Muslim women on this issue. Activists at United Women in Banja Luka (RS), who had not worked directly with rape survivors but with gender-based violence in other contexts, speculated that rape must be especially difficult for *Serb* women, because of the emphasis placed by Orthodox Christianity on women's sexual purity. This was in 2007, before these activists got involved in the state-level initiative for improving conditions for rape survivors. Wartime rape, even of Serb women, had not been a topic in RS political discourses up to then either. I took this unfamiliarity as a sign of just how buried this issue was in their cross-ethnic women's NGO and donor circles.

On the collective level, then, suffering and stigma were both emphasized and condemned. But what to do with the hundreds or thousands of individual war rape victims who had survived and were living in BiH?[12] No one argued for their social rejection, but there was also a sense that they had been so tainted by the experience of rape that one could not relate to them as normal members of society. They were not supposed to be visible. Women activists, including rape survivors themselves, by and large conformed to this avoidance. There was a notable silence around Srebrenica, for example. The main focus was on the murder of so many men. Rape, which had been part of the abuse and terror inflicted by the invading Serbs during the fall of the enclave, was never a subject associated with Srebrenica, even though emphasizing this might logically have intensified the sense of victimhood and injustice visited upon the Bosniacs in this region.[13] The enormity of the losses of the murdered men overshadowed the many atrocities this community had experienced.

"There was that, too, and then some," Ziba at Žene Srebrenice told me when I asked whether there had been rape in Srebrenica." But we don't talk about it." Fewer women survivors fell into this category, so the associations did not make it an issue, but even on an individual level, the activists explained, women with other experiences of suffering would sooner mention those, especially if they had lost loved ones. The women may have been raped, but they had survived. The activists related that one of their members had lamented about her lost son, "Why wasn't he female so that they would rape him but he would still be alive, rather than his being male and now not being here at all?" In the face of the loss of the men and all the other atrocities this population had endured, speaking about rape was considered unseemly.

The women at the two main Srebrenica women's associations thus acknowledged that rape had happened, but it was not a comfortable topic for them and certainly not a public one. It was also a topic that did not come up on its own, and on occasions when I brought it up, the women quickly switched back to the subject of their missing men and other pressing concerns. Even when accepted by their families, no woman wanted to be branded a raped woman in the community. As one member of Majke enklava put it, they "still had to live with people" (*treba živjeti dalje s narodom*). With another, more "respectable" experience of loss and victimhood—and in this case, one that held a prominent place in narratives of national victimhood—such women sought to win a measure of recognition for their suffering and to press moral claims in public without drawing attention to, and thus possibly inviting the questioning of, their own moral integrity. This was an option that other rape survivors did not necessarily have.

Rape Survivors and Activism

Although Medica had been publicly vocal about its work and the topic of wartime rape during the war itself, the organization also took pains to shield its clients from media and community scrutiny, which required a good deal of discretion and silence. After the end of the war, the few Bosnian organizations like Medica that dealt with the issue continued to treat and aid survivors but also turned to other pressing issues. Some of the survivors themselves did speak out but chiefly to therapists and war crimes investigators and eventually as witnesses, mostly with identities disguised, in war crimes trials in The Hague and later at the War Crimes Chamber in Sarajevo (see Mischkowski and Mlinarević 2009). Medica and other similar NGOs supported the survivors in this and spoke out at various round tables and conferences on the subject, but they only rarely brought the topic into any sort of public arena. Therapist Marijana Senjak and other Medica activists explained their priority as respecting the survivors and their wishes, even as they were aware that staying silent meant risking that these crimes would go unacknowledged and unpunished (Andrić-Ružičić 2003, 107). Many survivor-witnesses had retreated from even the limited public visibility of witnessing, bitter from their experience at the ICTY because they felt inadequately protected, that sentences were too short, or that they were not allowed to tell their stories in a way that would give them catharsis (Mertus 2004).

Thus, most of the advocacy around this issue was on behalf of victims rather than *by* victims themselves. There were a few exceptions in the first postwar years. In northwest BiH, Nusreta Sivac, a judge from Prijedor who had survived rape in the nearby Omarska camp, continued to be visible and active with women's NGOs and campaigns for justice in that area after her return to BiH. Sivac had spent the war in Zagreb, where she had also been active with women's NGOs. She and fellow Prijedoran Jadranka Cigelj had been featured in the 1996 documentary *Calling the Ghosts*, about mass rapes in BiH, in which the two women are shown traveling to The Hague to serve as ICTY witnesses. In 1999 Sivac told me she was unsure about whether her testimony and public visibility had been a good idea since those responsible for Omarska had not been brought to justice and she continued to suffer in many ways from being known as a rape survivor. But she was mostly threatened in her hometown of Prijedor, now in the Serb-controlled RS, for being a *vocal* victim working to bring to justice perpetrators of all aspects of ethnic cleansing and their supporters in the Serb nationalist leadership. Years later, in 2007, she was more optimistic that her tormenters would be punished and she declared that it had all been worth it.[14] Indeed, she continued to speak in a variety of forums about her experiences and the other tortures she witnessed.

Two major collections of testimonies by women rape survivors, published in Bosnian and English (Ajanović 1999; Tokača 1999),[15] also appeared relatively early. As we have seen, however, these were not books organized, presented, and framed by rape survivors themselves, even as the survivors had supported them. It was not until the mid-2000s that public advocacy for women war rape survivors began to be conducted also by the women themselves. They joined other women's NGOs, human rights activists, and feminists in BiH that were becoming more vocal on this issue, leading to productive cooperation on some levels but also to tension over who had the right to represent victims.

Engaging the State

Public activism on the issue of rape was generally focused on the pursuit of justice in some form. Many held out hope that the courts would bring historical, retributive justice and in the process establish the truth about what happened, an expectation that remained unsatisfied by the experiences of many trial witnesses (Mertus 2004; Mischkowski and Mlinarević 2009). Others were more concerned with social, or redistributive, justice, noting that many war victims, especially rape survivors, were living in poverty without permanent housing or health insurance and still coping with the physical and psychological effects of their ordeals. In 2003 Medica Zenica organized a round table titled "Wartime Rape, Ten Years Later," where it was noted that survivors were still not recognized by the state as civilian victims of war or provided for in any other capacity. For all the times that war rapes were evoked by Bosniac nationalists, politicians, or religious leaders, no one in government office or religious institutions had offered survivors more than words. Only NGOs had offered any sort of tangible aid.[16]

The state, or more precisely the parts of it over which Bosniac politicians had control (where resources and rhetoric were directed at all at the well-being of the population), was first of all concerned about the roles of men, or social categories defined as male, and above all with those roles and categories privileged by dominant national narratives, in this case primarily former war combatants.[17] This reflected the centrality of war in narratives of Bosniac and Bosnian nation-building. As elsewhere, the war as "the ultimate gendered act" (Kouvo and Levine 2008) in which male roles and actions—as soldiers, generals, or politicians—take on even more importance than in peacetime, had forged so many of the social categories upon which political and moral claims in the postwar period were based (Bougarel 2006; Bougarel et al. 2007b). Even during the war, the government had provided different forms of privileges and aid for soldiers, with directed aid for wounded soldiers and the dependents of Bosnian Army soldiers killed in the fighting—"*sehid*s and fallen combatants." With the end of the fighting and demobilization, former soldiers were given various forms of compensation for their service, while wounded veterans (*ratni vojni invalidi*, RVI) and the families of dead soldiers continued to receive monthly pensions from the state (see Bougarel 2006).[18] It was a loss of the male capacity as breadwinner and protector that was the crucial factor deemed necessary for compensation, whether in the case of wounded veterans who could no longer work to support their families, or the widows and families of fallen soldiers who had lost their male breadwinner and thus their source of income.[19]

In 1998, three years after the end of the war, a law on civilian war victims was passed granting the physically disabled a similar, though smaller, state pension tied to the percentage of disability they were determined to have sustained from war-inflicted wounds. Eligibility for this aid was restricted to victims with physical injuries such as missing limbs. The debilitating psychological effects

Figure 19 Painting honoring a fallen soldier/martyr (*šehid*) with the symbols of what he died defending: BiH and Mostar. Photographed July 1996. (photo by author)

of trauma were not recognized by the law, leaving survivors of war rape and of detention camps ineligible unless they also had serious physical injuries or, in very rare cases, were persistent enough and could convince the authorities that their ordeals had caused physical damage. Realizing that war rape would continue to be ignored as a legitimate category of disability, Besima Borić, a Federation parliamentary representative from the SDP and a close ally of many Bosnian women's activists, introduced a bill to amend the civilian victims law to include rape survivors. But her initiative fell flat, activists believed, because she belonged to a rival party from the ruling SDA.

Time passed, the SDA was voted out and then back in again, but successive further attempts also failed.[20] In retrospect, activists and politicians chalked this up to worries about financing. Although individual benefits for civilian victims of war would be small, no one could say how many war rape survivors there were who could potentially claim eligibility, which meant there could be no estimate of how much the new benefit would cost. The Federation budget was already hugely overburdened with similar entitlements, a large portion of which was taken up by payments to former soldiers and the families of those killed. The International Monetary Fund (IMF) had long been pressuring the Bosnian state to cut back on such social benefits, but when the short-lived SDP-led Federation government had attempted to redefine military benefits by need rather than as an across-the-board entitlement, thereby culling the rolls

Avoidance and Authenticity

significantly, the uproar was so great that the new law was largely reversed. As Xavier Bougarel has shown (2006), cutting benefits was seen as a great dishonor to those who had fought for Bosnia, even an insult to their masculinity, and the SDP was voted out in the next election.[21] From then on, politicians were especially wary of the power of the veteran population. In the meantime, the state was having difficulty distributing benefits (on time or at all) to retirees and the "regular" disabled. Other groups like unemployed workers harbored a sense of injustice stemming from socialist-era expectations that they should also be receiving aid in these difficult economic times. This was especially palpable in Zenica with its large population of unemployed industrial workers placed on waiting lists (*na čekanju*), scarcely hoping for reassignment or compensation.

All of these various moral claims were being made largely by males on behalf of male groups, or groups conceptualized as representing male roles. Although it was known at some level that men had suffered sexualized violence during the war, the category of war rape victims was almost always associated with women, women who were expected to be, and largely were, silent. One state official, Deputy Minister for Human Rights and Refugees Slobodan Nagradić, was quoted in a British newspaper expressing doubts that any woman speaking out about rape could be a true victim: "Women do not traditionally talk about rape here, he says, and those that do are using rape for political manipulation." With the prospect of rape survivors qualifying for a state pension, Nagradić also suggested that "many are very poor and may just be doing it for the money."[22]

Advocates for the victims reacted strongly in the press; this was doubly insulting, coming as it did from an official of the RS. Presumably no politician in the Federation would have suggested such a thing in public, but even here, according to activists in the Dignity campaign, similar suspicions had been murmured by politicians in the halls of Parliament—yes, rape was terrible but how had these women found themselves in this situation? Were they not somehow partially to blame themselves? Telling also was the skepticism I heard voiced by people in the Federation toward the most vocal rape victims. Yes, they were brave but were they perhaps not traumatized or a bit unhinged to be venting their anger so freely? Were they acting as pawns of the politically powerful rather than being truly needy themselves?

Rape survivors were therefore easy to ignore, whether because they were silent or, paradoxically, because those who were vocal were suspected of ulterior motives, political machinations, or psychological instability. When the issue finally gained public attention through women's NGOs, the financial situation made it easier for politicians to imply the reason why rape survivors had been ignored for so long: it was not that society did not care or valued their suffering less but that resources were scarce. I found no evidence that any public official commented on the ways in which socially disadvantaged groups, whether connected to wartime experiences or not, had been prioritized by the state, nor on why the government was acting only now in response to persistence from NGO activists, although several international bodies criticized these as government failures (Amnesty International 2009, 41). Giving precedence to veterans and their families went without saying and was in fact reflected in the relative amounts awarded, as it soon became clear.

.

"For the Dignity of Survivors"

Medica's 2003 round table on wartime rape was attended by Jasmila Žbanić, the young female film director who was then researching her first full-length film, *Grbavica*, about a Bosnian woman and her now adolescent daughter born of wartime rape. Marijana Senjak, an experienced therapist who had been with Medica from the beginning, advised Žbanić on the film, helping the director to depict the everyday realities of war rape survivors in a realistic, non-sensational way. With the round table highlighting the present material hardships faced by war rape survivors, the participants agreed to launch a new campaign for the recognition of war rape survivors as civilian victims of war. The organizing committee included Žbanić's film company Deblokada, Medica, the women's section of SULKS, and several other women's and therapy NGOs, some of whom had already begun to work on their own similar initiatives.[23] The title of the campaign, "For the Dignity of Survivors," deliberately avoided the connotations of passivity and social irrelevance that went with the label of victim. Consistent with Medica's established practice and feminist politics, the name sought to stress the continued humanity of this population whose ordeals, as the campaign pointed out in its public statements, should not be allowed to remain only in the memories of the survivors but should "concern all of us."[24] Furthermore, even though the campaign focused on *women* survivors and most assumed it was about *Bosniac* women as most of the survivors were, a few key activists also ensured that the wording of the amendment not specify sex or ethnicity in the eligibility criteria.

The Dignity campaign was limited to the Federation since the RS already had a law that nominally included survivors of wartime sexual violence. In light of the state-level campaign that began a few years later (2010–12), this decision seems fairly limited, both because of the severe inadequacy of the RS law (see Amnesty International 2009, 2012), and because it was later fully possible, if not entirely without problems, to engage activists and survivor organizations from the RS on the issue.[25] In 2006 and earlier, however, it was especially still the case that focusing on the Federation was much more straightforward than campaigning throughout BiH. Here it was assumed from the outset that "victims of wartime sexual violence" meant female Bosniac victims of rape by Serb (or Croat) forces. (There was some acknowledgement that men had also been abused sexually, but few were comfortable talking about this, least of all the survivors themselves. However, a number of them did register to receive benefits once the amendment passed.) There was a general consensus that this was a population deserving of sympathy and aid. There was no need to wade into the murky territory of contentious "ethnic" issues so studiously avoided by most women's activists working across entity lines but that also might destabilize alliances within the Federation itself. Ultimately, the important thing was to get the law passed at least in the entity where most survivors lived.

The campaign thus went forward engaging the state institutions of the Federation, mobilizing networks of allies built over years of political initiatives and activists' embeddedness in their communities. After having their requests sent to the many levels of government go unanswered, campaign activists engaged Nermina Kapetanović, an SDA representative in the Federal House of Representatives (Zastupnički dom) who was from Zenica and known to some of the Medica activists. Kapetanović was not a feminist or particularly interested in women's issues, but as a medical professional she saw herself as a humanitarian and champion of the socially underprivileged. As a Bosnian patriot, she saw the victims of those who had wanted to destroy BiH's multiethnic fabric as a particularly worthy cause. The campaign joined forces with Saliha Đuderija, a government lawyer who later became Assistant Minister of Human Rights and Refugees; she had previously begun formulating a similar initiative with ADL Barcelona, another women's NGO from Sarajevo. She drafted the amendment they wanted put forward in Parliament. Kapetanović in turn lobbied the speaker of the House of Representatives to cosponsor the bill. Although Kapetanović later insisted that the politicians involved had all had "good intentions," it took several more ignored proposals, false starts, objections about financing, and disagreements over who was behind it for the amendment to eventually pass in the spring of 2006.

Hierarchies of Victimhood

In the lead-up to the passage of the amendment, campaign organizers had first attempted to sideline questions about pension amounts or other provisions by making this a campaign for status. War rape survivors, they argued, had been ignored for too long; their suffering deserved state recognition as civilian war victims. Expectations of state responsibility toward vulnerable members of society were widespread locally, quite apart from compensation that might have been sought from the perpetrators, but it was also an expectation enshrined in the UN's Basic Principles (Amnesty International 2009, 43). Despite the fact that various NGO projects had been working with this population since reports of the rapes had first surfaced, their aid had never come close to reaching all the victims or addressing their problems in a systematic way. NGOs were neither as stable nor as predictable as the state, nor were they expected to be.

There was also a solid precedent for the privileging of the military, war veterans, and the surviving families of military dead, a category that had enjoyed generous state benefits in socialist Yugoslavia, including choice housing, land, and priority for employment (Bougarel 2006; Karge 2010).[26] After the recent war, military veterans occupied a more ambiguous position, with many demobilized veterans complaining, perhaps precisely in comparison with the socialist period, that their sacrifices were not appreciated or rewarded materially. In fact, during the war one group of wounded soldiers, many on crutches or in wheelchairs, descended on Medica Zenica loudly protesting that they were more deserving than women war victims of the funds they saw reaching Medica.[27] Rhetorically, however, and in terms of state benefits, veterans continued to occupy the top of the hierarchy. The Dignity campaign argued that rape survivors had been unjustly bypassed for state aid and that their suffering had been just as meaningful and should be officially recognized.

Financial issues soon came to dominate political discussions, however, sidelining the other provisions that were part of the amendment: in addition to the monthly pension, beneficiaries were also to be offered free job-skills training, access to psychological and legal aid as well as health care, and were to be given priority in hiring and housing allocation. The monthly payments became the focus of consideration with a consensus quickly reached that the maximum amount of the monthly pension should not exceed 70 percent of the maximum amount for which wounded army veterans (RVIs) were eligible. At the time, 70 percent of an RVI pension meant 513 KM (approx. US$335) per month, a meager but significant sum when the average monthly gross salary was 807 KM, retirement pensions 247 KM (International Labor Organization [ILO] 2009, 7–8), and much of the population was barely scraping by. As with other civilian war victims, RVIs, or society's "regular" disabled, most rape survivors would receive a still smaller portion of the maximum, according to the percentage of disability they were determined to have sustained. Still, something was better than nothing for the many struggling survivors.

Campaign activists, including victim associations, eventually agreed that it would be impractical to push for anything more than 70 percent. At ŽŽR they considered themselves "in the first group" of war victims deserving of aid, but were content with the 70 percent designation since "raped women are not invalids [disabled]," as their president put it in one conversation with me. SULKS, on the other hand, insisted for some time that rape survivors deserved the same amount as RVIs, arguing that the raped had also "defended Bosnia with their bodies" (Ajanović 1999). Equating these victims with wounded military veterans was the strongest possible framework in which to demand recognition, but precisely because there was such a strong popular consensus about privileging military veterans, Marijana of Medica thought it unwise to make such demands. She saw the difference as one of intentions: soldiers had knowingly put themselves in harm's way while rape survivors and camp detainees had not. Of course, much of the male population had been drafted, compelled into service both by army enforcement and by popular sentiment, the rest having volunteered out of a sense that they had no choice but to defend their homes. Marijana did not delve into such distinctions, but focused on what she saw was the most pragmatic course of action in settling for the 70 percent figure. The hierarchy of victimhood was thus translated into monetary values and ratified by state, political, and NGO actors alike.

Harnessing Patriotism

The success of Žbanić's film *Grbavica* raised the profile of the status campaign and energized supporters to finally see the amendment become law. But the enthusiasm was more than sympathy for rape victims in whatever form and for many may have had little to do with these crimes at all. When the Golden Bear prize was announced on February 18, 2006, in Berlin, the BiH Federation press gave it extensive coverage and commentators praised the award as a victory won on the world stage *for Bosnia*. Like the Academy Award for Best Foreign Language Film won by Danis Tanović in 2001 for *Ničija zemlja* (*No Man's Land*), *Grbavica*'s success was presented, completely apart from the much more subtle, even anti-nationalist messages in both these films, as a triumph for the nation and the country,[28] a reinforcement of Bosniacs'/Bosnia's status as victims of nationalist war aims, and, especially with Žbanić's public call while accepting the award for the arrest of the two most powerful Serb indicted war criminals still at large at the time, a reminder to the world of the viciousness and guilt of the Serb nationalist project.[29]

When Tanović won, a large banner was hung over a major intersection in Sarajevo proclaiming, "Screw the country that doesn't have an Oscar!"[30] This time, in covering the Sarajevo premier of the film, Federation Television repeatedly ran a short celebratory clip with aesthetics worthy of a European football advertisement: computer-generated fireworks graphics exploding over a picture of the Golden Bear trophy accompanied by the 1970s hit song "We Are the Champions!" by the British band Queen. This was followed by a few scenes from *Grbavica* trailers, the mood of which was, by contrast, tense, emotional, and subdued.[31] "We" was left unspecified, but was implied to mean "Bosnia," "Bosniacs," or possibly "victims of war," all of which could amount to the same thing. The actual content of the film and the victim/survivors themselves seemed quite secondary. Long-time rape survivor advocates like Marijana were aghast at how Federation politicians jumped onto the patriotic bandwagon to revel in the success of a film that was actually "a scathing critique of criminality and corruption in [postwar] Sarajevo, in Bosnia." As she told me when I visited her in June 2006, she and her fellow activists had asked themselves, "What are they celebrating? They're celebrating the fact that they haven't done anything! . . . I don't mean for the film, I mean for the women who survived war rape."[32]

Since before the Berlin award, the plan had been to collect signatures in support of the amendment at the showing of the film, which had yet to premier in BiH. Campaign organizers had contacted women's groups in various towns where the film was to be shown. Soon, however, they had requests from NGOs and even schools and other groups in many more places that wanted to help collect signatures and distribute flyers. The Sarajevo premier was moved from the National Theater's five-hundred-seat hall to Zetra, the rebuilt former Olympic stadium with seats for five thousand. In addition to the few screenings originally planned for other major towns (Zenica, Tuzla, Mostar), showings were arranged in many more, smaller places; where there was no cinema, they used the local House of Culture (*Dom kulture*).

The enthusiasm was not limited to the film and its success, as the requests directed at the status campaign showed. Marijana took this as a level of sympathy for and sensitivity to the problems of women war rape survivors. "Probably they also wanted to share in the success of the film," she acknowledged, "to participate in something that brought this kind of success to BiH, to be part of that. Which is good." But it was also "a kind of solidarity" the organizers had not expected, especially that all these people were volunteering time and resources to help the campaign, something rare in the world of Bosnian NGOs (see chapter 3). Medica and the other NGOs in the campaign with other sources of funding like Vive žene and Žene ženama had paid for the printing of the leaflets and other expenses, but most of the activists had volunteered their time and small expenses. This was not seen as an ordinary NGO project but a humanitarian and patriotic initiative in solidarity with the victims.

Regardless of the reasons, the sudden attention and enormous response led to the collection of 50,000 signatures, which campaign activists delivered to Parliament. After the amendment passed, there were those who dismissively quipped that the amendment would never have gone anywhere without the success of *Grbavica*, and the headlines in the Federation press implied just that. This irked the campaign's activists, including Žbanić herself, considering all they had done beforehand to prepare the amendment, not to mention the prior efforts of others. But they were satisfied with the end result. They all gathered at a well-attended press conference in Sarajevo to mark the end of the campaign and to hand out certificates of thanks to the numerous NGOs and individuals who had contributed.

Problems with Implementation

Once the amendment became law, new questions arose and the difficulties of implementation began. Who would determine victims' levels of disability or even certify eligibility in the first place? Would claiming benefits mean having to relive war trauma by (re)telling the details? Over a decade after the crimes, rape survivors rarely had physical wounds to show. Many had not been treated at the time and thus lacked medical paperwork, and memories of details were growing dim, clouded by lingering trauma. Those hoping to qualify for the new pensions were required to produce certification that they had indeed survived wartime rape. Inexplicably, when the law first went into effect, documentation from therapy organizations like Medica Zenica for those survivors who had had counseling was not deemed adequate. The primary gatekeeper for certification at first was the Association of Women Victims of War (ŽŽR). There was nothing in the amendment establishing ŽŽR's authority, and some survivors I met or heard about had established eligibility in other ways, but most survivors and advocates accepted this procedure even if it seemed worrying to some (e.g., Amnesty International 2009, 44–46; Mischkowski and Mlinarević 2009).

Bakira Hasečić, ŽŽR's president, had been instrumental in putting her group forward as the only organization that could verify claims. When I pressed her on how this could be done with certainty, she confidently stated that she and her members "knew who the victims were." If they did not, they could find someone from a claimant's community who knew the details. ŽŽR's public calls for victims to come forward ended with the assurance that "privacy is guaranteed." But the public and social nature of "knowing" about these women seemed like a potential obstacle to survivors' claiming much-needed aid. ŽŽR's method of taking testimony was also worrying, as I saw on one of the occasions in the summer of 2006 when I made the long trip to the periphery of Sarajevo's suburbs to where the organization had its office at the time. The municipality had allocated them a two-room office in a ground-floor retail space of a socialist-era apartment block now inhabited mostly by destitute refugees and socially marginalized Roma (Gypsies). The entrance door opened directly from the sidewalk into the main room, where, on that day, two puffy-eyed women sat on the couch clutching tissues while Hasečić sat at a desktop computer entering in what one of the women was saying. Hasečić's back was to the door with the screen in full view. The blinds were drawn but I was able to enter, expecting nothing more than my scheduled meeting.

Hasečić quickly stopped typing and rose to tell me we could not meet that day because these women had unexpectedly dropped by to apply for certificates and were giving their testimony. There was thus some effort to protect the women's privacy, at least from me, a foreigner whom Hasečić repeatedly mistook for a journalist. But I wondered about the other members of the organization who were also present. I could not know their relationship to the women giving testimony—was it assumed that other rape survivors would be supportive or otherwise did not pose a threat to the women giving testimony? My concern deepened when I returned soon after to talk with Hasečić and she told me some of the details of the rape ordeals suffered by the women I had seen giving testimony the time before. She also told me the full name of another woman who had come to ŽŽR for a certificate, a woman I happened to know well, effectively "outing" someone who was otherwise silent and considerably troubled about this episode in her past. Moreover, ŽŽR did not have a qualified mental health practitioner on hand to guide survivors through their testimony as therapy NGOs always did. The organization was in fact suspicious of psychological support, insisting that their members needed material aid rather than therapy.

Needless to say, all of this was problematic. I heard murmured rumors about ŽŽR accepting large sums of money in exchange for certificates or about their position being due to political patronage. Other survivor advocates worried that this system was open to abuse and began to lobby for the acceptance of certificates from other organizations and institutions. They were ultimately successful, but ŽŽR continued to assert its role as primary advocate for all of

Bosnia's raped women and to dismiss the efforts of other survivor and advocate organizations. The tension thus produced stemmed both from competition over scarce and dwindling resources for NGOs and from different approaches to public visibility and to claims of authenticity on the part of activists.

Speaking Out

ŽŽR's stated purpose was providing aid to survivors but an equally important part of its ultimate agenda was the arrest and prosecution of war crimes perpetrators. As Hasečić regularly told the media, her organization existed to pursue "justice and truth." She herself was very visible in the media, speaking out at every opportunity about wartime rape, massacres, camps, and other atrocities, especially those committed by Serbs and especially in her home region of Eastern Bosnia. She was particularly keen to see all the rape survivors her organization registered also testify against perpetrators in war crimes trials. When I first met her in 2005, she explained that "women who step forward publicly and try to do something are our priority, not those who sit around and wait for someone to give them money." On another occasion she declared that "she who conceals or stays silent about that is worse than the war criminal himself." Indeed, ŽŽR appears to have given many applicants for civilian victim status the impression that their certificate issued by ŽŽR was contingent on their promising to testify at the local BiH war crimes court (Amnesty International 2009, 45–46). As with the two women whose testimony I interrupted, ŽŽR collected the testimonies of hundreds of survivors who came to them for certification.

Alisa Muratčauš, then head of the women's section of SULKS, the other publicly visible association of rape survivors, also wanted women to testify, whether openly or as protected witnesses, because "the truth really has to come out, and every war criminal *must* be held responsible." The book *I Begged Them to Kill Me* had been an explicit step toward "truth and justice," the women's statements published not only in the interest of general knowledge but as a basis for legal prosecution (Ajanović 1999).[33] The mostly male editors had strongly encouraged women to tell their stories, asking them, much like Hasečić, "Dare we stay silent? Don't we know that silence about a crime is the same as the crime itself?" (ibid., 14). Informally, however, Muratčauš talked more about how difficult this was for women rape survivors, given the "patriarchal framework" in which they lived. Predictably, none of the women survivors I got to know were particularly keen on being publicly identified as raped women and, aside from the most vocal activists, most tried to avoid the spotlight even as they did testify in war crimes trials and talked outspokenly to journalists when approached. These were, however, only the few who had decided to speak out, usually as the price that had to be paid for the hope that justice would be served (in the courts). Many more stayed invisible publicly, some even in their everyday communities or families.

The opportunity to collect benefits was thus a double-edged sword for the survivors. Most of them were still displaced and many were living a precarious existence on the margins of society; a regular income, however meager, would make a world of difference. But to claim benefits they would have to risk not only calling attention to this aspect of their past and reliving the trauma—of rape but also of other forms of pain and loss—by telling the story out loud perhaps for the first time in many years, or ever. Claiming the pension also meant identifying, classifying oneself as a victim, in legal terms but, unavoidably, in social and moral terms as well (Ross 2003). The more public a woman's story was, the deeper these considerations became. It was these difficulties with making statements public that advocacy/therapy organizations like Medica and Vive žene were worried about. In their experience, survivors usually confided in a close female relative first, waiting much longer to tell husbands, fathers, or brothers, if they told them at all.[34] Still, given the collective nature of the violence and the small communities in which it occurred, family members often "knew"; there had been no need to tell the story to anyone in the way survivors were being required to now.

Moreover, as my encounters with survivors also confirmed, those who had spoken about their ordeals (with friends, family members, therapists, or even war crimes investigators) had done so most, and most intensively, in the years just after the war. Over a decade after these events, survivors had rebuilt their lives. However precarious their economic and material existence, most had settled into a social niche that was dependent on a tacit agreement among those around them about how to deal, or not deal, with the facts of their having been raped.[35] Few were in a position to refuse regular aid, but establishing eligibility could require a shift in their everyday sense of self and how that self was embedded in their social world. They would now have to acknowledge to themselves and to certain others their categorization as a rape victim and be reminded of that fact every month with the arrival of a benefit voucher. This aspect of the benefit scheme was perhaps unavoidable, but from the perspetive of the feminist therapy NGOs, ŽŽR's approach needlessly exacerbated the problems by pushing survivors to speak out more publicly than they may have wanted. Even more worrying, the first payment vouchers mailed out by the government indicated that recipients were survivors of sexualized violence, causing heightened anxiety and at least one rumored suicide among the survivor-beneficiaries.[36]

　　　　　　　　　　　　　　Avoidance and Authenticity

For Medica, the principles of their work—as therapists and as feminists—had always been to guard women's privacy and to leave them in control of what happens to information about them. They had seen the problems faced by their clients who had gone to testify at the ICTY and now felt inadequately protected, not only from the social stigma of rape but, as with survivors of any atrocity, from possible intimidation from perpetrators and their supporters. They further worried about the majority of survivors who had not received therapy. Moreover, Medica and similar NGOs had struggled for years to shield their clients from journalists wanting statements from raped women (Andrić-Ružičić 2003).[37] Medica activists had in fact declined the suggestion by their own feminist founders-donors to compile testimonies from rape survivors into a written record partly out of a fear that such a publication would become fodder for nationalist and political manipulation. As we saw in chapter 2, *I Begged Them to Kill Me* was a case in point.[38]

Somewhat paradoxically, then, the feminists at the therapy NGOs came down on the side of protection, discretion, and silence, while the non-feminist survivor-activists (at SULKS and ŽŽR) tended to favor public testimony, viewing it as a repudiation of the idea that female rape victims should remain shamed and silent—an otherwise common *feminist* stance. The survivors did not explain their position as opposition to patriarchal norms, much less as feminist, but simply as defiance of what were certain to have been the expectations of the perpetrators, that their victims be intensely shamed and remain silent. While many of the survivor-activists did say they felt humiliated, those speaking in public insisted that it was the perpetrators exclusively who should feel shame. Feminist therapy NGOs like Medica agreed but at the same time they were not as concerned with encouraging women survivors to speak publicly as individuals, even for the purpose of establishing justice. Advocacy could be pursued on behalf of survivors as a group, as in the campaign for status.

Survivors and their advocates thus shared basic aims but were often divided over how to attain them. The therapy NGOs tended to be very careful about how they represented survivors. After frustrating reactions from survivors when she testified at the ICTY,[39] Vive žene's Jasna Zejčević decided it was not her or the other activists' place to speak for victims because, she said, "I don't know what they really feel." Medica therapists had not testified directly but had advised the court and made their materials available. The reactions of some of the survivor-activists only heightened this caution.

At ŽŽR, even this low-key approach of advocacy and therapy NGOs was deemed to be misplaced. All NGOs were struggling for funding as well as public legitimacy but ŽŽR seemed to feel this competition most keenly. In all my conversations with Hasečić, she expressed deep suspicion about other

NGOs working on behalf of women rape survivors, above all because they were led by women "who hadn't experienced anything," that is, had not suffered atrocities during the war, particularly rape. She and some of her fellow members gathered in the ŽŽR office when I visited them in June 2006 even dismissed the women at SULKS, because not everyone there, including the women's leader at the time, had been raped. As one of ŽŽR's members boasted, theirs was the only organization that was run by "a woman who felt the suffering on her own skin." On this basis, ŽŽR complained that other organizations were illegitimately garnering attention and funds on behalf of rape survivors.

This politics of authenticity also tainted the organization of witnesses for war crimes trials as well as the process of certification for state benefits. In both cases, Hasečić claimed the right to speak for and represent rape survivors and regularly opposed cooperation with other groups of survivors or their advocates. At first, during and just after the campaign for status, other activists refrained from publicly voicing any criticism of ŽŽR. They wanted to keep the focus on winning benefits for and influencing public perceptions of rape survivors but there was also a consensus that, as a rape survivor, Hasečić deserved respect for bravely speaking out in public.

Rejecting Angelina Jolie

In the autumn of 2010, tensions between Hasečić and the other women's activists eventually became public after an incident involving the Hollywood film star Angelina Jolie, who was directing a new movie set in the Bosnian war, then known only as "Untitled Love Story."[40] Based on a rumor that the film would depict a Muslim rape victim falling in love with her Serb rapist, Hasečić successfully lobbied the Federation Minister of Culture to revoke Jolie's permit to film on location in BiH. Neither Hasečić nor the minister had seen the script, and the rumor about the rape/love plot seems to have been floated by Željko Mitrović, a Serbian television magnate close to Milošević's circles, who had previously boasted about having rejected Angelina Jolie when she was looking for local partners.[41] He had refused, he said, out of patriotism, since her film would once again "represent Serbs as the eternal bad guys" (Dežulović 2010; see also Arslanagić 2010b).

Instead of scrutinizing Mitrović's motives, most commentators in the local and international media focused on Jolie and on Hasečić as the voice of "Bosnian rape victims," prompting some to denounce Jolie as heartless and others to praise her as a great humanitarian—she had previously visited Bosnian refugees as a UNHCR goodwill ambassador. Hasečić once again made her opinion known in the local and international press, calling the film "an outrageous and humiliating misrepresentation of our ordeal" (Arslanagić 2010a). Local women's activists joined Sarajevo urban elites and the film industry who denounced the permit revocation as an attempt at censorship.

Even after Jolie and others refuted the rumor, Hasečić continued to condemn the film and its director, at times it seemed on the basis of the rape/love plot but at other times in more vague terms suggesting that *any* representation of the camps, rapes, or even of cross-ethnic romantic love in the Bosnian war would cause her and other rape victims distress. "What we have gone through cannot be filmed," she told the British *Independent* newspaper (Zimonjic 2010). In response to the officially released synopsis describing the film as depicting a Serb camp where Bosniacs were detained as the site of the love story between a Muslim woman detainee and Serb guard who fall in love *before* the war, Hasečić told reporters, "As far as we are concerned a love story could not have existed in a camp. Such an interpretation is causing us mental suffering" (Agence France-Presse 2010). She further added that the only love that could have been possible in a camp was that between a woman and her child.

On one level, it is understandable that people who went through such traumatic experiences as detention camps, rape, and other tortures would object to such a place becoming the scene of a love story. In September 2012 one survivor told me that she could never sit through a film that even suggested that love could exist in a rape camp, regardless of when the pair had met. Other survivors who did see the film and even praised it talked about how difficult it was to watch as it brought back vivid memories of their own ordeals. Ethnicity need not be part of such objections. In ŽŽR's reactions to the Jolie film, however, rape victims were defined ethnically as Bosniac (Muslim) women and Serb men were rapists, the latter being precisely what Mitrović had said he objected to.

What seemed to bother Hasečić and other members of ŽŽR the most was the idea that love or consensual sexual relationships could exist at all between Muslims (women) and Serbs (men) in such a war context. Croatian feminist Slavenka Drakulić began to open up this aspect (although she also weighed in against censorship) with a direct challenge to Hasečić. Drakulić argued that by denying the possibility of love or romance, ŽŽR was denying Serb men their humanity, precisely in the way they had dehumanized their victims. This framing, Drakulić wrote, paradoxically absolves the perpetrators of guilt for the rapes because, after all, "they are not human beings but monsters!" (Drakulić 2010). While this was an important intervention and a rare attempt to engage with the dynamics of sex and power in understanding the gendered dynamics of war, the more important part of the equation for Hasečić seems ultimately to have been the moral reputation of the victims rather than the depiction of the rapists. The more "beastly" and further from normal men the perpetrators were, the less likely it was that the morality or conduct of their victims would be questioned.

Hasečić saw rape in war as a completely different dynamic than other rapes, as she had made clear at the end of a visit to the ŽŽR office in summer 2006 when I asked her whether they would welcome non-war rape survivors into their organization. In fact, she expressed deep suspicion of women who were raped outside of the war context. Anyway, she continued, "That's not what we're here for. We're for truth and justice, that it's known what happened in the war." I then asked her whether men who had been sexually abused in the war might join her organization. Hasečić rejected this, too, explaining with the help of the other members of ŽŽR who were in their office that day that they could not have men appearing at their office lest their neighbors start to talk and suspect that they were sexually involved with these men. "Let them form their own organization," they said, echoing other women's NGOs who took social gender divisions for granted. "This is an organization for women." Not long after, however, after the passage of the status amendment, a few dozen men did join the organization, temporarily, Hasečić explained, so that they could establish eligibility for benefits. ŽŽR's ultimate focus was firmly on victimization in the war rather than the gendered aspects of violence.

All of this indicated that despite the overall condemnation of war rapes and their valued place in understandings of the brutality of Serb nationalist forces and the victimization of Bosniacs—a situation in which one might least expect suspicions about the women who had been attacked—there were still doubts about the sexual reputations of individual survivors. At least those like Hasečić clearly feared that their own reputations would be called into question through the suggestion that the boundary between force and love in a situation of armed conflict could be blurred and complicated. ŽŽR members were therefore disturbed by the potential for this film to disrupt a representation in which they were invested, that of the rapes as national victimization.

In the midst of the public outcry that followed, most of the women's NGOs, journalists, and others who had been advocating on behalf of rape survivors, including activists from Medica and other self-declared feminists, concentrated their public statements on opposing censorship rather than engaging the content of Hasečić's objections (many bemoaned the damage to Bosnia's world reputation and economic losses from Jolie's having to relocate most of the filming to Hungary).[42] A group of various women's activists including Medica issued a stern condemnation of censorship that also referenced the sensitivity of the issue of war rape in light of the history of media manipulation, asking, "What kind of message would ultimate canceling of filming send to the invisible women who also have traumatic war experiences but are not members of any associations nor do they agree with the stances of Bakira Hasečić?"[43] They thus made explicit their refusal to grant Hasečić the right to represent Bosnian rape survivors.

Underscoring this refusal, Enisa Salčinović, the head of the now officially constituted women's section at SULKS, gave statements to the media opposing Hasečić's and challenging her right to speak for all Bosnia's victims. Unlike the previous women's section representative, Salčinović was a rape survivor and had shared her story publicly.[44] She further stated that half of her members did not support Hasečić and that she should "not speak in all of our name." It was SULKS that specifically represented women *camp* survivors, the apparent subject of Jolie's film. Salčinović's comments were published by *The Observer*, whose headline announced provocatively, "Jolie Rape Film Divides Embittered Bosnia" (Beaumont 2010).

Around the same time, Belma Bećirbašić, a journalist at the independent weekly *Dani* who had regularly been writing about issues of gender and sexuality, published a scathing indictment of Hasečić titled "Trafficking in Victims' Emotions" (Bećirbašić 2010). Four years previously, Bećirbašić reported, she had uncovered evidence that Hasečić had been making false promises to victims in exchange for war crimes testimony and statements to the media, public attention that many did not want (Bećirbašić 2006). Bećirbašić explicitly stated that she had held back in the past from publishing any criticism of Hasečić or ŽŽR because she sensed that the social taboo against exposing the exploitation of victimhood would endure. I had been given a similar message from women's advocates at Medica and elsewhere. Despite concerns, it had been important to project a united front among women's activists, both out of (feminist) principles of solidarity with survivors and out of practical considerations for the success of their activities.

In response to the criticism, Hasečić focused on the suffering that she and other victims had endured and on countering accusations that she was acting alone.[45] ŽŽR members backed her up, insisting that "we are all Bakira" (Beaumont 2010). Hasečić continued her campaign, sending a letter over a month later to UNHCR, demanding that Jolie be removed as goodwill ambassador because of her "ignorant attitude toward victims," which also justified rape survivors' continued doubts about the film (Agence France-Presse 2010). *The Observer* implied that the women of ŽŽR were so bitter—about their wartime suffering and their postwar difficulties living on the margins of society—that they just wanted to call attention to their plight rather than express a particular position about the rapes or the film (Beaumont 2010).

Female Victim Identities and Public Activism

Both the categories of female war victimhood—the refugee and rape victim—carried with them certain stigma, while at the same time featuring prominently in national narratives of collective identity, morality, and justification for statehood. They were thus frequently and successfully mobilized, but less uncomfortably in the case of the refugee. Most rape survivors were living in isolation from each other, unable to find solace in collective airing of their traumas or to create public victim personae the way the women Srebrenica survivors and other refugees had done (Bećirbašić 2010). Refugees and Srebrenica survivors were less reluctant to speak in public even though they were more likely to be derided as ignorant, backward, and rural (and often such derision took gendered and sexualized forms). But rape victims were much more likely to shun any public recognition altogether. Those who did speak out could be considered brave, unhinged, or both.

The SULKS women's section offered a form of solidarity for some women under the cover of having suffered camp detainment, a setting that did not necessarily mean rape, even as camps were the site of the most notorious and systematic rapes in the Bosnian war. But it was just a handful of women who frequented their sewing workshop and were thus on hand to speak to visitors and journalists. It was an even smaller number that participated in public gatherings on the subject, most of them convened by women's NGOs or human rights organizations. At ŽŽR, the public face of wartime rape was one woman, Bakira Hasečić, who for a time largely monopolized the public face of the wartime rape victim even in the international press, despite the continued and sustained involvement of advocacy NGOs and international organizations with presumably better access to publicity channels.

Medica had years ago experienced the limits of popular understanding of wartime rape as gender-based violence. Regardless of the support generated for wartime rape survivors, when it came to "ordinary rape" and domestic violence after the war, sympathy was more readily offered to the male perpetrators, assumed to be war veterans, the defenders who had sacrificed so much for the nation. The widespread consensus that wounded veterans and veterans in general deserved the highest levels of state support was another aspect of this view. Understanding for men who drank heavily and assaulted their wives or children also stemmed from the knowledge that so many men had been put out of work by the war and market reforms that they were now unable to fulfill their roles as breadwinners and thus household authorities. A critique of gendered power that linked gendered violence in war and peacetime like that advanced by Medica should have called these assumptions into question.

But the time had evidently not yet come for critically examining the gender order that made sexualized violence in war such a powerful weapon.

A direct discussion of the nature of wartime rape with all its gendered and sexed as well as nationalist aspects had yet to take place among women's activists themselves, whether within the Federation, across BiH entities, or regionally. Even members of anti-nationalist feminist networks that could trace their alliances back to those who stood in the early 1990s against the nationalist appropriation of war rapes were far from united in the assumptions they brought to initiatives around wartime rape.

This was illustrated at a conference I attended in Sarajevo in September 2012 on improving the status of wartime rape survivors throughout the countries of what had been Yugoslavia.[46] The conference was organized by the Sarajevo office of the United Nations Population Fund (UNFPA), which had, along with Amnesty International, turned its attention to the topic starting in 2009 and 2010. Suddenly, with pressure from foreign agencies and EU politicians, there was movement on a state-level law to provide benefits to survivors in all parts of the country. And women's activists from the RS—from the cross-entity network of feminist-friendly NGOs—were now involved, as were representatives from war survivor organizations from both BiH entities.

Participants engaged in mostly practical exchanges about the particulars of prosecuting war crimes, and about NGO efforts in different countries to reduce stigma and provide material and psychological aid to survivors. There was also a lively discussion about how to best honor survivors through a monument, museum, or institute dedicated to women's experiences of war in the region. On one hand, it was encouraging to see such a varied group of feminist and antiwar activists, gender policy and women's rights officials, government war crimes prosecutors, war rape survivors, and international organization representatives finally come together across ethnicized boundaries to tackle the problem of aiding survivors. On the other hand, however, the sessions as well as informal conversations during coffee breaks revealed fundamental differences in assumptions about sexualized violence in war.

It was not surprising to hear survivors speak only in terms of security, trauma, and bringing perpetrators to justice. These were their central issues of concern and the focus of the conference. Survivor organizations had never focused on gender beyond invoking conservative notions of rape as ruination for women; they had clearly experienced rape as a brutal tool of ethnic cleansing and genocide. They thus sometimes referenced ethno-national collectivities but more frequently they spoke in ethnically neutral terms about trauma, recovery, and practical issues like income, schooling, and housing for victims. They did not engage in critiques of gendered power (nor would one necessarily expect them to). When, at the UNFPA conference, Vera from United Women in Banja Luka tried to frame a working group discussion about stigmatization of rape survivors in terms of patriarchal norms, participants from the RS and the Federation got hung up instead on the question of whether and how many survivors there might be in the RS (i.e., among Serb women) and on how trauma prevents many survivors from speaking to anyone about their ordeals. Attempts to discuss attitudes about female sexuality and honor were simply not understood by those not familiar with the feminist critiques of domestic violence and "ordinary" rape that informed Vera's questions as facilitator. Everyone knew what the consequences of "patriarchal society" were for women and their sexual reputation, but talking about challenges or alternatives never went beyond the agreement that these women were not to blame. It was, after all, a war, and one in which women had been attacked as members of a collective; they could not be blamed as individuals. The fundamentals of how notions of sexuality and honor shaped gendered power hierarchies and thus produced both violence and stigma remained unexamined no matter how hard Vera tried to return the group to these questions.

During the general presentations, one working group's emphasis on a "feminist approach" to aiding survivors and raising public awareness was not remarked upon. Nor was the mention by a veteran Croatian feminist from the Center for Women Victims of War of her organization's insistence that wartime rape be seen as a crime against *women* specifically. Participants similarly ignored the language used by an activist from Women in Black in Belgrade who stressed the importance of understanding war rapes as a weapon of (Serb-led) *genocide*, not only in Srebrenica but in the whole war. Even though Serbian feminists in the 1990s had stood in international forums against notions of genocidal rape, Women in Black's oppositional positioning in a Serbian society that was still dominated by denials of Serb-perpetrated atrocities and arguments equating all sides in the Bosnian war had now produced expressions of the opposite extreme in terms of the gender versus ethnicity debate.[47] Just as the question of whether mass rapes could have been committed without orders from above (discussed in chapter 4) had exposed disagreements among Bosnian activists, the different vocabularies used by presenters from Serbia and Croatia hinted at what several activists confirmed privately as the complete avoidance of discussion on this issue among otherwise closely allied anti-nationalist feminists across former Yugoslavia.

Yet these activists from Zagreb and Belgrade were at least explicit about their stances. Bosnian activists had not even broached the subject among like-minded anti-nationalist feminists in Bosniac-dominated areas, much less across the entity divide. They had thus not worked out a language with which to

Figure 20 Activists from Women in Black, Belgrade, at the annual burial and memorial service for Srebrenica victims in Potočari, Eastern Bosnia, July 11, 2003. Banners read: "Women in Black for Peace and Human Rights" and "Women in Black against War, Belgrade." (photo by author)

discuss the topic. It was much safer to "strategically avoid" questions that might trouble intensely felt convictions about the character of the war and of collective responsibility. Those activists interested in exposing and challenging patriarchal structures could do so more comfortably through issues of domestic violence; discrimination against women in politics, advertising, or workplaces; and even advocacy for war rape survivors, as long as these topics could be discussed without reference to conflicting war narratives. When activists in the Federation challenged the patriarchal logic of stigma against war rape survivors, whatever their personal intentions, their words were most readily understood through narratives of Bosniac victimhood, of collective innocence and moral righteousness in opposition to an illegitimate Serb (and Croat) secessionist project. This happened not only in the name of Bosniac nationalisms, whether religious or secular, but also in the name of support for a multiethnic BiH state, as each position saw Bosniac victims of Serb (and Croat) nationalist atrocities as the primary symbols of the forces they opposed (see Helms 2012).

It was thus no surprise when Jolie's film *In the Land of Blood and Honey* was finally released at the end of 2011 that assessments quickly fell into ethno-national camps. Serbian media condemned the film and its author as anti-Serb for portraying them as criminals and rapists. Members of SULKS and other Bosniac rape survivors praised the film as a true representation of what they had endured. Hasečić, not invited to the private pre-screening for survivors, fell silent, despite the fact that the relationship between the two protagonists of the film *did* suggest the possibility of love in such circumstances—elements that ŽŽR survivors had objected to from the start. The film also suggested, however, that the female lead in fact returns to a lengthy sexual captivity by her erstwhile boyfriend in his military headquarters as a spy for Bosnian resistance forces, not out of love at all. The film left things ambiguous enough, though, to enable discussions of the moral grey zone created by power asymmetries and set scripts of gender, sex, ethnicity, and violence associated with war. But as with the more sophisticated and realistic film *Grbavica*, public depictions of Jolie's film were framed solely by competing ethno-national narratives that allowed for characterizations of victims and perpetrators only as ethno-national collectivities.[48]

In this light, it was a major achievement that women's activists in 2006 had not only pushed for the passage of the civilian victims' law amendment to include survivors of sexualized violence in war, but they had also worked to ensure that the amendment's wording did not specify the sex or ethnicity of the victims. Formulating victimhood in terms of sexualized violence therefore included rape but also encompassed other forms of sexualized violence experienced by women as well as men, as such acts perpetrated against men had fallen much more commonly outside the category of rape. The later initiative supported by UNFPA kept the non-specification of sex or ethnicity and an expansive definition of the violence, moving the proposed law to the state level.[49] For activists as well as the general public, these all continued to be seen as initiatives on behalf of women and primarily Bosniacs. But their more expansive coverage, in addition to allowing aid to reach more survivors, opened up at least the conceptual space for a public discussion of the gendered elements of sexualized violence in all its forms, including the implication of gender ideologies that continued to shape understandings and experiences of the war well after its end.

Conclusion

Aren't you just a victim
selling your own trauma?
asked the Harvard blonde
with the brains worth half a million.
I couldn't find the words in English to say
Do you have any idea how right you are?
Nine deaths, bleeding eardrums,
Dodging bullets—It all fits in the word trauma.
And yes, I was unable to say in English,
I'm afraid
that's the only valuable thing I have.

Adisa Bašić, *Trauma-Market* (2004, 36)

Renouncing the "Victim Philosophy"

In the last days of 2008, speaking to the governing board of
the SDA as the leading Bosniac party, party president Sulejman Tihić, himself
a survivor of a Serb concentration camp during the war, called for a new set
of priorities in "Bosniac-Bosnian politics." They needed to set aside the "passive position of the victim and take up the active position and responsibility
of a relevant political factor."[1] Tihić assured his listeners:

We cannot forget the past, we will persistently search for the missing
up until the last one is found and given a dignified burial, we'll insist on
prosecuting those responsible for war crimes, but we have to work for the
present and a better future. So far a central place has been taken up by a
victim philosophy, stories of aggression, genocide, war criminals, and injustice perpetrated in BiH and against Bosniacs. We have to get beyond the

absurd politics that asks for and expects the international community, the high representative, the USA, Islamic and other countries to do our job and solve our problems. Those times have passed.[2]

Tihić spoke in the name of Bosniacs with a view toward achieving a multiethnic BiH state through compromise with the "other BiH peoples and citizens—Serbs, Croats, and others living in our country."[3] It was part of his effort to differentiate himself from his rivals within the party, especially Sarajevo mayor Nedžad Branković, who had styled himself as a champion of the veteran population in a period when state entitlements to veterans were fiercely debated. More broadly, it was also linked to the idea that Bosniacs could not become the leading force of a multiethnic BiH state from a position of victimhood.[4]

ŽŽR's Bakira Hasečić was among the representatives of victim groups, Bosniac public figures, and associations in other countries who reacted to Tihić with outrage and indignation, denouncing him as a "traitor to national interests" who was essentially "forcing victims to get used to the results of [wartime] crimes!" Challenging Tihić's right to speak in the name of the nation, they accused him of doing the bidding of Serb nationalist politicians, "equating the aggressors with the victims," and thereby "finalizing the work of the butchers for Greater Serbia."[5] Hasečić initiated a petition to "say NO to politicians who demand that we forget genocide."[6] She and other victims felt forgotten, abandoned, which was especially egregious coming from "our politicians."[7]

As in many instances before, a challenge to the centrality of uncomplicated victimhood was met with the charge of siding with the enemy perpetrators and ideologues of Serb nationalism. This framing was especially resonant in the face of complaints by RS leader Milorad Dodik published some months earlier in a Belgrade newspaper: "The basic concept of the Bosniac political elites is to make the Bosniacs the only victims of the war in Bosnia and Herzegovina in the eyes of the world. And when you achieve the halo of the victim then you have the right to everything."[8] The main opponent of Bosniac and pro-BiH politics had put his finger on exactly what he and "his people" lacked in the eyes of the world: the moral power of innocence that comes with the status of victim. Dodik was doubtless encouraging a popular sense of resentment among Serbs in the RS who nurtured long-standing *Serb* claims to victim status on the basis of past wars and injustices. There was a disingenuousness to this position, too, coming from the head of the entity that now existed thanks to the project of ethnic cleansing that had produced so many Bosniac victims in the first place.

Dodik of course had political reasons for belittling Bosniac victimhood. For proponents of a united BiH, his separatist politics were the biggest threat to achieving a functioning state. For those in the Bosniac-dominated areas of BiH, Bosniac victimhood was important to keep in focus not only out of respect for what victims had endured but also because it was a crucial element of the moral justification for the Bosnian cause politically, against the idea that the RS should remain a separate, even independent, and above all *Serb* polity. Any suggestion that collective ethnic victimhood should not be at the top of the agenda could thus be taken as an endorsement of anti-Bosniac and anti-Bosnian politics. As the Jolie affair, public discussions over *Grbavica*, and Medica's reaction to the German article about wartime rape had all shown, the characterization of the war and the place of its victims in ethnic terms remained stubbornly dominant fifteen years after the start of the war and beyond.

Nation and Masculinity: Rising from the Ashes

Idith Zertal begins her critical analysis of the role of the Holocaust in building a new Jewish/Israeli nationalism with a quote from the end of Benedict Anderson's well-known treatise on the social construction of nationalism: "From . . . remorselessly accumulating cemeteries, the nation's biography snatches exemplary suicides, poignant martyrdoms, assassinations, executions, wars and holocausts. But to serve the narrative purpose, these violent deaths must be remembered/forgotten as 'our own'" (Anderson 1983, 206, in Zertal 2005, 1). Zertal charts the ways in which the deaths of European Jews in the Holocaust were memorialized as "our own" and mobilized to build a new nation-state that excluded the possibility of sharing sovereignty, land, or citizenship with non-Jews in Palestine. Certainly critics of Israeli policies and military actions toward Palestinians and the occupied territories have not hesitated to note the irony of the once-victimized Jews turning now to victimize ethnic and religious others, just as Israel's defenders justify their actions on the basis of past victimhood and accuse their detractors of harboring hatred toward the Jews as a collective.[9]

Gender has been central to this transformation, particularly masculinity. As Cynthia Enloe memorably wrote, "nationalism has typically sprung from masculinized memory, masculinized humiliation, masculinized hope" (Enloe 1990a, 44; see also Nagel 1998). While this characterization takes for granted a particular aggressive, heterosexual, imperialist masculinity as the driving force of nationalism, this constellation has nevertheless functioned as an ideal in many nationalist projects.[10] Tamar Mayer (2000a) has traced how early Zionist leaders focused on the male population in their drive to create a "new

Jew," explicitly masculine and embodied as the "Muscle Jew" (see also Massad 1995). Jewish men were to transform from the weak, feminized ghetto-dwellers of European society to the forceful, masculine, muscle-bound leaders of a new, proud state with a well-equipped and tough army: "From Zero to Hero," as in Mayer's title. Mayer shows how such notions of ideal masculinity and nationhood conformed to the prevailing ideologies of the late nineteenth and early twentieth centuries in Germany, precisely the scientific-racist thinking that constructed Jews as feminized, weak, and inferior and that eventually fed into Nazism and the Holocaust (see also Mosse 1985). In other words, despite radically different behaviors and culpabilities among perpetrator and victim communities, they shared a fundamental set of ideas about gender, bodies, and nation, much as the ethno-national groups produced by the gendered violence of the Bosnian war operated within a set of shared meanings.

Mayer further shows how the cycle in Israel has continued: as the Holocaust formed the rationale for the formation of the Jewish state and its claims since 1948 to territory and security, present-day Israeli male soldiers look to aggressive military violence as an "invitation to manliness" (Mosse 1985, 114; see also Nagel 1998). One group of soldiers actually left their posts in late 1994 after the Oslo accords when it became clear that instead of asserting force over Palestinians they would be keeping the peace and "guard[ing] day-care centers" (Mayer 2000a, 283). There was no action or glory here: it was no way to become a real man.

Were similar tendencies to be found in Bosniac and Bosnian nationalisms? The notion of rising from the ashes recalls the rousing chorus of the popular patriotic wartime song "To My Dear BiH," a defiant call to resistance on behalf of a multi-ethnic Bosnia and Herzegovina that is nonetheless framed as being defined by strong Muslim traditions.[11] The song exhorts BiH in its whole territory, "a hundred times paid for in blood," to "rise up from the ashes / like a hundred times before." With reference to *sevdah*, the traditional Muslim "female" genre of laments and unhappy love songs (as opposed to the "male" epics of empire and armed resistance associated with Ottoman times), the song asserts that "every mother's heart knows that *sevdah* is woven only from sorrow." It reassures "the country of our grandfathers" that "as long as your sons exist you will be defiant, free, and proud." While women mourn the dead, the nation's sons—armed, strong, and determined—will defend the country at all costs.

These observations are not to single out Bosniac and Bosnian narratives as more dangerous than others or to suggest that such rhetoric necessarily leads to intolerance or violence. Indeed, the diversity of expressions of these stances in BiH suggested many possible outcomes. Similarities with the trajectory of

Israeli or Serb nationalist mobilizations, among others, might raise concern, however, as it did for those like the Bosniac friend with whom I attended the promotion of the book of war rape testimonies discussed in chapter 2, an event that was decidedly more Bosniac oriented than "To My Dear BiH." A refugee of Serb ethnic cleansing himself, my friend had witnessed Serb nationalists growing increasingly "fascist" (his word) in the days before their brutal attacks during the war, using the language of collective victimhood and genocide to underscore the Serbs' historical plight. This had been part of renewed mutual accusations in the 1980s of past genocides that had intensified nationalist mobilizations in the lead-up to war. Indeed, in her confession statement upon being sentenced for crimes against humanity by the ICTY, former RS president Biljana Plavšić explained Serb war atrocities through reference to the past victimization of Serbs, especially in World War II, as the reason for their zeal in trying to secure territories.[12] In his account of competing narratives of victimhood around Srebrenica, Ger Duijzings argues that postwar emphasis in Bosniac narratives on collective victimhood is a more recent phenomenon that reflects Bosniacs' relatively late-starting process of ethno-national consolidation. Such discourses, also invoking past genocides and the Holocaust, date from the late socialist period (see Bougarel 2010; Sorabji 2006) and, as Duijzings argues, have brought Bosniac narratives closer to the Serb way of "being in history," that is, interpreting all past events through ethnic notions of collective victimhood (2007, 146, quoting Bloch 1998, 67–84). My friend at the book promotion was alluding to just this mode of drawing lessons from war violence when he remarked after the speeches that Bosniacs were "starting to sound dangerously like *Četnik*s." To him and to others I knew, including many women's activists, the political manipulation of collective victimhood was a betrayal of that very victimhood

The Limits of Gender Rhetoric for Nationalism

The promotion of *I Begged Them to Kill Me* was saturated with concerns about male protection of the nation's women and thus its honor. It was precisely the role of protector that Muhamed Filipović was admonishing his fellow Bosniac men to step up and embrace in the face of new threats to Bosniac nationhood. But he was careful to say only that next time they would need to be prepared instead of leaving the nation's women "to the thieves and wolves" (see chap. 2). What he did not say, and what was never pointed out explicitly, was that the extent of the violence against women made plain that this time Bosniac men had *failed* in their roles as protectors. They had not lived up to the requirements of manhood in the logic of patriarchal nationalisms. By failing to stay alert to threats from ethnic others, they had even "allowed" themselves to be captured, held as helpless prisoners. What was worse, and even more silenced, some had also been sexually assaulted, reduced in the shared logic of gender and bodily integrity to the position of helpless victims, of women, and through castration the loss of what made them men (see Žarkov 2007). Indeed, one rape survivor whose husband had been murdered by Serb ethnic cleansers told me informally that she felt her town's Bosniac men had let them down. Had they been brave enough to organize an armed defense, things might have turned out differently. There were thus limits to the use of gender rhetoric for this formulation of nationalism, and particularly for the mobilization of ethno-national victim narratives.[13]

In BiH, but also wherever the logic of woman-as-nation/men-as-protector prevails, I suggest that the limits lie in the interpretation and representation of gendered violence, especially of wartime rape. Crucial to this argument is an understanding of gendered and sexualized constructions of both femininity/women and masculinity/men. The symbolism of female victimhood effectively invokes innocence and non-implication in the processes leading to conflict; female victims and mourning mothers easily stand in for the nation and its territory and point to the barbarity of the enemy in attacking "even" women and children. But care must be taken to impugn the humanity—the masculinity—*of the enemy*, as in the framing of *I Begged Them to Kill Me*, rather than dwell on how those women and children succumbed to such terror in the first place. It is the danger that "our" men will be implicated as not fulfilling their masculine duties, that the "dishonoring" of "our" women will come to light—a danger suggested only by the nationalist logic itself—that threatens whenever women victims become visible.

Recall from chapter 2 that in Croatian nationalist discourses the rapes of Muslim women were stressed. The Croat woman and thus the nation could then be spared the humiliation of sexual victimization even while stressing and condemning the brutality of the Serb enemy. Bosniac and Bosnian discourses did not have this option. The rape of women was emphasized at key points and for foreign audiences but soon ceased to play such a major role in collective victim narratives. At the same time, the enormity of the losses at Srebrenica, in addition to having been proclaimed genocide by an international court, also presented a more palatable yet still female face of ethno-national victimhood that in fact became the primary symbol of Bosniac and Bosnian moral claims (see Helms 2012).

In a similar way, the emphasis on the gender dimensions of Srebrenica is also not without its limits, which contributes to the reasons why the public visibility and vocality of the women survivors of Srebrenica have not been met with unconditional approval in Bosniac-dominated areas of BiH. Prejudices against the rural population have been frequently channeled into invective against Srebrenica survivors, especially as they were seen by urban anti-nationalists as the quintessential examples of rural people who blindly subscribed to SDA nationalism. Nevertheless, there are also indications that the Srebrenica women's groups initially directed anger at "their own" leadership, accusing Bosniac leaders of having "traded" Srebrenica for more easily incorporated land around Sarajevo, thus leaving them to the mercy of Mladić's army (Bougarel 2012). In other words, they blamed the nation's (male) leaders for not protecting them as civilians.

We must also consider the great efforts to classify the men killed at Srebrenica as civilians *only*, rather than acknowledging the presence of a Bosnian Army unit within the enclave when it fell (see Helms 2012). The systematic killings of these men, many of them shot with their hands bound, should make it irrelevant whether they were civilians or soldiers. But by the gendered logic through which this and armed conflicts everywhere are understood, armed men—or those deemed capable of taking up arms—become legitimate targets, while women and other "weak" members of society (children, the elderly) are by definition civilians and therefore a priori innocent, unimplicated victims (Carpenter 2006). Only as civilians can men be seen as victims. And because they are dead, these men can "safely" be lauded as national martyrs, even, through the stereotype of backward, simple, uneducated Eastern Bosnian villagers, as men who were meek and powerless. They become the passive sacrificial lambs for the nation, purified by death and unimplicated in the workings of political or military power, similar to Ivan Čolović's description of tributes to young men going off to war in Serbia (2002, 48–56). It is this unimplicatedness that becomes so important according to the logic that implicated or "noninnocent victims" (Ballinger 2003, 135) diminish the nation's claim to victimhood (see also Helms 2012; Power 1999).

The figure of the young, innocent boy "with the soul of a girl [virgin]" that Čolović analyzes was not, however, the dominant figure of the (living) masculine Serb warrior. In Serbia, a militarized, defiant, and tough masculinity has been associated with nationalism and war, in keeping with Serb narratives of ensuring that Serbs will never become victims again as in the past (see, for example, Bracewell 2000; Čolović 2002). Serb men were principally seen as victims of the deviant sexuality of "other" men who deprived them of their pure Serb offspring by impregnating Serb women (Žarkov 2007; see also Bracewell 2000). Losing in battle was not part of this image, notwithstanding

Figure 21 Names of those killed in the fall of Srebrenica are inscribed on endless panels of stone at the Potočari Memorial Complex. A young woman (sitting) wears a T-shirt that reads: "History is written with blood. Crimes must never be forgiven or history forgotten!" July 11, 2007. (photo by author)

the simultaneous nurturing of the myth of the Serb defeat at the Battle of Kosovo. That debacle was mythologized as a spiritual decision rather than a military defeat, making possible the face-saving slogan in terms of the masculine warrior that the Serbs win in war but lose in peace (see, for example, Čolović 2002; Živković 2011).

In the Croatian context, Michaela Schäuble (2009) has shown how a heroic, defensive warrior masculinity has been built upon narratives of collective victimhood, presenting a dilemma for dominant masculine ideals. As Schäuble argues, "to claim a collective 'victim identity' or 'victim status' without forfeiting all conventional attributes of masculinity is a rather delicate tightrope walk. In my view, the martyr is the only figure who simultaneously embodies notions of victimhood and of (male) heroism and effectively manages to combine the two" (182). In other words, victims cannot be properly masculine in the militarized, aggressive form of the warrior.

The figure of Naser Orić, the muscle-bound former policeman and bodyguard to Slobodan Milošević and later Bosnian Army commander of the Srebrenica enclave until just before it fell, brings this dilemma to light.[14] His supporters celebrate him as a strong defender of the Bosniac population in Srebrenica, but his Rambo-like image does not sit well with that of the reluctantly violent Bosniac male defenders portrayed by Fikreta or Azra (chapter 4) and especially not with that of Bosniac victimhood in the face of genocide in Srebrenica. During the war Orić's forces led a number of brutal assaults on Serbs, including civilians, precisely the source of Serb claims to victimhood in this area. Neither does his command over the enclave sit well with the image of noble defender of his people; in the desperate conditions for the refugee population crowded there, males were violently forced to serve on dangerous front lines and females were recruited into the exchange of favors for sex (Netherlands Institute 2002; Suljagić 2005). But Orić was not in Srebrenica during its fall, having been removed shortly before, with the effect that he was disconnected from the moment of ultimate tragedy. There was thus less chance that he might contaminate the purity of Bosniac narratives in the logic of all-or-nothing victimhood.

The victim is perceived as passive, devoid of agentive power, classified a priori as the object of protection, already a potential victim. From the perspective of nationalist logics, there is thus no shame in women's having become victims, even while sexualized violence conveys other sorts of shame. The shame belongs to the men who failed to protect them. Rape and sexual assault are at once defined as "dishonoring," but also as the expected and feared consequence of a failure to protect. As Žarkov put it, women were defined from the outset as "rapable" (2007, 172), while the loss of sexual integrity—penetration—of a male body meant the loss of masculinity itself (162–65). This is why the figure of the raped woman makes a better symbol of national suffering than a raped man. But it is also why there are limits to the use of gendered symbols and rhetoric for national narratives of victimhood. As long as the nation is identified with males as the leaders of a patriarchally defined nation, the powerful masculinity of its males and the (sexual) honor of its females will continue to be in need of shoring up.

From the perspective of the male-defined nation, Bosniacs and the defenders of BiH had in fact been in a frustrating position in the early years of the war before they found ways to circumvent the international arms embargo placed on the region. Poorly armed and up against a Serb army that had inherited all the hardware and munitions of the Yugoslav People's Army, the Bosnian Army was in the position of helpless men, forced to watch as their women were assaulted and dishonored. "If Europe wants to help the women of Bosnia, it has to send weapons to their men!" a representative of the Muslim humanitarian organization Merhamet blurted out in frustration at a gathering in Germany in the early months of the war (Benard and Schlaffer 1992 [my translation]). His outburst summed up the gendering of wartime roles and the threat to masculinity of Bosniacs' and BiH's wartime predicament.

We can thus understand Tihić's call to renounce victimhood in a new light. Given the classic gendering of passive and active roles, especially in relation to the nation, Tihić's emphasis on action, in contrast to the "passive position of the victim," points to the masculinization of "the active position and responsibility of a relevant political factor."[15] A nation associated with victimhood was passive and, as he also stressed, dependent on the international community like a damsel in distress. If Bosniacs were to take the lead in state-building, they could not assume such a feminized and thus powerless position.

The Limits of Victim Claims for Feminism

Critiques of feminist uses of affirmative essentialisms in the service of victim narratives are well established and apply as much to the Bosnian context as to the "West" or anywhere else. Essentialisms preclude change and variation. Victimhood implies a negation of responsibility, incites sympathy and solidarity with other victims (Minow 1992), and establishes a sense of moral "goodness" (Spasić 2000). Women come out looking good if they are seen as "essentially" nurturing, peace-loving, and tolerant of differences. But this implies—and it is often explicitly stated—that men are greedy, selfish, violent, nationalistic, and eager to wage war. These traits certainly describe some, even many, women and men respectively. But as feminist scholarship has shown repeatedly, these tendencies have more to do with socially constructed roles, models of behavior, and ideals of femininity and masculinity than with any natural "essence."

To this some feminists and women's advocates, including many I met in BiH, would likely counter that reasons are irrelevant if this discernable difference remains. Bosnian activists thus saw advantages to the strategic use of affirmative essentialisms, whether as implicit argument against masculinist dismissals or as a tactic to avoid alienating the community, while setting one's sights on long-term change. Many seemed to feel, especially in contact with foreign donor representatives, that victimhood—war victimhood—was "the only valuable thing they had," as in the epigraph. Indeed, in the ever-shrinking donor market, appealing to "foreign" sensibilities often carried material implications.

But as a strategy of representation, even passively, the notion of peaceloving women and warmongering men ultimately undermined feminist goals. In the context of the former Yugoslavia, only a few feminists have pointed to the ways in which affirmative victim narratives of women foreclose the possibility for women to be taken seriously as political subjects, agents, and citizens. As the Serbian feminist sociologist Marina Blagojević writes, "Releasing women of any blame for the war and 'crises' would be another trap of patriarchal narcissism. Where there is no guilt, there is no complicity and therefore no subjectivity" (1994, 475). Ivana Spasić, another sociologist from Serbia, noted that feminist analyses of the wars of Yugoslav secession had done little to critique the ubiquitous construction of women as victims (2000, 354). One problematic implication of this tendency was that in absolving women of responsibility, "both negative and positive," the victim narrative obscures the fact of women's citizenship, "the principal space wherein they can fight for themselves" (353). This was the dilemma that the women I described in chapter 5 were struggling to overcome as they argued for their relevance as political actors.

The stark division between peace-loving women and violent, corrupt men therefore also worked against the not-necessarily-feminist goals of foreign intervention agencies. For if it was "men" who were bad leaders out for selfish greed and promoting (ethnic) chauvinism, how was the male-dominated political sector to become properly democratic? While women were being encouraged to enter formal politics and to participate politically through NGOs, no one was under the illusion that they would soon rise to top decisionmaking positions in significant numbers, much less take over. Clearly, for most donors and foreign officials, affirmative essentialisms of women (whether believed or not) were strategic in terms of fulfilling short-term goals. This was a way to animate women as part of a larger effort to oust entrenched nationalist cabals from power. Arguments using gender essentialisms disappeared in appeals to other similarly marginalized groups such as youth, members of ethnic minorities, or NGO advocates for human rights or democratic values.

For feminists and other activists committed to challenging gendered power hierarchies, the implications were even more serious. If they were striving to be taken seriously as political actors, for their critiques and suggestions for change to count, then it was hardly useful to be cast outside the realm of the political, to be constructed as victims with all the passivity and assumptions about protection that this implied. What was more, this focus accentuated women's difference from men while glossing over differences among women. Ivana Spasić further writes: "By artificially hardening the boundaries between women and men as political subjects we blur the internal boundaries between differentially responding groups of women or, in the last analysis, individual women. Doing that, we basically reduce women to their 'biological substratum'—to being mothers" (353). Among the "differentially responding groups of women" were those who participated directly or indirectly in nationalist violence, those who resisted the reintegration of ethnic others into society or voted for exclusivist nationalists. Perhaps more ubiquitous were those who tried not to respond or who felt ambivalent about the processes in which they were swept up. There were also differently responding women's activists, like the range I have described in this book. How could a critical feminist voice be articulated if all women were lumped into the same basket when it came to stances on nationalism, politics, war, or social justice?

Further, reducing women to motherhood not only led back to conservative nationalist formulations of women as reproducers of the nation (and vulnerable to "ethnic" rape), but it also foreclosed other social roles for women, even those who were not mothers. I did know several Bosnian feminists who consciously enacted alternative scripts in their own ways of being mothers and nurturing family members (with or without male partners), not all of them living in larger towns or cosmopolitan spaces. But there was as yet no public space for motherhood in BiH that was not monopolized by nationalist or at least conservative (patriarchal) ideals of family and society. In the short run, this ensured that appeals to the moral standing of "women" were effectively mobilized around assumptions of present or future motherhood. In the long run, however, like many of the feminist denunciations of the nationalist mobilization of women in the final days of Yugoslavia in Žarkov's analysis (2007, 82), there was a significant risk that feminism would surrender motherhood to nationalism as the prevailing logic of social and political action.

Implications in Postconflict Settings

The Bosnian war only sporadically figures in international news anymore, but dominant representations of primitive, brutal violence remain. Gendered wartime violence has strongly shaped this image. Theorists of gender and armed conflict, transitional justice measures, and international law continue to invoke the distinctly gendered aspects of the Bosnian war and to apply its lessons to other conflicts and episodes of violence and their aftermaths. Despite the existence of some very well-grounded analyses, many inaccuracies and distorted conclusions have made it into the larger literature, not to mention into popular consciousness. Was there a way in which images could have been different? Are non-specialists, popular audiences, or policy makers incapable of grasping the complexities of local meanings and experiences? If the Bosnian case teaches us one thing, it is to remain skeptical of where information about atrocities and victims in armed conflicts comes from and how it is disseminated. In her discussion of this problem in the analysis of wartime rape in BiH, Rose Lindsey (2002) called for a shift in the debate from descriptions and proof of crimes to analyses of gendered social structures and ideologies that made such violence possible in the first place. This book has endeavored to contribute to such an approach. Crucially, it has not focused only on the ideologies and contexts of neighboring states that played a major role in inciting the violence, but has instead focused on the place and people toward whom the violence was directed. My aim was both to confirm the devastation of this victimhood and also to complicate simplistic views of good and bad, victim and perpetrator.

Echoing feminist concerns with "giving voice" to marginalized and "voiceless" subalterns, Lindsey also called for better attention to be paid to those working with war victims and especially to the testimonies of victims themselves. This approach is certainly laudable and a logical first step. On a practical level, it may well have minimized the level of distortion in reports on wartime rapes and other aspects of the Bosnian war. The inclusion of Bosnian women's voices represented as equally knowledgeable might have mitigated Orientalized images of powerless Muslim women victims. However, it raises further problems, starting with the thorny expectations of authenticity encountered in chapter 6. When one victim speaks out, she does not necessarily speak for all victims of similar crimes. Insisting on authentic victims' voices, too, means that highly knowledgeable and experienced practitioners, activists, and theorists can be easily dismissed for not having "felt the war on their own skin." Such a complex set of issues deserves a proper debate, accessible to the public and inclusive of a variety of voices, including but not restricted to those of victim-survivors.

There is also no escaping that Orientalizing constructions of victimhood often came from Bosnians, too, not least from victims themselves. These associations only intensified the sense of helplessness and distance from any possibility of action—in other words, of innocence. Serb or Croat women may also have been raped, this narrative implied, but since Muslim women suffered more intensely they have earned a higher moral standing that renders them as more deserving (see Spasić 2000). Accepted uncritically, such claims can (and did) lead to further ethnicizing of the postwar recovery and a distortion of the ways in which war rape gets analyzed, prosecuted, and compared to similar contexts in other times and places.

Local women's voices and activities were also alarmingly romanticized by donor representatives, as in the NGO rhetoric of peace activism, ethnic tolerance, and women's rights that masked profoundly patriarchal gender ideologies. As we saw in chapter 5, the overlap between opposition to nationalism and violence in general and a specific condemnation of the enemy slipped easily into discourses of fundamental ethnic differences understood in a hierarchy of morality: good us versus bad them. In such a reading, the nuances and complexities of the war and the politics of its aftermath are silenced, even appearing as ethically problematic for implying criticism of the "good" group, whether understood as Bosniacs, Bosnians, or women.

The extension of state benefits to survivors of sexualized violence in the war raised yet another set of questions about visibility and "voice." For there were many survivors who refused to speak or testify in public, or even to undergo the bureaucratic process of establishing status, no matter how much the meager payments may have meant. Unlike an increasing number of other postviolence countries in which truth commissions have been instituted to allow victims to relate the injustices done to them in a more cathartic way than that offered by the perpetrator-centered adversarial approach of war crimes trials (Mertus 2004), in BiH the space for public airing of victim experiences has been minimal, even while it is occasionally fetishized and put on display at international gatherings (see O. Simić 2008). But as yet another attempt at establishing a truth commission for BiH and the ex-Yugoslav region continues (the REKOM initiative) and a regional feminist "Women's Court" starts to come together, it is instructive to bear in mind the problems that have arisen in other contexts where truth commissions have endeavored to be "gender sensitive." After the South African Truth and Reconciliation Commission was reformed to be more inclusive of women, it was noted that women were testifying mostly about the suffering of others, especially their own male family members (Ross 2003).

The response in South Africa, and in places like Guatemala and Peru where gender-sensitive truth commissions were subsequently established, was to encourage women to talk about their own experiences, an encouragement that turned into expectations that women would talk about rape (Theidon 2007). As Fiona Ross (2003) also shows in the South African case, the special experience that women were deemed to bring to the picture of war and state violence was implicitly sexualized, erasing other forms of gendered war violence and reifying women as "rapable" objects of protection (Žarkov 2007), and as vulnerable wombs (R. Miller 2007), and thus the carriers of national honor and reproducers of the nation as patriarchal national ideologies construct them.

As Kimberly Theidon (2007) notes, this focus also allows for the perpetrators, men, and militarized masculinities to escape notice.[16] Men are never called on to narrate their participation in rape, to answer questions about the exact details of what they did with their bodies or the bodies of their victims. If postconflict justice is to have any reparatory function, then men and the forms of masculinity that produce such violence must be problematized. Not only should reparation entail redistribution to victims of resources to ensure they can get on with their lives but, Theidon argues, "it should also include the redistribution of shame to those who earned it" (2007, 475), that is, the male rapists. Bosnian activists have called for a similar "redistribution," and were even supported during the war by Islamic clergy and some male political leaders in arguing against the idea that women victims should bear shame for having been raped. But as I have shown, such support was offered within a decidedly ethno-national framework, raising the question again of how to prevent representations and critiques of ethnicized violence from sliding into narratives of national victimhood.

We must also consider silences and invisibility outside of the framework of shame and stigma as the polar opposite of agency and voice. As feminists like those at Medica have stressed with their insistence on talking about survivors rather than victims, these individuals may, and do, refuse to let their identities be defined solely by their victimhood, by the experience of rape. For giving in to the idea that a raped woman's life has been ruined by this form of victimization accepts the notion that the female social being must be defined by who has had access to her body. Survivors do not have to articulate a feminist critique of such ideologies to feel the need to resist the victim label. As Theidon suggests, in reflecting on the ways in which women in Peru talked and did not talk about sexualized and other forms of violence in the 1980s conflict there, it could be that many women choose not to discuss their victimization "as the core of who they are today" or even at all: "The word recover has many definitions, among them 'to take back; to get back what has been lost; to re-cover.' What if part of recovery is taking back some sense of the private, of the intimate sphere that was violated? In a woman's refusal to make rape the narrative core of her subjectivity, might we see an insistence on the right to opacity in this era of confessional obsession and the tyranny of transparency?" (2007, 474). There was a fine line between acknowledging gendered forms of suffering, whether to condemn and prosecute perpetrators or to initiate a critique of gendered ideologies and the harms they cause in concert with those of nation and collectivity, and causing more pain to those it affected. In fact, Veena Das has argued that silence about rape is itself a form of agency, perhaps the only form available to some women (1996). Sometimes allowing victims to remain silent and anonymous is a way to allow them to reclaim dignity and a sense of self. In this way, the intense public attention to the war rapes and their survivors in Bosnia, despite the best intentions of advocates, was not necessarily a straightforwardly positive development for those very victims.

At the crux of these considerations lie concepts of agency and its privileging by feminists. Despite the efforts of feminist campaigns on behalf of rape survivors to decouple victimhood from passivity and allow for innocence to exist alongside agency, these associations remain strong, especially because moves in this direction have been largely separate from initiatives around sexualized violence in war. Many feminist analyses of war, including the Bosnian war, have actually reinforced the idea that agency and victimhood are mutually exclusive. As Žarkov concludes in her analysis of Serbian and Croatian media representations before and during the war:

> I would argue that the recent prominence of the woman-as-war-victim is the direct, albeit paradoxical consequence of the centrality of the concept of agency, and its relation to empowerment and emancipation in feminist theorizing. Informed by modernist discourses that split the social realities of women along the lines of what is private and what public, the feminist struggle against oppression and victimization has been a struggle for public spaces, and agency has been, for a long time, recognized only when exercised visibly, in public. Thus, women's engagement in militaries and wars with weapons in their hands was easy to conceptualize within the framework of agency and link to emancipation and empowerment. At the same time, victimhood has been the mirror image of such an understanding of agency. And, because there have always been women and regions that have been seen as more empowered and more emancipated than others, it was also easy to perceive some of them through the prism of victimization. Not surprisingly, women in the Balkan and African wars have been among the latter. (2007, 225)

Thus, the absence of women in positions of political and military power was easy to generalize into claims of non-involvement and non-responsibility by women, in other words, victimhood and thus innocence. Those who sought to disrupt these associations, too, have remained fixed on notions of agency, even complicity in Blagojević's terms, in a way that continues to suggest a problematic division between passive innocence and active guilt.

It is also this reading of victimhood that explains why the focus on rape reduces women to victims only, since any suggestion of agency (sexual or otherwise), as in the ability to decide and to act, on the part of a target of rape still apparently calls into question the innocence of the victim. Objections to the rumored plot of Angelina Jolie's film revealed precisely this assumption—a form of agency of Muslim women in zones of Serb military control could not be imagined without sullying the innocence of Bosniac women, and thus of Bosniacs in general. Women's attempts to escape, to protect themselves and their loved ones, to fight back, even when it meant even harsher attacks, were thereby erased (see Hromadžić 2007; Theidon 2007). So, too, were the myriad choices and acts of the women who lived through the processes of nationalist domination, war, oppressive governments, and simply the unquestioning reproduction of social hierarchies (see Lilly and Irvine 2002; Spasić 2000; Žarkov 2007). The perceived impossibility of agency for victimhood also hampers the attempts of women's activists to counter images of women's passive victimhood; the contrasting emphasis on affirmative traits of working for peace, reconciliation, ethnic tolerance, and concern for the future lead to an abdication of responsibility, of full inclusion as citizens and members of society—and ultimately back into other forms of victimhood in the name of proving innocence.

And so, in the Bosnian context, discourses on women and gender systems all too easily become hijacked by national narratives. In this sense, women's activism that deliberately avoided potentially contentious "ethnic" issues was a refreshing contrast to grand politics in BiH. Activists like those at Infoteka could still engage in political and legal issues while debating the impact of the new labor law on women, challenging sexist advertisements, or arguing for the "normality" of Bosnian levels of domestic violence in comparison with other European countries that did not experience war. Still, there was a lot invested in the idea that the war had created special forms of Bosniac and Bosnian victimhood. Feminist campaigns against sexist advertisements were ridiculed by some as frivolous concerns in the face of a social structure crippled by war trauma and death.[17] In the case of the domestic violence data, both apologists and campaigners against domestic violence seldom failed to mention the war, availability of weapons, and the trauma that men had been through as "defenders of Bosnia" and even camp inmates, even though explanations inevitably also cited the difficulties in the postwar (and postsocialist) economy for men to fulfill expected breadwinner roles. When Medica's data did not show heightened rates of domestic violence, but levels commensurate with other European countries, it provided another example of the resistance to explanatory frameworks outside those of ethnicity and nationalism. A fairly typical issue for women's activism with many elements attributable to postsocialist transformations became yet another part of the specificity of the Bosnian war, for some in order to dismiss its importance (and the patriarchal ideologies behind its tolerance) and for others as yet another aspect of BiH's suffering that is deserving of foreign attention (and funding).

Pondering Hope and Emancipatory Politics

This book has clearly shown the problems with celebratory accounts of women as victims and peacemakers in a society emerging from armed conflict. What are the alternatives? A few, more grounded studies have interrogated women's public expression in BiH and its potential for challenging dominant conceptualizations of community, society, state, and politics.[18] Cynthia Cockburn, for example, found hope in the "anti-essentialist choices" made by some women's activists and NGOs in BiH, including Medica, along with women in similar cross-ethnic peace projects in Northern Ireland and Israel/Palestine (2000). While she found that some activists avoided the term "feminism," they were still clear that gender was a complicated and varied social construction: it was not a given that women would be peacemakers or that men were all violent. And within their stances against chauvinistic nationalisms, some of the women also embraced their own forms of nationalism, even calling themselves nationalists, as in the case of Northern Ireland where it made anticolonialist sense. But the forms of feminism and nationalism these activists chose were always anti-essentialist. Given these basic principles, activists could then employ the "transversal politics" developed by Italian feminists with its "rooting" in individual, located stances and simultaneous "shifting" to appreciate the perspectives of those positioned differently (Cockburn 2007, 1998, 8–9; Yuval-Davis 1997, 130–31).

Cockburn's is a sensitive, eloquent account of the difficulties of alliances across ethnicized borders in areas of armed conflict, but there is a need to push further. Cross-ethnic alliance was certainly possible in BiH, but rooting and shifting required a certain amount of "strategic avoidance" on top of a shared political commitment, involving the "choices about silence and speech" that Cockburn also attributes to this kind of activism (1998, 262). This meant that even those activists most committed to anti-essentialist positions avoided deep discussions about the very forces of ethnicity, religion, and nationalist politics against which they were jointly fighting. In the most concrete example, even anti-nationalist feminists had yet to initiate a dialogue across their networks about wartime sexual violence.

Similarly, while the criteria of rejecting essentialist thinking very usefully narrows the range of activists who can be seen as challenging patriarchal and nationalist norms, it remains difficult to distinguish between truly anti-essentialist positions and those made in all sincerity that nevertheless mask a lack of critical engagement with ideologies of gender, ethnicity, and class from which members of that group might benefit, even only in terms of moral satisfaction. In BiH, anti-nationalist and pro-women's rights positions were easy to state from the position of a member of a victimized collectivity. This is not at all to say that there were no critical, anti-nationalist and feminist activists in BiH, but that it was more difficult to recognize them, just as it was more difficult for them to act effectively—to be recognized—when it came to challenging established gender, ethnic, and other hierarchies. At the same time, this book has aimed to render intelligible the logic by which well-meaning activists and aid officials nevertheless reinforced such essentializing frameworks.

Furthermore, while Bosnian women's NGOs have successfully influenced legislation, social programs, and state practices in a number of important ways, the NGO sector was not always the force of dramatic grassroots movements or visible subversive politics that might lead to fundamental social change. Affirmative essentialisms put forth by activists, donors, and intervention agencies alike often reinforced patriarchal assumptions about women's domestic roles and inevitable/potential victim status even as they promoted liberal notions of women's human rights and gender equality that ultimately did little to fundamentally challenge the established gender regime. While acknowledging the important role of many NGO activists in this field, I would also argue for a wider view of where subversive activism might come from.

In this light, more recent developments in journalism, academia, and the arts, but also through NGOs, are encouraging. While sometimes involving the same people or being heavily influenced by NGOs and donors, these other areas have become key to emerging women's and feminist critiques of patriarchal norms in BiH. Critical journalists, many of them women, have increasingly taken on issues such as sexual harassment, sex trafficking, difficulties faced by women in politics, and open intolerance of homosexuality. Women directors have made films about women's war-related experiences but also about other phenomena such as religious revival, sex trafficking, and the objectification of female pop singers.[19] Other female visual artists, writers, and poets have brought forms of gender critique into public view (see below), as has the recurring women's art festival *PitchWise*, organized by the feminist foundation

CURE (Girls) in Sarajevo.[20] Bosnian academics, some with degrees from abroad, began from the mid-2000s to introduce women's and gender studies into university curricula (Mlinarević and Kosović 2011; Potkonjak et al. 2008), and a master's program in Gender Studies was started at the University of Sarajevo in 2006 with students that have included some of the very professionals, NGO activists, and journalists who had been driving the increase in visibility of women's and gender issues. Debates about gender issues have been further encouraged by increasing Internet traffic and content related to gender activism through social media, chat forums, and web portals. Many of the women involved in these developments are from a younger generation than those who originally formed NGOs just after the war, suggesting that awareness of feminist critiques and their impact on public opinion will only grow.

While the postwar NGO "boom" meant that critical awareness of gender issues reached a surprising number of smaller towns (Helms, forthcoming), much of this new activity was nevertheless concentrated in urban and highly educated circles, and dealt with abstract concepts of art, representation, and academic theory. There was therefore little sense of critical mass in terms of public opinion: "woman" as a mobilized identity has not been made "politically relevant" (Gal and Kligman 2000, 106). There was even less of a broad understanding of what feminist or gender critique might mean outside of liberal conceptions of women's rights campaigns. The larger public was more likely to respond to practical issues depicted in an accessible way, even when informed by theoretical principles. Journalism and art thus presented likely arenas in which such critiques might become more widespread.

Several women writers, artists, and filmmakers have offered some particularly challenging alternative visions (Arsenijević 2010; Hashamova 2012; Husanović 2009; Simmons 2010). Jasmina Husanović and Damir Arsenijević, part of a new generation of Bosnian feminist scholars, show how both the cultural production of these women as well as the everyday practices of war survivors challenge, and even render meaningless, the "identitarian matrices" (Husanović 2009, 103), particularly ethno-national frameworks, that dominate in postwar BiH society. Importantly, they call for explicitly political scholarly interventions that take into account the effects on society of neoliberal and postsocialist restructuring and the ways in which ethno-national structures have effaced these processes (Husanović and Arsenijević 2006).

These films, stories, and poems offer alternate readings of the postwar experience without eliding the realities, even "ethnic" ones, of the war. The epigraph to this chapter, for example, discussed by Arsenijević (2011a, 196–97), lays bare the normally unspoken and even unwanted "value" of the victim status in an unequal global hierarchy. Seen in this light, the economy of NGO-donor relations, indeed the politics of representation as a whole, complicate narratives of foreign saviors and deserving victims, but also cynical dismissals of "manipulative" victims. In an equally unflinching way, Šejla Šehabović's poem "Srebrenica, Potočari, 9.5.2004," evokes not only the devastation of the violence but also the discomfort of the scene as visibly rural women Srebrenica survivors welcome visitors with traditional hospitality to the mass graveyard in Potočari that has become their home (English translation in Arsenijević 2011b, 173–74). Through these and other examples, Arsenijević argues for the power of gender analysis to expose not only gender inequalities but those of class and rural/urban origin as well as to problematize ethno-national politics even in the face of horrific violence.

Husanović engages in a related project, turning a postcolonial feminist sense of critical hope onto "Bosnian feminist trajectories" themselves (2009). From BiH's particular historical and geopolitical position, she argues, feminist critique has the potential to "shake and reshuffle our quests for political transformation" (104). Such disruption, Husanović shows, can be found in the artistic production of several women, including Jasmila Žbanić with her film *Grbavica*. As I noted, this film was far from just a story about Bosniac victimhood, the war, or the atrocities. The film's focus was rather on the dilemmas of motherhood (Carpenter 2010, 154–61; Hashamova 2012) and womanhood in the context of the economic and material difficulties of the postwar period, the hypocrisy of (Bosniac and pro-Bosnian) political leaders, and the embeddedness of BiH in international webs of humanitarian aid, governance, and gendered exploitation. It centrally addresses the pain caused by a war atrocity usually depicted through ethno-national categories of guilt and innocence but is far more about a "tapestry of losses and solidarities" (Husanović 2009, 105) among women marginalized by multiple forces of injustice.

Like these scholars, part of my aim in this book has been to point to the potential of gender critique to destabilize ethno-national frameworks. And so I share their enthusiasm for the subversive potential of this kind of artistic production and join them in arguing for a shift in analysis to better account for inequalities and injustices that remain invisible from a perspective of ethno-national blocs. But I suspect these scholars and artists would agree that subversive art and activist challenges to dominant understandings in BiH have been limited, first in terms of audience. This is less about access, although certain forms of art and literature are simply not seen by the majority of the economically struggling population in BiH, and more about the receivability of such critiques. As we saw with *Grbavica* (or the far less subversive *In the Land of Blood and Honey*), films are widely available and talked about in BiH, but the mainstream press's mode of assessing them has been strictly in terms of competing ethno-national narratives. Similar dynamics are visible with critiques put forth by women's activists that aim to subvert the present gender and ethno-national order. The subtleties of shaking and reshuffling dominant framings may come through in some ways but they certainly have not become politically salient.

Another point of caution derives from the ambiguities of overlapping collective victimhood narratives, especially in the Bosniac-dominated areas of BiH where most of these feminist artists are based. The moral claims made possible by identification with victimhood were mobilized in the service of both (religious and secular) Bosniac nationalism and as support for a multiethnic BiH. Bosniac women victims served as symbols of both these positions as they called attention to the victimization of the Bosniac nation as well as the attempts by Serb and Croat nationalists to destroy the multiethnic fabric of Bosnian society and thus the prospects for a functioning BiH state. Both positions, furthermore, often rely on some of the same ethno-national thinking they deplore in the nationalisms they oppose, whether through generalizations of collective character or, as in the case of common forms of liberal, cosmopolitan anti-nationalism in the Federation, multiculturalist reifications of distinct, coexisting ethnic blocks living in tolerance of each other (see Arsenijević 2007; Hajdarpašić 2008). Denunciations of ethno-nationalism, ethnic cleansing, and genocide, therefore, do not all stem from the same political critique, as we saw in the case of some women's NGO activists. Whether neutrally formulated appeals for justice and aid to war victims or nuanced critiques of gendered power that challenge ethno-national frameworks, oppositional expressions are more often than not read through collective, ethno-national lenses as being about Serb perpetrators and Bosniac victims, even when voiced in the name of multiethnic tolerance (see Helms 2012).

The appeal to cosmopolitan anti-nationalism also masks the deep, class-inflected rural/urban divisions of BiH society. In fact, even in very small towns where cosmopolitan sensibilities are also nurtured, such appeals often had the effect of constructing a cultured, urban "us," that linked sophisticated, knowing artists and activists to the superior knowledge of a democratic "West" where citizenship was more egalitarian. This was opposed to the primitive, backward nationalists of rural areas and "mentalities" (Bougarel 1999; Živković 1997), a characterization often read as a condemnation of Serbs as attackers of urban areas like Sarajevo, thus ethnicizing the rural/urban divide. All of this compounded the deep-seated disdain held by many urbanites toward fellow citizens—even of the same ethno-national group—marked as rural and thus backward and uncultured (*nekulturni*) (see, for example, Helms 2008, 2012; Jansen 2005a, 2005b; Maček 2009; Stefansson 2007).

Figure 22 Graffiti on houses being rebuilt after the war: "Better [to be] a dead horse than a live peasant." Photographed in Gornji Vakuf, July 1996. (photo by author)

The material in this book should thus give us pause. Praise for tolerance, the rejection of nationalism, and affirmations of women's more peaceful qualities can often mask profoundly patriarchal gender ideologies and notions of irreconcilable ethno-national differences. Condemnations of nationalism can be restricted to the nationalisms of groups in whose name ethnicized attacks were carried out. Feminist critiques are interpreted through ethno-national lenses and are sometimes themselves constructed with such a view of the world. And the call for women to participate in traditionally male-dominated arenas can be based on the conviction that women should first (naturally) fulfill their roles as mothers and continue to shoulder the main responsibility for the upbringing of children and maintenance of households. These are affirmative moral claims that often reinforce the very ideologies and practices they purport to oppose. To meaningfully chip away at power hierarchies like those based on gender or ethno-national ideologies requires the persistent dismantling of essentialist representations, the exposure of such ideologies at work in disguised forms, and attention to how other social categories are mobilized in the formulation of social and political claims to morality and legitimacy. It also requires analytical attention to unstated implications that hide in the zones of ambiguity created by narratives of collective victimhood and the ways in which they produce moral claims to innocence.

Notes

Introduction

1. Karadžić was captured in July 2008 and Mladić in May 2011, both in Serbia. Each was extradited to The Hague to stand trial at the International Criminal Tribunal for the former Yugoslavia (ICTY).

2. In this book I follow popular usage in using the term "refugee" for what were also technically internally displaced persons (IDPs).

3. Activism is my term meant to indicate activities by people who were or who aspired to be visible and effective in a public or social sense, beyond their immediate neighborhoods and families. It was not necessarily a label used by all those I call activists themselves, as I discuss in chapter 3.

4. For casualty statistics from the Bosnian war, see Tabeu and Bijak (2005) and the data gathered by the Sarajevo Research and Documentation Center at http://www .idc.org.ba/ (accessed June 15, 2011).

5. See the reflections of Stef Jansen (2006) on the perceived disconnect between suffering and academic analysis in the postwar BiH context, as well as the careful approach of Michaela Schäuble in dealing with similar gendered victim narratives in postwar Croatia (2009, forthcoming).

6. Activists from Serb and Croat areas appear in this study as actors in the wider women's NGO scene. These areas, however, deserve to be studied in their own right, especially as they have been sorely neglected in the academic and activist literature (for discussion of some of the reasons for this, see Bougarel et al. 2007b, 18–19).

7. This is an approximate number gleaned from the estimate of 130,000 for the population of the municipality (from http://www.zenica.ba), since there has not been an official census since 1991 (see Markowitz 2006) and efforts to hold a new one have been repeatedly postponed. The town's population was down from the prewar level of 96,027 (the 1991 population of the municipality was 145,517). See the BiH Agency for Statistics, http://www.bhas.ba/new/, and the Federation (of Bosnia and Herzegovina) Bureau of Statistics, http://www.fzs.ba/ (accessed May 20, 2008).

8. British anthropologist Cornelia Sorabji noticed a marked change after the war in the more reserved way she was received in Sarajevo after having been treated as a novelty there in the mid-1980s (personal communication 2003).

Chapter 1. Victims and Peacemakers

1. The precise term used in the Bosnian language(s) is *narod*, "people" or "nation" ethnically defined, as enshrined in both the socialist Yugoslav and postwar Bosnian constitutions. Ethnic (*etnički*) and national (*nacionalno*) are also used, but in everyday usage, the term *nacija* comes closest to the English "ethnic group," with its connotations of religious and cultural background without necessarily having the political aspirations to statehood implied by "nation" (see Bringa 1995; Sorabji 1993, 1995). In this book, I use ethnicity and nation as distinct terms, with "ethno-national" indicating overlap of these meanings.

2. This right was granted by Annex 7 of the Dayton Agreement but significant returns did not begin until 1998 and had tapered off significantly by 2004 (see, for example, Ito 2001; Ó Tuathail and Dahlman 2004; Philpott 2005).

3. Also playing major roles were the Organization for Security and Cooperation in Europe (OSCE), which handled elections, democratization, and human rights monitoring; the International Police Task Force (IPTF) monitored police forces; the UN High Commissioner for Refugees (UNHCR) coordinated refugee return and relief; the Commission on Real Property Claims (CRPC) oversaw the restoration of confiscated real estate; and countless other governmental, intergovernmental, EU, and UN agencies attended to humanitarian aid, housing reconstruction, democratization projects, education, health, and so on.

4. Following Stef Jansen (2006), I avoid the phrase "international community" except as a locally understood term, since there was a much more diverse set of actors and interests than this term implies. What was meant by international community was also usually more Euro-American than truly international. Instead, I use versions of Jansen's "foreign intervention agencies," stressing his caveat that the "foreign" designation reflects more the ways in which these actors were seen and sought to portray themselves than an objective reality, as such actors were well integrated into local and regional networks, employing "locals" at many levels (see Lendvai and Stubbs 2009; Pugh 2003).

5. For different views on this phenomenon especially among Serbs, see Denich 1994; Gordiejew 2006; Hayden 2008b; MacDonald 2002; Živković 2000, 2011. Elsewhere, I analyze how this logic is reflected in the Bosniac/Bosnian context through visual representations of women that invoke genocide in Srebrenica (Helms 2012).

6. Xavier Bougarel (2010) traces the ways in which genocide in fact became a prominent label still used during the Yugoslav era to classify persecutions and mass killings of all of Yugoslavia's major ethnic groups. For differing arguments about the genocide designation and the Bosnian war, see Bećirević 2010; Hayden 2008a; Hoare 2010; Nielsen 2013.

7. Examples in a large literature include Mayer 2000b; McClintock 1995; Parker et al. 1992; Peterson 1999; Williams 1996; Yuval-Davis 1997.

8. The frequent conflation of "Bosnian" with "Muslim," especially common in the foreign press, thereby erases non-Muslims as inhabitants of BiH, especially those who support the idea of a multiethnic BiH and who fought for its survival in the Bosnian Army.

9. Bosniacs are the descendants of local Slavs who converted to Islam during Ottoman rule (1463–1878). Since the late nineteenth century, they, along with other Muslims in what was to become Yugoslavia, have been referred to as Muslims (with a capital M) in the ethno-national sense, as opposed to the religious designation (muslim with a small m), although this was recognized officially only in 1968. Before that, Muslims declared themselves as Serbs, Croats, undetermined, and other available categories. In September 1993, the Bošnjački sabor (Bosniac Assembly) declared Bosniac to be the new national name, a label that was incorporated into the BiH constitution in 1995 as part of the Dayton Agreement. Muslim Slavs in Serbia, Montenegro, and Kosovo have also adopted the term. Some confusion stems from the unsuccessful attempts by Austro-Hungarian authorities to apply the term *Bošnjak* to all Bosnians and Herzegovinians as a geographical identification that would counter Serbian and Croatian claims to Bosnian territory and its people. The ethnically neutral term is now Bosnian (*Bosanac*), though this is avoided by those who resist inclusion in a multiethnic BiH. On the history and meanings of national designations for Muslims in Bosnia, see Banac 1994, 360–62; Bringa 1995; Bougarel 1996; Burg 1983; Rusinow 1982. Following popular usage, I use the terms Muslim and Bosniac interchangeably, Bosniac especially for official designations since the recent war.

10. Also living in BiH were Roma (mostly of Muslim faith), a dwindling number of Jews, and others. Interestingly, other Catholics in BiH, such as Czechs, Hungarians, or Slovaks, have at times been subsumed under the ethno-national category of Croat, while Orthodox populations such as Ukrainians were sometimes counted as Serbs, and people of mixed parentage were encouraged to identify with one of the three officially recognized "constitutive peoples": Serbs, Croats, and Bosniacs (see Markowitz 2006, 2010).

11. As time passed, power and control over Bosniac representation in government began to be contested by the Party for Bosnia-Herzegovina (Stranka za Bosnu i Hercegovinu or SzBiH) under the leadership of former SDA insider Haris Silajdžić, as well as by others, but the SDA remained a strong nationalist force.

12. Cf. the Austrian occupation (from 1878) and eventual annexation (1908) of BiH from the Ottoman Empire, and efforts to build a regional Bosnian identity under the notion of *Bošnjaštvo* (Bosniac-ness) (see, for example, Banac 1994; Bringa 1995; Donia 1981).

13. For critiques of the "ancient hatreds" paradigm, see, for example, Bringa 2002, 2005; Carmichael 2002; Gagnon 2004; Živković 2011. On notions of the violence as premodern, see Sorabji 1995; on modernity and the Balkans in general, see Green 2005. Hansen (2006) reviews the major discursive paradigms about the Bosnian war and the ways in which they affected American and British policies.

14. Note, however, that Dunja Rihtman-Auguštin asserts for Yugoslav-era Croatian ethnology, honor and shame did not figure into local analyses (1999, 106, note 3).

15. For overviews of Mediterraneanist anthropology that argue for its relevance, though from different perspectives and time periods, see Albera 2006; Gilmore 1982.

16. Religious identities and practices in BiH are a good example of the ethnic coding bias; as covered women have become a marker of the political danger of Islam, women's Islamic dress and other visible markers of reconfigurations of gender norms for pious Muslims were frequently interpreted as expressions of ethno-national identity and political orientation, which many pious women bitterly resented.

17. Fleming (1999, 151–52) also finds a "surrogate orientalism" at work in Western constructions of Greece (see also Herzfeld 1987).

18. On forms of such metaphors in Greece, see Green 2005, 128–58; in Bosnia, see Moranjak-Bamburać 2001.

19. For more examples of such nesting in different post-Yugoslav contexts, see Helms 2008; Patterson 2003; Razsa and Lindstrom 2004; Živković 2011. On the positing of hybrid identities between East and West, see Ballinger 2004. On skepticism or ambivalence toward the West, see Čolović 2002, 39–47; Helms 2008; Jansen 2002; Lindstrom 2003.

20. Susan Gal and her colleagues have especially developed the notion of fractal recursion. See, for example, Gal 2002, 2005; Gal and Kligman 2000; Irvine and Gal 2000. For an illustration of these phenomena in Milošević-era Serbia, see Živković 2011.

21. Michael Herzfeld in fact proposed the notion of Mediterraneanism as a stereotyping discourse in the vein of Orientalism (1987, 64). On Mediterraneanist anthropology in relation to BiH, see Bringa 1995, 6–7; on Croatia, see the special issue of *Narodna umjetnost* (Čapo Žmegač 1999).

22. For an exception and critique of feminist positions, see Jones 1994, 2000.

23. For examples of such literature on conflict zones, see Cockburn 1998; Giles and Hyndman 2004; Iveković and Mostov 2002; Lentin 1997; Lorentzen and Turpin 1998; Waller and Rycenga 2000; on gender and peacekeeping missions, see, for example, Cockburn and Žarkov 2002; Mazurana, Raven-Roberts, and Parpart 2005.

24. For examples of the latter, see Einhorn 1996; Scott, Kaplan, and Keates 1997.

25. There are exceptions, some only partial, either because they include countries outside of former Yugoslavia or because they also frame their analyses in terms of nationalism and war. On gender and democratization, or women in politics in Balkan countries, see, for example, Brunnbauer 2000; Helms 2007; Irvine 1998; for even rarer analysis of women and the transitional labor market in Serbia, see the work of Tatjana Đurić Kuzmanović (e.g., 2001, 2002). One could arguably also mention the work of ex-Yugoslav feminists such as Slavenka Drakulić (1991) or Renata Salecl (1994), who wrote about gender and (post)socialism in CEE as a whole. However, Salecl concentrated much more on ex-Yugoslavia than on CEE in general, even though she did take seriously an analysis of ex-Yugoslavia as a postsocialist place, and Drakulić's attempts to represent experiences of socialism in all of CEE ultimately glossed over the diversity

of those experiences in the interest of stressing East European women's stark difference from Western women. For an insightful critique of Drakulić's changing depictions of socialism, see Drezgić and Žarkov 2005.

Chapter 2. Wartime

1. Feminism and nationalism have of course been part of the same movements in places struggling for independence from colonialism or other forms of domination (Jayawardena 1986; Moghadam 1994; West 1997). In the European context, however, especially in recent decades, nationalisms have represented profoundly traditionalistic and patriarchal gender regimes, often incurring feminists' opposition (G. Kaplan 1997). However, as places like Croatia, BiH, or Northern Ireland show, hostility between feminism and nationalism is not always a given in Europe, especially where the nation is perceived to be under threat (see Cockburn 1998).

2. Following general patterns of affiliation, a large proportion of these women were Serbs.

3. Analyses of other state-socialist countries reveal common shifts in ideology and policies that reflected fluctuating demands for present and future workers. These resulted in contradictory messages sent to women as both workers and mothers, i.e., reproducers of new generations of workers. See, for example, Gal 1994; Haney 2002; Kligman 1998.

4. In a large literature by academics and activists, see especially Denich 1995; Drakulić 1993b; Kesić 1994; Korać 1998; Milic 1993; Mostov 1995; Olujic 1998; Seifert 1996; Sofos 1996.

5. International Criminal Tribunal for the former Yugoslavia (ICTY) judgment, *Kunarac et al.*, 2001, IT-96-23 & 23/1, available at http://www.icty.org/case/kunarac/4. For an overview of prosecutions of sexualized violence in the Bosnian war, see Mischkowski and Mlinarević 2009.

6. For details, see the UN Commission of Experts' report, Annex 9, "Rape and Sexual Assault," compiled under the direction of M. Cherif Bassiouni, S/1994/674/Add.2, vol. 5 (December 28, 1994), available at: http://www.ess.uwe.ac.uk/comex pert/IX.htm (accessed December 21, 2011); see also Amnesty International 1993.

7. The Croatian camp Lora in Split was another notorious site of the sexual abuse of male prisoners, in that case Serbs.

8. This explanation was also applied to other conflicts, as when the rape of (shorter, darker) Bengali women by (taller, lighter) Pakistani troops in 1971 was said to be an army policy to "create a new race" (Brownmiller 1975, 86). In Rwanda, Hutu soldiers raped and mutilated Tutsi women, often cutting away long noses and long fingers associated with being Tutsi, as well as mutilating women's genitals, an attack on their femaleness and capacity to give birth (Nowrojee 1996, 62–65). One Tutsi woman reported Hutu soldiers exhorting each other to "Kill them, you have to kill them. They will make Tutsi babies" (ibid., 54). Sudan and other places are more recent examples (Carpenter 2010).

9. According to the website of the Patriotic League (http://www.plbih.info), 5,360 women were registered in the Bosnian Army, however there is no accounting of how many women served in combat positions. Not only were women not expected to fight, according to the MA research of Lejla Hadžiahmić (2010) on female combatants in the Bosnian Army who fought in Sarajevo, but women soldiers were also sometimes suspected of sleeping with male soldiers or otherwise had their sexual reputations called into question. After the war, women fighters were marginalized both symbolically and in real terms, leaving many of them feeling forgotten and unappreciated.

10. *Pita* is a savory rolled thin pastry that can be filled with meat, cheese, or vegetables like spinach or squash (or, less commonly, in a sweet version with apples) typical of Bosnian cooking.

11. Feminists from Slovenia, where some of the strongest academic and activist networks in Yugoslavia had been developed, were also vocal critics of nationalism and war violence, for the most part taking positions similar to feminists in Croatia. Here I mainly discuss feminist discourses from Zagreb and Belgrade since this is where the debates were centered. For details, see especially Benderly 1997b; Batinic 2001; Lindsey 2002; Žarkov 2002, 2007.

12. Veteran Yugoslav feminists had begun critiquing nationalism, and especially Serbian nationalism, only in the mid-1980s (Žarkov 2002).

13. In her classification of the 1990s literature on wartime rape in various conflicts around the world, including Croatia and BiH, Skjelsbaek (2001a) calls much the same approach essentialist, as opposed to what she identifies as structuralist and social-constructivist approaches.

14. This group included Kareta, Trešnjevka, Nona Women's Center, Bedem Ljubavi, and the Bosnian women's refugee groups Biser (Pearl) and Žena BiH (Woman BiH). Members of the latter two groups continued to be active in BiH itself after the war ended.

15. Many similar cases of rape in war, even on an "ethnic" basis, have been documented, including in the Rwandan genocide that took place at the same time as the Bosnian war. Brownmiller had already discussed many of them in 1975. Dulić (2005) mentions rapes committed by different forces in occupied and partitioned Yugoslavia in World War II: Ustaše rapes of (mostly Serb and Jewish) women in camps and in forced transit to camps, and *Četnik* rapes of women during raids on Muslim villages. Stories of rapes during village raids are also mentioned by Jancar-Webster in her study of women partisan fighters (1990, 131).

16. Batinic 2001, n.p.; see also "Women Express Concern Over Tour," *off our backs*, March 1993, 10–11.

17. Most notoriously, MacKinnon responded to a Serbian feminist at a UN human rights conference in Vienna in 1993 with the challenge, "If you are in opposition to the regime in Serbia, why aren't you already dead?" (Benderly 1997b, 67).

18. Organizations in the Zagreb anti-nationalist camp included the Center for Women War Victims, the Antiwar Campaign Croatia, Ženska Infoteka, B.a.B.e., as

well as individual feminists including the "witches" and other veterans of Yugoslav second-wave feminism.

19. Significantly, the women were accused of raping Croatia but not (also) Bosnia. As Žarkov has shown, the Croatian media put forth images of Bosnian Muslim women as victims of rape in order to show the barbarity of the Serbs, while "saving" the pure image of Croatian women (cf. Lie 1997). Yet the ultimate victim was Croatia itself (Žarkov 2007, 129–35; see also Kesić 1994; Mertus 1994, 19–20; Mostov 1995, 525).

20. The Serbian media also used the label of "witches" for women/feminists who spoke out against nationalism and the Milošević government (Kajosević 1995, 44).

21. They were objecting to the choice of Vesna Kesić and Đurđa Knežević as representatives of Croatia on the MADRE tour described below.

22. See especially Knežević 1993; Mladjenović 1999; the statements of antinationalist feminists around the MADRE tour; and Vesna Kesić's rebuttal (1994) to the nationalist feminists' ally Catherine MacKinnon, who was a vocal proponent of the genocidal rape thesis but also notoriously put forth shockingly unsubstantiated claims about how the accessibility of pornography in Yugoslavia had caused Serbs (and no one else!) to use rape as a weapon of war (MacKinnon 1993b, 1994). For related critiques, see Batinic 2001; Korać 1998; Žarkov 2007.

23. These classifications furthermore do not allow consideration of women's capacity to exercise agency, as all sexual relationships between men and women belonging to different warring ethnic/religious groups come to be defined as rape even when consent may be present (Hayden 2000; see also Buss 2007; R. Miller 2007). As authors working on several different conflicts have shown, the line between consent and coercion is often undetectable given the constraints of patriarchal gender rules and precarious material situations that obtain in addition to and beyond war (Burnet 2012a; Das 1995; Soh 2004).

24. While higher and lower numbers circulated, the most commonly cited figure is that of a European Commission finding, that 20,000 women had been raped. This, however, was an estimate based on a very limited investigation; a more reliable estimate may never be reached. See Lindsey 2002; Skjelsbaek 2001a.

25. The anxiety over rape was a major factor in the rise of Serbian nationalism and its emphasis on narratives of victimhood (Dragović-Soso 2002, 132–34; Ilić 2009; Živković 2011).

26. Some of these women did write and speak about genocidal rape, particularly Aida Džajić of Biser Sarajevo, but this did not register in the international media or feminist academia the way the texts quoted above did.

27. Almasa and her fellow refugees were wary of feminists but had worked with Kareta because of their strong condemnation of Serb crimes. In the same September 2000 conversation, she explained: "Organizations like Kareta, Bedem Ljubavi, etc., were more like feminists who would fight, even using force, for human rights. They were against men. They thought that only the men were guilty, even though many of them were married. So some of them left the groups at the end, some of the more

reasonable ones, mostly the ones with husbands. While our organization was there precisely because of what was happening in the war, not just to women but all human rights that were violated."

28. For example, on the MADRE tour described earlier, feminists from Zagreb and Belgrade seemed to fill slots for Croats and Serbs, respectively, while the one Bosnian speaker (a woman who had not lived in Bosnia for some time) was a Muslim, leaving Muslims to stand for all of Bosnia, as was often the case in general in the international press.

29. Some mention of these aspects in gendered terms, particularly nationalist concerns with "mixed marriages," can be found in a few academic analyses (e.g., Kaufman and Williams 2007; Korać 1994; Hayden 2000; Žarkov 2007). In BiH after the war, local feminist criticisms of nationalist authorities appeared but these made more of sexism and corruption than connections to nationalism or ethnic politics.

30. Even after the war, only a few Bosnian women activists who had been working with women war survivors got their work to wider audiences in English (e.g., Andrić-Ružičić 1997, 2003; Ostojić 1999; Senjak 1997; Giles et al. 2003). Such texts tended to focus more on therapy, overcoming trauma, and the problems of service provision, however, than on analysis of the rapes themselves. Moreover, as discussed below, Bosnian activists were anxious to move on to other issues after the war, rather than dwell on rape and ethnic cleansing.

31. Sarajevan sociologist Nada Ler-Sofronić was part of the Yugoslav feminist scene from the 1970s. She continued her activism when she returned to Sarajevo after spending the war years abroad and was not active in the debates I describe.

32. Charli Carpenter (2010) has compellingly shown that discourses and many policy responses to "rape babies" have furthermore framed the issue as having to do with women, utterly neglecting concerns about the well-being of these children and particularly disregarding children's human rights norms.

33. Journalistic reports on "war babies" also appeared during and just after the war, but these were less useful empirically and largely reproduced Orientalizing assumptions as well as a neglect for the well-being of the children, as Carpenter shows (2010, 55–79).

34. Carpenter (ibid.) only interviewed one such child, Alen Muhić, who was publicly known, especially when a local filmmaker made a film about him starring the boy himself.

35. Article 2, Convention on the Prevention and Punishment of the Crime of Genocide, UN General Assembly Resolution 260 A (3), adopted December 9, 1948. Text at http://www.ohchr.org/EN/ProfessionalInterest/Pages/CrimeOfGenocide.aspx (accessed May 20, 2013).

36. For example, Allen 1996; Fisher 1996; Nikolić-Ristanović 1999; MacKinnon 1993a; Stiglmayer 1994. For critiques, see, for example, Carpenter 2000, 2010; Bos 2006; Evangelista 2011, 111–12; R. Miller 2007.

37. I maintain a distinction between ethnic cleansing and genocide, with the emphasis on the logic of the violence rather than a reification of ethnic differences themselves or the cynical labeling game that Edina Bečirević rightly condemns in the

case of Western politicians seeking to avoid taking action in the face of mass violence (2010; see also Nielsen 2013). As articulated by Dulić (2005), ethnic cleansers may not shrink from hateful and racist rhetoric or committing mass murder, torture, and other atrocities, but their ultimate goal is the ridding of a territory of an unwanted group rather than their complete annihilation from the earth as in genocide. Determining precise intentions in practice is of course another matter.

38. ICTY, *Prosecutor v. Radislav Krstić*, August 2, 2001, IT-98-33-T, and appeal, ICTY, April 19, 2004, IT-98-33-A. For further gender analysis of this case and comparison with a key sexualized violence case at the International Criminal Tribunal for Rwanda (ICTR), see Buss 2007.

39. *Prosecutor v. Krstić*, 211–12. The targeted population was defined as "the Bosnian Muslims in Srebrenica" or "of Eastern Bosnia," rather than all Bosniacs. See Hayden 2008b.

40. The court did call on leaders of a women's therapy NGO (Viva Žene) to testify about the patriarchal norms among the Srebrenica women with whom they had been working, but the concept of patriarchal society was not questioned.

41. *Prosecutor v. Krstić*, 209.

42. *Prosecutor v. Krstić*, cited in Buss 2007, 11.

43. Many women had in fact married or remarried, especially those who had emigrated. There were war widows still in BiH who had taken up with new men but had not married, not necessarily or only out of fear of community disapproval or dishonor to the dead but also because they did not want to lose the aid they received as widows. In this way, the state and aid agencies were the ones upholding patriarchal norms as well as further locking survivors into the position of helpless victims.

44. ICTY, *Prosecutor v. Vidoje Blagojević and Dragan Jokić*, 2005, IT-02-60-T, cited and discussed in Buss 2007, 12.

45. Among the pan-Islamist core were some of the 11 men and one woman who had been tried and jailed along with Izetbegović in 1983 by Yugoslav authorities for posing a nationalist threat to the socialist state after Izetbegović published his "Islamic Declaration" (1983). This episode was seen by Bosniac nationalists as part of the Yugoslav effort to suppress the Bosnian Muslims and fed into the SDA's anti-communism.

46. Dovište bez žena, *Oslobođenje*, June 30, 1997, 4.

47. Women have since been allowed to take part in the Ajvatovica pilgrimage.

48. On women's dress and (sexual) demeanor as markers of ethnic difference, see, for example, Anthias and Yuval-Davis 1989; McClintock 1993; Schein 1996; C. Smith 1996.

49. One woman at the IZ told me that Bosnian women would never accept polygyny because they were European (Helms 2008, 104).

50. This was not specifically a religious magazine. I leave aside the very predictably conservative gender messages conveyed in the Muslim religious press. For other details, see Maček 2009, 100–101.

51. For example, Kasumagić 1997; Dž. Latić 1994; Spahić 1994; and collected articles in Hadžić 1996.

52. Medica itself employed a woman spiritual counselor trained as an Islamic teacher (*mu'alima*) to work with women war victims, the majority of whom were Bosniacs.

53. Derviš Ahmed Nuruddin, "Poruka silovanim ženama," Tuzla, March 1993, 3. Document in the author's files.

54. Message from Pope John Paul II to Bosnia's Cardinal Vinko Puljić, February 2, 1993. Reprinted at http://www.priestsforlife.org/magisterium/93-02-02poperape andab.htm (accessed August 23, 2011). See also the statement from Franciscan Fra. Luka Markešić, who urged compassion toward victims as women are "the mother of life," making crimes against them "crime[s] against life!" (1999, 461).

55. Nuruddin, "Poruka silovanim ženama," 3.

56. Ibid., 4.

57. *Hidžab* (Ar. *hijab*) is not simply the veil or headscarf, as it is frequently termed in the Western press, but Islamic modest dress including covering of the hair (with a headscarf) but also usually the chest and the arms and legs to the wrists and ankles. In BiH, the traditional rural dress of Muslim women is not referred to in this way even though such women wear headscarves, while styles that cover the face and hands are usually qualified further through reference to stricter forms of Islamic observance (see Helms 2008).

58. A *mevlud* (Turkish, from the Arabic for "birth") is a commemoration of the birth of the Prophet Muhammed. On Bosnian *mevlud*s, especially those conducted by women, see Bringa 1995; Sorabji 1989, 1994.

59. Tone Bringa's *Returning Home* (2001) shows how complicated the return process became as each family waited for another family to leave their house so that they could return to it.

60. This article appeared before refugee return began in earnest and before aid to rebuild houses was widely available from foreign donors. This family may not have been given priority for rebuilding aid, however, as their village had apparently remained under Bosnian Army control. The mention of a working mosque suggests that if it was damaged by shelling it had since been repaired, while the family's house had not. The complaint that money was being supplied (by Arab and Muslim donors and condoned by local authorities) to rebuild and build mosques rather than homes or factories in which people could find jobs was commonly voiced in Bosniac-dominated areas at the time.

61. In fact, this ambiguity may have been deliberate. The article hinted at the international community's responsibility for this state of affairs but perhaps did not want to invite readers to contemplate what more the SDA government might have done for the families of its "heroes."

62. Part of a speech to the UN Security Council, August 30, 1993. Cited in MacKinnon (1994), 195–96, note 7, although MacKinnon praises Sacirbey and the BiH state for likening the country's predicament in the war to that of a woman rape victim. Likewise, she characterizes BiH's lawsuit in the International Court of Justice against Serbia for "genocide, including rape" as the state's "standing up for women in a way no state ever has" (ibid., 194), despite the lack of emphasis on rape in reference to this suit by any BiH officials.

63. Anthropologist Azra Hromadžić, who spent the war in the Bihać enclave in northwestern Bosnia, reports a similar experience (2007).

64. The translation of this group's name into English has varied because of the difficulty of translating *logoraši*, or those detained in what Bosnians called *logori*, from the German *Lager*, meaning camp, with all its associations with the Holocaust. Concentration camp thus renders a similar association in English. At some points they called themselves simply "detainees." Later, they would translate *logoraši* as Concentration Camp Torture Survivors, reflecting the Union's advocacy of a state-level law on care for victims of torture that would recognize the suffering of *all* camp survivors, including those who survived sexualized violence (see chapter 6). See their website at http://www.accts.org.ba.

65. An essay in the book by Swanee Hunt, former US ambassador to Austria, subtly reinforces this ethno-national framing even as it acknowledges the anti-nationalist feminist critiques discussed earlier in this chapter. Her source on those critiques is my own MA thesis, which I had shared with her assistants while doing fieldwork in Sarajevo. An (intentional or unintentional) error in translation in the Bosnian-language publication distorts the criticism: in listing some of the "problematic issues," the first is the question, "Does the description of genocidal rape minimize other cases of rape *perpetrated by Serbs*, or rapes perpetrated by members of the same ethnic groups, as 'ordinary'?" (emphasis added) (Hunt 1999, 77). Of course the point should be that genocidal rape erases rapes perpetrated by those *other than* Serbs (or more accurately, those that do not fall within the ethnic scenario), but in this formulation it is implied that only Serbs were capable of rape, at least "ethnic" rapes. Hunt further implies that the questions raised by feminist critics are inauthentic, describing them as coming from "those people outside Bosnia" (ibid.). She then effectively dismisses all critical inquiry by describing the distress of Bosnian rape victims she has met in her work with women in BiH and the poignancy of the help she offered as a shoulder for them to cry on.

66. However, as Živković eloquently shows, the highlander/lowlander dichotomy, like other Balkanist and Orientalist oppositions, is repeated recursively or in nesting fashion within ethnic groups and territories, and the highlander can also take on positive attributes at the expense of negative descriptions of lowlanders as docile collaborators with Ottoman rulers (2011, especially chapter 3).

67. In a similar twist on this culturizing logic, in the 1990s Pamela Ballinger encountered Italian exiles from World War II–era violence in Istria who, with the backdrop of the wars of Yugoslav disintegration, described partisan atrocities against Italians as examples of typical *Slav* barbarity (2003, 146–56). See also Grossmann 1995 on the racialization of Soviet soldier rapists in World War II Germany.

68. Skender Kulenović, "Na pravi put sam ti, majko, iziš'o"; Ajanović 1999, 150–52. Ajanović's full sentence in the original from the transcript of the book promotion, November 16, 1999, Zenica, reads: "Ova blistava poema upučena majci, ushičenom pjesničkom rječju sina, više nego ijedna druga riječ, stih, pjesma, slika, oslikava i predstavlja bosansku ženu, njen patrijarhalni odgoj, njen skrušeni stid, obliven rumenilom koje izvire iz duše same Bosne i blista na čistom obrazu bosanske žene-Bošnjakinje, kazujući joj o svijetu oko nje."

69. During the war, Medica Zenica had even been singled out, again by one of the same Bosniac nationalists writing in *Ljiljan*, Nedžad Latić, as working *against* Bosnia and the Bosniac nation because of the involvement of Caritas and other Christian charities from Germany at a time when there was fierce fighting between Croats and Muslims in Central Bosnia. Ignoring the discrepancy that Caritas had explicitly refused to fund abortion services, Latić insinuated that Medica was performing abortions on Muslims on purpose, even on women who had not been raped, and complained that "in all leading positions are Serb and Croat women" in Medica. Most of the author's wrath was aimed at Monika Hauser, the founder of Medica, whom he called the "fake queen of dishonored women" (N. Latić 1994).

70. Anela Hakalović (2011) came to similar conclusions from the perspective of trauma, arguing that this book displaces the trauma of rape from the individual women to the nation.

71. Research and Documentation Center (IDC), http://www.idc.org.ba/ (accessed July 27, 2011).

72. These distinctions become especially blurry in situations where men (and some women) move between military formations and civilian life, or where civilians are also armed.

73. IDC statistics, http://www.idc.org.ba/ (accessed July 27, 2011). According to this well-respected study, the majority of those killed and missing were military (55.27 percent) rather than civilians (40.82 percent). The same source found civilian casualties to outnumber military ones among the Bosniacs, but only marginally at 51.64 percent. Another well-regarded estimate put overall civilian casualties at 54 percent over military deaths at 46 percent (Tabeu and Bijak 2005), but again, the difference is smaller than the strong emphasis on civilian casualties implies.

Chapter 3. The NGO Boom

1. One of Sarah Phillips's key informants used the same metaphor about NGOs in Ukraine (2008, 65) as NGOs were springing up all over postsocialist Eastern Europe and indeed, starting several years earlier, throughout the world. The term "NGO 'Boom'" in fact comes from Sonia Alvarez's critique of women's NGOs in Latin America (1999).

2. Cargo cults, described by anthropologists working in Melanesia and the Pacific islands, drove people to dream of riches (cargo) arriving for them by boat or plane in the same way they saw happening for colonizers and white traders. Adherents imitated white behaviors, even constructing fake harbors and landing strips out of bamboo so as to lure ships and planes full of cargo.

3. For overviews of activities engaged in by Bosnian women's NGOs in the immediate postwar period, see Cockburn, Hubić, and Stakić-Domuz 2001; Walsh 1998.

4. An interesting contrast can be observed with early Western policies in postsocialist countries outside of ex-Yugoslavia: there, the goal was to prevent a return to communism (Carothers 1996, 65), whereas, in BiH and other formerly Yugoslav

states, the emphasis was on multiethnic cooperation and opposition to separatist nationalisms, areas where former Communists were strongest.

5. On these questions in BiH, see, for example, Gilbert 2008; for analysis of other post-Yugoslav countries, see, for example, Deacon and Stubbs 1998; Stubbs 1999b, 2007.

6. During and after the war, due to their foreign language and clerical skills (cf. Ghodsee 2005), many women and young people of both sexes found often short-term and unsteady work as translators, office assistants, and drivers with foreign militaries, intervention agencies, and NGOs. This work was better paid than most local NGO positions, when the latter were paid at all, but locals were not nearly as well paid as the foreigners who relied on the local knowledge and language skills of Bosnians to do their jobs (see Baker 2013).

7. Nor were there any women involved in the peace negotiations; one woman, the head of the British delegation to the talks, witnessed the signing (Lithander 2000).

8. In this book "the 2000s" indicates the first decade of the twenty-first century rather than the entire century itself. The Gender Center of the Federation was established at the end of 2000, followed by the Gender Center of the Republika Srpska at the end of 2001 and the state level Agency for Gender Equality on February 19, 2004 (see http://gender.undp.ba/index.aspx?PID=3&RID=38 [accessed February 22, 2011]).

9. Local authorities eventually forced Medica to stop performing abortions with the argument that they were not sufficiently equipped. Medica women, however, suspected that the real motivation was financial; state institutions lost revenue to Medica's free services.

10. "Medica" in this book refers to Medica Zenica. Medica Mondiale kept its focus on women and war, advocating for visibility and justice for women rape victims from World War II in Germany and setting up therapy projects in other war zones like Kosovo, Afghanistan, and Liberia. See http://www.medicamondiale.org/.

11. Naš most had existed since 1994 but its direction and membership had been much different before Razija had taken over the leadership in 1997.

12. Ilidža and other suburbs had been controlled by Serb forces during the war and were only turned over to the Federation in early 1996 in accordance with Dayton, widely suspected as exchange for Srebrenica. Upon the turnover, Serb leaders had used violent methods to ensure that all Serbs fled these areas; it was these "empty" places into which the refugees of Srebrenica and other areas of Eastern Bosnia had moved, mostly relocating from the Tuzla area.

13. Žene s Podrinja also counted many Srebrenica survivors in their ranks, but their main task was to work for return and they were not well known to the public, in contrast with the two biggest Srebrenica survivor organizations.

14. In 2006 Hasečić told me that out of 1,026 members there were three Croat and two Serb women.

15. These organizations were peripheral to my research; I include them mainly for their public presence as vocal women and because they played such an important role in narratives of victimhood among the Bosniacs. For more in-depth studies of

Srebrenica survivors from different perspectives, see Leydesdorff 2011; Nettelfield 2010, 99–144; Wagner 2008.

16. This function was already being attempted by the independent press but many Bosnians noted wryly that the media's relentless exposure of scandals, hypocrisy, and corruption rarely had any repercussions for those in power.

17. The AFŽ was disbanded in 1953 after it had been deemed too independent of the party (and as the "woman question" had allegedly also been solved). It was replaced by the Union of Women's Associations and later (from 1961) the Yugoslav Conference for the Social Activity of Women under the umbrella of the National Front of the Working People (Jancar-Webster 1990, 166). These organizations were led by women high in the party hierarchy, many of whom were veterans of the partisan movement and the AFŽ (Dobos 1983; Sklevicky 1984). They became a highly decentralized, loose grouping of regional organizations, including the localized, unconnected *aktiv žena* groups (Sklevicky 1989a, 103). The AFŽ name has remained in colloquial speech as a pejorative or at best dismissively humorous label for any women's political initiative, outspokenness, or even, as I once experienced, merely for gatherings of women, unaccompanied by males, in public places.

18. Among women's activists, I heard no shortage of criticism of the effects of neoliberal logics, not in such terms but as complaints about "wild capitalism," the absence of state welfare programs, or other contrasts with what they saw as positive aspects of socialism.

19. However, the feminists at Infoteka were concerned about getting *too* close to the state because it might dull their "feminist edge." This was actually among the points of disagreement that led Infoteka to form an independent, explicitly feminist NGO in March 2009 while Medica continued its course of tighter cooperation with local state institutions.

20. Critique of similar depoliticizing processes have been constant in contexts of "Third World development" (e.g., Escobar 1995; Ferguson 1990).

Chapter 4. The Nationing of Gender

1. Interethnic "mixed marriages" in BiH, the highest in Yugoslavia, have been calculated for 1981 at 15.3 percent (Burg and Shoup 1999, 42) and 16.8 percent (Bogosavljević 1992, 32–33) and fluctuating from 9.5 to 12.2 percent in the period 1962–1989 (Botev 2000). The meaning of these statistics has been qualified, however, by authors who point out that high levels were confined to urban areas (for which Donia and Fine asserted that the percentage was as high as 30–40 percent by 1990 [1994, 9]) whereas endogamy remained the norm in the villages (Bougarel 2004; see also Bringa 1995), or that mixed marriage rates were quite high precisely in mixed ethnic regions (such as cities) (Gagnon 1994a, 1994b). Interestingly, however, Bogosavljević's finding that 95.3 percent of Muslim women and 92.9 percent of Muslim men married other Muslims (1992, 32–33) implies that mixed marriage rates involving Muslims were lower.

2. Many scholars have argued passionately and convincingly against Serb and Croat nationalist claims of the incompatibility of Bosnia's ethnic groups and against the "ancient hatreds" thesis (Bringa 2005; Živković 2011), some going too far in the other direction and painting prewar BiH as a multicultural paradise (e.g., Campbell 1998; Donia and Fine 1994; Sells 1996). More to the point, in my view, are studies that show how ethnic differences and divisions were far from historically given but were instead *produced* through war violence (Hayden 1996; Maček 2009; Sorabji 1995), media discourses (Žarkov 2007), and the political strategies of nationalist and Communist elites (Gagnon 2004). For an overview of explanatory paradigms of the Bosnian war among Western officials, see Hansen 2006; for a review of approaches in scholarship on ethnic conflict, see Gagnon 2004, 195–200.

3. See, for example, Bringa 1995, 12–36; Bougarel 1996; Burg 1983; Rusinow 1982, 1985.

4. Gagnon (2004, 40) offers the fascinating finding from 1990 that levels of nationalistic sentiment were higher among party members in BiH than among the regular population, giving credence to the late 1980s sketch by the popular comedy troupe Top Lista Nadrealista (The Top List of Surrealists) in which the sensors of a special nationalism detector are not only activated by folk-costumed (male) representatives of each major ethnic group but also, and most insistently, by the Communist Party membership card in the pocket of a party official observing the demonstration.

5. I even met a few people who maintained that the SDA was not a "Bosniac" party but should be embraced by members of all ethnic groups for its support of multiethnicity. While there was indeed no indication of ethnic affiliation in the party's name, it had always declared itself to be the protector of the interests of those belonging to the "Muslim cultural-historical sphere" (*muslimanski kulturno-povjesni krug*), used the color green and a crescent moon in its iconography, and had been formed and continued to be led by Izetbegović and other former members of the World War II–era Young Muslims and other members of the group convicted by the socialist authorities in 1983 for "Islamic fundamentalism" and "Muslim nationalism"—leaders who unequivocally promoted Bosniac identity and a central role of Islam in politics and social life (see Bougarel 1997, 2001).

6. For critical accounts of reconciliation initiatives, see the special section of *Focaal* 57 (2010) on reconciliation in BiH edited by Anders Stefansson and Marita Eastmond. In addition to reconciliation and refugee return, the prosecution of war criminals, recovery of the remains of the dead, and other issues of transitional justice were also high priorities of both local activists and foreign agencies, most notably through legal proceedings at the ICTY and, after 2002, through the Bosnian War Crimes Chamber in Sarajevo. Women, often as surviving witnesses, have played a major part in these processes (see Delpla 2007; Helms 2010a; Mischkowski and Mlinarević 2009; Wagner 2008).

7. Youth and children were additional social categories constructed as unimplicated in power and therefore innocent and against nationalist divisions. However, as younger generations were growing up in a now ethnically segregated society where

even schooling was often divided by ethnicity, there was just as much reason to suppose they would be increasingly *more* resistant to imagining an ethnically integrated society.

8. However, such policies also created the incentive for some NGOs to nurture ethnic tension in order to show donors that there continued to be a need for funding reconciliation projects. Ana Dević also noticed this phenomenon in her work with women's NGOs in Serbia (personal communication 2000).

9. These feminist donors were the Kvinna til Kvinna foundation from Sweden and the American STAR Project (Strategies, Training, and Advocacy for Reconciliation). STAR's mission statement described it as a project that "offers encouragement, technical help and financial support to non-nationalist women's groups that work toward social change in the successor states of the former Yugoslavia" (Kervatin 1998).

10. Groups of Serb women in the RS or Croat women in Croat-dominated areas could solicit funds from corresponding religious or ethnic sponsors abroad, as well as from local government and nationalist parties. This is not to say that nationalist parties in Bosniac areas did not also support women's groups, as was the case with Fatma, which was affiliated with the SDA. However, because of the prevailing ideologies I have explained, this was more frequent in Serb and Croat areas. (Moreover, Fatma was a women's group but its focus was on children and moral upbringing, not on women per se, except as mothers.) On Islamic foreign aid to another Balkan region populated by Slavic Muslims and its gendered effects, see Ghodsee 2009.

11. Here, she was referring as much to Western donors as to Islamic donors that demanded full face veils for women or other changes in practice from what the Kewser women considered their own Bosnian tradition. On contestations over Bosnian Islam and their gendered components after the war, see Helms 2008; Spahić-Šiljak 2007, 2012; on the socialist period, see Bringa 1995.

12. Medica employed a trained Islamic teacher (*mu'alima*) who wore *hidžab*. When I lived in Zenica in 1999–2000, she mainly focused on her job as spiritual counselor for Medica's clients, saving her public engagement for activities with the Islamska Zajednica. Several years later, her public profile increased, however, when she became president of Medica.

13. As she put it in a 1993 interview: Lejla Saraljić, "Rat je šansa za duhovno osvješćenje Muslimana," interview, *Ratna Nova Naša Riječ*, June 18, 1993, 8–9.

14. See also the work of the Transkulturna Psihosocialna Obrazovna Fondacija (Transcultural Psychosocial Educational Foundation), http://www.tpo.ba/eng/ifirst.htm (accessed December 12, 2012).

15. The picture she paints completely neglects the high rates of ethnically mixed marriages in BiH, especially in the socialist period. However, in the large village where she lived and its rural surroundings, ethnic endogamy was more the norm than in urban areas.

16. This position has obvious roots in the socialist period, especially for religious families and those not connected to the Communist Party, like many of the residents of Fikreta's town. It also recalls the "anti-politics" movement in the 1980s

among dissidents in many socialist countries of Central and Eastern Europe, which extolled the restorative promise of autonomy possible in the sphere of home and family, a vision that nevertheless assumed male authority over women and children (Goven 1993).

17. Izetbegović was still alive at the time. Plavšić was a prominent member of the leading Serb nationalist party and former president of the RS before her conviction at the ICTY for crimes against humanity. Marković, the widow of Serbian President Slobodan Milošević and head of her own political party in Serbia, was often accused of having goaded Milošević into extreme nationalism and ruthless violence.

18. With characteristic cheekiness, she also referred to the coffee made by males as "coffee with eggs (balls/testicles)"—*kafa s jajima*—thus putting men down for their lack of skill in what were considered female tasks.

19. There was also quite a sense of separate women's and men's spheres, which was underscored by the participation of a few men who spoke up in a manner I had often witnessed at other women's NGO meetings: they spoke of what "you women" needed to do to help repair society, as if men were merely spectators who could not by definition participate in women's activities. For example, a young man from a youth organization in nearby Zvornik addressed the Bratunac meeting, saying: "I'm glad we're here and talking about joint [cross-ethnic] activities. . . . *Women should* make a plan for a project at the break on the subjects of women against war, life together [*suživot*], two-way return, etc. *You* need to get out into the public with this, through radio programs and tribunals and get the politicians going. Now we *even* have a good number of women there [in politics]" (my emphasis).

20. After having spent the summer in BiH, in September 1996 I rode from Belgrade to Sarajevo with some Belgraders who were seeing the "Muslim" parts of BiH for the first time since the war. Everything they saw, especially the occasional "covered woman" and SDA election campaign material with its crescent moon logo, seemed to fit into their expectations that Sarajevo had become a "Muslim fundamentalist" town as they had been told by the Serbian media and rumor mill. They clung to these impressions even as they drank freely available alcohol and passed far more "uncovered" women on the streets than those in *hidžab*.

21. Her Serb colleagues who went from Medica had to deal with different feelings as they were challenged for having stayed in a "Muslim town" or assumed to be allies because of their (Serb) names.

22. Žena 21 was a group of educated Sarajevan women who put out a magazine of the same name and had strong ties to Ambassador Hunt. The magazine was in many ways typical of the region's women's magazines—it was full of beauty and relationship tips, recipes, profiles of "successful women" who combined work with motherhood, etc.—but also often contained critical articles on women and politics or coverage of women's and even feminist activism.

23. During this same stay in Banja Luka, I also spoke to a group of academics, among them a woman who spoke about the "former Bosnia." By this she meant the republic of BiH under the structure of socialist Yugoslavia. As far as she was concerned,

there was no present-day BiH. She and her colleagues also asked me sincerely about Zenica and life in the Muslim-dominated Federation. They wanted to know if it was true that the language there was being called "Bosniac" (*Bošnjački*) just as Croats called it Croatian and Serbs called it Serbian. When I told them it was being called Bosnian (*Bosanski*), they dismissed this as absurd, firmly rejecting the idea that Bosniacs, Serbs, and Croats could share anything in common, and further implying that all three ethno-national groups were equally separatist.

24. Croat-dominated areas also avoided the term "Bosnian." Cafés there typically did not even offer such coffee—espresso was the norm, part of the claim to modernity and Western-ness (see Jansen 2002).

25. Yael Navaro-Yashin chronicles a similar process of (political) identity declaration through consumption in 1990s Turkey (2002, 78–113), which entailed some of the same markers of opposition to Islamist lifestyles and politics as were found among secular Bosniacs and many Serbs and Croats in BiH.

26. There was both internal political disagreement *and* direct foreign military involvement by Serbia and Croatia, but neither civil war nor aggression alone adequately characterizes the conflict. In my view, such labels function as ideological simplifications that deliberately obfuscate many more complicated aspects of the conflict as well as reify the view of warring ethnic groups. On such complexities, see, for example, Andreas 2008; Burg and Shoup 1999; Nielsen 2013.

27. See Cockburn et al. (2001, 106–26) for an account of the difficulties United Women and Vidra, another Banja Luka women's NGO, had to endure for defying prevalent Serb nationalist politics in different ways.

28. This formulation clearly evokes Tone Bringa's *Being Muslim the Bosnian Way* (1995) but was also a common phrasing used by my informants: "I'm a feminist, but in a Bosnian way" (*feministkinja sam, ali na bosanski način*). See also Markowitz on how urban Sarajevans used the notion of the "Bosnian way" to stake claims to a cosmopolitan Bosnian identity (2010, 155–65).

29. The mood in the RS was entirely opposite. Many demonstrated against NATO and in solidarity with their fellow Serbs (see Cockburn et al. 2001, 110–11).

30. Most BiH feminists at the time were mostly concerned with issues of gender, violence, and nationalism. Other issues in the typical package for American feminists of my generation did not always register for Bosnian feminists. Rarely was class discussed beyond issues of rural vs. urban lifestyles; Infoteka activists were proudly anti-homophobic, but their awareness of racialized categories developed only gradually when their American volunteer initiated a project on the situation of Roma women (Medica Zenica 2001). However, they decisively rejected environmentalism; when asked why they didn't recycle paper, Duška replied, "What do I care how much forest there is? I'm concerned about women!"

31. Medica Mondiale, however, via Monika Hauser and a colleague who were visiting Kosovar Albanian refugees at the time, did publicly call for an end to the Serbian ethnic cleansing even if this meant bombing military positions (but not population centers) (Monika Hauser, personal communication 2012).

32. ICTY judgment, *Kunarac et al.*, 2001, IT-96-23 & 23/1, available at http://www.icty.org/case/kunarac/4.

33. Gabriela Mischkowski, "Ein Gräuel ohne Strategie," *Die Tageszeitung*, no. 6386, March 2, 2001, 11, 241. It should be noted that Medica Mondiale was no longer Medica Zenica's main donor by then.

34. My account is based on later interviews with some of the participants, as it occurred several months after my departure from Zenica. I am deliberately vague about those involved in order to avoid reopening sensitive wounds that have since been patched and smoothed over.

35. E-mail letter from Medica Zenica to Medica Mondiale, Köln, April, 3, 2001, in author's files.

36. Medica opposed the Žena BiH that had existed in Zagreb where it took part in the wartime rape debates, not the newer NGO of the same name in (East) Mostar. The Mostar group took a much more anti-nationalist stance on wartime violence. In fact, its Bosniac leader was one of the few activists to come to the Sarajevo meeting about how to express opposition to the NATO bombing in Serbia and Kosovo.

Chapter 5. Politics Is a Whore

1. Public/private has been shown to be particularly Euro-American in construct, while similarly gendered dichotomies (e.g., outside/inside, culture/nature, technological/spiritual) have been shown by feminist anthropologists to carry different meanings in other societies (Lamphere 1993; Moore 1988; Rosaldo 1980; Strathern 1980).

2. Figures here and below are from Organization for Security and Cooperation in Europe 1998; see also Ler-Sofronić 1998.

3. Interestingly, Massey et al. (1997) found that party membership did not give social or economic benefits to women to the degree they did for men, explaining at least one factor in women's low political participation levels under socialism.

4. Many Bosnians, including women, blamed women themselves for not joining political parties and running for election, and, as voters, for voting for male candidates. In the same way as political figures of different ethnicities were seen as representing "their people," women candidates were presumed to be the representatives of the female population.

5. The quota rule (Rule 7.50) mandated that 30 percent of candidate lists, including three out of the first ten, be "members of the minority gender," which meant women in all cases aside from that of the Women's Party (Stranka Žena BiH). (The Women's Party was required to list men in 30 percent of its candidate slots.) In the elections of 2000, however, a system of open lists was instituted, allowing voters to choose individual names from one party's list. Only 18 percent of those actually elected in 2000 were women, partially confirming activists' fears that voters would skip over female names.

6. After the quotas were introduced, many parties had difficulty finding enough women who would agree to stand for election, though some complained that "quality"

women were being passed over for top spots on election lists in favor of the wives and cousins of male leaders who would presumably be easy to manipulate into following the directives of the parties' men.

7. Ganić had forged somewhat of a reputation as a supporter of women's rights, reportedly because he had two daughters with whom he sympathized. This penchant, however, contributed to his reputation as a less-than-manly politician and no doubt to the laughter his suggestion provoked in the Parliament.

8. While Ganić's suggestion was reported briefly and without comment in the press, the reaction of the delegates was described to me by a Bosnian woman journalist who had witnessed the event.

9. "Women who haven't married and don't have children aren't successful women." Lidija Korać, the only woman member of the Central Election Commission of BiH, guest on the talk show *Korak* (*Step*), TV Hayat, June 27, 2006.

10. Paraphrased from field notes taken during the program cited earlier.

11. Debate with women candidates broadcast October 26, 2000, on the independent Open Broadcast Network (OBN).

12. The 2000 elections did in fact result in wins for the multiethnic, "civic"-oriented Social Democratic Party (SDP), which (with heavy international backing) formed a governing coalition called the Alliance for Change. After two rocky years, however, voters threw out the Alliance and voted the main nationalist parties back in. On this period, see Bougarel et al. 2007b.

13. See http://www.osce.org/bih/53004 (accessed March 23, 2011).

14. "In Her Own Name," TVBiH, March 8, 2000.

15. The Bosnian League of Women Voters was a network of women's NGO activists from all over BiH who had responded to the suggestion of US diplomat Swanee Hunt that they establish an organization like the US League of Women Voters. The Bosnian "Liga" was locally run, though sporadically financed from abroad. It encouraged women to vote and all voters to vote for women candidates. Its members included women politicians and NGO leaders, including Šehida from Bosanka in Zenica and Almasa from Srcem do mira in Kozarac. Ironically, the Bosnian name was formed with the masculine plural of the word "voters." After exposure to the insistence by many women's activists on the use of feminine grammatical forms when referring to females ("female language" or *ženski jezik*), Šehida told me she had decided this was a mistake and wanted to change the name to the feminine Liga Žene Glasačica. This never happened, however, and I never heard other Liga members mention this problem.

16. Mediha Filipović, prominent figure in the Stranka za BiH (Party for BiH), speaking in front of other women activists and politicians at a round table sponsored by the League of Women Voters.

17. Mira Štic (Democratic Socialist Party) and Amila Omersoftić (Women's Party) during the October 2000 OBN debate (see above note).

18. Sessions were held in municipalities throughout BiH. The Zenica session was held on November 6–7, 1999, a weekend, since most of the female participants had nine-to-five jobs during the week.

19. Some female politicians actively embraced this role. Elsewhere I described how two Zenica MPs, both teachers by profession, positioned themselves as scolding men who behaved badly (Helms 2007).

20. This "dealing with" (*baviti se*) the past referred to nationalists' focus on collective victimhood and was different from "facing the past" (*suočavanje s prošlošćem*). The latter was associated with efforts to acknowledge war guilt and crimes committed by one's own nation and evoked similarly labeled efforts in Germany to come to terms with its Nazi past.

21. See http://www.srebrenica.ba/index.en.php (accessed March 25, 2011).

22. Bratunac cannot be separated from the political and symbolic importance of Srebrenica. Less than ten kilometers from Srebrenica and along the most accessible route into the town, Serb-held Bratunac was a major barricade sealing off the wartime enclave. It also served as the headquarters of Serb troops during the siege and fall of Srebrenica and some of the mass killings of Bosniac men took place in and around the town (see Duijzings 2007).

23. Neither of these cases was without serious problems and there was some question as to whether refugee return would foster or complicate ethnic reconciliation. Indeed, as in the Kozarac case, return to many areas had been easier because they had been relatively ethnically homogeneous before the war. Return to urban areas, which were ethnically mixed before the war, was much more problematic and slower to realize due also to the much more complicated issues of property restitution in apartment blocks.

24. Bosnian feminism, as they explained it, also differed from Western varieties in its refusal to "reject men." This alluded to the importance of family (heterosexual marriage and children) and outward markers of femininity—wearing skirts, high heels, and makeup much more than did visiting foreign feminists.

25. Amila Omersoftić, president of the Women's Party, during a televised candidates' debate devoted to women, broadcast on OBN, October 26, 2000, just before general elections in November. Omersoftić repeated several times that she and her party were "not some kind of feminists" until the moderator pointed out that neither he nor anyone else in the studio had mentioned the word.

26. Suzana Andželić, "Žena u politici danas nije retkost, ona je incident," *Žena*, October 29, 1999, 5. Interview with Senka Nožica.

Chapter 6. Avoidance and Authenticity

1. Office space is provided by the Sarajevo Canton, which also gives space on the same floor to war veteran organizations and other groups.

2. Many former camp inmates qualified for free or discounted transportation passes from the city. Still, five KM was very little: just over three American dollars at the time.

3. One quarter of the 2,000 women members had survived rape (United Nations Population Fund [UNFPA] 2010, 9). The larger organization also included men who had been sexually abused, but they did not easily talk about this.

4. In 2006–7 the exchange rate was about 1.5 KM per US dollar.

5. The women's section was established officially, under the leadership of Enisa Salčinović, in 2009.

6. Collected papers and testimonies from the conference "Violation of the Human Rights of Women in Bosnia and Herzegovina during the War, 1992–1995," published in Bosnian and English (Tokača 1999).

7. As before, my research combined interviews with participant observation and analysis of media discourses and materials compiled by advocates. Due to time constraints and the understandable wariness of many of the victim association leaders toward researchers and journalists (because, they said, they never saw any concrete benefit from speaking to such people), I did not get to know these activists as well as I had during my previous work, and was less able to do participant observation among the organizations themselves. It is also important to note that, as in my previous research, I did not interview rape survivors about their war experiences but as leaders and members of organizations doing advocacy work.

8. This friend, to his credit, quickly reevaluated his assumptions when he recalled the stereotypes he had had to put up with as a DP in wartime Zenica. Because the DPs had lost everything, they were sent brand-new clothing from relatives who had fled abroad, while Zenica residents, still in their own homes with their own things, had to make do with their old clothes. The DPs had therefore failed to garner sympathy from the population because they did not conform to the image of destitute refugees (see Drakulić 1993a).

9. Xavier Bougarel (2007) shows how this term lost much of its religious meaning in the postwar period in favor of ethno-national connotations. Paradoxically, however, it also lent more of a religious tone to expressions of ethno-national allegiance.

10. Raped women cannot, however, be considered "true" *šehid*s in the way that (male) soldiers killed fighting are; soldiers killed in battle are "first level *šehid*s," or "*šehid*s in this world and in the other world," while other war victims, women who die in childbirth, and others are "titular *šehid*s," or "*šehid*s in the other world" only (Bougarel, personal communication 2005).

11. This comment was made during discussion after a public talk on war rape, violence, and women's experiences in BiH by Nirman Moranjak-Bamburać on October 7, 2004, as part of the series of lectures titled "Šta je nama rat?" ("What is war to us?"), organized through the "Inter Nos—Među nama" program at the Sarajevo bookstore/café Buybook/Karabit in 2004–5. The incident was related to me by one of the series' lecturers, Jasmina Husanović of the University of Tuzla.

12. As of 2008, when many had come forth to register for the new benefits, ŽŽR claimed over 3,000 members, now both in BiH and abroad. Many rape survivors, also victims of ethnic cleansing, had in fact resettled as refugees in other countries.

13. See ICTY judgment, *Prosecutor v. Radislav Krstić*, August 2, 2001, 14–15, IT-98-33-T; Netherlands Institute for War Documentation (NIOD) 2002, 1121–28. Witnesses also reported women, mostly younger ones, being pulled off buses of deportees

and never seen again. In one case, a whole busload of women disappeared. Given the pattern of rapes in other places attacked by Bosnian Serb forces, it is not a stretch to presume that those women were raped before being killed.

14. Sivac was especially concerned with the prosecution of the detention camp commander who raped her, Željko Mejakić. His case, bundled with those of several other Serb camp officials from the Prijedor region, was transferred in 2006 from the ICTY to the Court of Bosnia-Herzegovina. On May 30, 2008, after Sivac expressed her optimism, Mejakić was convicted and sentenced to twenty-one years of imprisonment (upheld on appeal). See http://www.sudbih.gov.ba/?opcija=predmeti&id=33&je zik=e (accessed December 29, 2011).

15. *I Begged Them to Kill Me* (Ajanović 1999) was also published in German.

16. A government official who participated in the Dignity campaign also held (foreign-funded) NGOs and the international community responsible for this delay, pointing out in one of our interviews (in July 2006) that foreign officials had had no trouble putting other priorities, such as combating human trafficking or fighting terrorism, on the domestic agenda.

17. Similar priorities held also in areas of Serb and Croat control.

18. Veterans got privatization certificates valued according to their time in the service, as well as promises of priority in hiring, tax exemptions for starting new businesses, and other advantages, few of which were ultimately valuable or realizable in practice, leading to a mass of disillusioned and impoverished veterans (see Gregson 2000).

19. Lejla Hadžiahmić (2010, 81–83) discusses the revealing case of a male Army veteran and father whose wife had been killed as a soldier and who was angrily refused benefits to the families of *šehid*s and fallen soldiers because, as a man, it was his duty to go out and work rather than to "beg for money and steal from the mouths of mothers and children who really need the help" (*Oslobođenje*, November 5, 2007, 8, cited in Hadžiahmić 2010, 82).

20. In the mid-2000s survivors in the Sarajevo Canton were granted some limited benefits and access to health insurance by the cantonal authorities, but many more survivors were living in the other, far poorer cantons and had no access to aid.

21. Bougarel (2006) describes how opponents, especially the SDA and its allies who were eager to discredit the SDP-led coalition, cast the way in which the reforms were presented as an insult to the masculinity of the veterans. Suada Hadžović, the minister of Veterans' Affairs who announced the cuts, was a woman, while, by contrast, the first commander of the Bosnian Army, Sefer Halilović, had been put in charge of the Ministry of Social Affairs.

22. Kate Holt and Sarah Hughes, "Bosnia's Rape Babies: Abandoned by Their Families, Forgotten by the State," *The Independent*, September 13, 2005.

23. Members of the "initiating group" were: Deblokada (film company), Sarajevo; Centar za žrtve torture (Center for Victims of Torture), Sarajevo; Sekcija bivših logorašica SULKS (Section of former Women Camp Detainees of the Sarajevo Canton), Sarajevo; Istraživačko dokumentacioni centar (Research and Documentation Center),

Sarajevo; Žene ženama (Women to Women), Sarajevo; Vive žene (Vive Women), Tuzla; Medica Zenica, Zenica. The Association of Women Victims of War (ŽŽR) had begun its own lobbying efforts on this issue and was briefly also part of the Dignity campaign but later stepped out.

24. Campaign press release, March 2006.

25. A few RS women's NGOs voiced support for the Dignity Campaign but for the most part they did not participate.

26. Then, as now, recognition and privileges were only afforded to those who had fought for, or at least not against, the "right" side, i.e., with the Communist partisans, or had been civilian victims of "fascist terror," i.e., by Nazi, Ustaše, or Četnik forces (Karge 2010).

27. Monika Hauser, personal communication 2012.

28. No Man's Land was a joint production involving several countries and Tanović was at the time living abroad, but the fact that he was a Bosnian (and a Bosniac) underscored the claim for BiH.

29. Federation media also gave wide coverage at the time to the refusal of RS cinemas to show the film and the objections of those in the RS to what they said was Žbanić's unnecessary mention of Karadžić and Mladić as war criminals.

30. The banner, hung over Titova Street at the Eternal Flame WWII Partisan memorial at the beginning of the Ferhadija pedestrian zone, was a riff on the well-known phrase from the socialist era, jebeš zemlju koju Bosne nema ("screw the country that doesn't have Bosnia"), referring to Bosnia's central position in Yugoslavia. In the banner, presumably as a gesture to public respectability, jebeš/screw was replaced with the Rolling Stones' logo of a mouth with protruding tongue, but any passerby would have known what it stood for.

31. I was not in BiH at the time; this incident was related to me some months later by feminist scholar Jasmina Husanović, who was following the story on Bosnian TV and who was incredulous for much the same reasons as Marijana.

32. In fact, aside from one minister of culture, government officials had refused to back the film financially but were happy to take credit for its success.

33. Another collection of rape survivors' testimonies and conference proceedings (Tokača 1999) also aimed at establishing "truth." While proclaiming it a sin to remain silent, however, it also acknowledged the risks of speaking out, as reflected in its title, Sin of Silence, Risk of Speech.

34. Reluctance to confide in male family members did not necessarily reflect a fear of being rejected or mistreated. Several therapists and survivors stressed survivors' desire to spare male relatives from the pressure to exact revenge and the fear that the men would be harmed if they did attempt such retaliation.

35. The adjustment of rape survivors as well as what little information is available about children born of the rapes both suggest a process similar to the "practical kinship" observed by Veena Das in the case of families recovering from abductions, rapes, and forced marriages of women across ethnic and newly formed state borders during the partition of India (Das 1995; and see chapter 2).

36. This system was soon improved and vouchers indicated only "civilian victims of war." However, as late as 2012, activists were asking why it was not possible in all municipalities to set up bank accounts for the receipt of funds rather than having to redeem a voucher.

37. Such requests continued after the war, especially from the mid-2000s when the media started to ask about the whereabouts of children born from rape now entering adolescence. I witnessed the persistence of such journalists on several occasions in the offices of Medica and ŽŽR, both of which refused to put journalists in touch with women survivors.

38. Medica Zenica also felt the need to move on from wartime topics, while Medica Mondiale in Germany was committed to the long-term struggle against wartime sexualized violence in various world conflict zones. The Zenica activists had been quiet at the publication of *I Begged Them to Kill Me*, mostly because they saw it as something produced by (and for) SDA circles of which they were decidedly not a part.

39. Zejčević and fellow Vive žene therapist Teufika Ibrahimefendić testified in the ICTY cases of Biljana Plavšić and General Radislav Krstić.

40. I was not in BiH at the time but followed the story in the Bosnian- and English-language press, Internet forums, and conversations with Bosnian acquaintances. In September 2012, on a brief visit to Sarajevo and Zenica, I was able to speak to activists about it in person.

41. Mitrović was the owner of TVPink, an entertainment network with channels across the former Yugoslavia that was often criticized for offering sensationalist news and kitschy entertainment.

42. For example, Radio Sarajevo, "Šta žene kažu o slučaju Hasečić—Grahovac—Jolie," October 14, 2010, http://www.radiosarajevo.ba/content/view/35388/32/ (accessed November 24, 2010); Jovanović 2010.

43. Letter dated October 21, 2010, titled "Aktivistice i članice ženskih udruženja u BiH protiv censure" (Women activists and members of women's associations in BiH against censorship), and circulated to the media and via e-mail. Copy in author's files.

44. Salčinović's story was presented in a short documentary made for UN-TV (see http://www.unmultimedia.org/tv/21stcentury/2010/10/bosnia-healing-the-wounds-of-war.html [accessed December 22, 2010]; and she subsequently made appearances on behalf of Bosnian rape survivors, organized by UNFPA, at UN headquarters in New York and international conferences in Europe.

45. Jolie was quoted as dismissing the controversy, referring to Hasečić and saying, "There's one person who has a gripe" (Irish 2010).

46. "Ensuring Justice, Reparations, and Rehabilitation for Victims of Conflict-Related Sexual Violence," Sarajevo, September 5–6, 2012.

47. According to longtime Belgrade activist Lepa Mlađenović, who in the 1990s participated as an anti-nationalist feminist in many international forums about wartime rape, feminists in Serbia had not internally discussed wartime rape either (personal communication, December 2012).

48. Jolie in fact explicitly described her characters as metaphors for their respective ethno-national groups. See her interview with Jasmila Žbanić, http://www.berlinale.de/de/archiv/jahresarchive/2012/02_programm_2012/02_Filmdatenblatt_2012_201 20035hp (accessed November 3, 2012).

49. Initially the UNFPA program was explicitly for women survivors but was expanded upon consultation with local organizations to cover victims of wartime rape, sexual abuse, and torture in BiH (personal communication with staff of UNFPA Sarajevo, September and November 2012).

Conclusion

1. See http://www.sarajevo-x.com/clanak/081224046 (accessed November 11, 2012).

2. See http://www.naslovi.net/2008-12-25/e-novine/tihicu-dosta-politike-zrtve/973703 (accessed November 11, 2012).

3. See http://www.sarajevo-x.com/clanak/081224046 (accessed November 11, 2012).

4. Thanks to Larisa Kurtović for sharing her observations from this period, the complex politics of which deserve a deeper analysis than space allows here.

5. All quotes comes from a statement by three Bosniac writers, Isnam Taljić, Zilhad Ključanin, and Fatmir Alispahić, published at http://bosnjaci.net/prilog.php?pid=30586 (accessed November 11, 2012).

6. See http://bih-x.info/2009/01/17/gradani-bih-ce-svojim-potpisima-kazati-da-li-mogu-zaboraviti-agresiju-i-genocid/ (accessed November 11, 2012).

7. "Bakira Hasečić: Tihić nam želi zabraniti da se sjećamo genocida i još nam prijete," http://www.svevijesti.ba/content/view/20350/218/ (accessed November 11, 2012).

8. *Politika*, July 26, 2008, quoted in "Biznis.ba—Tihić ispunio i posljednju naredbu Dodika: Bošnjaci od srijede nisu žrtve," http://www.svevijesti.ba/content/view/19445/215/ (accessed November 11, 2012). Dodik explicitly acknowledged that Bosniacs had made up the majority of those killed (by some measures an improvement over his predecessors and allies who denied even this) but stressed that many Croats and Serbs had also been victims. For more on Dodik's role in the politics of victimhood, see Nielsen 2013.

9. Israel is only one example of these dynamics. For example, Simon Turner (2010) examines the "politics of innocence" among Hutu refugees from Burundi who struggled to be perceived as innocent and deserving of aid in the face of preemptive killings of Tutsis by Hutus who had been victimized in the past.

10. For critiques of this easy association and examples of a much bigger variety of masculinities mobilized in the service of nationalism, see, for example, Altinay 2004; Bracewell 2000; Elliston 2008; Greenberg 2006; Kanaaneh 2005; Sasson-Levy 2005; Waetjen 2001.

11. "Mojoj dragoj BiH," by the band Drugi Način. The song, which appeared early during the war and which was listened to with emotional longing by the Bosniac

and Croat refugees I lived and worked with in 1993–94, does not mention any one ethnic or religious group. However, its embrace of BiH in its whole territory as well as the symbol of the golden *ljiljan* (lily), the *fleur-de-lis*, associates it with Bosniacs and supporters of a united BiH state. The band's video in fact uses religious markers to show both Bosniacs (women in green *hidžab*) and Croats (Franciscan monks in brown robes), but no similarly recognizable Serbs or symbols of Orthodoxy. The spot evokes both a cosmopolitan secularism through the longhaired rock musicians in their leather jackets and earrings, as well as religious identifications, ending with the simultaneous sounds of church bells and Islamic prayer.

12. Plavšić was not only the only woman to have held high office in BiH but also one of very few to be convicted of war crimes (see http://www.icty.org/case/plavsic/4). Her confession and guilty plea, also unique among top leaders indicted by the ICTY, appears to have been part of a strategy to get a lighter sentence and avoid the original charge of genocide.

13. "The limits of gender rhetoric for nationalism" is the title of an article by Thembisa Waetjen (2001), who locates the reasons for the "failure" of the Zulu nationalism of the Inkatha movement in South Africa in a particular gender politics that emphasized a highly patriarchal and militant masculinity. Inkatha's rural, tradition-based ideology lost out to the African National Congress, which was also male-dominated but was more successful in appealing to urban populations and the youth of both sexes. My argument is only indirectly about nationalisms competing for the loyalty of members of the same constructed nation and more about competition on "the world stage" for intervention and backing from more powerful states in regional political struggles.

14. Orić was convicted of war crimes by the ICTY in 2006, but released for time served and later acquitted of all charges on appeal. In 2009 he was sentenced to prison on illegal weapons charges.

15. See http://www.sarajevo-x.com/clanak/081224046 (accessed November 11, 2012).

16. Some useful steps toward understanding the relationship between masculinities and militarization in the context of the former Yugoslavia can be found, for example, in N. Bašić 2004; Cockburn and Žarkov 2002; Čolović 2002; Jansen 2010; Milićević 2006; Petrović 2009, 2012; Schäuble 2009; Senjković 2004. However, aside from the ongoing research of Gabriela Mischkowski into what war crimes trial transcripts can tell us about perpetrator masculinity, I know of no sustained and grounded study of how and why men (or women) committed sexualized violence, perhaps inevitably given the significant methodological challenges.

17. Such was the criticism by male veterans facing benefit cuts (through means testing) of the female minister of Veterans' Affairs when she signed on to a campaign condemning the use of women's bodies in billboard ads (Bougarel 2006, 487).

18. For example, Arsenijević 2010, 2011a; Cockburn 1998; Cockburn, Hubić, and Stakić-Domuz 2001; Husanović 2009, 2010, 2011; Simmons 2010. For an exception to these hopeful assessments focused on international intervention and NGOs, see Pupavac 2005.

19. Jasmila Žbanić belongs to this group (*Grbavica*, *Na Putu*/*On the Path*, 2010), as does Aida Begić (*Snijeg*/*Snow*, 2008) and Danijela Majstorović (*Posao snova*/*Dream Job*, 2006, and *Kontrapunkt za nju*/*Counterpoint for Her*, 2004).

20. One could also add the Queer (arts) Festival organized in September 2008 in Sarajevo by the LGBT NGO "Association Q," although the effects of this event for public visibility were very mixed: the festival attracted intense scrutiny and condemnation from nationalists for nearly a month before its start. It was ultimately canceled after opening night when anti-gay and (Islamic) religious thugs attacked the participants, but the media debate before and after the event featured many prominent citizens expressing support for the festival and what it stood for, albeit in a way that reinforced ideas of tolerant, liberal, European anti-nationalists in opposition to a backward, Balkan, chauvinist religious nationalism (see Kajinić 2010).

References

Abu-Lughod, Lila. 1990. "Can There Be a Feminist Ethnography?" *Women and Performance* 5 (1): 7–27.

Achkoska, Violeta. 2004. "Lifting the Veils from Muslim Women in the Republic of Macedonia following the Second World War." In Naumović and Jovanović 2004, 183–94.

Agence France-Presse. "Bosnian Wartime Rape Victims Slam 'Ignorant' Jolie." November 29, 2010.

Ahmed, Leila. 1982. "Western Ethnocentrism and Perceptions of the Harem." *Feminist Studies* 8 (3): 521–34.

Ajanović, Irfan, ed. 1999. *Molila sam ih da me ubiju: Zločin nad ženom Bosne i Hercegovine.* Sarajevo: Savez logoraša Bosne i Hercegovine, Centar za istraživanje zločina.

Albera, Dionigi. 2006. "Anthropology of the Mediterranean: Between Crisis and Renewal." *History and Anthropology* 17 (2): 109–33.

Alcoff, Linda Martin. 2000. "Who's Afraid of Identity Politics?" In *Reclaiming Identity: Realist Theory and the Predicament of Postmodernism*, edited by Paula M. L. Moya and Michael Roy Hames-García, 312–44. Berkeley: University of California Press.

Allen, Beverly. 1996. *Rape Warfare: The Hidden Genocide in Bosnia-Herzegovina and Croatia.* Minneapolis: University of Minnesota Press.

Altinay, Ayşe Gül. 2004. *The Myth of the Military Nation: Militarism, Gender, and Education in Turkey.* New York: Palgrave Macmillan.

Alvarez, Sonia E. 1999. "Advocating Feminism: The Latin American Feminist NGO 'Boom.'" *International Feminist Journal of Politics* 1 (2): 181–209.

———. 2009. "Beyond NGO-ization: Reflections from Latin America." *Development* 52 (2): 175–84.

Amnesty International. 1993. *Bosnia-Herzegovina: Rape and Sexual Abuse by Armed Forces.* New York: Amnesty International USA.

———. 2009. *Bosnia & Herzegovina: "Whose Justice?": The Women of Bosnia and Herzegovina Are Still Waiting.* London: Amnesty International.

———. 2012. *Old Crimes, Same Suffering: No Justice for Survivors of Wartime Rape in North-East Bosnia and Herzegovina*. London: Amnesty International.

Anderson, Benedict R. 1983. *Imagined Communities: Reflections on the Origin and Spread of Nationalism*. London: Verso.

Andjelic, Neven. 2003. *Bosnia-Herzegovina: The End of a Legacy*. London: Frank Cass.

Andreas, Peter. 2008. *Blue Helmets and Black Markets: The Business of Survival in the Siege of Sarajevo*. Ithaca, NY: Cornell University Press.

Andrić-Ružičić, Duška. 1997. "Women's Self-Organizing in Bosnia: Feminism from Necessity, or Necessity from Feminism." In Kašić 1997, 25–28.

———. 2003. "War Rape and the Political Manipulation of Survivors." In Giles et al. 2003, 103–13.

Anthias, Floya, and Nira Yuval-Davis. 1989. Introduction to *Woman—Nation—State*, edited by Nira Yuval-Davis and Floya Anthias, 1–15. London: Macmillan.

Appadurai, Arjun. 1986. "Theory in Anthropology: Center and Periphery." *Comparative Studies in Society and History* 28 (2): 356–61.

Arsenijević, Damir. 2007. "Against Opportunistic Criticism." *European Institute for Progressive Cultural Policies Multilingual Webjournal* (November). http://eipcp.net/transversal/0208/arsenijevic/en.

———. 2010. *Forgotten Future: The Politics of Poetry in Bosnia and Herzegovina*. Baden-Baden: Nomos.

———. 2011a. "Gendering the Bone: The Politics of Memory in Bosnia and Herzegovina." *Journal for Cultural Research* 15 (2): 193–205.

———. 2011b. "Mobilising Unbribable Life: The Politics of Contemporary Poetry in Bosnia and Herzegovina." In *Towards a New Literary Humanism*, edited by Andy Mousley, 166–80. London: Palgrave Macmillan.

Arslanagić, Sabina. 2010a. "Bosnia Suspends Permission for Jolie Film." *Balkan Insight*, October 14. http://www.balkaninsight.com/en/article/bosnia-suspends-filming-permission-for-jolie-s-directorial-debut.

———. 2010b. "Serbian Media Accused of Distorting Jolie Film Script." *Balkan Insight*, October 14. http://www.balkaninsight.com/en/article/serbian-media-mogul-accused-of-undermining-jolie-s-film.

Askin, Kelly D. 2003. "Prosecuting Wartime Rape and Other Gender-Related Crimes under International Law: Extraordinary Advances, Enduring Obstacles." *Berkeley Journal of International Law* 21: 288–349.

Baines, Erin K. 2004. *Vulnerable Bodies: Gender, the UN and the Global Refugee Crisis*. Burlington, VT: Ashgate.

Baker, Catherine. 2013. "Prosperity without Security: The Precarity of Interpreters in Postsocialist, Postconflict Bosnia-Herzegovina." *Slavic Review* 71 (4): 849–72.

Bakić-Hayden, Milica. 1995. "Nesting Orientalisms: The Case of Former Yugoslavia." *Slavic Review* 54 (4): 917–31.

Bakić-Hayden, Milica, and Robert M. Hayden. 1992. "Orientalist Variations on the Theme 'Balkans': Symbolic Geography in Recent Yugoslav Cultural Politics." *Slavic Review* 51 (1): 1–15.

Ballinger, Pamela. 2003. *History in Exile: Memory and Identity at the Borders of the Balkans.* Princeton, NJ: Princeton University Press.

———. 2004. "'Authentic Hybrids' in the Balkan Borderlands." *Current Anthropology* 45 (1): 31–60.

Banac, Ivo. 1994. *The National Question in Yugoslavia: Origins, History, Politics.* Ithaca, NY: Cornell University Press.

Bašić, Adisa. 2004. *Trauma-Market.* Sarajevo: Omnibus.

Bašić, Natalija. 2004. "Kampfsoldaten im ehemaligen Jugoslawien: Legitimationen des Kämpfens und Tötens." In *Gender, Identität und kriegerischer Konflikt: Das Beispiel des ehemaligen Jugoslawien,* edited by Ruth Seifert, 89–111. Münster: Lit Verlag.

Batinic, Jelena. 2001. "Feminism, Nationalism, and War: The 'Yugoslav Case' in Feminist Texts." *Journal of International Women's Studies* 3 (1): 1–23.

Beaumont, Peter. "Jolie Rape Film Divides Embittered Bosnia." *The Observer,* October 24, 2010.

Bećirbašić, Belma. 2006. "Muža su ubili, mene zlostavljali, a danas mi prijete!" *Dani Independent News Magazine,* January 10. http://www.bhdani.com/default.asp?kat= txt&broj_id=452&tekst_rb=9.

———. 2010. "Trgovanje emocijom žrtve." *Dani Independent News Magazine,* October 22. http://www.bhdani.com/default.asp?kat=txt&broj_id=697&tekst_rb=8.

Bećirbašić, Belma, and Dženana Šečić. 2005. "Invisible Casualties of War." *Institute for War and Peace Reporting, Balkan Crisis Report* 383. http://iwpr.net/report-news/ invisible-casualties-war.

Bećirević, Edina. 2010. "The Issue of Genocidal Intent and Denial of Genocide: A Case Study of Bosnia and Herzegovina." *East European Politics & Societies* 24 (4): 480–502.

Bejarano, Cynthia L. 2002. "Las Super Madres de Latino America: Transforming Motherhood by Challenging Violence in Mexico, Argentina, and El Salvador." *Frontiers: A Journal of Women Studies* 23 (1): 126–50.

Belić, Martina. 1995. "The Biggest Victims of the War." *War Report* 36:32–34.

Belloni, Roberto. 2001. "Civil Society and Peacebuilding in Bosnia and Herzegovina." *Journal of Peace Research* 38 (2): 163–80.

Benard, Cheryl, and Edit Schlaffer. 1992. "Kleiner als ein Stuck Dreck." *Der Spiegel,* December 7, 186. http://www.spiegel.de/spiegel/print/d-13682253.html.

Benderly, Jill. 1997a. "Feminist Movements in Yugoslavia, 1978–1992." In *State-Society Relations in Yugoslavia, 1945–1992,* edited by Melissa K. Bokovoy, Jill A. Irvine, and Carol S. Lilly, 183–209. New York: St. Martin's Press.

———. 1997b. "Rape, Feminism and Nationalism in the War in Yugoslav Successor States." In West 1997, 59–72.

Bieber, Florian. 2004. "Institutionalizing Ethnicity in the Western Balkans: Managing Change in Deeply Divided Societies." European Centre for Minority Issues (ECMI) Working Paper 19. http://www.ecmi.de/uploads/tx_lfpubdb/working_paper_19.pdf.

Blagojević, Marina. 1994. "War and Everyday Life: Deconstruction of Self-Sacrifice." *Sociologija* 36 (4): 469–82.

Bloch, Maurice E. 1998. *How We Think They Think: Anthropological Approaches to Cognition, Memory, and Literacy*. Boulder, CO: Westview.

Bogosavljević, Srdjan. 1992. "Bosna i Hercegovina u ogledalu statistike." In *Bosna i Hercegovina između rata i mira*, edited by Dušan Janjić, Paul Shoup, and Srdjan Bogosavljević, 24–40. Beograd: Dom Omladine.

Bonfiglioli, Chiara. 2008. "Belgrade, 1978. Remembering the Conference 'Drugarica Zena. Zensko Pitanje—Novi Pristup?'/'Comrade Woman. The Women's Question: A New Approach?' Thirty Years After." Master's thesis, University of Utrecht.

Böröcz, Jozsef. 2006. "Goodness Is Elsewhere: The Rule of European Difference." *Comparative Studies in Society and History* 48 (1): 110–38.

Bos, Pascale R. 2006. "Feminists Interpreting the Politics of Wartime Rape: Berlin, 1945; Yugoslavia, 1992–1993." *Signs* 31 (4): 995–1025.

Bose, Sumantra. 2002. *Bosnia after Dayton: Nationalist Partition and International Intervention*. New York: Oxford University Press.

Bosnian Women's Initiative. 1996. "Information Paper 3." September 12. UNHCR Bosnia-Herzegovina.

———. n.d. "Information Paper 1." UNHCR Bosnia-Herzegovina.

Botev, Nikolai. 2000. "Seeing Past the Barricades: Ethnic Intermarriage in Former Yugoslavia, 1962–1989." In *Neighbors at War: Anthropological Perspectives on Yugoslav Ethnicity, Culture, and History*, edited by Joel M. Halpern and David A. Kideckel, 219–33. University Park: Pennsylvania State University Press.

Bougarel, Xavier. 1996. "Bosnia and Hercegovina: State and Communitarianism." In *Yugoslavia and After: A Study in Fragmentation, Despair and Rebirth*, edited by David A. Dyker and Ivan Vejvoda, 87–115. London: Longman.

———. 1997. "From Young Muslims to Party of Democratic Action: The Emergence of a Pan-Islamist Trend in Bosnia-Herzegovina." *Islamic Studies* 36 (2–3): 533–49.

———. 1999. "Yugoslav Wars: The 'Revenge of the Countryside' between Sociological Reality and Nationalist Myth." *East European Quarterly* 33 (2): 157–75.

———. 2001. "L'Islam Bosniaque, entre identité culturelle et idéologie politique." In *Le Nouvel Islam balkanique: Les musulmans, acteurs du post-communisme, 1990–2000*, edited by Xavier Bougarel and Nathalie Clayer, 79–132. Paris: Maisonneuve & Larose.

———. 2003. "Islam and Politics in the Post-Communist Balkans, 1990–2000." In *New Approaches to Balkan Studies*, edited by Dimitris Keridis, Ellen Elias-Bursac, and Nicholas Yatromanolakis, 345–60. Dulles, VA: Brassey's.

———. 2004. *Bosna: Anatomija rata*. Translated by Jelena Stakic. Beograd: Fabrika knjiga.

———. 2005. "Balkan Muslim Diasporas and the Idea of a 'European Islam.'" In *Balkan Currents: Essays in Honour of Kjell Magnusson*, edited by Tomislav Dulić et al., 147–65. Uppsala: Centre for Multiethnic Research, Uppsala University.

———. 2006. "The Shadow of Heroes: Former Combatants in Post-War Bosnia-Herzegovina." *International Social Science Journal* 58 (189): 479–90.

———. 2007. "Death and the Nationalist: Martyrdom, War Memory and Veteran Identity among Bosnian Muslims." In Bougarel et al. 2007a, 167–92.

———. 2010. "Du code pénal au mémorandum: Les usages du terme génocide dans la Yougoslavie communiste." In *Peines de guerre: La justice pénale internationale et l'ex-Yougoslavie*, edited by Isabelle Delpla and Magali Bessone, 67–84. Paris: Editions de l'EHESS.

———. 2012. "Reopening the Wounds? The Parliament of Bosnia-Herzegovina and the Question of Bosniak Responsibilities." In *Investigating Srebrenica: Institutions, Facts, Responsibilities*, edited by Isabelle Delpla, Xavier Bougarel, and Jean-Louis Fournel, 104–30. New York: Berghahn Books.

Bougarel, Xavier, Elissa Helms, and Ger Duijzings, eds. 2007a. *The New Bosnian Mosaic: Identities, Memories and Moral Claims in a Post-War Society*. Aldershot, UK: Ashgate.

———. 2007b. Introduction to Bougarel et al. 2007a, 1–35.

Bracewell, Wendy. 1996. "Women, Motherhood, and Contemporary Serbian Nationalism." *Women's Studies International Forum* 19 (1–2): 25–33.

———. 2000. "Rape in Kosovo: Masculinity and Serbian Nationalism." *Nations and Nationalism* 6 (4): 563–90.

Bringa, Tone. 1995. *Being Muslim the Bosnian Way: Identity and Community in a Central Bosnian Village*. Princeton, NJ: Princeton University Press.

———. 2002. "Averted Gaze: Genocide in Bosnia-Herzegovina, 1992–1995." In *Annihilating Difference: The Anthropology of Genocide*, edited by Alexander Laban Hinton, 194–225. Berkeley: University of California Press.

———. 2005. "Haunted by the Imaginations of the Past: Robert Kaplan's Balkan Ghosts." In *Why America's Top Pundits Are Wrong: Anthropologists Talk Back*, edited by Catherine Besteman and Hugh Gusterson, 60–82. Berkeley: University of California Press.

Bringa, Tone, and Debbie Christie. 1993. *We Are All Neighbours*. Documentary Film. Granada Television, Disappearing Worlds series.

Bringa, Tone, with Peter Loizos. 2001. *Returning Home: Revival of a Bosnian Village*. Sarajevo: Saga film and video.

Brownmiller, Susan. 1975. *Against Our Will: Men, Women and Rape*. New York: Simon & Schuster.

Brubaker, Rogers. 2002. "Ethnicity without Groups." *Archives Européennes de Sociologie* 43 (2): 163–89.

Brunnbauer, Ulf. 2000. "From Equality without Democracy to Democracy without Equality? Women and Transition in South-East Europe." *South-East Europe Review* 3 (3): 151–68.

Burg, Steven L. 1983. "The Political Integration of Yugoslavia's Muslims: Determinants of Success and Failure." *The Carl Beck Papers in Russian and East European Studies* 203. doi:10.5195/cbp.1983.6.

Burg, Steven L., and Paul S. Shoup. 1999. *The War in Bosnia-Herzegovina: Ethnic Conflict and International Intervention*. Armonk, NY: M. E. Sharpe.

Burnet, Jennie E. 2012a. "Situating Sexual Violence in Rwanda (1990–2001): Sexual Agency, Sexual Consent, and the Political Economy of War." *African Studies Review* 55 (2): 97–118.

————. 2012b. *Genocide Lives in Us: Women, Memory, and Silence in Rwanda*. Madison: University of Wisconsin Press.

Buss, Doris E. 2007. "The Curious Visibility of Wartime Rape: Gender and Ethnicity in International Criminal Law." *The Windsor Yearbook of Access to Justice* 25:3–22.

————. 2009. "Rethinking 'Rape as a Weapon of War.'" *Feminist Legal Studies* 17 (2): 145–63.

Cacace, Rosaria, Arcangelo Menafra, and Agustino Miozzo. 1996. *This War Is Not Mine: From Women for Mostar*. Lissone, Italy: Cooperazione Italiana and the EU Administration of Mostar.

Campbell, David. 1998. *National Deconstruction: Violence, Identity, and Justice in Bosnia*. Minneapolis: University of Minnesota Press.

Čapo Žmegač, Jasna. 1999. "Ethnology, Mediterranean Studies, and Political Reticence in Croatia: From Mediterranean Constructs to Nation-Building." *Narodna umjetnost: Croatian Journal of Ethnology and Folklore Research* 36 (1): 33–52.

Carmichael, Cathie. 2002. *Ethnic Cleansing in the Balkans: Nationalism and the Destruction of Tradition*. London: Routledge.

Carothers, Thomas. 1996. *Assessing Democracy Assistance: The Case of Romania*. Washington, DC: Carnegie Endowment Book.

Carpenter, R. Charli. 2000. "Surfacing Children: Limitations of Genocidal Rape Discourse." *Human Rights Quarterly* 22 (2): 428–77.

————. 2003. "'Women and Children First': Gender, Norms, and Humanitarian Evacuation in the Balkans, 1991–95." *International Organization* 57 (4): 661–94.

————. 2006. *Innocent Women and Children: Gender, Norms and the Protection of Civilians*. Aldershot, UK: Ashgate.

————, ed. 2007. *Born of War: Protecting Children of Sexual Violence Survivors in Conflict Zones*. Bloomfield, CT: Kumarian Press.

————. 2010. *Forgetting Children Born of War: Setting the Human Rights Agenda in Bosnia and Beyond*. New York: Columbia University Press.

Carr, Cynthia. 1993. "Battle Scars: Feminism and Nationalism Clash in the Balkans." *The Village Voice* 38 (July 13): 25–32.

Cerić, Mustafa. 2006. "A Declaration of European Muslims." Speech, February 24, Zagreb. *Radio Free Europe/Radio Liberty*. http://www.rferl.org/content/article/1066751.html.

Chatterjee, Partha. 1989. "Colonialism, Nationalism, and Colonialized Women: The Contest in India." *American Ethnologist* 16 (4): 622–33.

Cockburn, Cynthia. 1998. *The Space between Us: Negotiating Gender and National Identities in Conflict*. London: Zed Books.

————. 2000. "The Anti-Essentialist Choice: Nationalism and Feminism in the Interaction between Two Women's Projects." *Nations and Nationalism* 6 (4): 611–29.

————. 2007. *From Where We Stand: War, Women's Activism and Feminist Analysis*. London: Zed Books.

Cockburn, Cynthia, Meliha Hubić, and Rada Stakić-Domuz. 2001. *Women Organizing for Change: A Study of Women's Local Integrative Organizations and the Pursuit of Democracy in Bosnia-Herzegovina*. Zenica: Medica Infoteka.

Cockburn, Cynthia, and Dubravka Žarkov, ed. 2002. *The Postwar Moment: Militaries, Masculinities, and International Peacekeeping*. London: Lawrence & Wishart.

Coles, Kimberley. 2007. *Democratic Designs: International Intervention and Electoral Practices in Postwar Bosnia-Herzegovina*. Ann Arbor: University of Michigan Press.

Collins, Patricia Hill. 1991. *Black Feminist Thought: Knowledge, Consciousness, and the Politics of Empowerment*. New York: Routledge.

Čolović, Ivan. 2002. *The Politics of Symbol in Serbia: Essays in Political Anthropology*. London: Hurst.

Cowan, Jane K. 1991. "Going Out for Coffee? Contesting the Grounds of Gendered Pleasures in Everyday Sociability." In *Contested Identities: Gender and Kinship in Modern Greece*, edited by Peter Loizos and Evthymios Papataxiarchis, 180–202. Princeton, NJ: Princeton University Press.

Dahlman, Carl, and Gearóid Ó Tuathail. 2005. "The Legacy of Ethnic Cleansing: The International Community and the Returns Process in Post-Dayton Bosnia-Herzegovina." *Political Geography* 24 (5): 569–99.

Daniel-Wrabetz, Joana. 2007. "Children Born of War Rape in Bosnia-Herzegovina and the Convention on the Rights of the Child." In Carpenter 2007, 21–39.

Das, Veena. 1995. "National Honor and Practical Kinship: Unwanted Women and Children." In *Conceiving the New World Order: The Global Politics of Reproduction*, edited by Faye D. Ginsburg and Rayna Rapp, 212–33. Berkeley: University of California Press.

———. 1996. "Language and Body: Transactions in the Construction of Pain." *Daedalus* 125 (1): 67–91.

Das, Veena, and Arthur Kleinman. 2000. Introduction to *Violence and Subjectivity*, edited by Veena Das and Arthur Kleinman, et al., 1–18. Berkeley: University of California Press.

———. 2001. Introduction to *Remaking a World: Violence, Social Suffering, and Recovery*, edited by Veena Das and Arthur Kleinman, et al., 1–30. Berkeley: University of California Press.

Deacon, B., and P. Stubbs. 1998. "International Actors and Social Policy Development in Bosnia-Herzegovina: Globalism and the 'New Feudalism.'" *Journal of European Social Policy* 8 (2): 99–115.

de Alwis, Malathi. 1998. "Motherhood as a Space of Protest." In *Appropriating Gender: Women's Activism and Politicized Religion in South Asia*, edited by Patricia Jeffery and Amrita Basu, 185–201. New York: Routledge.

Delpla, Isabelle. 2007. "In the Midst of Injustice: The ICTY from the Perspective of Some Victim Associations." In Bougarel et al. 2007a, 211–34.

Denich, Bette. 1974. "Sex and Power in the Balkans." In *Woman, Culture, and Society*, edited by Michelle Z. Rosaldo and Louise Lamphere, 243–62. Stanford, CA: Stanford University Press.

———. 1976. "Urbanization and Women's Roles in Yugoslavia." *Anthropological Quarterly* 49 (1): 11–19.

———. 1977. "Women, Work and Power in Modern Yugoslavia." In *Sexual Stratification: A Cross-Cultural View*, edited by Alice Schlegel, 215–44. New York: Columbia University Press.

———. 1994. "Dismembering Yugoslavia: Nationalist Ideologies and the Symbolic Revival of Genocide." *American Ethnologist* 21 (2): 367–90.

———. 1995. "Of Arms, Men, and Ethnic War in (Former) Yugoslavia." In *Feminism, Nationalism and Militarism*, edited by Constance R. Sutton, 61–71. Arlington, VA: American Anthropological Association.

De Pina-Cabral, João. 1989. "The Mediterranean as a Category of Regional Comparison: A Critical View." *Current Anthropology* 30 (3): 399–406.

De Soto, Hermine G. 1994. "In the Name of the Folk: Women and Nation in the New Germany." *UCLA Women's Law Journal* 5: 83–101.

De Soto, Hermine G., and Nora Dudwick, eds. 2000. *Fieldwork Dilemmas: Anthropologists in Postsocialist States*. Madison: University of Wisconsin Press.

Dević, Ana. 2000. "Women's Activism between Private and Public Spaces: The Case of the Women in Black in Serbia." In Slapšak 2000, 195–209.

Dežulović, Boris. 2010. "Angelina u Zemlji Stvarnosti." *Nezavisne novine*, October 20. http://www.nezavisne.com/komentari/kolumne/Angelina-u-zemlji-stvarnosti-705
41.html.

Dobos, Manuela. 1983. "The Women's Movement in Yugoslavia: The Case of the Conference for the Social Activity of Women in Croatia, 1965–1974." *Frontiers: A Journal of Women Studies* 7 (2): 47–55.

Donia, Robert J. 1981. *Islam under the Double Eagle: The Muslims of Bosnia and Hercegovina, 1878–1914*. New York: Columbia University Press.

Donia, Robert J., and John V. A. Fine. 1994. *Bosnia and Hercegovina: A Tradition Betrayed*. London: Hurst.

Dragović-Soso, Jasna. 2002. *Saviours of the Nation: Serbia's Intellectual Opposition and the Revival of Nationalism*. London: Hurst.

Drakulić, Slavenka. 1991. *How We Survived Communism and Even Laughed*. New York: W. W. Norton.

———. 1993a. *The Balkan Express: Fragments from the Other Side of War*. London: Hutchinson.

———. 1993b. "Women and the New Democracy in the Former Yugoslavia." In Funk and Mueller 1993, 123–30.

———. 2010. "Imaju li žrtve pravo na cenzuru?" *Komentari*, October 14. http://www.tportal.hr/komentari/91254/Imaju-li-zrtve-pravo-na-cenzuru.html.

Drezgić, Rada. 2000. "Demographic Nationalism in the Gender Perspective." In Slapšak 2000, 211–33.

———. 2004. "The Politics of Abortion and Contraception." *Sociologija* 46 (2): 97–114.

———. 2010. "Policies and Practices of Fertility Control under the State Socialism." *The History of the Family* 15 (2): 191–205.

Drezgić, Rada, and Dubravka Žarkov. 2005. "Feminističke nevolje s Balkanom." *Sociologija* 47 (4): 289–306.

Duijzings, Ger. 2007. "Commemorating Srebrenica: Histories of Violence and the Politics of Memory in Eastern Bosnia." In Bougarel et al. 2007a, 141–66.

Dulić, Tomislav. 2005. "Utopias of Nation: Local Mass Killing in Bosnia and Herzegovina, 1941–42." PhD diss., Uppsala University.

Đurić Kuzmanović, Tatjana. 2001. "From State Directed Non-Development and Organized Gender Violence to Transition in Vojvodina and Serbia." In *The Paradoxes of Progress: Globalization and Postsocialist Cultures*, edited by Rachael Stryker and Jennifer Patico, 27–35. Berkeley, CA: Kroeber Anthropological Society.

———. 2002. *Rodnost i razvoj u Srbiji: Od dirigovanog nerazvoja do tranzicije/Gender and Development in Serbia: From Directed Nondevelopment to Transition*. Dual language edition. Novi Sad: Budučnost and Ženske studije i istraživanje.

Einhorn, Barbara. 1996. "Gender and Citizenship in East Central Europe after the End of State Socialist Policies for Women's 'Emancipation.'" In *Citizenship and Democratic Control in Contemporary Europe*, edited by Barbara Einhorn, Mary Kaldor, and Zdenek Kavan, 69–86. Cheltenham, UK: Edward Elgar.

Elliston, Deborah. 2008. "A Passion for the Nation: Masculinity, Modernity, and Nationalist Struggle." *American Ethnologist* 31 (4): 606–30.

Engle, Karen. 2005. "Feminism and Its (dis)contents: Criminalizing Wartime Rape in Bosnia and Herzegovina." *The American Journal of International Law* 99 (4): 778–816.

Enloe, Cynthia H. 1990a. *Bananas, Beaches & Bases: Making Feminist Sense of International Politics*. Berkeley: University of California Press.

———. 1990b. "Womenandchildren: Making Feminist Sense of the Persian Gulf Crisis." *The Village Voice* 25 (September): 30–31.

Erjavec, Karmen, and Zala Volčič. 2010. "Living with the Sins of Their Fathers: An Analysis of Self-Representation of Adolescents Born of War Rape." *Journal of Adolescent Research* 25 (3): 359–86.

Escobar, Arturo. 1995. *Encountering Development: The Making and Unmaking of the Third World*. Princeton, NJ: Princeton University Press.

Evangelista, Matthew. 2011. *Gender, Nationalism, and War: Conflict on the Movie Screen*. Cambridge: Cambridge University Press.

Ferguson, James. 1990. *The Anti-Politics Machine: "Development," Depoliticization, and Bureaucratic Power in Lesotho*. Cambridge: Cambridge University Press.

Filipović, Muhamed. 1999. "Sociopsihološka i antropološka analiza zločinačkog karaktera, osobito zločina ispoljenih prema Bošnjacima i Bošnjakinjama tokom Srpske agresije na Bosnu i Hercegovinu." In Ajanović 1999, 61–69.

Fisher, Siobhán K. 1996. "Occupation of the Womb: Forced Impregnation as Genocide." *Duke Law Journal* 46 (1): 91–133.

Fisher, William F. 1997. "Doing Good? The Politics and Antipolitics of NGO Practices." *Annual Review of Anthropology* 26 (1): 439–64.

Fleming, Katherine E. 1999. *The Muslim Bonaparte: Diplomacy and Orientalism in Ali Pasha's Greece*. Princeton, NJ: Princeton University Press.

———. 2000. "Orientalism, the Balkans, and Balkan Historiography." *The American Historical Review* 105 (4): 1218–33.

Fox, Richard G. 1996. "Gandhi and Feminized Nationalism in India." In Williams 1996, 37–49.

Fraser, Nancy. 1997. *Justice Interruptus: Critical Reflections on the "Postsocialist" Condition*. New York: Routledge.

Fridman, Orli. 2006. "Alternative Voices in Public Urban Spaces: Serbia's Women in Black." *Ethnologia Balkanica* 10:291–303.

———. 2011. "'It Was Like Fighting a War with Our Own People': Anti-War Activism in Serbia during the 1990s." *Nationalities Papers* 39 (4): 507–22.

Funk, Nanette, and Magda Mueller, eds. 1993. *Gender Politics and Post-Communism: Reflections from Eastern Europe and the Former Soviet Union*. New York: Routledge.

Gagnon, V. P., Jr. 1994a. "Reaction to the Special Issue of AEER War among the Yugoslavs." *Anthropology of East Europe Review* 12 (1): 79–81.

———. 1994b. "Reply to Simic." *Anthropology of East Europe Review* 12 (2): 51–52.

———. 2002. "International NGOs in Bosnia-Herzegovina: Attempting to Build Civil Society." In *The Power and Limits of NGOs: A Critical Look at Building Democracy in Eastern Europe and Eurasia*, edited by Sarah E. Mendelson and John K. Glenn, 207–331. New York: Columbia University Press.

———. 2004. *The Myth of Ethnic War: Serbia and Croatia in the 1990s*. Ithaca, NY: Cornell University Press.

Gal, Susan. 1994. "Gender in the Post-Socialist Transition: The Abortion Debate in Hungary." *East European Politics & Societies* 8 (2): 256–86.

———. 2002. "A Semiotics of the Public/Private Distinction." *Differences* 13 (1): 77–95.

———. 2003. "Movements of Feminism: The Circulation of Discourses about Women." In *Recognition Struggles and Social Movements: Contested Identities, Agency and Power*, edited by Barbara Hobson, 93–118. Cambridge: Cambridge University Press.

———. 2005. "Language Ideologies Compared: Metaphors of Public/Private." *Journal of Linguistic Anthropology* 15 (1): 23–37.

Gal, Susan, and Gail Kligman. 2000. *The Politics of Gender after Socialism: A Comparative-Historical Essay*. Princeton, NJ: Princeton University Press.

Ghodsee, Kristen Rogheh. 2005. *The Red Riviera: Gender, Tourism, and Postsocialism on the Black Sea*. Durham, NC: Duke University Press.

———. 2009. *Muslim Lives in Eastern Europe: Gender, Ethnicity, and the Transformation of Islam in Postsocialist Bulgaria*. Princeton, NJ: Princeton University Press.

Gilbert, Andrew. 2006. "The Past in Parenthesis: (Non) Post-Socialism in Post-War Bosnia-Herzegovina." *Anthropology Today* 22 (4): 14–18.

———. 2008. "Foreign Authority and the Politics of Impartiality in Postwar Bosnia-Herzegovina." PhD diss., University of Chicago.

Gilbert, Andrew, Jessica Greenberg, Elissa Helms, and Stef Jansen. 2008. "Reconsidering Postsocialism from the Margins of Europe: Hope, Time and Normalcy in Post-Yugoslav Societies." *Anthropology News* 49 (8): 10–11.

Giles, Wenona M., Malathi de Alwis, Edith Klein, and Neluka Silva, eds. 2003. *Feminists under Fire: Exchanges across War Zones*. Toronto: Between the Lines.

Giles, Wenona M., and Jennifer Hyndman, eds. 2004. *Sites of Violence: Gender and Conflict Zones*. Berkeley: University of California Press.

Gilmore, David D. 1982. "Anthropology of the Mediterranean Area." *Annual Review of Anthropology* 11 (1): 175–205.

Gordiejew, Paul B. 2006. "Playing with Jews in the Fields of Nations: Symbolic Contests in the Former Yugoslavia." *Social Identities* 12 (3): 377–400.

Goven, Joanna. 1993. "Gender Politics in Hungary: Autonomy and Antifeminism." In Funk and Mueller 1993, 224–40.

Grandits, Hannes. 2007. "The Power of 'Armchair Politicians': Ethnic Loyalty and Political Factionalism among Herzegovinian Croats." In Bougarel et al. 2007a, 101–22.

Green, Sarah F. 2005. *Notes from the Balkans: Locating Marginality and Ambiguity on the Greek-Albanian Border*. Princeton, NJ: Princeton University Press.

Greenberg, Jessica. 2006. "'Goodbye Serbian Kennedy': Zoran Đinđić and the New Democratic Masculinity in Serbia." *East European Politics & Societies* 20 (1): 126–51.

———. 2011. "On the Road to Normal: Negotiating Agency and State Sovereignty in Postsocialist Serbia." *American Anthropologist* 113 (1): 88–100.

Gregson, Kendra. 2000. *Veterans' Programs in Bosnia-Herzegovina*. Sarajevo: World Bank.

Grødeland, Åse Berit. 2006. "Public Perceptions of Non-Governmental Organisations in Serbia, Bosnia & Herzegovina, and Macedonia." *Communist and Post-Communist Studies* 39 (2): 221–46.

Grossmann, Atina. 1995. "A Question of Silence: The Rape of German Women by Occupation Soldiers." *October* 72:43–63.

Hadžiahmić, Lejla. 2010. "Women-Combatants in Defense of Sarajevo: Agents or Victims." Master's thesis, University of Sarajevo, Center for Interdisciplinary Postgraduate Studies, Gender Studies Program.

Hadžić, Mehmedalija, ed. 1996. *Mješoviti brakovi*. Sarajevo: Svjetlost štampa.

Hajdarpašić, Edin. 2008. "Museums, Multiculturalism, and the Remaking of Postwar Sarajevo." In *(Re)Visualizing National History: Museums and National Identities in Europe in the New Millenium*, edited by Robin Ostow, 109–39. Toronto: University of Toronto Press.

Hakalović, Anela. "Žrtvovanje Žrtve: Kako Modeli Svjedočenja o Ratnim Silovanjima od Individualne Traume Prave Traumu Kolektiva." *Puls Demokratije*. http://arhiva .pulsdemokratije.net/index.php?id=2140&l=bs.

Haney, Lynne Allison. 2002. *Inventing the Needy: Gender and the Politics of Welfare in Hungary*. Berkeley: University of California Press.

Hansen, Lene. 2006. *Security as Practice: Discourse Analysis and the Bosnian War*. New York: Routledge.

Harrington, Carol. 2010. *Politicization of Sexual Violence: From Abolitionism to Peacekeeping*. Gender in a Global/Local World. Farnham, UK: Ashgate.

———. 2011. "Resolution 1325 and Post-Cold War Feminist Politics." *International Feminist Journal of Politics* 13 (4): 557–75.

Hashamova, Yana. 2012. "War Rape: (Re)Defining Motherhood, Fatherhood, and Nationhood." In *Embracing Arms: Cultural Representation of Slavic and Balkan Women in War*, edited by Helena Goscilo and Yana Hashamova, 233–51. Budapest: Central European University Press.

Haskić, Sabiha. 2000. "Žene autori i tematizacija islamskih problema kroz Pereporod i Glasnik 1970–1980 god." Bachelor's thesis, University of Sarajevo, Faculty of Islamic Sciences.

Hayden, Robert M. 1994. "Recounting the Dead: The Rediscovery and Redefinition of Wartime Massacres in Late- and Post-Communist Yugoslavia." In *Memory, History, and Opposition under State Socialism*, edited by Rubie S. Watson, 167–84. Santa Fe, NM: School of American Research Press.

———. 1996. "Imagined Communities and Real Victims: Self-Determination and Ethnic Cleansing in Yugoslavia." *American Ethnologist* 23 (4): 783–801.

———. 2000. "Rape and Rape Avoidance in Ethno-National Conflicts: Sexual Violence in Liminalized States." *American Anthropologist* 102 (1): 27–41.

———. 2002. "Antagonistic Tolerance: Competitive Sharing of Religious Sites in South Asia and the Balkans." *Current Anthropology* 43 (2): 205–31.

———. 2008a. "'Genocide Denial' Laws as Secular Heresy: A Critical Analysis with Reference to Bosnia." *Slavic Review* 67 (2): 384–407.

———. 2008b. "Mass Killings and Images of Genocide in Bosnia, 1941–5 and 1992–5." In *The Historiography of Genocide*, edited by Dan Stone, 487–516. New York: Palgrave Macmillan.

Helms, Elissa. 2003. "Women as Agents of Ethnic Reconciliation? Women's NGOs and International Intervention in Postwar Bosnia-Herzegovina." *Women's Studies International Forum* 26 (1): 15–33.

———. 2006. "Gendered Transformations of State Power: Masculinity, International Intervention, and the Bosnian Police." *Nationalities Papers* 34 (3): 343–61.

———. 2007. "'Politics Is a Whore': Women, Morality, and Victimhood in Post-War Bosnia-Herzegovina." In Bougarel et al. 2007a, 235–53.

———. 2008. "East and West Kiss: Gender, Orientalism, and Balkanism in Muslim-Majority Bosnia-Herzegovina." *Slavic Review* 67 (1): 88–119.

———. 2010a. "The Gender of Coffee: Women and Reconciliation Initiatives in Post-War Bosnia and Herzegovina." *Focaal: Journal of Global and Historical Anthropology* 57 (Summer): 17–32.

———. 2010b. "Justice et genre: Mobiliser les survivantes de guerre Bosniaques." In *Peines de guerre: La justice pénale internationale et l'ex-Yougoslavie*, edited by Isabelle Delpla and Magali Bessone, 249–65. Paris: Editions de l'EHESS.

———. 2012. "'Bosnian Girl': Nationalism and Innocence through Images of Women." In *Retracing Images: Visual Culture after Yugoslavia*, edited by Daniel Šuber and Slobodan Karamanić, 195–222. Leiden: Brill.

———. Forthcoming. "The Movement-ization of NGOs? Women's Organizing after the Bosnian War." In *Theorizing NGOs: States, Feminisms, and Neoliberalisms*, edited by Victoria Bernal and Inderpal Grewal. Durham, NC: Duke University Press.

Henderson, Sarah L. 2003. *Building Democracy in Contemporary Russia: Western Support for Grassroots Organizations.* Ithaca, NY: Cornell University Press.

Heng, Geraldine, and Janadas Devan. 1992. "State Fatherhood: The Politics of Sexuality, Nationalism and Race in Singapore." In Parker et al. 1992, 343–64.

Herzfeld, Michael. 1980. "Honour and Shame: Problems in the Comparative Analysis of Moral Systems." *Man* 15 (2): 339–51.

———. 1987. *Anthropology through the Looking-Glass: Critical Ethnography in the Margins of Europe.* Cambridge: Cambridge University Press.

Heywood, Leslie, and Jennifer Drake, eds. 1997. *Third Wave Agenda: Being Feminist, Doing Feminism.* Minneapolis: University of Minnesota Press.

Hilhorst, Dorothea. 2003. *The Real World of NGOs: Discourses, Diversity, and Development.* London: Zed Books.

Hoare, Marko A. 2004. *How Bosnia Armed.* London: Saqi Books.

———. 2010. "Bosnia-Hercegovina and International Justice: Past Failures and Future Solutions." *East European Politics & Societies* 24 (2): 191–205.

hooks, bell. 1984. *Feminist Theory: From Margin to Center.* Boston: South End Press.

Hromadžić, Azra. 2007. "Challenging the Discourse of Bosnian War Rapes." In *Living Gender after Communism*, edited by Janet Elise Johnson and Jean C. Robinson, 169–84. Bloomington: Indiana University Press.

Hrycak, Alexandra. 2006. "Foundation Feminism and the Articulation of Hybrid Feminisms in Post-Socialist Ukraine." *East European Politics & Societies* 20 (1): 69–100.

Hunt, Swanee. 1999. "Silovanje." In Ajanović 1999, 75–78.

———. 2004. *This Was Not Our War: Bosnian Women Reclaiming the Peace.* Durham, NC: Duke University Press.

Husanović, Jasmina. 2009. "The Politics of Gender, Witnessing, Postcoloniality and Trauma." *Feminist Theory* 10 (1): 99–119.

———. 2010. *Između traume, imaginacije i nade: Kritički ogledi o kulturnoj produkciji i emancipativnoj politici.* Beograd: Fabrika knjiga.

———. 2011. "Culture of Trauma and Identity Politics—Critical Frames and Emancipatory Lenses of Cultural and Knowledge Production." In *Cultural Identity Politics in the (Post-) Transitional Societies: Cultural Transitions in Southeastern Europe*, edited by Aldo Milohnić and Nada Švob-Ðokić, 61–68. Zagreb: Institute for International Relations.

Husanović, Jasmina, and Damir Arsenijević, eds. 2006. *Na tragu nove politike: Kultura i obrazovanje u Bosni i Hercegovini.* Tuzla: Centar Grad.

Ilić, Dejan. 2009. "Kruna od trnja." *Peščanik*, March 1. http://pescanik.net/2009/03/kruna-od-trnja/.

Inglis, Shelley. 1998. "Re/Constructing Right(s): The Dayton Peace Agreement, International Civil Society Development, and Gender in Postwar Bosnia-Herzegovina." *Columbia Human Rights Law Review* 30:65–121.

International Bureau for Humanitarian Issues (IBHI). 1998. *Human Development Report: Bosnia and Herzegovina.* Sarajevo: IBHI and UNDP.

International Labor Organization (ILO). 2009. *Report on the Pension Reform in Bosnia and Herzegovina: First Assessment*. Budapest: International Labor Office.

Irish, John. 2010. "Angelina Jolie Defends Bosnian Directorial Debut." *Reuters*, December 2. http://www.reuters.com/article/idUSTRE6B12A920101202.

Irvine, Jill. 1998. "Public Opinion and the Political Position of Women in Croatia." In Rueschemeyer 1998, 215–34.

Irvine, Judith T., and Susan Gal. 2000. "Language Ideology and Linguistic Differentiation." In *Regimes of Language: Ideologies, Polities, and Identities*, edited by Paul V. Kroskrity, 35–83. Santa Fe, NM: School of American Research Press.

Ishkanian, Armine. 2000. "Gender and NGOs in Armenia." *The Anthropology of East Europe Review* 18 (2): 17–22.

———. 2003. "Importing Civil Society? The Emergence of Armenia's NGO Sector and the Impact of Western Aid on Its Development." *Armenian Forum: A Journal of Contemporary Affairs* 3 (1): 7–36.

Ito, A. 2001. "Politicisation of Minority Return in Bosnia and Herzegovina—The First Five Years Examined." *International Journal of Refugee Law* 13 (1–2): 98–122.

Iveković, Rada. 1993. "Women, Nationalism and War: 'Make Love Not War.'" *Hypatia* 8 (4): 113–26.

———. 1997. "Women, Politics, Peace." In Kašić 1997, 95–106.

Iveković, Rada, and Julie Mostov, eds. 2002. *From Gender to Nation*. Ravenna: Longo Editore.

Izetbegović, Alija. 1983. "The Islamic Declaration." *South Slavic Journal* 6 (1): 55–89.

Jalušič, Vlasta. 2004. "Gender and Victimization of the Nation as Pre- and Post-War Identity Discourse." In *The Violent Dissolution of Yugoslavia: Causes, Dynamics, and Effects*, edited by Miroslav Hadžić, 145–65. Belgrade: Centre for Civil-Military Relations.

———. 2007. "Organized Innocence and Exclusion: 'Nation-States' in the Aftermath of War and Collective Crime." *Social Research: An International Quarterly* 74 (4): 1173–200.

Jancar, Barbara. 1988. "Neofeminism in Yugoslavia: A Closer Look." *Women and Politics* 8 (1): 1–30.

Jancar-Webster, Barbara. 1990. *Women & Revolution in Yugoslavia, 1941–1945*. Denver, CO: Arden Press.

Jansen, Stef. 2002. "Svakodnevni Orijentalizam: Doživljaj 'Balkana'/'Evrope' u Beogradu i Zagrebu." *Filozofija i društvo* (18): 33–72.

———. 2003. "Why Do They Hate Us? Everyday Serbian Nationalist Knowledge of Muslim Hatred." *Journal of Mediterranean Studies* 13 (2): 215–37.

———. 2005a. *Antinacionalizam: Etnografija otpora u Beogradu i Zagrebu*. Beograd: Biblioteka XX vek.

———. 2005b. "Who's Afraid of White Socks? Towards a Critical Understanding of Post-Yugoslav Urban Self-Perceptions." *Ethnologia Balkanica* 9:151–67.

———. 2006. "The Privatisation of Home and Hope: Return, Reforms and the Foreign Intervention in Bosnia-Herzegovina." *Dialectical Anthropology* 30 (3): 177–99.

————. 2007. "Troubled Locations: Return, the Life Course, and Transformations of 'Home' in Bosnia-Herzegovina." *Focaal: Journal of Global and Historical Anthropology* 49 (Summer): 15–30.

————. 2009. "After the Red Passport: Towards an Anthropology of the Everyday Geopolitics of Entrapment in the EU's 'Immediate Outside.'" *Journal of the Royal Anthropological Institute* 15 (4) (December): 815–32.

————. 2010. "Of Wolves and Men: Postwar Reconciliation and the Gender of Inter-National Encounters." *Focaal: Journal of Global and Historical Anthropology* 57 (Summer): 33–49.

Jansen, Stef, and Elissa Helms. 2009. "The 'White Plague': National-Demographic Rhetoric and Its Gendered Resonance after the Post-Yugoslav Wars." In *Gender Dynamics and Post-Conflict Reconstruction*, edited by Christine Eifler and Ruth Seifert, 219–43. Frankfurt: Peter Lang.

Jašarević, Larisa. 2007. "Everyday Work: Subsistence Economy, Social Belonging and Moralities of Exchange at a Bosnian (Black) Market." In Bougarel et al. 2007a, 273–93.

Jayawardena, Kumari. 1986. *Feminism and Nationalism in the Third World*. London: Zed Books.

Jones, Adam. 1994. "Gender and Ethnic Conflict in Ex-Yugoslavia." *Ethnic and Racial Studies* 17 (1): 115–34.

————. 2000. "Gendercide and Genocide." *Journal of Genocide Research* 2 (2): 185–211.

Jovanović, Nebojša. 2010. "Untitled Censorship Story." *Mediacentar_Online.* http://www.media.ba/bs/etikaregulativa-novinarstvo-etika/untitled-censorship-story.

Kabeer, Naila. 1994. *Reversed Realities: Gender Hierarchies in Development Thought.* London: Verso.

Kajinić, Sanja. 2010. "'Battle for Sarajevo' as 'Metropolis': Closure of the First Queer Sarajevo Festival according to Liberal Press." *Anthropology of East Europe Review* 28 (1): 62–82.

Kajosević, Indira. 1995. "Women sans Frontiers." *War Report* 36 (September): 43–44.

Kaldor, Mary. 2007. *New and Old Wars: Organized Violence in a Global Era.* 2nd ed. Stanford, CA: Stanford University Press.

Kalosieh, Adrienne. 2003. "Consent to Genocide: The ICTY's Improper Use of the Consent Paradigm to Prosecute Genocidal Rape in Foca." *Women's Rights Law Reporter* 24 (2): 121.

Kanaaneh, Rhoda. 2005. "Boys or Men? Duped or 'Made'? Palestinian Soldiers in the Israeli Military." *American Ethnologist* 32 (2): 260–75.

Kaplan, Gisela. 1997. "Feminism and Nationalism: The European Case." In West 1997, 3–40.

Kaplan, Robert D. 1993. *Balkan Ghosts: A Journey through History.* New York: St. Martin's Press.

Kapur, Ratna. 2002. "The Tragedy of Victimization Rhetoric: Resurrecting the 'Native' Subject in International/Post-Colonial Feminist Legal Politics." *Harvard Human Rights Journal* 15:1–37.

Karge, Heike. 2010. "Transnational Knowledge into Yugoslav Practices? The Legacy of the Second World War on Social Welfare Policy in Yugoslavia." *Comparativ: Zeitschrift für Globalgeschichte und vergleichende Gesellschaftsforschung* 5 (10): 75–86.

Karić, Enes. 2002. "Is 'Euro-Islam' a Myth, Challenge or a Real Opportunity for Muslims and Europe?" *Journal of Muslim Minority Affairs* 22 (2): 435–42.

Kašić, Biljana. 2000. "The Aesthetic of the Victim within the Discourse of War." In Slapšak 2000, 271–84.

Kasumagić, Ismet. 1997. "Fafaron u Rahat-lokumu." *Dnevni avaz*, May 30.

Kaufman, Joyce P., and Kristen P. Williams. 2007. *Women, the State, and War: A Comparative Perspective on Citizenship and Nationalism.* Lanham, MD: Lexington Books.

Kervatin, Miriam. 1998. *Javno zagovaranje: Žene za društvene promjene u zemljama sljednicama bivše Jugoslavije.* Zagreb: STAR/Delphi International.

Kesić, Vesna. 1994. "Response to Catherine MacKinnon's Article 'Turning Rape into Pornography: Postmodern Genocide.'" *Hastings Women's Law Journal* 5:267–80.

———. 1995. "From Respect to Rape." *War Report* 36 (September): 36–38.

———. 1997. "Confessions of a 'Yugo-Nostalgic' Witch." In *Ana's Land: Sisterhood in Eastern Europe*, edited by Tanya Renne, 195–200. Boulder, CO: Westview Press.

Kligman, Gail. 1998. *The Politics of Duplicity: Controlling Reproduction in Ceausescu's Romania.* Berkeley: University of California Press.

Knežević, Djurdja. 1993. "Abused and Misused: Women and Their Political Exploitation." *Connexions* 42:12–13.

Kolind, Torsten. 2007. "In Search of 'Decent People': Resistance to the Ethnicization of Everyday Life among the Muslims of Stolac." In Bougarel et al. 2007a, 123–41.

Korać, Maja. 1994. "Representation of Mass Rape in Ethnic Conflicts in What Was Yugoslavia." *Sociologija* 36 (4): 495–514.

———. 1998. "Ethnic Nationalism, Wars and the Patterns of Social, Political and Sexual Violence against Women: The Case of Post-Yugoslav Countries." *Identities* 5 (2): 153–55.

Kouvo, Sari, and Corey Levine. 2008. "Calling a Spade a Spade: Tackling the 'Women and Peace' Orthodoxy." *Feminist Legal Studies* 16 (3): 363–67.

Kuehnast, Kathleen. 2000. "Ethnographic Encounters in Post-Soviet Kyrgyzstan: Dilemmas of Gender, Poverty, and the Cold War." In De Soto and Dudwick 2000, 100–118.

Kurtović, Larisa. 2011. "What Is a Nationalist? Some Thoughts on the Question from Bosnia-Herzegovina." *Anthropology of East Europe Review* 29 (2): 242–53.

———. 2012. "Politics of Impasse: Specters of Socialism and the Struggles for the Future in Postwar Bosnia-Herzegovina." PhD diss., University of California, Berkeley.

Lamphere, Louise. 1993. "The Domestic Sphere of Women and the Public World of Men: The Strengths and Limitations of an Anthropological Dichotomy." In *Gender in Cross-Cultural Perspective*, edited by Caroline Brettell and Carolyn Fishel Sargent, 82–92. Englewood Cliffs, NJ: Prentice Hall.

Lang, Sabine. 1997. "The NGOization of Feminism: Institutionalization and Institution-Building within the German Women's Movements." In *Transitions,*

Environments, Translations: Feminisms in International Politics, edited by Cora Kaplan, Debra Keates, and Joan Wallach Scott, 101–20. New York: Routledge.

Latić, Džemaludin. 1994. "Bezbojni." *Ljiljan*, June 10, 40.

Latić, Nedžad. 1993. "Pobjeda ili časna smrt!" *Ljiljan*, September 29, 26–27.

———. 1994. "Lažna kraljica obeščašćenih žena." *Ljiljan*, January 19, 21.

Lazarevska, Alma. 1995. "Hewers of Wood and Carriers of Water." *War Report* 36 (September): 46.

Lendvai, Noemi, and Paul Stubbs. 2007. "Policies as Translation: Situating Trans-National Social Policies." In *Policy Reconsidered: Meanings, Politics and Practices*, edited by Susan M. Hodgson and Zoë Irving, 173–89. Bristol, UK: Policy Press.

———. 2009. "Assemblages, Translation, and Intermediaries in South East Europe." *European Societies* 11 (5) (December): 673–95.

Lentin, Ronit, ed. 1997. *Gender and Catastrophe*. London: Zed Books.

Ler-Sofronić, Nada. 1998. "Women." In *Human Development Report: Bosnia and Herzegovina*, by International Bureau for Humanitarian Issues (IBHI). Sarajevo: IBHI and UNDP.

Leydesdorff, Selma. 2011. *Surviving the Bosnian Genocide: The Women of Srebrenica Speak*. Bloomington: Indiana University Press.

Lie, John. 1997. "The State as Pimp: Prostitution and the Patriarchal State in Japan in the 1940s." *Sociological Quarterly* 38 (2): 251–63.

Lilly, Carol S., and Jill A. Irvine. 2002. "Negotiating Interests: Women and Nationalism in Serbia and Croatia, 1990–1997." *East European Politics & Societies* 16 (1): 109–44.

Lindsey, Rose. 2002. "From Atrocity to Data: Historiographies of Rape in Former Yugoslavia and the Gendering of Genocide." *Patterns of Prejudice* 36 (4): 59–78.

Lindstrom, Nicole. 2003. "Between Europe and the Balkans: Mapping Slovenia and Croatia's 'Return to Europe' in the 1990s." *Dialectical Anthropology* 27 (3): 313–29.

Lithander, Anna, ed. 2000. *Engendering the Peace Process: A Gender Approach to Dayton—and Beyond*. Stockholm: Kvinna till kvinna.

Lockwood, William G. 1975. *European Moslems: Economy and Ethnicity in Western Bosnia*. New York: Academic Press.

Lórand, Zsofia. Forthcoming. "Learning a Feminist Language: The Intellectual History of Feminism in Yugoslavia in the 1970s and 1980s." PhD diss., Central European University, Budapest.

Lorentzen, Lois Ann, and Jennifer E. Turpin, eds. 1998. *The Women and War Reader*. New York: New York University Press.

MacDonald, David Bruce. 2002. *Balkan Holocausts? Serbian and Croatian Victim-Centered Propaganda and the War in Yugoslavia*. Manchester, UK: Manchester University Press.

Maček, Ivana. 2005. "Sarajevan Soldier Story." In *No Peace, No War: An Anthropology of Contemporary Armed Conflicts*, edited by Paul Richards, 57–76. Athens: Ohio University Press.

———. 2009. *Sarajevo under Siege: Anthropology in Wartime*. Philadelphia: University of Pennsylvania Press.

MacKinnon, Catherine A. 1993a. "Crimes of War, Crimes of Peace." *UCLA Women's Law Journal* 4:59–86.

———. 1993b. "Turning Rape into Pornography: Postmodern Genocide." *Ms. Magazine* 4 (1) (July/August): 24–30.

———. 1994. "Rape, Genocide, and Women's Human Rights." *Harvard Women's Law Journal* 17:5–17.

Malkki, Liisa H. 1995. *Purity and Exile: Violence, Memory, and National Cosmology Among Hutu Refugees in Tanzania*. Chicago: University of Chicago Press.

———.1996. "Speechless Emissaries: Refugees, Humanitarianism, and Dehistoricization." *Cultural Anthropology* 11 (3): 377–404.

Mamdani, Mahmood. 2002. "Good Muslim, Bad Muslim: A Political Perspective on Culture and Terrorism." *American Anthropologist* 104 (3): 766–75.

Markešić, fra. Luka. 1999. "Zločin nad ženom, majka života." In Ajanović 1999, 459–62.

Markowitz, Fran. 2006. "Census and Sensibilities in Sarajevo." *Comparative Studies in Society and History* 49 (1): 40–73.

———. 2010. *Sarajevo: A Bosnian Kaleidoscope*. Urbana: University of Illinois Press.

Massad, Joseph. 1995. "Conceiving the Masculine: Gender and Palestinian Nationalism." *The Middle East Journal* 49 (3): 467–83.

Massey, Garth, Jennifer Leach, and Dusko Sekulic. 1997. "Women in the League of Yugoslav Communists." *Women & Politics* 18 (1): 1–25.

Mayer, Tamar. 2000a. "From Zero to Hero: Masculinity in Jewish Nationalism." In Mayer 2000b, 283–307.

———, ed. 2000b. *Gender Ironies of Nationalism: Sexing the Nation*. London: Routledge.

Mazurana, Dyan E., Angela Raven-Roberts, and Jane L. Parpart, eds. 2005. *Gender, Conflict, and Peacekeeping*. War and Peace Library. Lanham, MD: Rowman & Littlefield.

McClintock, Anne. 1993. "Family Feuds: Gender, Nationalism and the Family." *Feminist Review* 44:61–80.

———. 1995. *Imperial Leather: Race, Gender and Sexuality in the Colonial Contest*. New York: Routledge.

Medica Zenica. 2001. *How We Live(d): Research on Status of Roma Women in Zenica Region*. Zenica: Medica Zenica Infoteka.

Merry, Sally Engle. 2006a. *Human Rights and Gender Violence: Translating International Law into Local Justice*. Chicago: University of Chicago Press.

———. 2006b. "Transnational Human Rights and Local Activism: Mapping the Middle." *American Anthropologist* 108 (1): 38–51.

Mertus, Julie. 1994. "'Woman' in the Service of National Identity." *Hastings Women's Law Journal* 5 (1): 5–23.

———. 2004. "Shouting from the Bottom of the Well: The Impact of International Trials for Wartime Rape on Women's Agency." *International Feminist Journal of Politics* 6 (1): 110–28.

Mertus, Julie, Jasmina Tešanović, Habiba Metikos, and Rada Borić, eds. 1997. *The Suitcase: Refugee Voices from Bosnia and Croatia*. Berkeley: University of California Press.

Meznarić, Silva. 1985. "Theory and Reality: The Status of Employed Women in Yugoslavia." In Wolchik and Meyer 1985, 214–20.

———. 1994. "Gender as an Ethno-Marker: Rape, War, and Identity Politics in the Former Yugoslavia." In *Identity Politics and Women: Cultural Reassertions and Feminisms in International Perspective*, edited by Valentine M. Moghadam, 76–97. Boulder, CO: Westview Press.

Milic, Andjelka. 1993. "Women and Nationalism in the Former Yugoslavia." In Funk and Mueller 1993, 109–22.

Milićević, Aleksandra Sasha. 2006. "Joining the War: Masculinity, Nationalism and War Participation in the Balkans War of Secession, 1991–1995." *Nationalities Papers* 34 (3): 265–87.

Milišić, Senija. 1999. "O pitanju emancipacije muslimanske žene u Bosni i Hercegovini." *Prilozi Instituta za Istoriju Sarajeva* 28:225–41.

Miller, Paul B. 2006. "Contested Memories: The Bosnian Genocide in Serb and Muslim Minds." *Journal of Genocide Research* 8 (3): 311–24.

Miller, Ruth A. 2007. *The Limits of Bodily Integrity: Abortion, Adultery, and Rape Legislation in Comparative Perspective*. Aldershot, UK: Ashgate.

Minow, Martha. 1992. "Surviving Victim Talk." *UCLA Law Review* 40:1411–45.

Mischkowski, Gabriela, and Gorana Mlinarević. 2009. ". . . And That It Does Not Happen to Anyone Anywhere in the World": The Trouble with Rape Trials—Views of Witnesses, Prosecutors and Judges on Prosecuting Sexualised Violence during the War in the Former Yugoslavia*. Köln: Medica Mondiale.

Mladjenović, Lepa. 1999. "Beyond War Hierarchies." *Women & Therapy* 22 (1): 83–89.

Mlinarević, Gorana, and Lamija Kosović. 2011. "Women's Movements and Gender Studies in Bosnia and Herzegovina." *Aspasia* 5:128–38.

Moghadam, Valentine M., ed. 1994. *Gender and National Identity: Women and Politics in Muslim Societies*. London: Zed Books.

Mohanty, Chandra Talpade. 1988. "Under Western Eyes: Feminist Scholarship and Colonial Discourses." *Feminist Review* (30): 61–88.

Mookherjee, Nayanika. 2006. "'Remembering to Forget': Public Secrecy and Memory of Sexual Violence in the Bangladesh War of 1971." *Journal of the Royal Anthropological Institute* 12 (2): 433–50.

Moore, Henrietta L. 1988. *Feminism and Anthropology*. Minneapolis: University of Minnesota Press.

Moranjak-Bamburać, Nirman. 2001. "The Privileged Crossroads: The Metaphor and Discourse of Space." *Forum Bosnae* 11:233–46.

Morokvasić, Mirjana. 1986. "Being a Woman in Yugoslavia: Past, Present and Institutional Equality." In *Women of the Mediterranean*, edited by Monique Gadant, 120–38. London: Zed Books.

Mosse, George L. 1985. *Nationalism and Sexuality: Respectability and Abnormal Sexuality in Modern Europe*. New York: Howard Fertig.

Mostov, Julie. 1995. "'Our Women'/'Their Women': Symbolic Boundaries, Territorial Markers, and Violence in the Balkans." *Peace and Change* 20 (4): 515–29.

Mujkić, Asim. 2007a. *Mi, građani etnopolisa*. Sarajevo: Šahinpašić.

———. 2007b. "We, the Citizens of Ethnopolis." *Constellations* 14 (1): 112–28.

Murdock, Donna F. 2003. "That Stubborn 'Doing Good?' Question: Ethical/Epistemological Concerns in the Study of NGOs." *Ethnos* 68 (4): 507–32.

Nagel, Joane. 1998. "Masculinity and Nationalism: Gender and Sexuality in the Making of Nations." *Ethnic and Racial Studies* 21 (2): 242–69.

Narayan, Uma. 1997. *Dislocating Cultures: Identities, Traditions, and Third-World Feminism*. Thinking Gender. New York: Routledge.

Naumović, Slobodan, and Miroslav Jovanović, eds. 2004. *Gender Relations in South Eastern Europe: Historical Perspectives on Womanhood and Manhood in 19th and 20th Century*. Münster: Lit Verlag.

Navaro-Yashin, Yael. 2002. *Faces of the State: Secularism and Public Life in Turkey*. Princeton, NJ: Princeton University Press.

Netherlands Institute for War Documentation (NIOD). 2002. "The Internal Political Relations in the Enclave." In *Srebrenica: Reconstruction, Background, Consequences and Analyses of the Fall of a "Safe" Area*, 1121–28. Amsterdam: NIOD. http://www.srebrenica.nl/Content/NIOD/English/srebrenicareportniod_en.pdf.

Nettelfield, Lara J. 2010. *Courting Democracy in Bosnia and Herzegovina: The Hague Tribunal's Impact in a Postwar State*. Cambridge Studies in Law and Society. New York: Cambridge University Press.

Nielsen, Christian A. 2013. "Surmounting the Myopic Focus on Genocide: The Case of the War in Bosnia and Herzegovina." *Journal of Genocide Research* 15 (1): 21–39.

Nikolić-Ristanović, Vesna. 1999. "Living without Democracy and Peace." *Violence against Women* 5 (1): 63–80.

———. 2000. *Women, Violence and War: Wartime Victimization of Refugees in the Balkans*. Budapest: Central European University Press.

Nizich, Ivana. 1994. "Violations of the Rules of War by Bosnian Croat and Muslim Forces in Bosnia-Herzegovina." *Hastings Women's Law Journal* 5:25–52.

Nordstrom, Carolyn. 2004. *Shadows of War: Violence, Power, and International Profiteering in the Twenty-First Century*. Berkeley: University of California Press.

Nowrojee, Binaifer. 1996. *Shattered Lives: Sexual Violence during the Rwandan Genocide and Its Aftermath*. New York: Human Rights Watch.

Olsen, Mary Kay Gilliland. 1990. "Redefining Gender in Yugoslavia: Masculine and Feminine Ideals in Ritual Context." *East European Quarterly* 23:431–44.

Olujic, Maria B. 1998. "Embodiment of Terror: Gendered Violence in Peacetime and Wartime in Croatia and Bosnia-Herzegovina." *Medical Anthropology Quarterly* 12 (1): 31–50.

Omerdić, Muharem. 2002. "The Position of the Islamic Community on the Care for Children of Raped Mothers." In *Pokidani Pupoljci/The Plucked Buds: Zbornik radova međunarodne konferencije održane u Sarajevu, 10. i 11. septembra 2001, godine pod nazivom Djeca—Žrtve rata i mira/Collection of Reports from International Conference held in Sarajevo—September 10–11, 2001—titled Children: Victims of War and Peace*, edited by Mirsad Tokača. Sarajevo: Komisija za prikupljanje činjenica o ratnim zločinima u Bosni i Hercegovini.

Oosterveld, Valerie. 2009. "Prosecution of Gender-Based Acts of Genocide under International Law." In *Plight and Fate of Women during and following Genocide*, edited by Samuel Totten, 205–18. New Brunswick, NJ: Transaction Publishers.

Organization for Security and Cooperation in Europe (OSCE). 1998. *Women's Representation in Elections in Bosnia and Herzegovina: A Statistical Overview 1986, 1990, 1996, 1997.* Sarajevo: OSCE.

Ostojić, Edita. 1999. "Some Pitfalls for Effective Caregiving in a War Region." In *Assault on the Soul: Women in the Former Yugoslavia*, edited by Sara Sharratt and Ellyn Kaschak, 161–66. New York: Haworth Press.

Ó Tuathail, Gearóid, and Carl Dahlman. 2004. "The Effort to Reverse Ethnic Cleansing in Bosnia-Herzegovina: The Limits of Returns." *Eurasian Geography and Economics* 45 (6): 439–64.

Parker, Andrew, Mary Russo, Doris Sommer, and Patricia Yaeger, eds. 1992. *Nationalisms and Sexualities.* New York: Routledge.

Pateman, Carole. 1988. *The Sexual Contract.* Stanford, CA: Stanford University Press.

Patterson, Patrick H. 2003. "On the Edge of Reason: The Boundaries of Balkanism in Slovenian, Austrian, and Italian Discourse." *Slavic Review* 62 (1): 110–41.

Penezić, Vida. 1995. "Women in Yugoslavia." In *Postcommunism and the Body Politic*, edited by Ellen E. Berry, 57–77. New York: New York University Press.

Peterson, V. Spike. 1999. "Sexing Political Identities: Nationalism as Heterosexism." *International Feminist Journal of Politics* 1 (1): 34–65.

Petrović, Tanja. 2009. "Becoming Real Men in Socialist Yugoslavia: Photographic Representations of the Yugoslav People's Army Soldiers and Their Memories of the Armed Service." *Centre for Advanced Study Sofia Working Paper Series* 2:3–17.

———. 2012. "Contested Normality: Negotiating Masculinity in Narratives of Service in the Yugoslav People's Army." In *Negotiating Normality: Everyday Lives in Socialist Institutions*, edited by Daniela Koleva, 83–102. New Brunswick, NJ: Transaction Publishers.

Phillips, Sarah D. 2008. *Women's Social Activism in the New Ukraine: Development and the Politics of Differentiation.* Bloomington: Indiana University Press.

Philpott, Charles. 2005. "Though the Dog Is Dead, the Pig Must Be Killed: Finishing with Property Restitution to Bosnia-Herzegovina's IDPs and Refugees." *Journal of Refugee Studies* 18 (1): 1–24.

Potkonjak, Sanja, Damir Arsenijević, Ajla Demiragić, and Jelena Petrović. 2008. "Između Politike Pokreta i Politike Znanja: Feminizam i Ženski/rodni Studiji u Hrvatskoj, Bosni i Hercegovini i Sloveniji." *Studia Ethnologica Croatica* 20 (1): 57–96.

Power, Samantha. 1999. "To Suffer by Comparison?" *Daedalus* 128 (2): 31–66.

Pugh, Michael. 2003. "Protectorates and Spoils of Peace: Political Economy in South-East Europe." In *Shadow Globalization, Ethnic Conflicts and New Wars: A Political Economy of Intra-State War*, edited by Dietrich Jung, 47–69. London: Routledge.

———. 2005. "Transformation in the Political Economy of Bosnia since Dayton." *International Peacekeeping* 12 (3): 448–62.

Pupavac, Vanessa. 2005. "Empowering Women? An Assessment of International Gender Policies in Bosnia." *International Peacekeeping* 12 (3): 391–405.

Radić, Radmila. 1995. *Verom protiv vere: Država i verske zajednice u Srbiji, 1945–1953*. Beograd: INIS.

Ramet, Sabrina Petra. 1996. *Balkan Babel: The Disintegration of Yugoslavia from the Death of Tito to Ethnic War*. Boulder, CO: Westview Press.

———. 1999. "In Tito's Time." In *Gender Politics in the Western Balkans: Women and Society in Yugoslavia and the Yugoslav Successor States*, edited by Sabrina Petra Ramet, 89–105. University Park: Pennsylvania State University Press.

Raudvere, Catharina. 2011. "Textual and Ritual Command: Muslim Women as Keepers and Transmitters of Interpretive Domains in Contemporary Bosnia and Herzegovina." In *Women, Leadership, and Mosques: Changes in Contemporary Islamic Authority*, edited by Masooda Bano and Hilary Kalmbach, 259–78. Leiden: Brill.

Razsa, Maple, and Nicole Lindstrom. 2004. "Balkan Is Beautiful: Balkanism in the Political Discourse of Tuđman's Croatia." *East European Politics & Societies* 18 (4): 628.

Rees, Madeleine. 2002. "International Intervention in Bosnia-Herzegovina: The Cost of Ignoring Gender." In Cockburn and Žarkov 2002, 51–67.

Ries, Nancy. 1997. *Russian Talk: Culture and Conversation during Perestroika*. Ithaca, NY: Cornell University Press.

Rihtman-Auguštin, Dunja. 1999. "A Croatian Controversy: Mediterranean-Danube-Balkans." *Narodna umjetnost: Croatian Journal of Ethnology and Folklore Research* 36 (1): 103–20.

Rosaldo, Michelle Z. 1980. "The Use and Abuse of Anthropology: Reflections on Feminism and Cross-Cultural Understanding." *Signs* 5 (3): 389–417.

Ross, Fiona C. 2003. *Bearing Witness: Women and the Truth and Reconciliation Commission in South Africa*. London: Pluto Press.

Rueschemeyer, Marilyn, ed. 1998. *Women in the Politics of Postcommunist Eastern Europe*. Revised and Expanded Edition. Armonk, NY: M. E. Sharpe.

Rusinow, Dennison I. 1982. *Yugoslavia's Muslim Nation*. Hanover, NH: Universities Field Staff International.

———. 1985. "Nationalities Policy and the National Question." In *Yugoslavia in the 1980s*, edited by Sabrina P. Ramet, 134–61. Boulder, CO: Westview Press.

Said, Edward W. 1978. *Orientalism*. 1st ed. New York: Pantheon Books.

Salecl, Renata. 1994. *The Spoils of Freedom: Psychoanalysis and Feminism after the Fall of Socialism*. London: Routledge.

Sampson, Steven. 1996. "The Social Life of Projects: Importing Civil Society to Albania." In *Civil Society: Challenging Western Models*, edited by Chris Hann and Elizabeth Dunn, 121–43. New York: Routledge.

———. 2003. "Weak States, Uncivil Societies, and Thousands of NGOs: Benevolent Colonialism in the Balkans." In *The Balkans in Focus: Cultural Boundaries in Europe*, edited by Sanimir Resić and Barbara Tornquist-Plewa, 27–44. Chicago: Nordic Academic Press.

Samuel, Kumundini. 2003. "Activism, Motherhood, and the State in Sri Lanka's Ethnic Conflict." In Giles et al. 2004, 167–80.

Šantić, Slavko. 1994. "Žirinovski među nama." *Oslobođenje*, June 16, 2.

Sasson-Levy, Orna. 2005. "Constructing Identities at the Margins: Masculinities and Citizenship in the Israeli Army." *The Sociological Quarterly* 43 (3): 357–83.

Savić, Alenka. 2000. *Positive Outcomes of the Bosnian Women's Initiative Programme in Terms of Promoting Tolerance, Reconciliation, and Dialogue in Multi-Ethnic Societies*. Tuzla: Mercy Corps Europe/Scottish European Aid.

Schäuble, Michaela. 2009. "Contested Masculinities: Discourses on the Role of Croatian Combatants During the 'Homeland War' (1991–1995)." In *Gender Dynamics and Post-Conflict Reconstruction*, edited by Christine Eifler and Ruth Seifert, 169–97. Frankfurt: Peter Lang.

———. Forthcoming. *Narrating Victimhood: Gender, Religion, and the Making of Place in Post-War Croatia*. Oxford: Berghahn Books.

Schein, Louisa. 1996. "'Multiple Alterities: The Contouring of Gender in Miao and Chinese Nationalisms." In Williams 1996, 79–102.

Schneider, Elizabeth M. 1993. "Feminism and the False Dichotomy of Victimization and Agency." *New York Law School Law Review* 38:387–99.

Scott, Joan Wallach. 1999. *Gender and the Politics of History*. Rev. ed. New York: Columbia University Press.

Scott, Joan Wallach, Cora Kaplan, and Debra Keates, eds. 1997. *Transitions, Environments, Translations: Feminisms in International Politics*. New York: Routledge.

Seifert, Ruth. 1996. "The Second Front: The Logic of Sexual Violence in Wars." *Women's Studies International Forum* 19:35–43.

Sells, Michael A. 1996. *The Bridge Betrayed: Religion and Genocide in Bosnia*. Berkeley: University of California Press.

Senjak, Marijana. 1997. "Women's Self-Organising in Bosnia: How We Felt When Supplying Psychological Help to Traumatized Women." In Kašić 1997, 29–30.

Senjković, Reana. 2004. "Romanticising Rambo: Masculinity and Social Perceptions of War in Croatia 1991–1995." In Naumović and Jovanović 2004, 287–304.

Šestić, Džemaludin. 1994. "O mješovitim brakovima." *Muallim*, September–October, 24–25.

Sharma, Aradhana. 2008. *Logics of Empowerment: Development, Gender, and Governance in Neoliberal India*. Minneapolis: University of Minnesota Press.

Siegel, Deborah L. 1997. "Reading between the Waves: Feminist Historiography in a 'Postfeminist' Moment." In Heywood and Drake 1997, 55–82.

Silliman, Jael. 1999. "Expanding Civil Society: Shrinking Political Spaces—the Case of Women's Nongovernmental Organizations." *Social Politics: International Studies in Gender, State & Society* 6 (1): 23–53.

Silverman, Carol. 2000. "Researcher, Advocate, Friend: An American Fieldworker among Balkan Roma, 1980–1996." In De Soto and Dudwick 2000, 195–218.

Simić, Andrei. 1983. "Machismo and Cryptomatriarchy: Power, Affect, and Authority in the Contemporary Yugoslav Family." *Ethos* 11 (1/2): 66–86.

Simić, Olivera. 2008. "A Tour to a Site of Genocide: Mothers, Borders and Bones." *Journal of International Women's Studies* 9 (3): 304–14.

————. 2012. "Challenging Bosnian Women's Identity as Rape Victims, as Unending Victims: The 'Other' Sex in Times of War." *Journal of International Women's Studies* 13 (4): 129–42.

Simmons, Cynthia. 2010. "Women Engaged/Engaged Art in Postwar Bosnia: Reconciliation, Recovery, and Civil Society." *The Carl Beck Papers in Russian and East European Studies* 2005:1–45.

Skjelsbaek, Inger. 2001a. "Sexual Violence and War: Mapping Out a Complex Relationship." *European Journal of International Relations* 7 (2): 211–37.

————. 2001b. "Sexual Violence in Times of War: A New Challenge for Peace Operations?" *International Peacekeeping* 8 (2): 69–84.

————. 2004. "The NATO Stabilization Force in Bosnia and Herzegovina: A Military Intervention Facing New Civilian Challenges." In *Gender Aspects of Conflict Interventions: Intended and Unintended Consequences*, edited by Inger Skjelsbaek, Elise Fredrikke Barth, and Karen Hostens, 25–38. Report to the Norwegian Ministry of Foreign Affairs. Oslo: PRIO.

————. 2006. "Victim and Survivor: Narrated Social Identities of Women Who Experienced Rape during the War in Bosnia-Herzegovina." *Feminism & Psychology* 16 (4): 373–403.

Sklevicky, Lydia. 1984. "Karaktaristike organizirano djelovanja žena u Jugoslaviji u razdoblju do drugog svjetskog rata." *Polje* 308 and 309 (October and November): 415–17, 454–56.

————. 1989a. "Emancipated Integration or Integrated Emancipation: The Case of Post-Revolutionary Yugoslavia." In *Current Issues in Women's History*, edited by Arina Angerman, Geerte Binnema, Annemieke Keunen, Vetie Poels, and Jaqueline Zirkzee, 93–108. London: Routledge.

————. 1989b. "More Horses Than Women: On the Difficulties of Founding Women's History in Yugoslavia." *Gender & History* 1 (1): 68–73.

Slapšak, Svetlana, ed. 2000. *War Discourse, Women's Discourse: Essays and Case-Studies from Yugoslavia and Russia.* Ljubljana: ISH.

Smillie, Ian. 1996. "Service Delivery or Civil Society? Non-Governmental Organizations in Bosnia and Herzegovina." A Report for CARE Zagreb.

Smith, Anthony David. 1988. *The Ethnic Origins of Nations.* Oxford: Basil Blackwell.

Smith, Carol A. 1996. "Race/Class/Gender Ideology in Guatemala: Modern and Anti-modern Forms." In Williams 1996, 49–77.

Sofos, Spyros A. 1996. "Inter-Ethnic Violence and Gendered Constructions of Ethnicity in Former Yugoslavia." *Social Identities* 2 (1): 73–92.

Soh, C. Sarah. 2004. "Aspiring to Craft Modern Gendered Selves: 'Comfort Women' and Chŏngsindae in Late Colonial Korea." *Critical Asian Studies* 36 (2): 175–98.

Sorabji, Cornelia. 1989. "Muslim Identity and Islamic Faith in Sarajevo." PhD diss., Cambridge University.

———. 1993. "Ethnic War in Bosnia." *Radical Philosophy* (63): 108–27.

———. 1994. "Mixed Motives: Islam, Nationalism and Mevluds in an Unstable Yugoslavia." In *Muslim Women's Choices: Religious Belief and Social Reality*, edited by Camillia Fawzi El-Solh and Judy Mabro, 108–27. Oxford: Berg.

———. 1995. "A Very Modern War: War and Territory in Bosnia-Hercegovina." In *War: A Cruel Necessity? The Bases of Institutionalized Violence*, edited by Robert A. Hinde and Helen Watson, 80–99. London: Tauris Academic Studies.

———. 2006. "Managing Memories in Post-War Sarajevo: Individuals, Bad Memories, and New Wars." *The Journal of the Royal Anthropological Institute* 12 (1): 1–18.

———. 2008. "Bosnian Neighbourhoods Revisited: Tolerance, Commitment and Komsiluk in Sarajevo." In *On the Margins of Religion*, edited by Frances Pine and João de Pina-Cabral, 97–112. Oxford: Berghahn Books.

Sorisio, Carolyn. 1997. "A Tale of Two Feminisms: Power and Victimization in Contemporary Feminist Debate." In Heywood and Drake 1997, 134–54.

Spahić, Mustafa Mujki. 1994. "Gore od silovanja: Zlo mješovitih brakova." *Ljiljan*, August 10, 22.

Spahić-Šiljak, Zilka. 2007. *Žene, religija i politika: Analiza utjecaja interpretativnog religijskog nasljeđa judaizma, kršćanstva i islama na angažman žene u javnom životu i politici.* Sarajevo: IMIC Zajedno.

———. 2008. "The Image of Woman in Religious Community Magazines in Bosnia-Herzegovina." In *Images of the Religious Other: Discourses and Distance in the Western Balkans*, edited by Christian Moe, 157–77. Novi Sad: CEIR.

———. 2010. "Images of Women in Bosnia, Herzegovina, and Neighboring Countries, 1992–1995." In *Muslim Women in War and Crisis: Representation and Reality*, edited by Faegheh Shirazi, 213–26. Austin: University of Texas Press.

———, ed. 2012. *Contesting Female, Feminist and Muslim Identities: Post-Socialist Contexts of Bosnia and Herzegovina and Kosovo.* Sarajevo: Center for Interdisciplinary Postgraduate Studies, University of Sarajevo.

Spahić-Šiljak, Zilka, and Rebeka Jadranka Anić. 2009. *I vjernice i građanke.* Sarajevo: TPO Fondacija i CIPS-Univerziteta u Sarajevu.

Spasić, Ivana. 2000. "Woman-Victim and Woman-Citizen: Some Notes on the 'Feminist' Discourse on War." In Slapšak 2000, 343–57.

Spivak, Gayatri Chakravorty. 1993. *Outside in the Teaching Machine.* New York: Routledge.

Stacey, Judith. 1988. "Can There Be a Feminist Ethnography?" *Women's Studies International Forum* 11:21–27.

Stefansson, Anders H. 2007. "Urban Exile: Locals, Newcomers and the Cultural Transformation of Sarajevo." In Bougarel et al. 2007a, 59–78.

Stetz, Margaret D. 2000. "'Woman as Mother in Headscarf': The Woman War Refugee and the North American Media." *Canadian Woman Studies* 19 (4): 66–70.

Stiglmayer, Alexandra, ed. 1994. *Mass Rape: The War against Women in Bosnia-Herzegovina*. Lincoln: University of Nebraska Press.

Strathern, Marilyn. 1980. "No Nature, No Culture: The Hagen Case." In *Nature, Culture, and Gender*, edited by Carol P. MacCormack and Marilyn Strathern, 174–222. New York: Cambridge University Press.

Stubbs, Paul. 1996. "Nationalisms, Globalization and Civil Society in Croatia and Slovenia." *Research in Social Movements, Conflicts and Change* 19:1–26.

———. 1997. "NGO Work with Forced Migrants in Croatia: Lineages of a Global Middle Class?" *International Peacekeeping* 4 (4): 50–60.

———. 1999a. *Displaced Promises: Forced Migration, Refuge and Repatriation in Croatia and Bosnia-Herzegovina*. Uppsala: Life & Peace Institute.

———. 1999b. "Social Work and Civil Society in Bosnia-Herzegovina: Globalisation, Neo-Feudalism and the State." In *Social Work and the State*, edited by Bogdan Lesnik, 55–64. International Perspectives in Social Work. Brighton, UK: Pavilion.

———. 2003. "International Non-State Actors and Social Development Policy." *Global Social Policy* 3 (3): 319–48.

———. 2007. "Civil Society or Ubleha?: Reflections on Flexible Concepts, Meta-NGOs and New Social Energy in the Post-Yugoslav Space." In *20 Pieces of Encouragement for Awakening and Change: Peacebuilding in the Region of the Former Yugoslavia*, edited by Helena Rill, Tamara Šmidling, and Ana Bitoljanu, 215–28. Belgrade: Centre for Nonviolent Action.

Sudetic, Chuck. 1998. *Blood and Vengeance: One Family's Story of the War in Bosnia*. New York: W. W. Norton.

Suljagić, Emir. 2005. *Postcards from the Grave*. Translated by Lejla Haverić. London: Saqi in association with the Bosnian Institute.

Tabeu, Ewa, and Jakub Bijak. 2005. "War-Related Deaths in the 1992–1995 Armed Conflicts in Bosnia and Herzegovina: A Critique of Previous Estimates and Recent Results." *European Journal of Population* 21:87–215.

Tax, Meredith. 1993. "Five Women Who Won't Be Silenced." *The Nation*, May 10, 624–27.

Taylor, Diana. 1994. "Performing Gender: Las Madres de la Plaza de Mayo." In *Negotiating Performance: Gender, Sexuality, and Theatricality in Latina/o America*, edited by Diana Taylor and Juan Villegas Morales, 275–305. Durham, NC: Duke University Press.

———. 1997. *Disappearing Acts: Spectacles of Gender and Nationalism in Argentina's Dirty War*. Durham, NC: Duke University Press.

Theidon, Kimberley. 2007. "Gender in Transition: Common Sense, Women, and War." *Journal of Human Rights* 6 (4): 453–78.

Todorova, Maria Nikolaeva. 1997. *Imagining the Balkans*. New York: Oxford University Press.

Tokača, Mirsad, ed. 1999. *Grijeh šutnje, rizik govora/The Sin of Silence, Risk of Speech*. Sarajevo: Komisija za prikupljanje činjenica o ratnim zločinima u Bosni i Hercegovini.

Toomey, Christine. 2003. "Cradle of Inhumanity." *Sunday Times of London*, November 9.

Turner, Simon. 2010. *Politics of Innocence: Hutu Identity, Conflict and Camp Life*. Oxford: Berghahn Books.

United Nations Population Fund (UNFPA). 2010. *From Conflict and Crisis to Renewal: Generations of Change*. State of World Population Reports. UNFPA.

Verdery, Katherine. 1994. "From Parent-State to Family Patriarchs: Gender and Nation in Contemporary Eastern Europe." *East European Politics & Societies* 8 (2): 225–55.

———. 1999. *The Political Lives of Dead Bodies: Reburial and Postsocialist Change*. New York: Columbia University Press.

Visvanathan, Nalini, Lynn Duggan, Laurie Nisonoff, and Nancy Wiegersma, ed. 1997. *The Women, Gender, and Development Reader*. London: Zed Books.

Visweswaran, Kamala. 1994. *Fictions of Feminist Ethnography*. Minneapolis: University of Minnesota Press.

Vranić, Seada, ed. 1996. *Breaking the Wall of Silence: The Voices of Raped Bosnia*. Zagreb: Izdanja Antibarbarus.

Waetjen, Thembisa. 2001. "The Limits of Gender Rhetoric for Nationalism: A Case Study from Southern Africa." *Theory and Society* 30 (1): 121–52.

Wagner, Sarah E. 2008. *To Know Where He Lies: DNA Technology and the Search for Srebrenica's Missing*. Berkeley: University of California Press.

Waller, Marguerite R., and Jennifer Rycenga, eds. 2000. *Frontline Feminisms: Women, War, and Resistance*. New York: Garland.

Walsh, Martha. 1998. "Mind the Gap: Where Feminist Theory Failed to Meet Development Practice—A Missed Opportunity in Bosnia and Herzegovina." *European Journal of Women's Studies* 5 (3–4): 329–43.

———. 2000. *Aftermath: The Role of Women's Organizations in Postconflict Bosnia and Herzegovina*. USAID Working Paper No. 308. July. http://www.microfinancegateway.org/gm/document-1.9.29606/2783_file_02783.pdf.

Watson, Peggy. 1993. "Eastern Europe's Silent Revolution: Gender." *Sociology* 27 (3): 471–87.

Wedel, Janine R. 2001. *Collision and Collusion: The Strange Case of Western Aid to Eastern Europe*. New York: Palgrave.

West, Lois A., ed. 1997. *Feminist Nationalism*. New York: Routledge.

Williams, Brackette F., ed. 1996. *Women Out of Place: The Gender of Agency and the Race of Nationality*. New York: Routledge.

Wolchik, Sharon L., and Alfred G. Meyer, eds. 1985. *Women, State, and Party in Eastern Europe*. Durham, NC: Duke University Press.

Women in Black/Žene u crnom. 1999. *Women for Peace: Anthology*. Belgrade: Women in Black.

Woodward, Susan L. 1985. "The Rights of Women: Ideology, Policy, and Social Change in Yugoslavia." In Wolchik and Meyer 1985, 234–54.

———. 2000. "Violence-Prone Area or International Transition? Addressing the Role of Outsiders in Balkan Violence." In *Violence and Subjectivity*, edited by Veena Das and Arthur Kleinman, et al., 19–45. Berkeley: University of California Press.

World Bank. 2002. *Bosnia and Herzegovina: Local Level Institutions and Social Capital Study*. Washington, DC: World Bank.

Yanagisako, Sylvia Junko, and Carol Lowery Delaney, eds. 1995. *Naturalizing Power: Essays in Feminist Cultural Analysis*. New York: Routledge.

Yuval-Davis, Nira. 1997. *Gender and Nation*. London: Sage Publications.

Zalihić-Kaurin, Azra. 1994. "The Muslim Woman." In Stiglmayer 1994, 170–73.

Zanca, Russell. 2000. "Intruder in Uzbekistan: Walking the Line between Community Needs and Anthropological Desiderata." In De Soto and Dudwick, 153–71.

Žarkov, Dubravka. 1991. "The Silence Which Is Not One: Sexuality, Subjectivity and Social Change in a Feminist Rethinking of Research on Peasant Women." Master's thesis, Institute of Social Studies, The Hague.

———. 1995. "Gender, Orientalism and the History of Ethnic Hatred in the Former Yugoslavia." In *Crossfires: Nationalism, Racism, and Gender in Europe*, edited by Helma Lutz, Ann Phoenix, and Nira Yuval-Davis, 105–20. London: Pluto Press.

———. 1997. "War Rapes in Bosnia: On Masculinity, Femininity and the Power of the Rape Victim Identity." *Tijdschrift voor Criminologie* 39 (2): 140–51.

———. 2001. "The Body of the Other Man." *Victims, Perpetrators or Actors?: Gender, Armed Conflict, and Political Violence*, edited by Caroline O. N. Moser and Fiona C. Clark, 69–82. London: Zed Books.

———. 2002. "Feminism and the Disintegration of Yugoslavia: On the Politics of Gender and Ethnicity." *Social Development Issues* 24 (3): 59–68.

———. 2007. *The Body of War: Media, Ethnicity, and Gender in the Break-Up of Yugoslavia*. Durham, NC: Duke University Press.

Zertal, Idith. 2005. *Israel's Holocaust and the Politics of Nationhood*. Translated by Chaya Galai. Cambridge: Cambridge University Press.

Zimonjic, Vesna Peric. "Rape Victims Tell Angelina Jolie to Leave Stories Untold." *The Independent*, November 1, 2010.

Živković, Marko. 1997. "Violent Highlanders and Peaceful Lowlanders: Uses and Abuses of Ethno-Geography in the Balkans from Versailles to Dayton." *Replika* (Special Issue: Ambiguous Identities in the New Europe): 107–19.

———. 2000. "The Wish to Be a Jew: The Power of the Jewish Trope in the Yugoslav Conflict." *Cahiers de l'URMIS* 6:69–84.

———. 2011. *Serbian Dreambook: National Imaginary in the Time of Milošević*. Bloomington: Indiana University Press.

Zvizdić, Memnuna. 1996. "The Workshop." In *Surviving the Violence: War and Violence against Women Are Inseparable*, by Medica Zenica, 32–33. Köln: Medica Mondiale.

Index

ancient ethnic hatreds thesis, 37, 263n2

Andrić-Ružičić, Duška, 74; critique of donor policies, 129–30; on cross-entity activism, 147; on environmentalism, 266n30; on gender essentialisms, 176, 183–86; on NATO bombing of Serbia, 153; on speaking out in public, 115. *See also* feminism; Infoteka; Medica Zenica

anti-militarism. *See* feminism: and (anti)militarism; Medica Zenica: and feminism; Women in Black (Žene u crnom) Belgrade

anti-nationalism, 124, 150, 246. *See also* feminism: anti-nationalist

anti-nationalist feminists: alliances across borders of, 61, 94, 129, 151–55, 156–57, 207, 221–22, 242; in Croatia, 61–63, 254n18; in Serbia, 61; stances on war rape, 61–63, 156, 221, 222, 243. *See also* Medica Zenica; Women in Black (Žene u crnom) Belgrade; United Women (Udružene Žene, organization)

anti-politics (of late socialism in Central Europe), 264–65n16

Antonija (organization), 131

Appadurai, Arjun, 37–38

Arsenijević, Damir, 244–45

art: as vehicle for social critique, 244–45

associations of citizens (*udruženje građana*), 107

authenticity: claims on behalf of victims, 212–13, 216, 237, 259n65

Baines, Erin, 95

Bakić-Hayden, Milica, 41

Balkanism, 6, 19, 40–41; and gender, 42–43; and the rural, 42

Ballinger, Pamela, 32–33, 259n67

Banja Luka, 145, 265–66n23, 266n27. *See also* Republika Srpska (RS); United Women (Udružene Žene, organization)

Baščaršija. *See* Sarajevo

Bašić, Adisa, 225, 235

Bećirbašić, Belma, 219

Bećirević, Edina, 256–7n37

benefits, state: for the disabled, 208–9; for survivors of torture, 221; for survivors of wartime sexualized violence, 4, 105, 195–97, 203–16, 224, 238. *See also* veterans: state benefits for

birth. *See* motherhood; rape in war: children born of; reproduction (births), and nationalism

Biser (organization), 156, 254n14, 255n26

Blagojević, Marina, 235, 241

border crossing (ethnicized), 144–46

Borić, Besima, 193, 204Bosanka (organization), 14, 98–100, 172; and League of Women Voters, 268n15; as mixing old and new styles of activism, 112

Bosfam (organization), *114*

Bosnia and Herzegovina (BiH): political structure of, 28, 120; support for, as multiethnic state, 28–29, 35–36, 73, 124, 134, 148, 246, 251n8. *See also* Bosnian; Dayton peace agreement; multiethnicity; Federation of Bosnia and Herzegovina; Republika Srpska (RS)

Bosniac: as national name, 35, 251n9; overlap with Bosnian identification, 36, 131, 134; standing for Bosnian, 65, 256n28. *See also under* ambiguity

Bosniac-dominated areas of BiH: and difficulty for non-Bosniacs to voice

coffee (*continued*)
139. See also *kafana* (pub/coffee house)
conscientious objectors, 152, 153
corruption, political, 10, 159, 161, 168, 210. *See also* politics; *and under* men
covered women: prejudice against, 132. *See also* veiling (of Muslim women)
čovjek/ljudi (man/men, person/people), 164–65
Croat-controlled areas of BiH, 53, 96, 149, 264n10, 266n24, 271n17
Croat(ian) nationalism: gendered, 34, 52, 57, 233; goals of, 72–73
cross-entity/cross-ethnic activism, 129, 144–51, 207, 242; as central to feminism, 144; perceived as a way to garner donor funds, 105. *See also* strategic avoidance; anti-nationalism
cryptomatriarchy, 182
culture: culture talk, 40; culturizing discourses, 6, 136; as explanatory lens, 6, 27, 66–69. *See also* gatekeeping concepts; rape in war: as particularly difficult for Muslim women
cultured/uncultured (*kulturno/nekulturno*) opposition, 30, 246. *See also under* rural
CURE (Girls, organization), 243–44
Cyrillic: vs. Latin script, 145

Das, Veena, 68, 240, 272n35; and Arthur Kleinman, 30
Dayton peace agreement: 28, 38, 145; and attention to gender, 93; criticisms of, 148; contradictions of, 120; and ethno-territorial delineations, 95; and logic of ethnic political representation, 120; obstruction of, 29, 92. *See also* refugee return

dead body politics, 31–33. *See also* victimhood: as gendered in relation to living and dead
democratization, 92–93, 109, 160. *See also* elections; OSCE
dichotomies, of social classifications, 30, 41. *See also* public/private dichotomy; *and specific dichotomous pairs*
Dignity campaign (Za Dostojanstvo Preživjelih), 3–4, 197, 206–11, 216
dimije, 26, 83
Dodik, Milorad, 226
domestic violence, 11,16, 42, 115, 184; as focus of women's NGO activism, 97, 144, 154, 197, 220, 222; politics of, after war, 155, 186, 241–42. *See also* Medica Zenica; NGOs, women's; violence against women
donors: approaches to gender/women, 93–95; dependence on, 116; diversity of, 94; dominant agendas of, 29, 90–92; drawn to BiH by publicity of war rapes/victimhood of women, 47, 91; dwindling NGO funding from, 98, 213; early focus of Federation on, 96; emphasis on reconciliation and return, 139, 160; feminist, 94, 130, 264n9; as guarantors of safety in cross-entity activism, 145; from Muslim countries, 29, 102, 131–32, 264nn10–11; promotion of multi-ethnicity/anti-nationalism, 129–30; promotion of women in politics by, 160, 170, 235–36; in Serb and Croat areas of BiH, 264n10; use of affirmative essentialisms, 94–95, 125–29, 191. *See also* foreign intervention agencies; NGOs: unfunded; OSCE

Drakulić, Slavenka, 217, 252–53n25; as anti-Croatia "witch," 62

dress, women's: as concern of Bosniac nationalism, 74–75; and feminists, 269n24; as marker of ethnic differences, 144; in politics, 187–88. See also *dimije*; headscarves, as symbols; veiling (of Muslim women)

Đuderija, Saliha, 207

Duga (organization), 145

Duijzings, Ger, 229

Dulić, Tomislav, 254n15, 257n37

Džajić, Aida, 255n26

East/West dichotomy, 41–42. See also Balkanism; Europe; Orientalism

elections, 159; as chance to force out nationalists, 170–71; and quota for women candidates, 163, 172, 267n5, 268n7. See also OSCE; politics; politics, women in

embargo, arms, 53, 234

employment: balancing with family, 167; of women under socialism, 50–51. See also NGOs: as employment

Engle, Karen, 66

entity border line: crossing of, just after Dayton, 144–46

essentialisms. See affirmative essentialisms; strategic essentialisms; feminists: and strategic use of essentialisms; men; representations; women

ethnic cleansing: compared with genocide, 69, 256–57n37; gendered patterns of, 56–57. See also Bosnian war; refugee return; war violence; World War II (in Yugoslavia): and inter-ethnic killings

ethnic key (*ključ*), 123

ethnic rape: as criminal offense, 63. See also rape in war

ethnicity: as coding bias, 38, 238; as dominant explanatory paradigm in BiH, 5, 29, 38–39, 242, 244, 246–47; ignorance of ethnic difference, 75, 122; and mixed parentage, 68; and names, 21, 122; and NGO membership, 129; and peaceful coexistence (life together, *suživot*) in BiH, 35, 121, 142; as produced by gender and sexuality distinctions, 52–53; as produced by war violence, 31, 52–53; as simplification of subjective identity, 20–21; and women's NGO agendas, 16. See also ancient ethnic hatreds thesis; cross-entity/cross-ethnic activism; multiethnicity; national narratives; patrilineality; religion: conflated with ethnicity; socialism: ethnicity and political organization under Europe: identification with, 31, 276n20. See also Balkanism; East/West dichotomy; Orientalism

Fatma (organization), 264n10

Federation of Bosnia and Herzegovina: as entity of BiH, 28; economic pressures on, 204–5. See also Bosniac-dominated areas of BiH; benefits, state

feminism: and analyses of Bosnian war, 43–44; and (anti-)militarism, 61, 66, 141, 151–55; anti-nationalist, 129, 154; Bosnian, 11, 113–15, 151, 184–86; 255–56n27, 266n30, 269n24; and environmentalism, 266n30; and essentialisms, 234–36; global feminist position, 61; impact of Bosnian war on, 47; influence on perceptions of wartime rapes, 198; Islamic, 133; as movement, 115, 118–9; and nationalism, 47, 253n1; negative reputation of,

feminism (*continued*)
109, 177; in prewar BiH, 65; and
race, 266n30; radical, 61; rejections
of/reluctance to identify with, 99,
101, 108, 118, 144, 187, 242,
269n25; and representations of
violence, 7; seen as political, 158,
184–85; as shaped by personal ties,
118, 151; in socialist Yugoslavia, 43,
51; and treatment of rape survivors,
215; and victimhood, 6–7, 234–36;
and wartime rape, 60–64, 155–57,
222. *See also* activism, women's;
cross entity/cross ethnic activism;
feminists; Medica Zenica
feminists: and all-women spaces, 111;
in BiH, 118, 144,; in Croatia, 61–
64, 222; debates over wartime
rapes, 60–64, 155–57, 222;
emphasis on women's active roles
in national processes/war, 126;
feminist alliances across BiH,
Croatia, and Serbia, 151, 153, 156–
57, 221–22; and NATO bombing
of Serbia, 154; obstacles to BiH
feminists in publicly challenging
national narratives, 154, 186; public
protests of conservative statements,
167; and research ethics, 16;
responses to war in former
Yugoslavia, 52, 60, 65; in Serbia,
61, 155; and strategic use of
essentialisms, 146, 149, 174, 184–
85, 191. *See also* anti-nationalist
feminists; feminism; Medica
Zenica; nationalist feminists;
United Women (Udružene Žene,
organization); Women in Black
(Žene u crnom) Belgrade
Filipović, Muhamed, 84–86
film, and national/patriotic sentiments, 209–11, 223–24, 245–46; as
vehicle for social critique, 243

Foča, sexualized war violence in, 56.
See also *Kunarac et al.* (ICTY
"Foča" trial)foreign intervention
agencies, 28–29, 250nn3–4;
agendas of, 92–93, 170–71, 177;
and gender issues, 93–94, 125–29,
130–31, 235–36; leaving BiH, 36.
See also democratization; donors;
OSCE; refugee return
foreigners, gaze of, 36; working in
BiH, 19, 29
Fox, Richard G., 7–8
fractals: Balkan, 41; copies, 42;
recursions, 41, 252n20
fundamentalism, Muslim/Islamic, 14,
132, 263n5, 265n20

Gagnon, V. P., 123
Gal, Susan, 36, 252n20; and Gail
Kligman, 4–5, 244, 252n20
Ganić, Ejub, 165, 268n7
gatekeeping concepts, 37–38
gender: as category of analysis, 4–5;
differences naturalized/naturalizing,
5, 8, 10, 81, 93–94, 110–11, 138,
161; in national narratives, 26;
roles as active, 27; and rural/urban
differences, 50, 66–67, 110, 182;
separate gendered spheres and
NGOs, 110–11, 139–40, 181–82,
218, 265n19; separate social spheres
designated by, 110, 135–38, 140;
and state benefits, 271n19. *See also*
cryptomatriarchy; men; nationalism, gendered; women
Gender Equality Agency and Gender
Centers (of BiH government), 93,
261n8
gender studies, 244
generation, 99, 110, 244, 263–64n7,
266n30
genocidal rape, 61, 63, 156, 222,
255n26

genocide, 69; forced pregnancy as, 70–71; gender and, 69–72. *See also* genocidal rape; Krstić ICTY trial; Srebrenica, women survivors of

Ghodsee, Kristin, 15, 261n6, 264n10

Gilbert, Andrew, 39–40, 45

Grbavica (film), 3–4, 194, 197, 206, 209–11, 224, 245. *See also* Žbanić, Jasmila

Green, Sarah, 19, 41

guilt, collective, 84–85, 134–36, 150. *See also* innocence; victim: noninnocent victims

Hadžiahmić, Lejla, 254n9, 271n19

Hadžović, Suada, 271n21

Halilović, Sefer, 271n21

Hasečić, Bakira, 105–6, 197; and implementation of benefits to war rape survivors, 211–13; and objections to Jolie film, 216–19, 224; and objections to notion of moving beyond collective victimhood, 226; as public face of Bosnian war rape survivors, 216, 220; stance on rape survivors speaking out, 215–16. *See also* Žene žrtve rata (ŽŽR), udruženje (organization)

Hauser, Monika, 97, 260n69, 268n31

Hayden, Robert, 57

headscarves, as symbols, 25, 37, 71, 79, 83, 99. *See also* dress: women's; *hidžab* (Ar. *hijab*); veiling (of Muslim women)

Helsinki Citizens' Assembly Banja Luka (organization), 147

Herzfeld, Michael, 252n21

hidžab (Ar. *hijab*), 258n57. *See also* dress, women's; headscarves; veiling (of Muslim women)

Hilhorst, Dorothea, 108

Holocaust, 32, 83, 227–28, 229. *See also under* camps

homosexuality, 57, 243, 276n20

honor and shame, as traits of Mediterranean societies, 38; in analyses of Bosnian war, 43. *See also* rape in war: honor and

Hotel Fontana (Bratunac), 141

Hromadžić, Azra, 259n63

humanitarianism, 207, 216; as opposite of politics, 30, 108, 159, 177–78, 182. *See also* NGOs: as humanitarian

humor, black, 153

Hunt, Swanee, 259n65; and League of Women Voters, 268n15; *This Was Not Our War* (book), 126–27; and *Žena 21*, 145, 265n22

Husanović, Jasmina, 244–45, 270n11, 272n31

I Begged Them to Kill Me (Ajanović, ed.): collective demonization of the (male) enemy in, 84–85,136; female/national honor in, 67, 199, 229; and male duty to protect the nation/women, 86, 229–30; and the nation as collective victim, 83, 86–87; publication and promotion of, 82–87, 273n38; on testimonies as public visibility of war rape, 195, 197, 213

ICTY (International Criminal Tribunal for the former Yugoslavia), 197, 202, 215, 229, 275n12, 275n14. *See also* Krstić ICTY trial; *Kunarac et al.*

Ilidža, 261n12

Infoteka, 15, 262n19, 146. *See also* Andrić-Ružičić, Duška; Medica Zenica

innocence: as facet of victimhood, 4–5, 32–33, 79, 149–50, 157, 230,

innocence (*continued*)
247; as incompatible with agency,
240–41; power of, as tied to
collective victimhood, 226; tainted
by association with political engagement, 178–79, 231. *See also* guilt,
collective; victim: noninnocent
victims; victimhood
internally displaced persons (IDPs).
See refugees
international community, 250n4. *See
also* donors; foreign intervention
agencies
International Women's Day, 102, 109,
111, 112, 172
In the Land of Blood and Honey (film),
216–19, 223–24, 241, 245
Ishkanian, Armine, 9
Islam: European, 42; Islamic
feminism, 33; political role of, in
Bosniac nationalism, 35, 73. *See
also* Muslim clerics in BiH
Islamska Zajednica (Islamic Community of BiH), 74, 158–59, 264n12
Iveković, Rada, 31–32, 52; as anti-
Croatia "witch," 62
Izetbegović, Alija, 35, 73–74, 146,
257n45, 265n17; wife of, 137

Jalušić, Vlasta, 33
Jansen, Stef, 39, 249n5, 250n4
Jolie, Angelina, 216–19. See also *In
the Land of Blood and Honey*
journalism. *See* media
justice, 173, 202–3, 213–14, 215. *See
also* ICTY (International Criminal
Tribunal for the former Yugoslavia);
rape survivors, wartime: as war
crimes witnesses; transitional justice; War Crimes Chamber, Bosnian

kafana (pub/coffee house), 188
Kapetanović, Nermina, 207

Kaplan, Robert, *Balkan Ghosts*, 37. *See
also* ancient ethnic hatreds thesis
Karadžić, Radovan, 210, 272n29
Kareta (organization), 254n14
Kesić, Vesna, 255n22; as anti-Croatia
"witch," 62, 255n21
Kewser (organization), 102–3, 132
Kleinman, Arthur: and Veena Das, 30
Kligman, Gail: and Susan Gal, 4–5,
244, 252n20
knitting projects (of women's NGOs),
100, 112–13. *See also* psychosocial
NGO activities
Korać, Lidija, 167
Kosovo: Albanian women's activists in,
154; and reports of rape, 63. *See
also* ethnic rape; Serbia: NATO
bombing of
Kozarac, 103–4, 181, 269n23. *See also*
Srcem do mira (organization)
Krstić ICTY trial, 71. *See also*
genocide; patriarchal society
Kulenović, Skender, 85
Kunarac et al. (ICTY "Foča" trial),
155, 197
Kunosić-Vlajić, Mevlida, 173
Kurtović, Larisa, 121

language: and ethno-national
differences, 20–21, 265–66n23.
See also script
Latić, Džemaludin, 76
Latin. *See* script
Lazarevska, Alma, 59
League of Women Voters (Bosnian
organization), 100, 172–73, 188,
189, 268n15
legitimacy, claims to, 5, 7, 10, 30–32,
89, 160, 247. *See also* affirmative
essentialisms; victimhood
Ler-Sofronić, Nada, 256n31
Lindsey, Rose, 237
logoraši, 82–83, 87, 259n64

Lora (camp in Croatia), 253n7
Lovrić, Jelena, 62

Maček, Ivana, 10, 30
MacKinnon, Catherine, 61, 254n17, 258n62
MADRE speaking tour, 62–63, 256n28
Majke Enklava Srebrenice i Žepe, Pokret (Mothers of the Enclaves of Srebrenica and Žepa, Movement of) (organization), 71, 106, 180
Malkki, Liisa, 66
March 8th. *See* International Women's Day
Marković, Mirjana (Mira), 137, 265n17
marriage, and nationalist prescriptions, 34, 52. *See also* mixed marriages
masculinity: in Balkanist representations, 43; and imperative to protect (women/nation), 86, 229–31, 233–34; of military veterans, 205; nationalism and, 57–58, 81, 227–34; and politics, 166, 168; threatened by inability to fulfill breadwinner roles, 186, 220, 241; as topic of research in BiH, 44; urban, 166; of war dead, 81, 231–34. See also *logoraši*; men; patriarchal society; sexualized violence against males; war: and normative gender roles
Mayer, Tamar, 227–28
media: and ethnic differences, 136, 145; gender critiques in, 243; images of Bosnian women in, 25–26, 37, 79–82, 99, 107; journalism as platform for gender critique, 243; journalists seeking out war survivors, 194–95, 215, 273n37; manipulation of war rape in, 62, 87, 156, 218; nationalist coverage

of films, 209–10, 223–24, 245–46; presence of Bosnian women's activists in, 65, 71–72, 82, 185; reports of corruption in, 159, 262n16; social media, 115, 244. *See also* Bećirbašić, Belma; Hasečić, Bakira; *In the Land of Blood and Honey* (film); representations; Srebrenica, women survivors of; visibility, public; Žarkov, Dubravka
Medica mondiale, 98, 113, 155, 261n10, 268n31. *See also* Hauser, Monika
Medica Zenica, 14–15, 97–98, 110; and abortion services, 97, 260n69, 261n9; and alliances with Zagreb and Belgrade feminists, 129, 145, 151, 156–57 (*see also* anti-nationalist feminists); and (anti-)militarism, 152–55; and (anti-)nationalism, 129–30; and cross-entity activism, 129–30, 145–51, 242; and ethnic makeup, 129–30; and feminism, 112–15, 118, 129, 144–45, 151, 176, 186–87, 206; as professionalized service NGO, 117–18; program for schooling refugee girls, 199; protection of survivors' privacy by, 87, 201, 215; and public advocacy on behalf of war rape survivors, 197–98, 201, 203, 206, 211, 218; and public/political activities, 113–14, 150–51, 155, 158–59; relationship with the state, 116, 262n19; reputation of, in local community, 108, 112, 177, 208; and stance on collection of war rape testimonies, 273n38; and stance toward Bosnian war rapes, 155–57; and treatment of rape survivors, 83, 86, 211; wider impact of activists from, 118; and work against domestic violence, 98, 115,

Medica Zenica (*continued*)
155, 157, 184, 186, 220. *See also*
Dignity campaign (Za Dostojanstvo
Preživjelih); Hauser, Monika;
Infoteka; rape survivors, wartime:
therapy for
Mediterranean, as culture area, 38
Mejakić, Željko, 271n14
men: and alcohol consumption, 75; as
breadwinners, 88, 181, 203 (*see also
under* masculinity); as camp
detainees, 241, 253n7; as civilians,
87–88, 231; as corrupt and violent,
161, 171, 234, 235; as defenders
(not aggressors) in war, 138, 147,
149, 155, 186, 233; as politicians/
political, 177, 181, 188; presumed
as soldiers, 56, 86, 88, 144–45,
203; as protectors of nation/
women, 86, 229–31; roles of, in
nationalist narratives, 25, 34, 52,
57, 81; as rude and competitive
(in politics), 173–75; as self-
interested and corrupt (in politics),
189, 191, 235; serving "coffee with
balls," 265n18; social spheres of,
110; as symbols of national victimhood, 83, 88–89; as victims of
gender order, 138. See also *logoraši*;
masculinity; rapists (perpetrators of
war rape); sexualized violence
against males; veterans (former
combatants); war: and normative
gender roles
Merjem (organization), 102, 111
Merry, Sally Engle, 184
militarism. *See* feminism: and (anti-)
militarism; Medica Zenica: and
feminism; Women in Black (Žene u
crnom) Belgrade
military: conscription of men into,
58–59; women in, 49, 58–59. *See
also* Bosnian Army: women in

Milošević, Slobodan, 101, 137, 151–
53, 216, 233, 265n17. *See also*
Marković, Mirjana
Mischkowski, Gabriela, 155–57,
275n16
Mitrović, Željko, 216, 217
mixed marriages: children of, 68;
condemnations of, by Bosniac
nationalists, 75–77; effects of war
on, 59, 76; in prewar BiH, 262–n1,
264n15; and women, 76–77
Mlađenović, Lepa, 273n47
Mladić, Ratko, 210, 272n29
modernity, 55; of discourses on
women's rights, 9, 10, 175; of
Europeanness, 31, 107, 266n24;
and the urban, 30, 110; and
Yugoslavia, 15, 31, 43, 66
Mookherjee, Nayanika, 198
moral claims, 10–11; of women as
collective actors, 95, 108, 126, 247.
See also morality; victimhood: as
moral category
morality: and gendered purity, 81;
moral hierarchies of ethnic differences, 136–38; moral judgments/
hierarchies and gendered categories,
10, 85, 136–38; moral worlds after
war, 30; and social transformation,
5. *See also* victimhood: and moral
superiority
mosques: attendance at, 75; postwar
rebuilding of, 74, 258n60; in
skyline of Sarajevo, 122; wartime
destruction of, 53, 54, 83
Mostar, 81, 96, 127, 144–45, *204*
Mostov, Julie, 31–32
motherhood: as active role in the
nation, 87; conflated with womanhood, 85, 127, 135–36, 167,
175–76, 236; mourning mothers
as symbols of national victimhood,
72, 230; and nationalism, 8–9, 52,

OSCE: NGO initiatives of, 96; promotion of women in politics by, 163, 170–71, 172–74; and "Women Can Do It!" political skills training for women, 173–76, 187, 191. *See also* elections: and quota for women candidates

pacifism, 152. *See also* feminism: and (anti-)militarism; Medica Zenica: and feminism; Women in Black (Žene u crnom) Belgrade
pan-Islamists, 74, 257n45
Partizanke (female partisans, WWII), 49
patriarchal society: benevolent patriarchy, 136–38; as explanation for severity of/stigma against rape in war, 25, 195, 200, 222; as support for Srebrenica genocide judgment, 71–72. *See also* Balkanism; Orientalism; rape in war: as particularly difficult for Muslim women
patrilineality: and children born of rape, 58, 68–69, 70; and mixed marriage, 76–77
perpetrators. *See* rapists (perpetrators of war rape)
Planinc, Milka, 162, 163
Plavšić, Biljana, 63–64, 137, 229, 265n17, 275n12; as exception to lack of women in high-level politics, 163; as unmarried and childless, 169
politics: blamed for everything negative, 159; different models of doing, 113–14, 186; as dirty/corrupt, 108, 160, 172–73; distancing from, in order to achieve political goals, 108–9, 160, 177–78, 190; as male, 160, 161–66 (*see also under* men); and motherhood, 167–69; as not respectable for women, 136–37,

166–70, 182; as opportunism/way of pursuing personal interests, 121, 159; primarily associated with formal politics, 158–59, 161; wider meanings of the political, 158–59; women and the political, 158–92; women as meddling in, 52, 137, 177, 182, 187. *See also* feminism: seen as political; men; NGOs: as humanitarian; politics, women in
politics, women in, 103, 162, 165, 166–67, 187–90; concern that they "remain women," 187; forced by crises to engage in politics, 189; as forces for positive change, 171, 172–73, 190; as homemakers, 188; as mothers, 171, 175–76; as non-nationalist peacemakers, 171; promotion of, by foreign intervention agencies and donors, 170, 235–36; and respectability, 188; as those who can clean up politics/uncorrupt, 172–73, 175, 188. *See also* democratization; dress, women's; NGOs: as humanitarian; politics; OSCE; visibility, public; whore
polygyny, 75
postsocialism, 29, 242; in analyses of BiH, 39–40; and analyses of gender, 45–46; democratization projects, 90; transformations of, in BiH, 10, 12, 29–30. *See also* masculinity: threatened by inability to fulfill breadwinner roles
Potočari Memorial Complex, *179, 223, 232, 245*
pregnancy, forced: in rape camps, 56, 57, 67; trauma of, 78. *See also* rape in war: children born of
professionalization. *See* NGOization
property restitution, and refugee return, 39, 258n59, 269n23
pseudonyms, usage in this book, 20

psychosocial NGO activities: as aid to women war victims, 104, 106; knitting/weaving/sewing programs, 112–13, 193–94. See also therapy, psychological

public/private dichotomy: as gendered spheres, 135, 161; and general political transformations, 5, 161; in postwar BiH, 9–10

quota. See elections: and quota for women candidates

radne akcije (socialist work actions), 117

rape (non-war), 198, 218, 220, 222, 259n65. See also ethnic rape

rape camps, 56, 58, 106, 202, 217, 219. See also pregnancy, forced

rape in war: in Bosnia in WWII, 254n15; children born of, 58, 67, 68–69, 272n35, 273n37; compared to mixed marriages, 76; in Croatian nationalist narratives, 57; as drawing donors to BiH, 47; honor and, 86, 199, 222; as less serious than the killings of men in war, 201; as marker of brutality of ethnic others/enemies, 84–85; as nationalist metaphor, 34, 52; Orientalist representations of, 65–66, 69; as particularly difficult for Muslim women, 66–67, 195, 199–200, 238; as part of Bosniac/Bosnian victim narratives, 3–4, 26–27, 82–87, 186, 218; proposed commemoration of victims of, 221; public visibility of, 196–97, 238; as quintessential form of women's victimization in war, 83, 239; of Serb women, 60–61, 62–63; stance of religious officials on, 77–78; as unaddressed topic of women's activism, 200; as weapon of ethnic

cleansing, 56–57, 155, 221. See also feminism: and wartime rape; feminists: debates over wartime rapes; genocidal rape; Kunarac et al.; patrilineality: and children born of rape; pregnancy, forced; rapists (perpetrators of war rape); sexualized violence against males; war: sex and power during

rape survivors, wartime: assumed to be Bosniacs, 206, 207, 224; assumed to be women, 205, 206, 207, 224; Bosnian government and, 3–4, 78, 202–6; popular solidarity with, as a group, 198, 210–11; postwar lives of, 3–4, 67, 194, 196–97, 203, 214, 219, 221; protection of privacy of, 87, 201, 215; published testimonies of, 82–83, 106, 195, 202, 215, 272n33; reaction to Jolie film, 216–18, 224; and relationships with family members, 67–68, 214, 272n34, 272n35; research among, 270n7; and shame, 83, 205, 215, 233; social rejection of/stigma against, 66–67, 198–201, 214, 222; speaking out/staying silent in public, 83, 87, 195–96, 202, 205, 213–16, 238; as "speechless emissaries," 66; state benefits for, 4, 105, 195, 197, 203–16, 238; status as civilian war victims recognized, 208; suspicions about authenticity of claims of, 205; as symbols of national victimhood, 88, 196, 234 (see also rape in war: as part of Bosniac/Bosnian victim narratives); therapy for, 194, 211, 221, 256n30; unease toward, 198–99; as war crimes witnesses, 201–2, 213, 215, 219. See also Dignity campaign (Za Dostojanstvo Preživjelih); I Begged Them to Kill Me (Ajanović, ed.);

rape survivor organizations; SULKS (Union of Concentration Camp Torture Survivors, Sarajevo Canton): women's section of; therapy, psychological: therapy NGOs; Žene žrtve rata (ŽŽR), udruženje (organization)

rapists (perpetrators of war rape): depictions of, 217–18, genetic input of, 68, 69; and motivation to rape, 155, 199, 223–24; and shame, 85, 239; taunts to victims of, 58, 70–71, 78

reconciliation: employment as key to, 141; as focus of international intervention, 124, 139; survivors too bitter for, 140; women as agents of, 94, 124–29, 142

refugee return, 29, 79–80, 95, 143; NGO strategies to achieve, 181–83; as political, 160, 171, 181–83; as priority of international intervention, 93, 95, 124; as reversal of ethnic cleansing, 39, 124; right to, as inscribed in Dayton, 28; women predominant in, 124, 160; women targeted to lead, 95, 125, 160. See also property restitution, and refugee return; reconciliation; Srcem do mira (organization); Srebrenica, women survivors of; NGOS, women's: of/for refugees; Žene s Podrinja (organization)

refugees: assumptions about appearance of, 270n8; evictions of, 79; women, 25, 47, 194, 220. See also NGOs, women's: of/for refugees; refugee return; rural: as refugee widows

religion: adherence to, suspected as opportunism, 132; and anti-communism, 36; conflated with ethnicity, 35, 39, 78, 133, 137, 140;

as marker of ethnic difference, 35; and monoethnic NGOs, 101–3; and nationalism, 133–34; and (re)traditionalization, 36; under socialism, 49, 257n45, 264–65n16; and women's NGOs/activism, 130–34. See also Islam; secularism; veiling (of Muslim women)

representations: of Bosnian/Bosniac women, 6, 25–27, 37, 43, 64, 65, 237–38; by Bosnians themselves, 26; essentialized, 9–10, 34, 126, 161, 171, 173–76, 234–36; of non-Western women, 6; rejection of media images of Bosnian women, 25–26, 99, 107; romanticized, of BiH, 126–27; of Serbs/Serb men, 216–17, 223–24. See also affirmative essentialisms; Balkanism; culture; men; Orientalism; refugees; rural; women

reproduction (births), and nationalism: 34, 52; in BiH, 58, 75; in Croatia, 73; in Serbia, 58, 73. See also patrilineality; pregnancy, forced; rape in war: children born of

Republika Srpska (RS): atmosphere of, during NATO bombing of Serbia, 266n29; benefits for war survivors in, 206; delay in foreign agency/donor activity in, 96, 145; as entity of BiH, 28; marginalization of anti-nationalist feminists in, 150, 266n27; response to Grbavica in, 272n29; response to Jolie film in, 224–25; separatist atmosphere in, 145, 265–66n23. See also United Women (Udružene Žene, organization)

research, and travel/movement, 18–19; and researcher positionality, 19–20

respectability: and ethnicized gender roles, 136–38; and forms of

respectability (*continued*)
gendered victimhood, 201, 230;
and sexuality, 111, 190; and women
in politics, 168–69, 188; and
women's public personae, 191–92;
and women's social activities, 110–
11. *See also* politics; sexuality; whore
Ross, Fiona, 239
Rukavina, Mary Ann, 172
rural: prejudices against population of,
in BiH, 26, 99, 231; as primitive,
42; as refugee widows, 79–82;
rural/urban divisions, 87, 220, 246,
247; to urban migration, 50;
women, 59

Salčinović, Enisa, 219
Salecl, Renata, 252n25
Sarajevo: as center of foreign intervention, 14, 96; as European Jerusalem,
122; old town of (Baščaršija),193–
94; siege of, 30, *48*, 53, 59, 81, 83,
96
Schäuble, Michaela, 32, 233, 249n5
script: use of Cyrillic or Latin in BiH,
145
SDA (Stranka Demokratske Akcije),
14, 35, 74, 102, 169, 207, 257n45;
and anti-communism, 74–75, 76,
257n45; as Bosniac nationalist
party, 263n5; election campaign of,
163–64; as ruling party, 14–15, 35–
36, 204–5; and victimhood philosophy, 225; women's organization of
(Fatma), 264n10
SDP (Socijaldemokratska Partija),
164–65, 204–5, 268n12, 271n21
secularism: under socialism, 122–23,
132. *See also* Bosniac nationalism:
secular
Šehabović, Šejla, 245
šehidi (martyrs), 77; fallen soldiers as,
203, *204*; war rape survivors as,

198, 199, 270n10. *See also* masculinity: of war dead
Senjak, Marijana, 201, 206, 209
Serbia: gendered nationalism in, 34,
58, 231–33; nationalist goals of,
72–73, 135; NATO bombing of
(including Kosovo), 151–55,
266n31. *See also* Serb(ian)
nationalism
Serb(ian) nationalism: as obsessed
with the past, 136; as responsible
for the war, 135–36
Serbs: as war victims, 44, 60–61, 62–
63, 142–43. *See also* Četniks: as
distinguished from all Serbs; rape in
war: of Serb women
sevdah, 228
sexuality: in ethnicized war context,
217, 224; questioned for women
engaged in mixed company/male
pursuits, 111, 168–69, 199; of rape
survivors, 218, 222; as source of
political influence for women, 182–
83. *See also* honor; rape in war;
respectability; sexualized violence
against males
sexualized violence. *See* rape in war;
sexualized violence against males
sexualized violence against males, 52,
57, 64, 230; silence about, 67, 83,
205, 230; state benefits and, 207,
224
shame. *See under* rape survivors,
wartime; victimhood
silence: and activist alliances, 139; as
agency, 240; and reconciliation,
141; strategic choices about, 139,
148; of war rape survivors, 214,
215, 238–40. *See also* strategic
avoidance
Simić, Andrei, 182
Sivac, Nusreta, 202, 271n14
Skjelsbaek, Inger, 64, 254n13

205; protesting donor money going to women war victims, 208; state benefits for, 203, 204–5, 208, 220, 271n18, 272n26; wounded, 203, 208–9, 220

victim: civilian war victims, 203; as label, 10–11; noninnocent victims, 32–33, 231; as passive, 27. *See also* authenticity: claims on behalf of victims; rape survivors, wartime; Srebrenica, women survivors of; victimhood

victimhood: and agency, 240–41; all-or-nothing logic of, 12, 69, 143, 156, 233; collective versus individual, 5, 11; competing, 32–33, 63, 69, 143, 226–27, 229; female victimhood images, 25–27, 220–24, 230; as gendered in relation to living and dead, 88–89, 181, 231–33; as grounds for claiming collective innocence/unimplicatedness, 5, 32–33, 160, 191–92, 230, 231, 234–35, 240–41; as justification for victimizing others, 33, 227–29; as moral category, 10, 160; and moral superiority, 31, 33, 104, 140, 149, 157, 191–92, 234, 238; and national narratives, 5, 7; political (mis)use of, 12, 229; and shame, 233–34, 226; and suffering, 5, 11, 238; valuable asset, 235; as weak (feminized) political position, 225–26, 234. *See also* innocence: as facet of victimhood; national narratives; victim

violence against women: in peace and war, 61; as women's NGO focus, 150. *See also* domestic violence

visibility, public: skepticism of publicly visible/political women, 108, 137, 150, 177; of women's activists, 115, 155, 178, 185–86;

of women war victims in nationalist narratives, 230. *See also* activism, women's; media; Medica Zenica: and feminism; Medica Zenica: and public/political activities; politics, women in; rape survivors, wartime: speaking out/staying silent in public; voice, of war survivors

Vive žene (organization), 25–26, 211, 214, 257n40, 271–72n23. *See also* Zejčević, Jasna; therapy, psychological

voice, of war survivors, 64–66, 202, 237–38

volunteerism, and NGOs, 116–17, 211. *See also* activism, women's: and dedication to cause

Vukovar, 149

war: as analytical lens, 37; as crucible of social categories, 30, 39; everyday life in, 59; and normative gender roles, 34, 54, 81, 87–89, 181, 203, 209, 234; sex and power during, 217–18, 224. *See also* Bosnian war; rape in war; sexualized violence against males; victimhood; war crimes; war violence

war crimes: by Bosniacs, 124; trials for, 197, 263n6; by various militaries in Bosnian war, 53–54. *See also* ethnic cleansing; genocide; ICTY (International Criminal Tribunal for the former Yugoslavia); rape survivors, wartime: as war crimes witnesses; War Crimes Chamber, Bosnian

War Crimes Chamber, Bosnian, 194, 201, 213, 263n6

war violence: against civilians, 53; gendered logic of, 54, 72, 230; gendered patterns of, in Bosnian war, 53–59

Western political and economic
models, 31. *See also* activism,
women's: competing notions/
models of; civil society, and
democratization; donors; foreign
intervention agencies; NGOs
whore: girls going to school as, 50; as
opposite of respectable behavior
for women, 30, 71, 111; politics
as a, 158, 159, 168, 183. *See also*
sexuality
widows of war, rural, 59, 79, 127. *See
also* refugees: women; Srebrenica,
women survivors of
witches, feminists labeled as: in
Croatia, 62, in Serbia, 255n20
women: as anti/non-nationalist,
127, 150, 171, 172–73; as biggest
victims of the war, 87–89, 92; as
citizens, 235; as civilians, 33, 88,
181; as by definition apolitical, 144,
146, 150, 177, 181–83; as family
breadwinners, 167; as focus of feminist analysis in former Yugoslavia,
44; as innocent victims of war, 72,
88, 126–27, 181; models of ideal
Bosnian women, 188; as nation/
territory, 34, 62, 63, 85; non-
Western, 6; as peacemakers, 94,
126, 127, 138, 139–44, 171, 172–
73; as presupposed victims of
rape, 64; as primary caretakers of
children and households, 167, 168–
69, 170, 190; as reproducers of
the Bosniac nation, 73–74; as
responsible for war, 134–38, 142;
rural, 59; suspicion of public/
political activity of, 116, 118–19,
177, 184; as symbols of nation,
33, 57, 163, 230; as symbols of
national victimhood, 47, 246; as
unconnected to war, 126, 146,
150, 172–73; as uncorrupt/morally

pure, 127, 173–74, 188, 235;
victim images of, 6, 25–26. *See
also* military: women in; moral
claims: of women as collective
actors; motherhood; NGOs,
women's; politics, women in;
reconciliation: women as agents
of; reproduction (births), and
nationalism; respectability; sex-
\uality; war: and normative gender
roles
Women Victims of War, Center for
(organization, Zagreb), 222. *See also*
Žene žrtve rata (ŽŽR), udruženje
(organization)
Women's Court (Ženski Sud), 238
women's issues: as home and family,
170, 190
"Women Can Do It!" *See* OSCE
Women in Black (Žene u crnom)
Belgrade, 129, 141, 151–53, 154,
186, 222, *223*
Women of Podrinje (organization).
See Žene s Podrinja
(organization)
Women of Srebrenica (organization).
See Žene Srebrenice
(organization)
Women's Party (Stranka Žena), 169,
170, 175, 188, 267n5
work. *See* employment
World War II (in Yugoslavia): and
interethnic killings, 33, 122, 136;
and rape, 254n15

youth, 164; as forces for change in
politics, 171; as represented by
foreign intervention agencies, 128,
236, 263–64n7; actions after World
War II, 117
Yugoslavia: and abortion, 49, as
between East and West, 42–43;
and modernization, 49; and

privileging of military, 208. *See also* socialism
Yugoslav People's Army (Jugoslovenska Narodna Armija), 84, 149, 234

zar and *feredža*. See veiling (of Muslim women): banning of, by socialist Yugoslavia
Žarkov, Dubravka, 52–53, 56–57, 58, 64; on Croatian media depiction of Muslim rape victims, 255n19; on feminists surrendering ethnicity to nationalism, 133; on gendered constructions of victims and protectors, 233–34; on Orientalist representations of Muslim women, 66–67; on women's agency and victimhood, 240
Žbanić, Jasmila, 3–4, 194, 197, 206, 209–10, 245. See also *Grbavica* (film)
Živković, Marko, 32, 252n20, 259n66
Zejčević, Jasna, 25–26, 215. *See also* Vive žene (organization)

Žena 21 (organization), 265n22; 1996 women's conference in Sarajevo, 145–46
Žena BiH (organization), 64, 103, 156, 254n14, 255–56n27, 267n36
Žene s Podrinja (organization), 104–5, 109–10, 139–44, 181–83
Žene Srebrenice (organization), 106, 178, *180*, 181, 200
Žene u crnom. *See* Women in Black (Žene u crnom) Belgrade
Žene ženama (Women to Women, organization), *96*, 110, 211
Žene žrtve rata (ŽŽR), udruženje (organization), 105–6, 197, 209, 220; and implementation of state benefits to rape survivors, 211–13; stances on rape survivors speaking out, 214–16. *See also* Hasečić, Bakira
Zenica, 14–15; atmosphere in, during NATO bombing of Serbia, 152; unemployment in, 205; as wartime refugee collection point, 96, 97; women's NGO tour of, 112

Critical Human Rights

Court of Remorse: Inside the International Criminal Tribunal for Rwanda
THIERRY CRUVELLIER; translated by CHARI VOSS

*How Difficult It Is to Be God: Shining Path's Politics of
War in Peru, 1980–1999*
CARLOS IVÁN DEGREGORI; edited and
with an introduction by STEVE J. STERN

*Innocence and Victimhood: Gender, Nation, and
Women's Activism in Postwar Bosnia-Herzegovina*
ELISSA HELMS

Torture and Impunity
ALFRED W. MCCOY

Human Rights and Transnational Solidarity in Cold War Latin America
Edited by JESSICA STITES MOR

Remaking Rwanda: State Building and Human Rights after Mass Violence
Edited by SCOTT STRAUS and LARS WALDORF

*Beyond Displacement: Campesinos, Refugees, and
Collective Action in the Salvadoran Civil War*
MOLLY TODD

*The Politics of Necessity: Community Organizing and
Democracy in South Africa*
ELKE ZUERN